MOODY GOSPEL

JOHN

COMMENTARY

MOODY GOSPEL
JOHN
COMMENTARY

J. CARL LANEY
Paul Enns, General Editor

MOODY PRESS
CHICAGO

© 1992 by
J. Carl Laney

All Scripture quotations, unless indicated, are taken from the *Holy Bible: New International Version*. Copyright © 1973, 1978, 1984 International Bible Society. Used by permission of Zondervan Publishing House. All rights reserved.

ISBN: 0-8024-5621-9

3 5 7 9 10 8 6 4 2

Printed in the United States of America

DEDICATED TO NANCY,
whose life glorifies God

CONTENTS

Maps/Illustrations

PREFACE

The gospel of John is the first book I read from in my Greek New Testament as a seminary student. The book has remained one of my favorites for study and exposition through twenty years of ministry. The Greek text can be read and translated by a beginning student, yet the most knowledgeable theologians still ponder the profound truths of the fourth gospel.

I have not engaged in my study of John's gospel alone. Being a student of this book has made me a student of many great commentators who have carefully expounded this text. Westcott, Tenney, Morris, and Bruce have become my friends and colleagues. I have gone to their books with my questions and have appreciated their helpful exegetical insights. And so this commentary is not a totally new contribution. I stand on the shoulders of the many authors I quote and footnote.

And yet this commentary is distinctive. I have sought to write not only a commentary on the biblical text but to provide a geographical and cultural background for the life of Christ as presented in the fourth gospel. I have emphasized the historical and cultural background of the Samaritans, the Jewish leaders, and the biblical festivals. Time and space have been given to the identification and description of biblical sites like Cana of Galilee, Sychar, and Bethsaida-Julias. Following the lead of Tenney, the thematic focus of this commentary is on the development of belief and unbelief—the positive and negative responses to the Person of Christ. In John's gospel we see the beginnings of belief, the opposition to belief, the strengthening of belief, and the culmination of belief as the disciples come to believe in the resurrected, divine Messiah.

I thank my colleague, Gerry Breshears, for taking the time to read sections of the manuscript and for his thoughtful remarks and insights. I am very grateful to my good friend, Dr. Paul Enns, who carefully edited the complete manuscript. His corrections and comments have added significantly to this work. I owe a debt of gratitude to Nancy, my wife, whose love, cheerful spirit, and commitment to our family and ministry is a continual source of joy and encouragement. I thank my Savior for the blessings of the New Covenant, the privilege of being a student of His Word, and for the wonderful opportunity to share the fruits of my studies with others. For students of John's gospel I have adapted the prayer of Psalm 119:18, "Open our eyes that we may see wonderful things in your Word."

INTRODUCTION

TITLE

The title of the fourth gospel is *Kata Iōannēn*, "According to John," reflecting the early tradition that it is the record of the gospel as recounted by the apostle John.

AUTHOR

There are two major views regarding the authorship of the fourth gospel. Most evangelicals believe that the book was written by John the apostle.[1] A slight modification of this view is that John the apostle was the witness of the events recorded but that some other person actually wrote the gospel.[2] Others have held that the author was a certain "John the elder" mentioned by Papias.[3] The most prominent view among nonevangelicals today is that the author of John is unknown.[4]

1. Leon Morris, *The Gospel According to John*, NICNT (Grand Rapids: Eerdmans, 1971), pp. 8-30.
2. R. V. G. Tasker, *The Gospel According to St. John*, TNTC (Grand Rapids: Eerdmans, 1960), p. 11.
3. A. M. Hunter, *The Gospel According to John*, The Cambridge Bible Commentary (Cambridge: At the University Press, 1965), pp. 13-14.
4. For further study, see Donald Guthrie's *New Testament Introduction* (Downers Grove, Ill.: InterVarsity, 1971), pp. 241-71.

JOHN THE APOSTLE

Though the gospel of John is anonymous, both internal and external evidence point to John the apostle, the son of Zebedee, as the author of the work.

Internal evidence indicates that the author was a Palestinian Jew for he quotes the Old Testament (6:45; 13:18; 19:37), has a knowledge of Jewish ideas and traditions (2:6; 5:1; 10:22), and has a knowledge of Palestine (1:44; 2:1; 5:2; 9:7; 11:18). The author clearly presents himself as an eyewitness of the events he recorded (1:29, 35, 43; 2:6; 4:40, 43; 5:5; 12:1, 6, 12). John 21:20, 24 indicates that the author is the "disciple whom Jesus loved," the one who "leaned" on Jesus' breast at the Passover supper (cf. 13:23; 19:26; 20:2; 21:7). The author was one of the inner circle of the disciples and had a close association with Peter, as did James and John, the sons of Zebedee (13:23, 24; 20:2-10; 21:2, 7, 20). Because James had long since been martyred (Acts 12:1-5), and Peter appears as a different person from the beloved disciple (21:7), only John is left to be that disciple and author of the gospel.

External evidence from the time of the church Fathers reflects an early belief that the apostle John wrote the fourth gospel. Irenaeus (A.D. 120-202) wrote, "Afterwards, John, the disciple of the Lord, who also had leaned upon His breast, did himself publish a gospel during his residence at Ephesus in Asia" (*Against Heresies* 3.1.1). As for the reliability of Irenaeus, Eusebius says his authority was Polycarp (A.D. 70-155/60), who had personally heard the apostles (*Historia Ecclesiastica* 4:14). Theophilus of Antioch (A.D. 115-188), Clement of Alexandria (A.D. 190), Origen (c. A.D. 220), Hippolytus (A.D. 225), Tertullian (c. A.D. 200), and the Muratorian Fragment (A.D. 170) agree in attributing the fourth gospel to John, the son of Zebedee.

JOHN THE ELDER

Some scholars have suggested that a disciple of the apostle John, perhaps the "elder" John mentioned by Papias, bishop of Hierapolis (A.D. 70-155), wrote the gospel and was later confused with the apostle. Eusebius quotes Papias as mentioning both "John" and "the elder John" (*Historia Ecclesiastica* 3:39). Some have concluded from this statement that "John the apostle" must be distinguished from "John the elder," and that the latter may have been the author of the gospel. The following arguments are given in favor of this view.

1. An unlettered man (Acts 4:13) could not have written a work as profound as the fourth gospel. However, the meaning of "unlettered" is calculated from the viewpoint of formal training in rabbinic schools and does not mean "unlearned."

2. A fisherman's son would not have known the high priest (John 18:15-16). However, all fishermen cannot be assumed to be from the lower classes. John may well have been of a priestly family (cf. Eusebius *Historia Ecclesiastica* 3:31; Mark 15:40 with Matt. 27:56; Luke 1:36; John 18:15-16; 19:25).

3. An apostle would not have designated himself as an elder, as the writer of 2 and 3 John does. However, the apostle Peter calls himself an elder (1 Pet. 5:1), so why should John not do so?

4. Because the writer of the fourth gospel used Mark (so some argue), the author could not have been John because an apostle would not have depended on the work of one who was not an apostle. Yet many argue that Matthew, an apostle, used Mark. But this point is never used as an argument against Matthean authorship of the first gospel.

A careful reading of Papias reveals that he used "elder" in an apostolic sense and that both references to John are to the same individual. John is seen in two situations: first associated with the other apostles and presumably laboring in Palestine, and then as accessible to Papias at a time when the other apostles had passed from the scene. It may well be that this shadowy figure "John the Elder" may "never have existed at all."[5]

BIOGRAPHY OF JOHN

John was the son of Zebedee and brother of James (Mark 1:19). He was a partner with his father, brother Andrew, and Peter in a fishing business on the Sea of Galilee (Matt. 4:21; Luke 5:10). His mother's name was Salome, as a comparison of the parallel passages of Matthew 27:56 and Mark 15:40 indicates. His mother may have been the sister of Mary the mother of Jesus (Mark 15:40; John 19:25). His brother James was probably older because he is always named first.

John was an early disciple of John the Baptist and followed Christ after encountering Him at Bethany beyond the Jordan (John 1:35-42). John accompanied Jesus on His first tour in Galilee (2:2) and later

5. Everett F. Harrison, *Introduction to the New Testament*, rev. ed. (Grand Rapids: Eerdmans, 1965), pp. 220-21.

with his partners quit the fishing trade to become a fisher of men (Matt. 4:19-21). John and his brother James were called "sons of thunder" (Mark 3:17; Luke 9:54) by Jesus. John and his brother James were at the Transfiguration (Matt. 17:1). John occupied a place of privilege at the Last Supper (John 13:23). He witnessed the trial and crucifixion of Jesus and assumed responsibility for Jesus' mother after He committed her to his care (John 19:26-27).

John is associated with Peter in a number of events in Acts (3:1-11; 4:3-21; 8:14-25). He was regarded with Peter and James as a pillar of the early church (Gal. 2:9). Irenaeus writes that John resided at Ephesus, where he served as bishop and wrote his gospel (*Against Heresies* 3.1.1). Polycarp, bishop of Smyrna, testifies to a personal acquaintance with John and relates how John once went into a bath at Ephesus and, seeing the heretic Cerinthus (c. A.D. 100), ran out without bathing, exclaiming, "Let us flee lest the bath should fall in, as long as Cerinthus, that enemy of the truth is within" (Eusebius *Historia Ecclesiastica* 4:14).

John wrote his epistles from Ephesus, probably around A.D. 90. Later, in the fifteenth year of Domitian (A.D. 81-96), he was exiled to the island of Patmos (*Historia Ecclesiastica* 3:18) where, at the close of Domitian's reign (Irenaeus *Against Heresies* 5.3.3) he wrote Revelation (Rev. 1:9). Victorinus of the third century records in his commentary on Revelation 10:11 that John wrote Revelation on Patmos and was liberated when Domitian was assassinated in A.D. 96. Upon his return from Patmos, John took up residence again in Ephesus (*Historia Ecclesiastica* 3:20) and spent his closing years visiting the Asian churches, ordaining elders, and ministering (*Historia Ecclesiastica* 3:25). Irenaeus records (*Against Heresies* 2.22.5; 3.3.4) that John lived in Ephesus until the time of the emperor Trajan (A.D. 98-117). Polycrates, bishop of Ephesus (A.D. 189-198), states that John was buried in Ephesus (*Historia Ecclesiastica* 3:31).

READERS

The Hebrew terms and background indicate that the fourth gospel is the product of Jewish thought and reflects a concern for the Jews outside the land of Israel (1:41; 4:25; 7:35; 10:16; 11:52; 20:31).

Although the author may have had the Jews of the Diaspora in mind, its univeral tone (3:16; 10:16; 12:32) suggests that the circle of readers should not be too narrowly restricted. The readers also would include the Christian church and mankind in general.

DATE OF WRITING

Those who assume that John did not write the gospel generally advocate a late date for the work (A.D. 110-170). It is argued that John's references to "the Jews" point to a time when they had become confirmed enemies of the church. However, there was plenty of opposition and conflict between the disciples of Jesus and the Jewish establishment even before the crucifixion. It is also thought that the highly developed theology of John would indicate a late date of writing. But the theology is no more developed than that of Romans, which was written by Paul in A.D. 56/57.

The discovery in Egypt of the Rylands Papyrus 457, a fragment of John's gospel dating from the early second century A.D., requires that the date of composition be pushed back at least into the first century. It is presumed that it would take several decades for the document to be disseminated from Ephesus and come to acceptance in a place as distant as Egypt.

The traditional view among evangelicals is that the gospel was written around A.D. 85-90. It may be argued that John's gospel supplements the other gospels and thus was written after the synoptics. It has also been pointed out that John makes no reference to the fall of Jerusalem in A.D. 70, which may suggest a date of writing some time after that event.

Some scholars are suggesting that the gospel should be dated before the fall of Jerusalem in August A.D. 70.[6] It is argued that John writes as though he has not seen the synoptics. And he refers to the followers of Jesus as disciples rather than apostles. One of the most facinating arguments for an early date is John 5:2, where John writes "there is," not "there was" a pool. This may indicate a composition before the A.D. 70 destruction of Jerusalem. Later in 18:1 he writes, "There was an olive grove." Although not present in the city (see below), it is possible that John wrote when Jerusalem was under siege by the Romans (spring A.D. 70). The groves and gardens on the hillsides had been destroyed, but the city had not yet been taken.

6. John A. T. Robinson, *Redating the New Testament* (Philadelphia: Westminster, 1976), pp. 254-311; Morris, *The Gospel According to John*, pp. 34-35.

HISTORICAL SETTING

According to Irenaeus (*Against Heresies* 3.1.1) the gospel was written at Ephesus, John's residence and place of burial. He had been ministering in Ephesus for twenty to twenty-five years, and the elders of the Asian churches may have requested a written record of his teaching before he died. Ephesus was located three miles from the Aegean Sea on the Cayster River. In New Testament times it was the greatest commercial city of Asia Minor. It ranked with Alexandria and Syrian Antioch among the three greatest cities of the East. It was also a political center, being the seat of the Roman administration of the province of Asia. As a religious center, Ephesus was the guardian of the temple of Artemis and her image, which, according to legend, fell from heaven (Acts 19:35).

John's gospel has a somewhat different geographical emphasis than the synoptics. John emphasizes the Judean ministry of Christ whereas the synoptics present more about Christ's Galilean ministry. John records Christ's ministry in Galilee (chap. 2; 4:3; chaps. 6 and 21), Samaria (chap. 4), and Judea and Jerusalem (chap. 5; chaps. 7-20).

The chronological scheme of John's gospel is organized around the Jewish religious calendar.[7] Many of the major events of the gospel are linked to some religious festival celebrated by the Jews in Jerusalem. The controversy over the Person of Christ grew with His appearances at these feasts. His initial presentation to the people of Jerusalem occurred at Passover (2:13). Controversy over His Sabbath healing and personal claims took place at an unnamed feast (5:1), perhaps Tabernacles. The feeding of the five thousand and discourse in the synagogue at Capernaum occurred at Passover (6:4). The Jewish leaders sought to arrest Jesus when He was in Jerusalem for the Feast of Tabernacles (7:2). At the Feast of Dedication, His enemies tried to stone Him (10:22-31). And Jesus' death and resurrection took place at Passover (11:55; 13:1; 18:28).

John is not concerned about giving a full chronology of Christ's life, but he does provide sufficient detail to enable the reader to tie the life of Jesus with first-century dates and events. The record begins with the commencement of Jesus' public ministry at the Jordan in the

---

7. Merrill C. Tenney, "The Old Testament and the Fourth Gospel," *Bibliotheca Sacra* 120 (1963), pp. 306-7.

summer or autumn of A.D. 29. The gospel records the life of Christ, including His death, April 3, A.D. 33.[8] Chronological pinpoints include:

Commencement of Ministry (1:29-51)	Summer/Autumn, A.D. 29
First Passover (2:13-22)	April 7, A.D. 30
Ministry in Samaria (4:35)	January/February, A.D. 31
Feast of Tabernacles (5:1)	October 21-28, A.D. 31
Third Passover (6:4)	April 13/14, A.D. 32
Feast of Tabernacles (7:2, 10)	September 10-17, A.D. 32
Feast of Dedication (10:22)	December 18, A.D. 32
Royal Entry (12:1-19)	March 30, A.D. 33
Fourth Passover; Death (chap. 19)	April 3, A.D. 33

PURPOSE

The purpose of John's gospel has been the subject of much discussion. A growing number of scholars is recognizing the significance of John 20:31 in considering the historical purpose of the fourth gospel.[9] John writes, "But these are written that you may believe that Jesus is the Christ, the Son of God, and that by believing you may have life in his name" (20:31). John's purpose is clearly evangelistic. He designed the gospel to present the orthodox doctrine of the Person and work of Christ, inspiring faith and life in Him.

"THESE [SIGNS]"

The pronoun "these" refers to the "miraculous signs" mentioned in 20:30. Jesus performed many signs that are not recorded in this gospel. But these that John mentions are recorded for a definite purpose. The word "sign" (*sēmeion*) is the term most often used by John to refer to Christ's miracles. The word indicates that the miracles signify something. They are the insignia of Christ's deity and messiahship. The word indicates that the miracle is designed to lead people beyond the work itself to some great truth about the miracle worker (cf. 3:2; 20:30-31).

What miracles does John refer to? There are seven recorded in the gospel, exclusive of the resurrection and the miraculous catch of

---

8. The dates provided in this commentary are based on the research of Harold W. Hoehner, *Chronological Aspects of the Life of Christ* (Grand Rapids: Zondervan, 1970).

9. D. A. Carson, "The Purpose of the Fourth Gospel: John 20:31 Reconsidered," *JBL*, 106 (1987): 639-51.

fish recorded in the epilogue (21:4-11). Each miracle is intended to reveal something about the Person of Christ: (1) changing water to wine (2:1-11)—Christ as creator; (2) healing the nobleman's son (4:46-54)—Christ as healer; (3) healing the lame man (5:1-9)—Christ as restorer; (4) feeding the five thousand (6:1-14)—Christ as provider; (5) walking on the water (6:16-21)—Christ as protector; (6) healing the blind man (9:1-12)—Christ as illuminator; and (7) raising of Lazarus (11:1-46)—Christ as life-giver. It is quite clear that the miracles of Jesus had an instructive purpose and were recorded by John to reveal truths concerning the Person of Christ.

"THAT YOU MAY BELIEVE"

The miracles recorded in John's gospel are purposive. They are intended to elicit belief in the reader. The present subjunctive refers to the entire process of coming to faith and continuing to believe.[10]

The word "believe" (*pisteuō*), used ninety-eight times in the gospel, essentially means "to trust." In John's gospel, belief in Christ is equivalent to receiving Him (1:12), obeying Him (3:36), and abiding in Him (15:1-11; cf. 1 John 4:15). "Believing" in Christ does not merely refer to intellectual assent to a proposition about Christ. Rather, the biblical concept of "belief" involves a personal response and commitment to Christ's Person.

There is strong evidence in John's gospel to indicate that belief is progressive. This is not to discount the significance of a point-in-time decision to trust Christ. Yet from John's viewpoint, belief does not necessarily take place instantaneously but is aroused, nurtured, strengthened, and confirmed. This is seen in the case of the nobleman of Capernaum who appealed for his son's healing on the basis of what he had heard about Christ's miracles. He believed the word of Jesus (4:50), and that belief was confirmed and strengthened by the miracle that led him to put faith in Christ's Person (4:53). The progress of belief is also observed in the blind man who believed Jesus to be a "prophet" (9:17), to be "from God" (9:33), and finally that Jesus was the "Son of Man" (9:35-38).

The clearest evidence of the progress of belief is seen in the disciples. Nathanael believed in Jesus as Son of God and King of Israel when Christ revealed His omniscience before him (1:50). The disciples are said to have "believed" in Christ following the miracle at

10. Ibid., p. 640.

Cana (2:11). It was after the resurrection that the disciples believed the Scripture and Christ's words concerning His death (2:22). Evidence of their growing, developing belief is seen in John 6:69; 16:30; and 17:8. Christ allowed Lazarus to die that the disciples might "believe" (11:15). After the resurrection John saw the empty tomb and "believed" (20:8).

Belief among the disciples was initiated by the testimony of John the Baptist (1:35-41). That belief was confirmed as they saw the miracles—the insignia of His deity (2:11; 6:69). The belief of the disciples was consummated by the resurrection and resurrection appearances of Christ (2:22; 20:8; 20:25-29). Tenney summarizes well the concept of the progress of belief in John:

> The growth of belief depicted in the Gospel of John thus moves from an initial acceptance on the testimony of another to a personal knowledge marked by loyalty, service, and worship; from assumption of the historicity and integrity of Jesus to a personal trust in Him; from an outward profession to an inward reality; from attending to His teachings to acknowledging His lordship over life. Full belief may not be attained instantly; yet the incipient and tentative belief is not to be despised. The groping inquiry of Nicodemus, the wistful outreach of the woman of Samaria, the untaught earnestness of the blind man, the erratic committments of Peter, the blunt incredulity yet outspoken loyalty of Thomas, were reshaped by Christ into a living faith that conducted the power of God.[11]

The gospel of John presents the reader with something of an enigma. In the progress of belief there is a stage that falls short of consummated faith resulting in salvation. This is first in evidence in 2:23 where many at Passover "believed" as a result of Christ's signs, yet He did not "believe" (trust) them (2:23-25). Christ discerned that their faith was superficial, based only on the miracles they had seen. Later in 7:31, during the Feast of Tabernacles, many of the multitude "believed in Him" but apparently not as Messiah. In 8:31 Jesus spoke to the Jews "who had believed Him" and accused them of seeking to kill Him (8:40). He later accused the same Jews of unbelief (8:45-46). Evidence of this enigma, the "belief of unbelief," is also seen in John 12:11, 37.

---

11. Merrill C. Tenney, "Topics from the Gospel of John, Part IV: The Growth of Belief," *Bibliotheca Sacra*, 132 (1975): 357.

Tenney refers to this belief that falls short of genuine faith as "superficial."[12] Morris calls it "transitory belief," which is not saving faith.[13] It seems to be based merely on outward profession, not coupled with regeneration. The problem with this "belief" is its object. It appears to have been based primarily on miracles and is not rooted in a clear understanding of the Person of Christ as Messiah and Son of God. Many were inclined to "believe" something about Jesus but were unwilling to yield their allegiance to Him, trusting Him as their personal Sin-bearer.

"THAT JESUS IS THE CHRIST, THE SON OF GOD"

The key to belief is its content. Belief that issues in saving faith must rest in an orthodox understanding of the Person and work of Christ. The term "Christ" (*Christos*), properly translated "Messiah" (anointed one), is actually a title, not a proper name. The miracles are designed to show that Jesus is indeed the anticipated Messiah of Old Testament prophecy.

The miracles also serve to authenticate His deity. Jesus is the "Son of God." He calls God His Father 106 times in the gospel of John and appeals to His "works" (miracles) to prove His claims (5:36; 10:25, 38; 14:11). Even Christ's enemies understood His claims to deity (5:18).

"THAT . . . YOU MAY HAVE LIFE IN HIS NAME"

Belief in Jesus, the divine Messiah, results in life (*zōē*). Jesus claimed to be the resurrection and the life (11:25). He has life in Himself (5:26) and can give life to whom He wishes (5:21). This "life" is defined as "eternal" (3:16). The concept of eternal life includes both a quantity (3:16; 3:36) of life as well as a quality of life (5:24; 10:10; 17:3). Eternal life precludes perishing and issues in spiritual life and blessing. Eternal life results from entering into a personal relationship with God through faith in Christ.

THEME

John's gospel is the "Gospel of Belief." The word *believe* (*pisteuō*) occurs 98 times in the gospel. The theme of the book is reflect-

12. Ibid., p. 351.
13. Morris, *The Gospel According to John*, p. 603.

ed in the purpose statement of 20:30-31, "belief in Jesus, the Messiah and Son of God."

STRUCTURE

Various suggestions have been made as to the plan or structure of the gospel. The book divides itself into three major sections: the prologue (1:1-18), the narrative (1:19–20:31), and the epilogue (21:1-25). Both Dodd and Brown divide the narrative into two sections: the book of signs (1:19–12:50) and the book of "passion" or "glory" (13:1–20:31).[14] Tenney observes a "symphonic structure" in which the major themes (signs, sonship, messiahship, and eternal life) run concurrently through the gospel "like the melodies of a symphony."[15] According to Tenney, these interwoven themes, fluctuating in emphasis but always progressive in development, lead steadily forward to accomplish John's purpose of providing an incentive to faith. Accordingly, the *signs* provide the basis of belief, the *Person of Christ* is the object of faith, and *eternal life* is the result of belief. In another intriguing study, Staley argues that the symmetrical shape of the prologue (1:1-18) sets the tone for the structure of the narrative to follow.[16] Staley divides the gospel into five sections that radiate concentrically, developing key themes of the prologue.

It has been suggested by some that the outline of the book ought to follow the major events of the life of Jesus. This approach, however, does not work well in the gospel of John. The apostle John is quite obviously not writing a biography of Jesus. As a biographer, he would not leave out such major events as Christ's birth, baptism, temptation, Sermon on the Mount, transfiguration, and ascension. The last ten chapters of the book are devoted to the last week of Jesus' life and the resurrection appearances. A biography would not have such an imbalanced approach. Most scholars agree that John's gospel is a thematic study that focuses on selected incidents in the life of Jesus.

The overview and outline sections that follow reflect something of a synthetic approach to the structure and development of the gos-

---

14. C. H. Dodd, *The Interpretation of the Fourth Gospel* (Cambridge: At the University Press, 1953), p. x; Raymond E. Brown, *The Gospel According to John*, 2 vols. (Garden City, N.Y.: Doubleday, 1966, 1970), 1:cxxxviii.

15. Merrill C. Tenney, "The Symphonic Structure of John," *Bibliotheca Sacra* 120 (1963): 125.

16. Jeff Staley, "The Structure of John's Prologue: Its Implications for the Gospel's Narrative Structure," *Catholic Biblical Quarterly* 48 (1986): 241-63.

pel. Between the prologue (1:1-18) and epilogue (21:1-25) John develops the theme of belief, which shows the beginnings of faith among Jesus' disciples (1:19– 4:54), the development of unbelief among His rejectors (5:1–12:50), the strengthening of belief in the lives of the twelve (13:1–17:24), the consummation of unbelief as seen in the trial and crucifixion (18:1–19:41), and the confirmation of belief resulting from the resurrection (20:1-31).

OVERVIEW

I. THE PROLOGUE, 1:1-18

The prologue presents the thesis and digest of the book. It summarizes the essential facts concerning the life of Christ, emphasizing His deity (1:1), incarnation (1:14), and the response to His coming —belief (1:12) and unbelief (1:11). The prologue shows that Christ came to reveal the Father (1:18) and redeem man (1:12). The great themes of the gospel—belief, unbelief, light, darkness—have their inception in the prologue.

II. THE BEGINNINGS OF BELIEF, 1:19–4:54

Following the prologue, John presents the positive response to the Person of Christ. In this section we see the beginnings of belief among the disciples, Nicodemus (a religious leader), the Samaritans (religious outcasts), and the nobleman (Gentile). The positive response to Jesus from those of diverse backgrounds demonstrates that Jesus is not just the Savior of the Jews but of the whole world.

III. THE DEVELOPMENT OF UNBELIEF, CHAPS. 5-12

Having presented the beginnings of belief, John presents the other response to the Person of Christ (1:11)—rejection and unbelief. There are three major developments within this section:

A. Controversy, chaps. 5-6

Controversy over the Person of Christ centers on two miracles, each of which issues in a discourse.

B. Conflict, chaps. 7-11

Conflict with the Jewish religious establishment focused on the issue of Christ's identity. Christ's claim to deity incited the anger of the Jewish authorities. Four times in this section it is said the Jews sought to kill Jesus (7:19, 25; 8:37; 11:53).

C. Crisis, chap. 12

Chapter 12 is the turning point in the development of the argument. The long awaited "hour" (12:23; cf. 2:4; 7:6, 30; 13:1; 17:1) has come. This chapter also shows the transition from Jesus' public ministry to a night of private teaching with His disciples (12:36).

IV. THE STRENGTHENING OF BELIEF, CHAPS. 13-17

In this section Christ seeks to strengthen and confirm the belief of His followers in preparation for His crucifixion. Here Jesus teaches His disciples major truths (about service, love, prayer, heaven, abiding, persecution, the Holy Spirit, joy, victory, unity) that will enable them to be more effective in their ministries in those areas after His departure.

Chapter 15 is central to this great discourse. Here Jesus focuses on the theme of relationships—relationships between the Father and Son (identity), between Christ and the disciples (abiding), between the disciples and one another (love), between the disciples and the world (hostility), and between the disciples and the Holy Spirit (co-witnesses).

V. THE CONSUMMATION OF UNBELIEF, CHAPS. 18-19

The consummation of unbelief is seen in the rejection and crucifixion of Christ. Christ is seen not as the victim but the victor. He was in absolute control of the events that issued in His arrest, trial, and crucifixion. He delivered His own disciples from the arresting authorities (18:8-9), and in the garden He could not be touched except by His permission (18:6). Even in death, His life was not taken from Him, but He voluntarily yielded His Spirit (19:30).

VI. THE CONFIRMATION OF BELIEF, CHAP. 20

The resurrection of Christ from the dead confirmed the belief of the disciples (20:8, 27-28, 31). The resurrection, and its authentication by Jesus' resurrection appearances, became the central theme of the apostolic proclamation (1 Cor. 15:4-5).

VII. THE RESPONSIBILITIES OF BELIEF, CHAP. 21

Chapter 21 balances with the prologue and is intended to show readers how belief is to be applied. Belief is to issue in service, motivated by one's love for Christ (21:15-17).

OUTLINE

I. **The Prologue, 1:1-18**
  A. The Essential Nature of the Word, 1:1-5
    1. In relation to God, 1:1-2
    2. In relation to creation, 1:3
    3. In relation to man, 1:4
    4. In relation to evil, 1:5
  B. The Manifestation of the Word, 1:6-13
    1. Announced by John, 1:6-9
    2. Rejected by His own, 1:10-11
    3. Received by individual believers, 1:12-13
  C. The Incarnation of the Word, 1:14-18
    1. The incarnate Word, 1:14
    2. The witness of John, 1:15
    3. The revelatory Word, 1:16-18

II. **The Beginnings of Belief, 1:19—4:54**
  A. The Witness of John the Baptist, 1:19-34
    1. The identification of John, 1:19-28
    2. The Lamb of God, 1:29-34
  B. The First Disciples, 1:35-51
    1. Andrew, John, and Peter, 1:35-42
    2. Philip and Nathanael, 1:43-51
  C. The First Miracle at Cana, 2:1-12
    1. The marriage at Cana, 2:1-5
    2. The miraculous provision, 2:6-10

3. The results of the miracle, 2:11
4. The visit at Capernaum, 2:12

D. The First Temple Cleansing, 2:13-22
  1. The cleansing of the Temple, 2:13-17
  2. The riddle about the Temple, 2:18-20
  3. The explanation by John, 2:21-22
  4. The response at Passover, 2:23-25

E. The Interview with Nicodemus, 3:1-21
  1. Nicodemus and new birth, 3:1-15
  2. Reflections on the Son of God, 3:16-21

F. The Testimony of John the Baptist, 3:22-36
  1. The question of purification, 3:22-26
  2. The humility of John the Baptist, 3:27-30
  3. Reflections on the issues of life, 3:31-36

G. The Interview with the Samaritan Woman, 4:1-42
  1. The reason for leaving Judea, 4:1-3
  2. The divine appointment at Jacob's well, 4:4-6
  3. The conversation with the woman, 4:7-26
  4. The testimony in Sychar, 4:27-30
  5. The priorities of Christ, 4:31-38
  6. The belief of the Samaritans, 4:39-42

H. The Healing of the Nobleman's Son, 4:43-54
  1. The departure to Galilee, 4:43-45
  2. The request of the nobleman, 4:46-47
  3. The progress of faith, 4:48-54

III. **The Development of Unbelief, chaps. 5-12**

A. The Healing of the Lame Man, 5:1-18
  1. The miraculous healing, 5:1-9
  2. The response to the miracle, 5:10-18

B. The Discourse on Christ's Authority, 5:19-47
  1. The basis of Christ's authority, 5:19-23
  2. The extent of Christ's authority, 5:24-30
  3. Witnesses to Christ's authority, 5:31-47

C. The Feeding of the Five Thousand, 6:1-15
  1. The occasion of the miracle, 6:1-4
  2. The test of faith, 6:5-9
  3. The miraculous feeding, 6:10-13
  4. The response to the miracle, 6:14-15

  5. The response to the miracle, 11:45-53
  6. The wilderness retreat, 11:54
  7. The Passover pilgrimage, 11:55-57
 L. The Close of Christ's Public Ministry, chap. 12
  1. The anointing at Bethany, 12:1-8
  2. The hostility of the priests, 12:9-11
  3. The royal entry, 12:12-19
  4. The prediction of Jesus' death, 12:20-36
  5. The explanation for unbelief, 12:37-43
  6. The consequences of unbelief, 12:44-50

IV. **The Strengthening of Belief, chaps. 13-17**
 A. The Example of Humble Service, 13:1-20
  1. The circumstances at the supper, 13:1-3
  2. The example of humble service, 13:4-11
  3. The explanation of the foot washing, 13:12-17
 B. The Prediction of Jesus' Betrayal, 13:18-30
  1. The announcement to the disciples, 13:18-22
  2. The identity of the betrayer, 13:23-27
  3. The departure of Judas, 13:28-30
 C. The Preparation for Departure, 13:31–14:31
  1. The new commandment, 13:31-35
  2. The question of Peter, 13:36–14:4
  3. The question of Thomas, 14:5-7
  4. The question of Philip, 14:8-21
  5. The question of Judas (not Iscariot), 14:22-24
  6. The concluding words of encouragement, 14:25-31
 D. The Believer's Relationships, chap. 15
  1. The relationship with Christ, 15:1-11
   a. The allegory, 15:1-2
   b. The application, 15:3-6
   c. More about remaining in Christ, 15:7-11
  2. The relationship with disciples, 15:12-17
  3. The relationship with the world, 15:18-25
   a. The reasons for the hostility, 15:18-21
   b. The prediction of hostility, 15:22-25
  4. The relationship with the Holy Spirit, 15:26-27
 E. The Ministry of the Holy Spirit, 16:1-15
  1. The persecution of the disciples, 16:1-4
  2. The departure of Jesus, 16:5-7

VI. **The Confirmation of Belief, chap. 20**
  A. The Empty Tomb, 20:1-10
  B. The Appearance to Mary Magdalene, 20:11-18
  C. The Appearances to the Ten, 20:19-23
  D. The Appearance to Thomas, 20:24-29
  E. The Purpose of the Gospel, 20:30-31

VII. **The Responsibilities of Belief, chap. 21**
  A. The Appearance in Galilee, 21:1-14
    1. The return to fishing, 21:1-3
    2. The miraculous catch, 21:4-11
    3. The breakfast with Jesus, 21:12-14
  B. The Instruction of Peter, 21:15-19
  C. The Correction Concerning John, 21:20-23
  D. The Authentication of the Record, 21:24-25

HOMILETICAL SUGGESTIONS

Many of those who study John's gospel are desirous of preaching its great truths. A preacher could simply begin with John 1:1 and preach through to 21:25. But this could be rather tedious and may not be the best way to develop the major themes and teachings of the book.

I suggest that preachers divide the book into reasonable sections and preach several shorter sermon series rather than a single lengthy one.

In my own preaching from the fourth gospel, I have found it helpful to begin with the prologue (1:1-18). This section presents the deity and incarnation of Jesus. From the prologue I proceed to the purpose statement (20:30-31). This states John's purpose in writing and reveals his approach to the book. After these introductory messages, I suggest preaching a series of messages on the seven miracles of John's gospel (cf. pp. 19-20). John's purpose statement (20:30-31) indicates that these miracles were presented to elicit belief. Such a series should focus on the Person of Christ as shown by His mighty deeds.

A later series from John could be developed from the Upper Room discourse (chaps. 13-17). Here John presents wonderful teachings of Jesus with which every disciple should be familiar—teachings on ministry, love, heaven, prayer in Jesus' name, peace, abiding in Christ, the ministry of the Holy Spirit, and many more.

A spring series of messages could be developed from John 18-20, presenting the trial, crucifixion, and resurrection of Jesus. Such a series could be scheduled to conclude on Easter Sunday with a message on the resurrection appearances of Jesus.

Other homiletical suggestions will be included in the commentary to help stimulate the preacher's own creative thinking.

Study Guide

The following questions are designed to help students master the major issues of John's gospel. Suggested answers may be found in the commentary. An annotated bibliography, at the end of this volume, provides further resources for study and research.

1. What is the theme of John and purpose of the book? How does John go about accomplishing the purpose of his gospel (20:31)?
2. What are the views on the date of John's gospel? What evidence is there for the date you advocate?
3. What are the major interpretive problems in John?
4. What is the textual issue of John 7:53–8:11? What evidence can you present for inclusion?
5. In what geographical area does most of John's gospel take place? How is this different from the synoptics?
6. How does John develop the gospel thematically? Can you point out the key turning points and significant developments as related to the themes of belief and unbelief?
7. What does John mean by the term *believe*? What words are used as synonyms for *belief*?
8. What would the term *logos* have meant to the Jews and Greeks of John's day? How does John use and develop this familiar term?
9. What is the chronological problem of the Passover in John 19:28? What is a likely solution to this problem?
10. What is your interpretation of the meaning of the foot washing in John 13:1-20? What is the major lesson of the analogy of the vine in John 15:1-11?
11. What is the significance of chapter 12 in relationship to the argument of John?

12. What key topics are discussed in each chapter of the Upper Room discourse (John 13-17)?
13. What unique contribution does John's gospel make to the record of the trial of Jesus?
14. How does chapter 21 fit into the argument of John's gospel? What is the major lesson Jesus was teaching Peter in 21:15-17?

Abbreviations

JBL	*Journal of Biblical Literature*
JETS	*Journal of the Evangelical Theological Society*
NICNT	New International Commentary on the New Testament
NICOT	New International Commentary on the Old Testament
TNTC	Tyndale New Testament Commentaries

JOHN
CHAPTER
ONE

BEGINNINGS OF THE GOSPEL

THE PROLOGUE, 1:1-18

The prologue of the fourth gospel presents a summary of the book. Here the essential facts concerning the life of Jesus the Messiah are declared: His deity, incarnation, and mission. John declares that the incarnate God has entered into human life to bring life and light to as many as believe in Him. The rest of the gospel unfolds, elaborates, and demonstrates this truth.

There are many divergencies among scholars over the analysis and interpretation of the prologue.[1] But there is a growing consensus that the repetition of key words ("Word," "life," "light") within the prologue reflects the poetic character of Hebrew parallelism.[2] It has been further argued that the prologue is chiastic in structure. Chiasm may be defined as a literary figure or structural principle that consists of "placing crosswise" words, ideas, sentences, or passages to provide symmetry and emphasis. Culpepper presents a convincing study on

---

1. J. S. King, "The Prologue to the Fourth Gospel: Some Unresolved Problems," *Expository Times* 86 (1975): 372-75.
2. Eldon Jay Epp, "Wisdom, Torah, Word: The Johannine Prologue and the Purpose of the Fourth Gospel," in *Current Issues in Biblical and Patristic Interpretation*, ed. Gerald F. Hawthorne (Grand Rapids: Eerdmans, 1975), p. 129.

35

the conceptual parallels of the prologue and offers the following analysis:[3]

A. Word with God, 1-2
   B. What came to be through the Word: creation, 3
      C. What we receive through the Word: life, 4-5
         D. John sent to testify, 6-8
            E. Incarnation; response of the world, 9-10
               F. The Word and His own, 11
                  G. Those who accept the Word, 12*a*
                     H. Become children of God, 12*b*
                  G.' Those who believed in the Word, 12*c*
               F.' The Word and His own, 13
            E.' Incarnation; response of the community, 14
         D.' John's testimony, 15
      C.' What we have received from the Word: grace, 16
   B.' What came to be through the Word: grace and truth, 17
A.' Word with God, 18

The chiastic structure of the prologue focuses on v. 12*b* and reflects John's leading concern to bring the readers to a faith-relationship with God as His spiritual children (cf. John 20:31).

THE ESSENTIAL NATURE OF THE WORD, 1:1-5

John opens his gospel with several declarations concerning the "Word" (*Logos*). The logos was an established, first-century philosophical concept that John drew upon, added to, and enriched to communicate something about the Person of Christ (cf. 1:14; 1 John 1:1; Rev. 19:13).[4]

Scholars debate whether the concept of the logos has its roots in Jewish or Hellenistic thought. God creates by His word (Gen. 1:3; Ps. 33:9), and in the Hebrew Scriptures the *word* of God is often personi-

---

3. R. Alan Culpepper, "The Pivot of John's Prologue," *New Testament Studies* 27 (October 1980): 1-31.

4. For further study on the logos, see Donald Guthrie, *New Testament Theology* (Downers Grove, Ill.: InterVarsity, 1981), pp. 321-29; Leon Morris, *The Gospel According to John*, NICNT (Grand Rapids: Eerdmans, 1971), pp. 115-26; G. A. Turner, "Logos," in *The Zondervan Pictorial Encyclopedia of the Bible*, ed. Merrill C. Tenney (Grand Rapids: Zondervan, 1975), 3:953-58.

fied as an instrument for the execution of His will (Pss. 33:6; 107:20; 119:89; 147:15, 18). This concept also appears in the Apocrypha (Ec'us. 1:1-20; 24:1-22; Wisdom 9:1) and Jewish Targums (paraphrastic translations of portions of the Old Testament into Aramaic), where the Aramaic term *memra* ("word") is substituted for the divine name of God. Thus, in Jewish thought, the logos concept is associated with the personification of God's revelation.

Philo (c. 20 B.C.-A.D. 54), an Alexandrian Jew, also made frequent use of the term *logos*. Philo accepted the philosophical ideas of the day and attempted to bring about a synthesis of Greek philosophy with Old Testament theology as he interpreted the Hebrew Scriptures. In his writings, Philo used the word *logos* to denote the intermediate agency by which God created material things and communicated with them. The logos was conceived of as a bridge between the transcendent (holy) God and the material (evil) universe. For Philo and those of Hellenistic (Greek) worldview, the logos constituted a mediating principle between God and matter.

In the past, many scholars were persuaded that John drew primarily upon Hellenistic thought in his use of the logos concept. More recently, scholars are giving greater credence to the possibility that John drew his logos concept from Jewish thought. Considering the data, it seems likely that John drew upon a concept familiar in both Greek and Jewish thought.

There are various shades of meaning of this term that would have theological and philosophical significance to both Jews and Greeks of John's day. John drew upon this familiar logos concept but gave it new and fuller meaning.

For John, the logos is no mere mediating principle; the Logos is a personal being. For John, the logos is no mere personification of God's revelation; the Logos is God's revelation in the flesh. In his use of logos, John amplifies and applies a familiar concept. He identifies the Logos as a divine Person who reveals God to man.

IN RELATION TO GOD, 1:1-2
1:1   The prologue is "bracketed at the beginning and end with assertions of the deity of the Logos."[5] John begins by affirming the eternal existence (v. 1*a*), personal distinctiveness (v. 1*b*), and divine nature

5. Ed L. Miller, "The Logos Was God," *The Evangelical Quarterly* 53 (April-June 1981), p. 68.

of the Logos (v. 1c). John first declares that the Logos antedates time and goes back to eternity past. He existed with God since the beginning of time.

John goes on to state that the Logos was "with" (*pros*), but distinct from, God (v. 1b). The Logos is seen to be a separate entity from God—not a mere attribute or extension of the Father. This distinctiveness is with regard to personality, not divine essence. The word *with* speaks of a "face to face" relationship. The Logos is in a close relationship (fellowship) with God, yet exists as a distinctive Person.

John concludes his trilogy on the Logos by revealing that the Logos is no mere personification or principle (v. 1c). The Logos, he declares, is truly a divine Person.

The *New World Translation* of the Bible, published by the Jehovah's Witnesses, translates this third affirmation "the Word was a god." It is argued that the absence in the Greek text of the definite article ("the") with *theos* ("God") means that the Logos (Jesus) is merely "a god," a "semi-deity." The deity of Christ and the doctrine of the Trinity are thus denied.

But the apostle John expressed the truth in the best way possible. Had he used the article with *theos* he would have expressed the error of the third-century heretic Sabellius, who held that the Father and the Son were one Person. This would have contradicted John's previous statement, which distinguished God the Father and the Logos. Having just asserted that the Logos was "with" God, John could not now say that the Logos was identical with God.[6] The Logos is not to be identified as God the Father but has the same divine essence or attributes. The absence of the article emphasizes the character and the divine quality of the Logos. As Kent notes, "By placing *theos* first in the clause, John gave it the emphatic position, and by employing it without the article, he stressed the qualitative sense of the noun."[7] For a similar construction without the article, see John 4:24.

1:2   In v. 2, John combines the first and second clauses of v. 1 ("in the beginning" and "with God") to emphasize that the Logos did not come to have a relationship with God but was with God *from the beginning*.

---

6. Ibid., p. 73.
7. Homer A. Kent, Jr., *Light in the Darkness* (Grand Rapids: Baker, 1974), p. 7.

IN RELATION TO CREATION, 1:3

1:3 In relationship to creation, the Logos is revealed to be the active agent, the Creator of "all things." Paul expresses the same thought in Col. 1:16-17 (cf. 1 Cor. 8:6; Heb. 1:2). Every created thing came into being by the activity of the Logos.

IN RELATION TO MAN, 1:4

1:4 John introduces two themes that will be developed throughout the gospel—life and light. The Logos has life in Himself and is a source of both physical life (John 5:25; 11:25) and spiritual life (14:6) to others. The word *life* (*zōē*) occurs thirty-six times in John. Seventeen times it is used with the adjective *eternal* (*aiōnios*) with no apparent difference in meaning. John's purpose in writing was to elicit belief that would issue in life (20:31), both in its quantitative (10:28) and qualitative aspects (10:10). Believers in Jesus Christ enjoy spiritual life in Him because of the new birth (quality of life) and eternal life after death because of the resurrection (quantity of life).

The Logos is "the light of men." The term *light* is used metaphorically in John to refer to the illumination from God that penetrates spiritual darkness to bring spiritual light. Jesus is the light personified (John 8:12; 9:5) and is a source of spiritual light to mankind. Because Ps. 36:9 indicates that God is the ultimate source of light and life, v. 4 supports John's affirmation that the Logos is divine (1:1).

IN RELATION TO EVIL, 1:5

1:5 Verse 5 introduces another major theme in John's gospel—the opposition of light and darkness. *Darkness* is used by John to refer to the realm of spiritual evil—the satanic world system set in opposition to God and His people (John 12:35). Unbelievers love the darkness (3:19), but believers have no part in it (8:12). Jesus, the Logos, is the light of the world (8:12; 9:5), which penetrates the world's darkness.

The last phrase, best translated "the darkness has not overcome (or overtaken) it," indicates that in this spiritual conflict darkness is not able to extinguish the light. Light is preeminent over the darkness. Though opposed, Christ was victorious in His mission of bringing the spiritual illumination of His Person to the unbelieving world set against God.

The contemplation of God, His character, and His creative work in vv. 1-5 should not simply fill our minds with theological facts. When

God revealed Himself to Moses, he bowed low and worshiped (Ex. 34:6-8).

The Manifestation of the Word, 1:6-13

The Logos has been identified and described. Now John recounts Jesus' presentation to the world and reports the two responses—rejection by His own and acceptance by others.

ANNOUNCED BY JOHN, 1:6-8

John the Baptist was sent from God to prepare the way for the coming of the Logos. The announcement of His coming and circumstances of His birth are recorded in Luke 1:5-25. The angel declared to Zacharias that John would minister in the "spirit and power of Elijah" to lead people to repentance and "to make ready a people prepared for the Lord" (Luke 1:17).

1:6 Verse 6 marks a significant stage in redemptive history—the coming of John, the introducer of the Messiah (cf. John 1:19-34). The apostle tells of the origin of John's mission. Like other prophets (Ex. 3:10-15; Isa. 6:8), he did not come on his own but was commissioned and sent "from God" (cf. Mal. 3:1).

1:7 The purpose of John's ministry is to "testify concerning that light." The words "as a witness" focus on John's activity and introduce another major theme in the fourth gospel. The noun "witness" (*marturia*) occurs fourteen times in John, and the verb "to bear witness, testify" (*martureō*) occurs thirty-three times. The primary usage of this term is with reference to the character and significance of the Person of Christ. Charles notes that the apostle's task is to build his case for who Jesus is. He accomplishes this by using key witnesses, even up to the final courtroom appearance before Caiaphas and Pilate.[8] John the Baptist is the first key witness (cf. John 1:29-34).

1:8 The ultimate purpose of John the Baptist's witness is to elicit belief in Jesus, the Light. The word *believe* (*pisteuō*) introduces the major theme of John's gospel, the gospel of belief. *Believe* occurs ninety-eight times in John and means essentially "trust." The biblical concept of belief moves beyond mere intellectual assent to reliance, commitment, and obedience to the Person of Christ (cf. John 3:36).

---

8. J. Daryl Charles, "'Will the Court Please Call in the Promise Witness?': John 1:29-34 and the 'Witness'-Motif," *Trinity Journal* 10 (1989): 72.

The theme of belief and its anthesis (unbelief) can be traced throughout the gospel.

Lest any should mistake John the Baptist for the Messiah (cf. John 1:20), the apostle clarifies that he was only the witness, not "the Light" Himself.

1:9   The divine Logos is identified in v. 9 as the "true light" in contrast to false claimants. Belief itself does not save. The object of faith is essential. A faith that saves must be placed in truth. Truth is another of John's favorite concepts.[9] The adjective "true" (*alēthinos*) appears nine times and is used of that which is genuine, not counterfeit.

The words "that gives light to every man" should be understood to refer to general illumination (cf. Ps. 19:1-6; Rom. 1:20), not universal salvation (cf. John 5:29).

It is debatable whether the phrase "coming into the world" refers to "every man" or to "the true light." Because it is used elsewhere with clear reference to Jesus (cf. John 3:19; 6:14; 12:26; 17:37), John probably intends it to refer to the incarnation, a subject he will introduce shortly (1:11).

Verse 9 contains the first appearance of a significant word in John's writings—*kosmos* ("world"). This word is used by John in several different ways. It can refer to the entire created order (John 17:5) and the earth in particular as the dwelling place of mankind (11:9; 16:21). By extension (i.e., metonymy), *kosmos* can refer to the people who inhabit the world (3:16; 12:19). John also uses the word *kosmos* to refer to the fallen and alienated humanity at enmity with God (1:10; 7:7; 17:25). Although there is nothing intrinsically evil about the *kosmos*, it has turned away from its Creator and shown its hatred for Christ.

REJECTED BY HIS OWN, 1:10-11

1:10   John records that even though the incarnate Logos was the Creator of the world (John 1:3), mankind failed to recognize and acknowledge Him as such. Used with reference to persons, the Greek word *ginōskō* ("recognize") means to realize and acknowledge what one is or claims to be. The unbelieving world did not recognize its own Creator.

1:11   Not only was He ignored by the world in general, He was rejected by His own Jewish people. "That which was his own" refers

9. See Morris's helpful analysis of this concept (*The Gospel According to John*, pp. 293-96).

to all that He had a right to possess—a land, a people, a throne—all that was His by covenant promise (cf. 2 Sam. 7:12-16). Yet His own people did not "receive him." The word "receive" (*paralambanō*) is used in Matthew 1:24 of Joseph taking Mary as his wife. A relationship of trust and committment is implied. Such a relationship with Christ was what the Jewish people refused.

Many people experience rejection in life. Due to various circumstances, they face rejection by friends, co-workers, and family members. It is some consolation to know that Jesus has walked this path. He experienced rejection and knows how to comfort His own.

RECEIVED BY INDIVIDUAL BELIEVERS, 1:12-13

1:12   Verse 12 describes the blessing that comes to those who "receive" Christ. Such persons are privileged to enter into God's own family. The words "received him" are further defined by the phrase "to those who believed in his name." John uses a distinctive faith-formula, "believe into" (*pisteuein eis*), meaning to "believe into Jesus." Used with *pisteuō*, the conjunction *eis* ("into") implies personal surrender and commitment. Although John does not even mention the words *repent* or *repentance,* belief "into" suggests the same turning from the sin of unbelief that repentance involves.[10]

John speaks of believing "in His name." In ancient times, one's name was more than just a personal designation. It was a reflection of one's character and attributes. People were often named or renamed for some noticeable character trait (cf. Num. 13:16; Matt. 16:18; Luke 1:31). The name of Jesus speaks of His person, His attributes, all that He stands for in relationship to His deity and messiahship. To believe in the name of Jesus is to trust in His person as God-man and Redeemer. This involves personal relationship, not merely intellectual assent.

Those who take this personal step of faith have the rightful authority to become "children of God" (*tekna theou*), sharers in the spiritual life of the Father. The importance of this truth is highlighted by its prominence as the center of the prologue (see p. 36). Two important phrases are used in the New Testament to describe the believer's relationship with God: "children of God" and "sons of God." The latter emphasizes the believer's heritage and position. The former emphasizes the believer's nature and character. As a child shares certain

10. George Allen Turner, "Soteriology in the Gospel of John," *JETS* 19 (Fall 1976): 273.

characteristics or features with his natural father, so believers by new birth "participate in the divine nature" (2 Pet. 1:4). This is not to suggest that they become "gods." Rather, they partake in the moral and spiritual nature of God. True children of God will reflect in their own lives some of the characteristics of their Father (cf. Gal. 5:22-23).

1:13   John explains in v. 13 how one becomes a member of God's family. The three expressions "natural descent," "human decision," and "husband's will" are all ways of referring to conception and physical birth. The Jews placed a lot of stock in their physical heritage. They believed that God would favor them merely because of their Abrahamic ancestry. John repudiates such a view. It is not through physical descent but through spiritual birth that one enters God's family. The word *born* (cf. John 3:1-8) is a strong metaphor for a completely new beginning.

The theological point here is that becoming "children of God" takes place as a result of God's work, not ours. New life is of God's initiation and power.

THE INCARNATION OF THE WORD, 1:14-18

John proceeds to demonstrate how the coming of the Logos fits into God's plan to reveal Himself to man.

THE INCARNATE WORD, 1:14

1:14   The most astounding fact of history is that the divine Logos took on humanity while giving up nothing of His deity (cf. Phil. 2:6-8). The term "flesh" (*sarx*) refers here to physical, human life. Jesus, the God-man, partakes of the fullness of deity and the fullness of humanity. The words "and made his dwelling among us" (a powerful metaphor for God's presence) can be traced back to Noah's prayer that God would "dwell in the tents of Shem" (Gen. 9:27). Indeed, God dwelt among the descendents of Shem when He manifested His presence in the Tabernacle during the wilderness wanderings (Ex. 40:34-38). As the Shekinah had dwelt among the Israelites, so the Logos dwelt among humanity ("us").

John testifies that he personally saw the glory of the Logos. The word "glory" (*doxa*) can refer literally to brightness or splendor or metaphorically to fame and renown. John witnessed both. He was with Jesus at the transfiguration (Matt. 17:1-8) and saw His reputation magnified by His miracles and teaching (John 2:11).

The expression "the One and Only" (NIV) or "only begotten" (NASB) is a translation of the Greek word *monogenēs.* There is some debate as to whether *genēs* is derived from *gennaō* ("beget") or *genos* ("kind"). Jesus is either the "one-begotten" or the "one-kind" divine Logos. Because the same term is used of Isaac (Heb. 11:17), who was not Abraham's only son (cf. Gen. 16:15-16), it is most likely that it refers to a "unique" or "one-of-a-kind" Logos. The weight of the linguistic evidence supports this conclusion.[11] The expression emphasizes the deity of the Logos and His unique relationship with the Father (cf. John 1:18; 3:16, 18).

The incarnate Logos is described as "full of grace and truth." Although "grace" (*charis*) occurs only three times in John (1:14, 16, 17), it is one of the great themes of the Bible. The word speaks of favor, help, or goodwill that one grants to another. "Truth" (*alētheia*) is one of the major themes of the fourth gospel. The word occurs twenty-five times and may refer to reality as opposed to mere appearance, or describe fidelity of character.

The words "grace and truth" are reminiscent of the frequently occurring word group in the Hebrew Scriptures "love and faithfulness" (*hesed we'emeth*; cf., Ex. 34:6; Ps. 86:15). Taken together, these words emphasize the attributes of kindness and fidelity reflected in the character of God. These attributes have the fullest and most exquisite display in Jesus. He incarnates God's favor and communicates God's truth. As Messiah and Savior, Jesus is the totally dependable reality.

THE WITNESS OF JOHN, 1:15

1:15 The apostle has described the ministry of John the Baptist (John 1:6-8), and now he records his testimony. To understand the inherent riddle in John's testimony one must realize that in antiquity most people believed chronological priority meant superiority. The older were honored and revered because of their age. This principle seems not to apply in the case of John and Jesus. John was older than Jesus by six months (cf. Luke 1:26, 36). Yet the divine Logos is the superior of the two because He existed before John the Baptist's incarnation. John testifies to the preeminent and preexistent Logos.

11. For further study, see Colin Brown, *Dictionary of New Testament Theology* (Grand Rapids: Zondervan, 1976), 2:75-76; J. V. Dahms, "The Johannine Use of Monogenes Reconsidered," *New Testament Studies* 29 (April 1983): 222-32.

As the introducer of Jesus, John the Baptist was a man of great privilege. But with privilege John shows great humility. God can trust humble people with privileged ministry because He is assured of receiving glory.

THE REVELATORY WORD, 1:16-18

1:16   It is not at all clear whether v. 16 continues the testimony of John the Baptist (cf. v. 15) or contains the reflections of the apostle. Comparing vv. 15-16 with vv. 30-31 would suggest that the apostle interrupts John the Baptist's words in v. 16 with his own concluding reflections (vv. 16-18).

John declares that the fullness of grace found in the divine Logos has provided an abundance of blessing for believers. Christ is the source of the believers' blessings. The word *fullness* suggests the abundance of His resource. The expression "one blessing after another" translates the words "grace in place of grace." The idea is that of an unending supply of divine grace. As one gracious blessing is appropriated, another is made available in its place.

It has been suggested that Exodus 33:13 (NASB) provides the background for the expression "Now therefore, I pray Thee, if I have found favor [grace] in Thy sight, let me know Thy ways, that I may know Thee, so that I may find favor [grace] in Thy sight." The implication is that favor is given to one who has already received favor.[12] In his careful study of this phrase, Hodges favors this approach and suggests that Israel's national history could truly be summed up as the story of "grace after grace."[13]

1:17   The "grace and truth" that is said to characterize the Logos (see comments on v. 14) is given further emphasis in v. 17. John compares the Mosaic revelation ("the law") with that which God reveals in Christ. John is making more of a comparison than a contrast. There was, of course, grace (Gen. 6:8; Ex. 33:17) and truth (Ex. 34:6) in the old, or Mosaic, economy. But this revelation was of a "preliminary character."[14] Now through God's revelation in Jesus Christ, grace and

---

12. Morna D. Hooker, "The Johannine Prologue and the Messianic Secret," *New Testament Studies* 21 (October 1974): 53.

13. Zane C. Hodges, "Grace After Grace—John 1:16," *Bibliotheca Sacra* 135 (January-March 1978): 44.

14. W. J. Dumbrell, "Law and Grace: The Nature of the Contrast in John 1:17," *The Evangelical Quarterly* 58 (January 1986): 34.

truth have come to their greatest realization. Jesus incarnates the fullest measure of divine grace and truth.

Verse 17 contains John's first use of the designation "Jesus Christ." Jesus is the name Gabriel instructed Mary to name her son (Luke 1:31). It is the Greek form of the Hebrew name *Joshua* and means "salvation of Yahweh." The term *Christ* is the Greek translation of the Hebrew *Messiah*, meaning "anointed one." This word is used in the Hebrew Bible to refer to anointed priests and kings. The anointing of a public leader was a religious act that gave recognition to the spiritual dimension of the office. The anointed official served to represent God in the outworking of His theocratic purposes. The term is used in Psalm 2:2 and Daniel 9:25-26 of the promised descendant of David (2 Sam. 7:12-16), destined to rule the nation of Israel. The double title is used only twice in John (1:17; 17:3), but it is used frequently in Acts and the epistles. John uses it here in a solemn and climactic way to emphasize that Jesus is the promised one who comes as God's official representative and ruler.

1:18   John concludes the prologue by revealing the purpose of the incarnation—to give those in darkness a revelation of the truth of God. Because God is spirit (John 4:24), His essential being cannot be seen. He has manifested Himself by glorious appearances in times past (cf. Ex. 33:18–34:8; Isa. 6:1-5), but never was He fully revealed. Yet the incarnation has provided a means for God to be fully revealed and known.

There is a significant textual issue here in verse 18. Some manuscripts read *monogenēs huios* ("one-of-a-kind Son"), and others read *monogenēs theos* ("one-of-a-kind God"). With the acquisition of the Bodmer Papyri, particularly P⁶⁶ and P⁷⁵, both of which read *monogenēs theos,* the external support for this reading has been notably strengthened. The text strongly supports a Johannine affirmation of Christ's deity. Jesus *is* God.

As the Logos shares deepest intimacy with God, He is thus in a position to reveal deep truths about the Father. The words "at the Father's side" may be literally rendered "in the bosom of the Father." This divine Logos has fully explained and revealed the Father. Jesus literally "leads the way to" and "declares" (*exēgeomai*, from which *exegete* is derived) the character of God.

In the prologue John has summarized the advent of the Messiah in words that would communicate to both Jew and Gentile of the first century. John introduces the major themes of his gospel and shows how Christ came to deliver man from spiritual darkness and reveal the fulness of God's grace.

THE BEGINNINGS OF BELIEF, 1:19–4:54

The first chapters of John's gospel focus on the beginnings of belief. Here the first disciples are introduced and the first miracles are recounted. The response to Christ's Person is initially quite positive. Two of John the Baptist's disciples follow Him. Nathanael acknowledges Jesus as the "Son of God," the "King of Israel." In these chapters John records the positive response to Jesus by Jews, Samaritans, and by a Gentile nobleman.

THE WITNESS OF JOHN THE BAPTIST, 1:19-34

John the Baptist functioned as Jesus' introducer. It was his job to prepare a believing remnant of Jews to welcome the Messiah when He should appear on the scene (cf. Matt. 3:1-6 and Isa. 40:3; Luke 1:13-17 and Mal. 4:5).

THE IDENTIFICATION OF JOHN, 1:19-29

1:19   While John was ministering (cf. John 1:7-8, 15), representatives of the relgous establishment approached him to investigate his activities and claims. They regarded it as their responsibility as religious leaders to examine prophets to see if they were of God (cf. Deut. 13:1-5; 18:20-22). The priests were descendants of Aaron who had authority to minister at the altar in the Temple (Ex. 28:1). The Levites were descendants of Levi who had been appointed by God to assist the priests (Num. 8:19, 26). They came with the simple question, "Who are you?" (NASB). The officials in Jerusalem wanted to know more about him.

1:20   Although nothing had been said about John's being the Messiah, the first-century Roman rule of Palestine lent itself to considerable messianic expectancy. John wanted it to be emphatically clear that he laid no claim to the office of Messiah. John used the emphatic pronoun to strengthen his statement "I am not the Christ!"

1:21   The priests and Levites inquired further, "Are you Elijah?" Their question was based on the prophecy of Malachi 4:5, which predicted the coming of Elijah before the day of the Lord. It was commonly believed among Jews of the first century that Elijah the Tishbite

would return in the flesh to restore Jewish families to purity in anticipation of Messiah's coming. The Septuagint's translation of Malachi 4:5
reads "Elijah the Tishbite," not simply Elijah, which would have encouraged this idea. John made it clear that he was definitely not Elijah
the Tishbite.

John's response has raised questions about his fulfilling Malachi's predictions (Mal. 3:1; 4:5-6). On the basis of John 1:21, some
hold that Elijah must personally come again to fulfill these prophecies. Those who hold this viewpoint often identify one of the two witnesses of Revelation 11:3-6 as Elijah. Others are more impressed by
the rather clear indications in the synoptic gospels that John the Baptist fulfilled Malachi's prophecies (cf. Matt. 11:10-14; 17:10-13; Mark
9:11-13; Luke 1:17, 76).

It seems that John denied being Elijah the Tishbite whom the
Jews anticipated. But he fulfilled Malachi's prophecies—in an unexpected way. He came in the "spirit and power of Elijah" (Luke 1:17).
Malachi uses the name Elijah (Mal. 4:5) to refer to the prophetic office
of Elijah. As restorer of God's people, John fulfilled this office and
ministry (Matt. 3:4-6).

Still perplexed, the priests and Levites asked, "Are you the
Prophet?" This question is based on God's promise in Deuteronomy
18:15, 17 to raise up for Israel a prophet like Moses. The Jews of the
first century were expecting a great meditorial person in the tradition
of Moses to appear on the scene before the coming of Messiah. John
assured them that he was not this expected prophet.

1:22   Having exhausted their own list of possibilities and in need of
an answer to give the religious authorities, John's interrogators asked
him to explain himself. "What are you saying about yourself?"

1:23   John answered by quoting Isa. 40:3, which both identifies him
and tells of his mission. John was the "voice" spoken of by Isaiah.
Strangely, Isaiah predicted that the voice would be "calling in the desert." This is the first indication that things were not quite right in Jerusalem. The religious establishment of first-century Judaism was
corrupt. The voice had abandoned Jerusalem and was calling out in
the desert.

The message, "Make straight the way for the Lord," recalls the
preparation made by subjects for a king's passage through their land.
A few days before his travel, they would sweep the road, clear away
debris, and fill the potholes in preparation for the king's use. In a
similar way, John was preparing the nation for the coming of Messiah.

1:24   Whereas the priests and Levites led in the first phase of John's interrogation, the delegation of Pharisees took over in v. 24. The Pharisees were a leading sect within first-century Judaism. They are described by Josephus as having the reputation of "excelling the rest of their nation in the observances of religion, and as exact exponents of the laws" (*Jewish Wars* 1.110). The Pharisees had broken ranks with the Hasmoneans (descendants of the Maccabees) over their abandoning certain traditions and over the legitimacy of the Hasmonean priesthood. The Pharisees held that rabbinic tradition was as valid as the written law of Moses. They were generally middle class Jews who were quite rigorous in the exercise of their religion. The doctrines of the Pharisees were orthodox, although they were condemned by Jesus for not practicing what they preached (Matt. 23:3).

1:25   Matthew reports that John was baptizing in the Jordan River as people "confessed their sins" (Matt. 3:6). John's baptism was an immersion (from *baptizō*, "to dip, immerse, sink") that expressed the repentance of the one submitting to the ritual and his anticipation of forgiveness, which the coming Messiah would grant (Mark 1:4; Luke 3:3).

The Pharisees wanted John to explain his baptism. They were not unfamiliar with ritual immersion. Self-baptism was a common cleansing ritual among the Jews and was required of converts to Judaism. But the Pharisees wondered why John was baptizing, inasmuch as he made no claim to be the Messiah, or Elijah, or the expected Prophet.

1:26   John explained that his baptizing was preparatory for the Messiah's work. It gave people an opportunity to express their desire for cleansing and identify themselves with John, who would introduce Messiah to Israel. The words "among you stands one you do not know" indicate that the Messiah was present on the scene but had not yet been identified. His introduction to Israel was imminent.

1:27   Verse 27 reflects John's view of himself as a subordinate in relationship to the Messiah (cf. 1:15). The removal of a master's sandals was regarded as the duty of a slave. According to an early rabbinic saying, not even a disciple was permitted to perform this task. "Every service which a slave performs for his master shall a disciple do for his teacher except the loosing of his sandal thong."[15] John, a man of genuine humility (cf. John 3:27-30), saw himself as below the status of a slave—not even worthy to unlatch the Messiah's sandal.

---

15. Cited by Morris, *The Gospel According to John*, p. 141.

1:28   The apostle reports that John's interaction with the religious leaders regarding his identity took place at "Bethany on the other side of the Jordan," where John was baptizing. The location of Bethany (cf. John 10:40-41) has been the subject of much debate. By the third century A.D. there was confusion regarding the identification of the site. On the basis of his allegorical interpretation of Scripture, Origen suggested that the proper reading was Bethabara ("house of preparation") and that the site was located west of the Jordan. But the reading "Bethany" is attested by overwhelming documentary evidence. And the phrase "beyond the Jordan" clearly distinguishes it from the Bethany near Jerusalem (Matt. 21:17; Mark 11:1), placing the site east, not west, of the Jordan.

The name Bethany is probably derived from *bet aniyyah*, meaning "house of the boat/ship." This would be an appropriate name for a ford community on the Jordan. Two such fords are represented on the Madaba mosaic map (c. A.D. 560). Although the remains of such ford communities would have long since washed away, there is a strong tradition from the earliest times that links Jesus' ministry with the Hajlah ford in the vicinity of the Wadi el-Kharrar, about seven miles southeast of Jericho.[16] Bethany was a little village situated on the Jordan noted primarily as a ford and a place of refreshment for weary travelers.

THE LAMB OF GOD, 1:29-34

1:29   On the day following the investigation by the religious delegation, John identified Jesus as the Lamb of God. This testimony occurred after Jesus' baptism and temptation and should not be confused with it. (The baptism took place earlier, probably in the summer or autumn of A.D. 29.[17]) What John records here is the first public declaration by John the Baptist that Jesus is the Messiah, the Lamb of God.

There are two basic dimensions of Christ's messianic mission —redemptive and kingdom. He came to redeem and to reign. Here the emphasis is on the Messiah's work of redemption. By referring to Jesus as the "Lamb of God," John is drawing deeply upon the Old Covenant theology of sacrifice. In the Hebrew Scriptures, a lamb is

16. Clemens Kopp, *The Holy Places of the Gospels*, trans. Ronald Walls (New York: Herder and Herder, 1963), pp. 113-29.

17. Harold W. Hoehner, *Chronological Aspects of the Life of Christ* (Grand Rapids: Zondervan, 1970), pp. 29-44.

THE LOCATION OF BETHANY BEYOND THE JORDAN
John 1:28

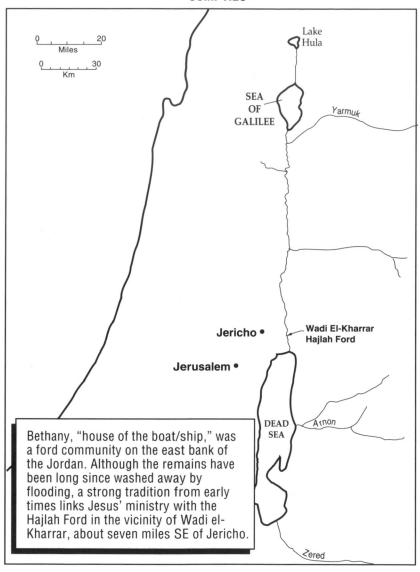

Lake Hula

0 ____ 20
Miles

0 ____ 30
Km

SEA OF GALILEE

Yarmuk

Jericho •

Wadi El-Kharrar
Hajlah Ford

Jerusalem •

DEAD SEA

Arnon

Bethany, "house of the boat/ship," was a ford community on the east bank of the Jordan. Although the remains have been long since washed away by flooding, a strong tradition from early times links Jesus' ministry with the Hajlah Ford in the vicinity of Wadi el-Kharrar, about seven miles SE of Jericho.

Zered

51

associated with many sacrificial offerings: Passover (Ex. 12:3-14), the daily Temple sacrifice (Ex. 29:38-41), the burnt offering (Lev. 1:10), the peace offering (Lev. 3:7), sin offering (Lev. 4:32), the purification of a leper (Lev. 14:13), the lamb sacrifices for the Feast of Trumpets, Tabernacles, and Day of Atonement (Num. 29:1-40). It is probable that the Lamb of God designation focuses not on one particular Old Testament metaphor but on God's sacrificial provision in a collective sense.[18] Yet it is not without purpose that John develops much of his material around the Passover Feast.

The Passover taught that deliverance was effected through the shedding of blood—the death of the innocent in behalf of the guilty (Ex. 12:1-14). Jews hearing John speak would likely link his remark to the Passover lamb. John was saying, "Jesus is God's sacrificial lamb." He was the Lamb Abraham had said God would provide (Gen. 22:7-8). Paul would later write, "For Christ, our Passover lamb, has been sacrificed" (1 Cor. 5:7).

The words "who takes away the sin of the world" are laden with theological significance. The verb "takes away" (*airō*) means "to lift up," "to carry away," "to remove." As the scapegoat identified with sin and carried it with him from the camp of Israel, so Jesus was "sin for us" (2 Cor. 5:21) and carried it to the cross. The penalty He bore was sufficient to provide redemption for "the world"—lost humanity.

1:30   John clarifies in verse 30 that the "Lamb of God" was none other than the superior and pre-existent Messiah about whom he had testified (John 1:15).

1:31   The key to vv. 31-34 is the twice repeated phrase "I myself did not know him" (1:31, 33). Although the NIV varies the translation, the phrases are identical in the Greek. The words "I myself did not know him" should not be taken to imply that John the Baptist did not know Jesus at all. The infancy narrative in Luke 1:36-45 indicates that John and Jesus were related. What John was saying was that he did not recognize Jesus as the Messiah until He was divinely revealed. It was in connnection with John's ministry of baptizing that this took place. In fact, John's ministry of baptism was inaugurated for the specific purpose (*hina*, "that," "in order that") of revealing the Messiah to Israel.

1:32   The apostle records the Baptist's testimony, "I saw the Spirit come down from heaven as a dove and remain on him." This oc-

18. Charles, "John 1:19-34 and the 'Witness'-Motif," p. 78.

curred when Jesus was baptized by John in the Jordan. The apostle testifies to this event, as do the synoptics (Matt. 3:16; Mark 1:10; Luke 3:22). Luke also referred to this when he wrote of how "God anointed Jesus of Nazareth with the Holy Spirit and power" (Acts 10:38).

The phrase "as a dove" describes the descent of the Spirit (literally, "coming down as a dove from heaven"). There is some debate as to whether the Spirit actually took the form of a dove in His manifestation. Luke's use of the word "bodily" (Luke 3:22) provides rather convincing evidence that the Spirit took the visible, physical form of a dove. As to the symbolic significance of the dove, several Jewish writings use the dove as an image of the Spirit of God (Talmud *Hagigah* 15*a*, Targum to Canticles 2:12).

1:33 God had revealed to John the Baptist that the Messiah would be identified by a manifestation of the Spirit's descending and remaining upon Jesus. The Lord also revealed to John that the Spirit-anointed Messiah would "baptize" others "with the Holy Spirit." Jesus spoke of this ministry with His disciples just before His ascension: "For John baptized with water, but in a few days you will be baptized with the Holy Spirit" (Acts 1:5; cf. Luke 24:49; Acts 2:33). John had identified people with his messianic movement through water baptism. Jesus would identify believers with Himself through the ministry of the Holy Spirit (Rom. 8:9, 14; 1 Cor. 12:13). Jesus' possession of the Spirit (1:32) and baptizing of others with the Spirit signals the imminent commencement of the long-awaited messianic age (cf. Isa. 11:1-2; 42:1; 61:1-2; Ezek. 36:25-27; Joel 2:28-32).[19]

1:34 Verse 34 brings the reader to the climax of John's testimony. The gospel of John was written to bring people to the recognition that Jesus is the divine Messiah (John 20:31). John the Baptist concluded his initial public testimony concerning Jesus by aligning himself with that purpose. What John had seen and heard at the baptism of Jesus, including God's announcement from heaven (cf. Matt. 3:17; Mark 1:11; Luke 3:22), serves as convincing evidence that Jesus was God's divine Son ("the Son of God"). Several manuscripts read instead "the chosen one of God," but the age and diversity of witnesses support the reading "Son of God," a phrase more in harmony with the theological terminology of the gospel.[20]

---

19. Walt Russell, "The Holy Spirit's Ministry in the Fourth Gospel," *Grace Theological Journal* 8 (Fall 1987): 230.

20. Cf. Bruce M. Metzger, *A Textual Commentary on the Greek New Testament* (London: United Bible Societies, 1971), p. 200.

The phrase "son of God" (*huios theou*) appears eleven times in the gospel of John. The purpose statement (20:31) indicates the gospel was written that people might believe that Jesus is the Son of God. Believers may become "sons of God" (1:12; 11:52), but Jesus' sonship stands apart from all others. As "son," Jesus has a special relationship (5:20; 6:47) with the Father and a unique knowledge of the Father (10:15). The words of Jesus in 8:58; 10:30; and 14:6 indicate that the term "son of God" affirms His deity (cf. 5:18).

THE FIRST DISCIPLES OF JESUS, 1:35-51

It was at Bethany beyond the Jordan that Jesus made His first disciples. This took place as an outgrowth of John's declaration that Jesus was the "Lamb of God" and "Son of God." As a result of John's testimony, some of his followers left him and began to follow Jesus.

ANDREW, JOHN, AND PETER, 1:35-42

It was John's mission to point men to the Messiah (John 1:7). On the day following his identification of the "Lamb of God" (John 1:19), he had the opportunity to direct two of his disciples to Jesus.

1:35 The two disciples with John were Andrew (1:40) and probably the apostle John. John's pattern in the fourth gospel is to refer to himself only indirectly (cf. 13:23). These two men had traveled from Galilee to the wilderness of Judea in response to John the Baptist's ministry (cf. Matt. 3:5-6). They had listened to his preaching of repentance and had responded to his message.

1:36 John is seen here to be carrying out his work of witness (cf. 1:7). When he saw Jesus passing by, he once again declared, "Look, the Lamb of God."

1:37 Two of John's disciples who heard this witness were prepared to respond. Andrew and John acted on the Baptist's testimony and "followed Jesus." The aorist of *akolutheō* is ingressive, focusing on the commencement of their action. The term is used elsewhere of committed discipleship (cf. Matt. 8:22; Luke 9:61). Yet it can also be used of those whose interest and commitment is only temporary. Many of Jesus' followers withdrew upon hearing His difficult teachings (cf. 6:2, 66). It is uncertain as to the measure of commitment being manifested by Andrew and John at this time. The call to become fishers of men occurred later (cf. Matt. 4:18-22).

1:38   Realizing that He was being followed, Jesus turned and spoke to the two, "What do you want?" (literally, "What are you seeking?"). The two disciples of John responded to Jesus' question with a question of their own, "Where are you staying?" The question implied that they wanted to go with Him and sit under His teaching. They were interested in becoming associated with Him in a teacher-disciple relationship. The term *rabbi* is a transliteration from the Hebrew term meaning "my master." It was used by the Jews as a respectful designation for their religious teachers.

1:39   Jesus responded positively to their query inviting them to "come and see." They followed Jesus to the place where He was staying and spent the rest of what must have been a very memorable day with Him.

John provides the reader with the first of several time notices in the gospel (John 4:6, 52; 19:14). It was the "tenth hour of the day" when Andrew and John joined Jesus. The Jews of the first century reckoned the days from sunset to sunset. From the Babylonians they learned to divide the daylight period into twelve hours beginning at 6:00 A.M. According to this system of reckoning, the "tenth hour" would be 4:00 P.M. For legal and contractural purposes, the Romans reckoned their days from midnight to midnight. Accordingly, the tenth hour would be 10:00 A.M. Yet Roman sundials, in popular use by the common people, designated noon as the sixth hour of the day.

By either Jewish reckoning or Roman sundials, the tenth hour would be 4:00 P.M. Yet John says that the disciples "spent that day with him." How could this be true if there were only two hours left in the day? It was commonly understood in Jewish society that any part of the day would be regarded as the whole for purposes of reckoning time (Jerusalem Talmud, *Shabbath* 9.3). John is telling the reader that the disciples spent the rest of the day with Jesus and that the time spent was significant.

1:40   Although John does not mention himself, he identifies Andrew, Simon Peter's brother, as one of the two disciples who had followed Jesus. Andrew and Peter, natives of Galilee, were from the city of Bethsaida (John 1:44) but made their home in Capernaum (Mark 1:21). They were fishermen by trade and were in partnership in a fishing enterprise on the Sea of Galilee with James and John, sons of Zebedee (Matt. 4:18; Luke 5:10).

1:41   The afternoon interview with Jesus must have provided Andrew with sufficient evidence of His messianic Person because he immediately sought out his brother, Peter, and reported, "We have found the Messiah." He used the Jewish term for God's anointed one. John the apostle translates the term into Greek (*Christos*, or "Christ") for the benefit of non-Jewish readers.

1:42 Andrew is remembered because he was one of the first to acknowledge Jesus as Messiah and because he had the heart of an evangelist. He did not just report his findings; he brought Peter to Jesus. Andrew wanted his brother to know the Lord. The greatest gift anyone can receive is the good news of the gospel. The greatest gift anyone can give is the same precious truth.

When Andrew's brother came to Jesus he was given a new name. People were often named or renamed in the biblical period to ac- knowledge a character trait or significant event (cf. Num. 13:16). Pe- ter's Jewish name was Simon ben John ("Simon son of John"). But Jesus gave him the name "Cephas," which in the Aramaic language means "stone." Peter (*Petros*) is the Greek translation of the Aramaic name. The renaming of Simon foreshadowed the character and signif- icance of his person as a disciple of Jesus (cf. Matt. 16:16-19)—he was to become Peter, "the rock," steadfast and firm in faith.

PHILIP AND NATHANAEL, 1:43-51

1:43 On the day following his renaming of Peter, Jesus resolved to leave for Galilee. It was not yet time for his ministry to commence in Jerusalem. Galilee is the name applied to the northern district of Isra- el that was surrounded on three sides by foreign nations. The term literally means "circle" or "district," the fuller expression of which is "district of the Gentiles" (Isa. 9:1). According to Josephus, Galilee was divided into upper and lower regions (*Jewish Wars* 3.35-40). Upper, or northern, Galilee does not enter much into biblical history. Lower Galilee served as the location for most of Christ's ministry as recorded in the synoptic gospels. Galilee's fertility was highly praised by Jose- phus, who states that no part of the land was left uncultivated.

Before departing for Galilee, Jesus found Philip and said, "Fol- low me." The imperative is best translated "Keep on following me." Jesus intended for Philip to become a disciple.

1:44 Like Andrew and Peter, Philip was from the Galilean town of Bethsaida. Many Bible atlases and maps have indicated that there were two Bethsaidas, one in Galilee and the other east of the Jordan in Gaulanitis. Josephus tells how Philip the Tetrarch advanced the village of Bethsaida, near the northeast shore of the Sea of Galilee, to the status of a "city" (*polis*) by strengthening its fortifications, increasing its population, and naming it Julias (after the emperor's daughter). This site has been identified as et-Tell, situated about a mile and a half north of where the Jordan River empties into the Sea of Galilee. Early pilgrim tradition knows of only one Bethsaida-Julias, and no evidence for a western Bethsaida appears until the time of the Crusades, when sites were moved in wholesale fashion to suit the convenience of pilgrims.

Bethsaida-Julias was a double site with a fishing village suburb on the Galilean lakeshore (el-'Araj) within reasonable proximity of the fortified city of et-Tell. A Roman road and an aquaduct join the two sites.[21]

1:45 Verse 45 reflects the evangelistic principle of multiplication. As Andrew brought Peter, so Philip led Nathanael to the Messiah. He reported to Nathanael that he had found the prophesied Messiah, the one written of by Moses (cf. Gen. 3:15; 22:8; 28:12; 49:10; Num. 21:9; 24:17) and the prophets (Isa. 7:14; 9:6; 52:13–53:12; Mic. 5:2; Zech. 9:9). Philip identified the Messiah in terms of His earthly relationships—Jesus, from the city of Nazareth and the adopted son of Joseph (cf. Matt. 1:18; Luke 1:34).

Nathanael seemed shocked at the mention of Nazareth. Nazareth was so insignificant and relatively unknown that it was not even mentioned in the Hebrew Scriptures. But Nathanael's question, "Can any good come from there?" suggests that insignificance was not the only problem. There was something unclean about the place. This was due to its geographical proximity to Sepphoris, the Roman capital of Galilee. Sepphoris was located just four miles north of Nazareth. When the Roman rulers of this region needed workmen, they drew from the laborers of Nazareth. Some of the citizens of Nazareth exploited this opportunity for personal gain. And so the people of Nazareth were disdained by many Jews. It was an insignificant place with a questionable reputation.

There is a time to debate issues, and there is a time to let the issues speak for themselves. Philip recognized that it was a time for the latter. He simply responded, "Come and see."

1:47 Seeing Nathanael approaching, Jesus made a statement that reflects supernatural insight into the character of the man. He de-

---

21. J. Carl Laney, "Geographical Aspects of the Gospel," in *Essays in Honor of J. Dwight Pentecost*, ed. Stanley D. Toussaint and Charles H. Dyer (Chicago: Moody, 1986), pp. 81-82.

clared, "Here is a true Israelite in whom there is nothing false." Nathanael was a man of integrity. The word "false" appears in extrabiblical text to refer to "bait" or a "snare." There was not a hidden hook or trap in Nathanael's character.

1:48 Surprised to hear these words spoken by a stranger, Nathanael inquired, "How do you know me?" He wondered, perhaps, if they had met before. Had their paths crossed at a festival or village market? Jesus demonstrates in His response that His knowledge of Nathanael's character was of supernatural origin. He had seen Nathanael while he was still sitting under the fig tree, before he had been called by Philip.

1:49 Nathanael was a man who did not need a lot of convincing. According to Trudinger, knowing the thoughts of men was one of the expected accomplishments of the ideal King (as in Wisdom 7:20).[22] Faced with the Person and knowledge of Jesus he exclaimed, "Rabbi, you are the Son of God; you are the King of Israel." Nathanael was recognizing Jesus as the divine Messiah who had a right to the royal throne of David (cf. 2 Sam. 7:12-16). The prophets had anticipated the coming of this messianic king and the establishment of His kingdom. Jacob announced that He would come through Judah (Gen. 49:10). Micah had predicted His birth in Bethlehem (Mic. 5:2). Isaiah prophesied His virgin birth (Isa. 7:14) and His ministry in Galilee (Isa. 9:1-2). Nathanael realized that the promised ruler had come. He could be expected to assume His rightful, royal office.

1:50 Nathanael had taken the first step of faith. This was a faith that would be encouraged, undergirded, and enlarged through the three and one-half years of his association with Jesus. Knowing what was ahead, Jesus responded, "You will see greater things than that." Nathanael had not seen anything. The best was yet to come.

1:51 Jesus then made an exciting promise to Nathanael and the others. The word translated "you" (*humin*) is the plural form. The promise is set off by the words "I tell you the truth," literally, "Amen, amen" ("truly, truly," NASB). This phrase is used twenty-five times in John and appears nowhere else in the New Testament. It is used by the author to introduce a truth of special solemnity and importance.

What is the meaning of Jesus' promise that Nathanael and the others would see heaven open and "the angels of God ascending and descending on the Son of Man"? Jesus is undoubtedly drawing imagry

---

22. L. Paul Trudinger, "An Israelite in Whom There Is No Guile: An Interpretative Note on John 1:45-51," *The Evangelical Quarterly* 54 (April-June 1982): 119.

from the vision Jacob had at Bethel (Gen. 28:12). As he slept, Jacob dreamed of angels ascending and descending upon a ladder that reached from earth to heaven. Jesus is saying that Jacob's dream has become a reality through His incarnation. The divine Messiah is the ladder, the bridge, the mediator between heaven and earth (1 Tim. 2:5). He is the one through whom man can have access to and fellowship with God.

The expression "Son of Man," appearing twelve times in John, is the favorite self-designation of Jesus. There is considerable debate among scholars as to whether Jesus drew upon Ezekiel's use of this term (Ezek. 2:1-3) to emphasize His humanity or upon Daniel's use of the term (Dan. 7:13) to emphasize His messiahship.

It seems that the issue of Jesus' humanity was never debated by those He ministered among in the first century. The crucial and debated issue was His messiahship. Yet the term *messiah* had such political connotations in the first century that it was difficult to use without arousing rebellion against Roman rule. The Jews were looking for a political messiah—one who would overthrow Rome and establish an independent Jewish state.

Most likely Jesus appropriated the term *Son of Man* from the glorious vision of Daniel 7:13. Those with genuine interest and biblical awareness would not be likely to miss the allusion to Jesus' messiahship. Yet those who were rejecting Him could have taken the term simply as a reference to His own humanity. Like the parables, the term *Son of Man* could be understood on a surface and superficial level as well as a deep and theological level.

HOMILETICAL SUGGESTIONS

The prologue of the gospel (1:1-18) provides an excellent opportunity for expounding the deity of Christ. He is the divine Logos who came to reveal God to mankind. The verses that follow present the messianic forerunner, John the Baptist (1:19-28), and then focus once again on Jesus.

John's great purpose in this first section of the gospel is to introduce the reader to the Person and manifold diminsions of the Messiah. There are eight different terms used for Christ in vv. 29-51. He is designated the "Lamb of God," "Son of God," "Rabbi," "Messiah," "Jesus of Nazareth," "son of Joseph," "King of Israel," and "Son of Man." These eight terms could be expounded in a single message or in a sermon series.

JOHN
CHAPTER
TWO

MINISTRY AND MIRACLE

THE FIRST MIRACLE AT CANA, 2:1-12

At strategic times throughout biblical history miracles have been used as messengers from God to authenticate His message. It was during the period of Christ's earthly ministry that miracles had their mightiest display. There are two primary purposes for these miracles. First, they were designed to authenticate that Jesus was who He claimed to be—the Messiah and Son of God (John 20:31). Second, they were designed to authenticate Christ's message. In John 10:38 Jesus appealed to the miracles to substantiate His message concerning His oneness with the Father. In John 8:12 He claimed to be the light of the world. In John 9 He proved that claim by giving sight to the man born blind.

An additional and significant purpose of Christ's miracles was to foreshadow, in a brief display, conditions of the future messianic kingdom. Isaiah anticipates a day when "the eyes of the blind will be opened," "the ears of the deaf will be unstopped," the lame will "leap like a deer," and the mute tongue will "shout for joy" (Isa. 35:5-6). These basic purposes of Christ's miracles must be kept in mind in studying the seven great miracles of John's gospel.

THE MARRIAGE AT CANA, 2:1-5

2:1 The miracle at Cana took place "on the third day" after Jesus' departure from Bethany (John 1:28). The distance between Bethany and Cana is about seventy-five miles. In the biblical period, when most travel was done on foot, it was not uncommon for travelers to average twenty-five miles per day.

The location of Cana of Galilee is a matter of considerable debate. Kefr Kenna ("the village of Kenna") makes a fairly convincing claim to authenticity. The Franciscan church in the heart of the village is reportedly built on the actual remains of the house in which the miracle took place. Tourists may view an old water jar that is said to have held wine after the miracle. The earliest pilgrim tradition, however, points to a site about nine miles north of Nazareth called Khirbet Kana ("ruin of Cana"). Josephus refers to Cana as his military quarters and then later describes his quarters as being in the Plain of Asochis, now known as the Bet Netofa Valley (*Life* 86, 207). The analysis of the name *Cana* ("place of reeds") would also suggest Khirbet Kana, located on a hill overlooking the marshy stretches of the Bet Netofa Valley. Although the site has not been excavated, surface exploration has led to the discovery of ruins from the Roman period, including ancient tombs, wall foundations, and thirty-one cisterns. Future excavation at the site may serve to confirm the identification.

A Jewish wedding was an occasion of great joy and festivity and was the culmination of a long process toward marriage. On the evening of the marriage the bride was led, usually by torchlight procession, from the home of her parents to her new husband. There the marriage formula was pronounced and legal documents signed. After the prescribed washings and benedictions the marriage feast would begin. It could last one day or continue on for a week, depending on the resources of the new husband.

Jesus' mother was attending this marriage celebration. The directions she gave the servants (John 2:5) suggest that she was helping with the wedding, perhaps as a friend of the family.

2:2   Jesus and the disciples had also been extended an invitation and had come to the wedding. Although the term "invited" is singular ("he was invited"), this does not necessarily indicate the disciples had come as uninvited guests. It has been shown that in Semitic Greek it was not uncommon to have a singular subject followed by a singular verb to which a plural subject would be linked by *and* (*kai*).[1]

---

1. Barclay M. Newman and Eugene A. Nida, *A Translator's Handbook on the Gospel of John* (London: United Bible Societies, 1980), p. 56.

THE LOCATION OF CANA OF GALILEE
John 2:1

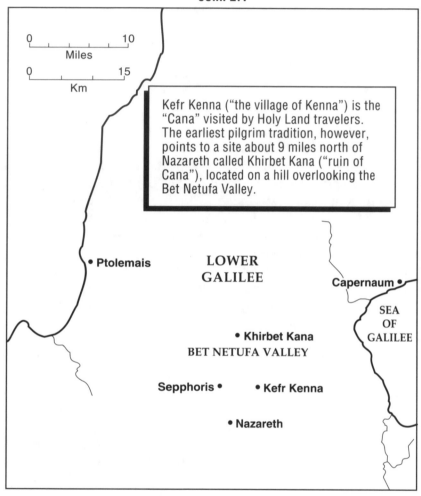

Kefr Kenna ("the village of Kenna") is the "Cana" visited by Holy Land travelers. The earliest pilgrim tradition, however, points to a site about 9 miles north of Nazareth called Khirbet Kana ("ruin of Cana"), located on a hill overlooking the Bet Netufa Valley.

0   10
Miles

0   15
Km

• Ptolemais

LOWER GALILEE

Capernaum •

SEA OF GALILEE

• Khirbet Kana

BET NETUFA VALLEY

Sepphoris •

• Kefr Kenna

• Nazareth

The "disciples" refers to those who had followed Jesus from Bethany to Galilee. They had not yet committed themselves to Him (Matt. 4:18-22; Mark 1:16-20) but were interested in learning more about Him.

2:3   A serious breach of hospitality took place during the marriage feast at Cana—the wine ran out. The discovery of this fact by the guests would certainly have been an embarrassment to the host and his family. Mary quickly brought the matter to Jesus' attention. Her words, literally, "They are having no wine," seem to suggest her wish that He would do something about it. She knew that her Son had been divinely appointed to a messianic task. She had treasured in her heart the wonderful words of Gabriel concerning His birth (Luke 1:26-33) and had contemplated the evidences of His supernatural character. As Toussaint observes, His appearance with the disciples whom He had called would point to the beginning of His public ministry.[2]

Confident that He was the Messiah, she expected Him to do such signs as Moses had done, to manifest Himself to the Jewish people. When would be a more opportune time both to demonstrate His messiahship and meet the needs of the wedding guests?

2:4   Jesus' response to Mary, literally, "What to me and to you, woman?" may sound disrespectful to modern ears. Yet Jesus addressed Mary as "woman" when He committed her to John's care at the cross (John 19:26). It is evident the term could be used to express affection and respect. Jesus was saying in effect, "Dear woman, your maternal authority does not extend into the realm of My messianic work." Jesus' view of His mother's authority is in stark contrast to the Catholic view of Mary. Although Jesus respected His mother, He did not submit to her maternal authority, nor did He worship her. Christians should honor but not venerate Mary.

Jesus then added the words "My time has not yet come." The coming "time" or "hour" (*hōra*) is an important theme in the approaching culmination of Jesus' ministry (John 7:6, 30). When the hour does come (13:1), His betrayal and crucifixion are imminent.

2:5   Mothers have a way with their children, and Mary was no exception. She remained confident that Jesus would somehow respond and meet the need. She placed the household servants at His disposal and instructed them, "Do whatever He tells you."

2. Stanley Toussaint, "The Significance of the First Sign in John's Gospel," *Bibliotheca Sacra* 134 (January-March 1977): 48.

THE MIRACULOUS PROVISION, 2:6-10

Jesus performed thirty-six specifically detailed miracles during His earthly ministry. Many others are referred to in general terms. A miracle is simply "an extraordinary event, a creative deviation from God's normal and natural way of working."[3]

Miracles are done by God's power and are out of the ordinary realm of human experience. Miracles in the Bible are purposive, usually for authenticating a person or a message.

2:6   At the wedding feast were six stone water jars that had been placed there for use in ritual purification. Mark 7:1-4 indicates that this kind of ceremonial washing was of great importance to the Jews. Each jar had a capacity of two to three *metrētai*, a unit of measure estimated at about nine gallons. Thus, the jars could hold between eighteen and twenty-seven gallons each.

2:7   At the request of Jesus, the pots were filled with water. John notes they were filled "to the brim." There could be no mistake as to the original contents of these vessels.

2:8   Jesus then instructed the servants to draw from the vessels and take a portion to the "master of the banquet." This term appears only here in the New Testament. The term could refer to a slave who was responsible for managing the banquet, such as a headwaiter or butler. In this context, however, the banquet master appears to have a role more like a "master of ceremonies."[4] It is unlikely that a slave would call the bridegroom aside to commend the wine.

2:9   The servants knew what they had filled the vessels with. Then the master of the banquet declared what the water had become. A miracle had taken place. The spring water of Cana incredibly had turned into wedding wine. Christ is Lord over His creation and is able to use His supernatural resources to meet man's need.

2:10   Calling the bridegroom aside, the master of the banquet remarked that it was the universal custom for a host to put out the best wine first. Only after the sense of taste was rendered less discerning by earlier portions would the cheaper wine be put out. The words "after the guests have had too much to drink" translates *methuskō* in the passive, "to drink freely," "to get drunk." John, however, is not suggesting that Jesus created more wine for drunken guests. Rather,

---

3. John R. Stott, *Baptism and Fullness: The Work of the Holy Spirit Today* (Downers Grove, Ill.: InterVarsity, 1976), p. 96.

4. Leon Morris, *The Gospel According to John*, NICNT (Grand Rapids: Eerdmans, 1971), p. 184.

he records the comment to highlight for the reader the *quality* of the wine Jesus produced. It made even the best wine appear inferior by comparison.

Concern for the abuse of alcoholic beverages has led some expositors to conclude that Jesus created grape juice rather than wine. However, the word used here (*oinos*) is the normal word for fermented juice of the grape. The normal Greek word in the biblical period for unfermented grape juice is *trux*. It is important for believers to appreciate that the same Bible that condemns drunkenness (Eph. 5:18) and cautions against a misuse of alcoholic beverages (Prov. 23:29-35; 1 Tim. 3:3, 8) recognizes wine as one of God's gifts (Ps. 104:15; Eccles. 9:7).

It is of considerable significance that in antiquity wine was diluted with water. Only barbarians would drink unmixed wine. This custom is referred to in the epilogue of 2 Maccabees, where the writer states, "Just as it is injurious to drink wine by itself, or again water, whereas wine mixed with water is pleasant and produces a delightful sense of well-being, so skill in presenting the incidents is what delights the understanding of those who read the story" (2 Macc. 15:38-39). Although the ratio varied, one part wine was usually mixed with three parts water.[5]

As a result, the alcoholic content of wine used in the first century was considerably reduced. Undiluted wine in use today is not the same as that which was served at the wedding at Cana. Scripture provides guidelines for dealing with such questionable issues as wine-drinking (cf. 1 Cor. 6:12, 19; 8:13; 10:31; Col. 2:20-23; 1 Tim. 3:2; 1 Pet. 2:9).

Every Christian must make a decision whether to use or avoid alcoholic beverages. There is no prooftext for total abstinence, nor is there any text advocating social drinking. One must be guided by one's conscience and by principles of the Word. This is an issue where consciences may differ (Rom. 14:1-5), and the application of the scriptural principles may vary, depending on the situation at hand.

Some may conclude that the wisest course of action for a present-day American Christian is to avoid the use of alcoholic beverages. Others may decide on a moderate use of alcohol in celebration (Gen.

---

5. Robert H. Stein, "Wine-Drinking in New Testament Times," *Christianity Today* (June 20, 1975), pp. 9-10.

14:18; John 2:1-11), worship (Ex. 29:40; Matt. 26:27; 1 Cor. 11:25-26), or during intimate moments (Song of Sol. 1:2; 8:2). Both decisions are biblically acceptable and defensible.

The principle of "love limits liberty" must be kept in view when making a decision on this matter. The use of wine can be seen as a matter of liberty—a matter for which there is not a specific scriptural prohibition. Yet Paul points out that Christian liberty should always be exercised with love and restraint (1 Cor. 8:9-13). He specifically declares, "It is good not to eat meat or to drink wine, or to do anything by which your brother stumbles" (Rom. 14:21).

The difficulty and potential danger revolving around this issue should not be ignored. If a believer does feel the liberty to use alcohol, he should not set such an example that would lead a brother or sister to sin. At times, Christians must forgo certain activities out of concern for the spiritual life of others. Again, Paul declares, "For if because of food your brother is hurt, you are no longer walking according to love. Do not destroy with your food him for whom Christ died" (Rom. 14:15).

The apostle Peter challenged the Jewish Christian readers of his first epistle, "Keep your behavior excellent among the Gentiles" (1 Pet. 2:9). This has application both to those who use alcoholic beverages and those who do not.

If those believers who use alcohol must set a good example of moderation and discretion, then those who do not use alcohol must beware of censorious words or actions. They must guard against legalism (Gal. 5:1) and the danger of giving man's viewpoints and traditions greater consideration than the statements of Scripture (Mark 7:13). They must also guard against prideful, holier-than-thou attitudes regarding this issue. Finally, those who totally abstain must guard against asceticism (Col. 2:20-23) and the failure to appreciate that everything created by God is good (1 Tim. 4:4-5).

The miracle at Cana not only authenticated Christ's Person to His newly called disciples. It gave them a preview of the joy that would be theirs in the messianic kingdom. In the Hebrew Scriptures wine is often associated with joy. According to the psalmist, wine "gladdens the heart of man" (Ps. 104:15). Lack of wine reflects the absence of joy (cf. Isa. 16:10; Joel 1:5, 12). Joel prophesied that in the future messianic kingdom "the vats will overflow with new wine" (Joel 2:24). Abundant wine was one of the anticipated blessings of the kingdom (cf. Isa. 25:6; 27:2-6; Jer. 31:12; Hos. 2:22; Joel 3:18; Amos 9:13-14).

The turning of water to wine was an indication that the Messiah was present and the kingdom was imminent. The miracle gave the wedding guests a brief foretaste of the abundance of joy that would be theirs in Messiah's kingdom. The old wine of Judaism, perverted by the legalism and traditions of the Pharisees, had run out, and Jesus the Messiah was to bring in the new.[6]

THE RESULTS OF THE MIRACLE, 2:11

2:11   John concludes the account by reporting that this was the first of Jesus' miracles. The Greek reads, "This he did (as) a beginning of signs." The word "signs" (*sēmeiōn*) is used throughout John's gospel to refer to supernatural signs—the miracles of Jesus. The word suggests that the miracles were not ends in themselves. They signified something. They were designed to lead observers to an understanding of the Person of Christ.

Two results of this first miracle are noted by John. First, Jesus "revealed his glory." The word "glory" (*doxa*) is used here to refer to Jesus' true character or divine attributes. Through the miracle Jesus disclosed to the disciples His inherent divine nature and Person. Second, the disciples believed (*pisteuō*). They had learned enough about Jesus at Bethany to follow Him to Cana. But now they put their trust in Him. This was the first step in a developing faith that would culminate in full understanding of His Person as resurrected Redeemer (cf. John 20:8).

THE VISIT AT CAPERNAUM, 2:12

2:12   After the wedding feast at Cana, Jesus went down to Capernaum for a short stay. His mother, brothers (Matt. 12:46; John 7:3, 5), and disciples accompanied Him. The reference to Jesus' brothers indicates quite clearly that Joseph and Mary had other children after the birth of Jesus (cf. Mark 6:3). Capernaum ("village of Nahum"), located on the northwest shore of the Sea of Galilee, became the center for Christ's ministry after His rejection at Nazareth (cf. Matt. 4:12-14). He performed some of His greatest miracles there (Mark 2:1-12; John 4:46-54) and taught in its synagogue. Although originally from Bethsaida (John 1:44), Peter made his home in Capernaum (Matt. 8:5, 14). John gives no indication as to what took place during this brief visit.

6. Stanley Toussaint, "The Significance of the First Sign in John's Gospel," *Bibliotheca Sacra* 134 (January-March 1977), p. 50.

THE REGION OF GALILEE
John 2:12

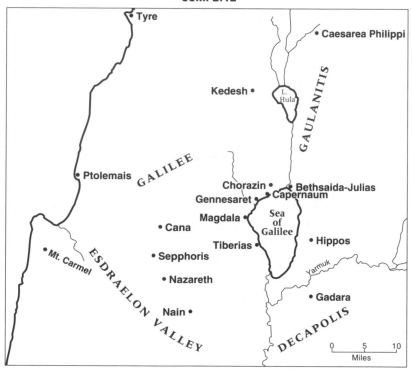

"Galilee" is the name applied to the northern district of Israel. The term literally means "circle" or "district," fuller expression of which is "district of the Gentiles" (Isa. 9:1). Galilee is surrounded on three sides by foreign nations. The region is divided into a series of east-west valleys and basins. Galilee's fertility is highly praised by Josephus, who states that no part of the land was left uncultivated.

THE FIRST TEMPLE CLEANSING, 2:13-22

Jesus cleansed the Jerusalem Temple twice—early in His public ministry and after His royal entry (cf. Matt. 21:12-17). On both occasions Jesus' actions demonstrated His messianic authority over His Father's house.

THE CLEANSING OF THE TEMPLE, 2:13-17

2:13   It was in anticipation of the approaching Passover that Jesus went up to Jerusalem. According to Hoehner's chronology, the year was A.D. 30.[7]

Passover took place in A.D. 30 on Friday, April 7. This is the first of three Passovers mentioned by John (cf. John 6:4; 12:1). It is significant that Jesus' ministry took place in connection with feasts of the Jews, which had redemptive and messianic significance. John wants the reader to appreciate that Jesus comes in fulfillment of the Jewish hopes and expectations expressed by such feasts.

For the Jews, Passover commemorated God's deliverance of His people from the plague of death and bondage of Egypt (Ex. 12:25-28; 13:11-16). It was one of the three great pilgrim feasts (Deut. 16:16) for which Jews throughout the land would travel to Jerusalem to worship. The words "went up to Jerusalem" reflect the ascent in elevation as one travels from the surrounding regions to reach the city (2,425 feet elevation).

2:14   The people who came to Jerusalem for Passover needed an animal to sacrifice, usually a lamb (Ex. 12; Mishnah: *Pesahim*). For the annual Temple offering (Ex. 30:13-16; Mishnah: *Shekalim*), they also needed to have their Roman money exchanged for the Jewish half-shekel. Because every Jew was required by law to spend one tenth of his income in Jerusalem (Deut. 14:23-27), the so-called second tithe, the citizens of Jerusalem were more than willing to provide for the needs of visitors, usually at inflated prices.

Verse 14 reveals how the court of the Temple had been turned into a bazaar, complete with livestock for sacrifice and money changers to provide worshipers with the approved currency. The area of the Temple being used in this manner was the Court of the Gentiles, sur-

---

7. Harold W. Hoehner, *Chronological Aspects of the Life of Christ* (Grand Rapids: Zondervan, 1970), p. 143.

rounded by colonnaded porches and encompassing the Sanctuary (*naos*) where the Holy of Holies was located.

2:15   The desecration of the holy Temple with cattle, manure, and greedy money changers demanded a response on the part of Jesus the Messiah. The Jewish Temple was God's house—the place where He had determined that His reputation should be magnified. Yet this holy place had become a dirty, noisy market.

Jesus made a whip out of cords or rushes and drove the merchants and their animals from the Temple court. He overturned the tables of the money changers, scattering their coins on the pavement.

2:16   Jesus commanded the dove sellers, "Get these out of here!" His verbal rebuke reveals why He responded in such a forceful manner. "How dare you turn my Father's house into a market?" Jesus was exercising His rightful authority over God's house through the messianic act of the Temple cleansing.

Although the church building is not the equivalent of the Herodian Temple, some principles may apply. Should the local church building be used as a vehicle for commerce and financial profit? Such did not please our Lord. Church boards should study the issue carefully before allowing common and ordinary uses for a place set apart for worship.

2:17   At a later time as the disciples reflected on Jesus' cleansing of the Temple they recalled the words of David in Psalm 69:9, "Zeal for your house will consume me." The quote is directly from the Septuagint, although it uses the second aorist tense ("has consumed") instead of the future ("will consume"). Although these words express the heart of David, they find their ultimate fulfillment in the Person of Christ. The cleansing of the Temple gave evidence of Jesus' consuming zeal for God's reputation and worship.

Do we have such a zeal for God's house? God's kingdom? God's work? This kind of zeal is generated through a deep, personal relationship with Him through Christ.

THE RIDDLE ABOUT THE TEMPLE, 2:18-20

2:18   The Jews did not question the legitimacy of the action taken by Jesus against the merchants and money changers, but they did question His authority. Who did He think He was? The Jews demanded of Jesus a miraculous sign to authenticate His status and prove His right to take such action.

2:19   Jesus responded to the demand of the Jews by propounding a riddle, "Destroy this temple, and I will raise it again in three days." Jesus, the master teacher, did not reveal all the facts clearly and simply. He used a riddle to stimulate the thinking of the learners. Through questions and answers He let the disciples participate in the process of discovery. The word translated "temple" (*naos*) refers to the sanctuary, or Holy Place, as distinguished from the Temple precincts (*hieron*), including the court He had just cleansed. The statement lent itself to misinterpretation and was later used against Jesus during His trial before Caiaphas and the Sanhedrin (cf. Matt. 26:59-61; Mark 14:58; 15:29).

2:20   The misunderstanding of the Jews is reflected in their comment regarding Herod's remodeling of the second Jerusalem Temple. The second Temple was built by the Jews after their return from Babylonian Captivity. Although begun in 536 B.C., it was not completed until 515 (cf. Ezra 3:1–6:15). This Temple served the Jewish worshipers throughout the intertestamental period. It was Herod, the Idumean king of the Jews, who decided to enhance his own reputation by enlarging and refurbishing the Temple. According to Josephus, Herod began this project in 20/19 B.C. (*Antiquities* 20.219). The sanctuary (*naos*) was completed in 18/17 after one and one-half years of work (*Antiquities* 15.421). The work on the Temple precincts was not completed until Albinus's procuratorship (A.D. 60-62; *Antiquities* 20.219).

In view of this historical data, what did the Jews mean by "It has taken forty-six years to build this temple"? The Temple was not to be completed until around A.D. 62. At the time of Jesus' discussion with the Jews, the Temple precincts (*hieron*) were still under construction, but the sanctuary (*naos*) had stood for forty-six years (from 18/17 B.C. until A.D. 29/30). Hoehner convincingly argues that the word "build" lays emphasis on the end of the action (effective aorist) rather than the beginning.[8]

Therefore, "the Jews were asking Jesus how He would be able to raise up in three days the temple edifice which had stood for forty-six years."[9] Such a massive and enduring structure was not likely to be destroyed and rebuilt in three days.

8. Ibid., pp. 38-43.
9. Ibid., p. 42.

THE EXPLANATION BY JOHN, 2:21-22

2:21   John explains in v. 21 that Jesus was not talking about the Jerusalem Temple at all. He was speaking of the "temple" (*naos*, "sanctuary") of His own body (cf. 1 Cor. 3:16; 6:19; 2 Cor. 6:16).

2:22   John adds that it was not until after the resurrection that the disciples recalled the words of Jesus and understood the riddle. It was then that they believed the Scripture—that it predicted Messiah's resurrection (Ps. 16:10; Isa. 53:12)—and the words Jesus had spoken. This verse anticipates the culmination of the disciples' belief (cf. John 20:8). It is clear that only after Jesus was raised from the dead did the disciples truly understand and fully place their trust in Christ.

THE RESPONSE AT PASSOVER, 2:23-25

2:23   During the Passover feast in Jerusalem many visitors witnessed the miraculous signs Jesus was performing as evidence of His messiahship. As a result of beholding the miracles, many "believed on His name" (v. 23). Yet Jesus was not overly enthusiastic about this apparent expression of faith.

2:24   John reports that "Jesus would not entrust Himself to them, for He knew all men." The words translated "believed" (v. 23) and "entrust" (v. 24) in the NIV are the same word in the original (*pisteuō*). Those who saw the miracle believed in Jesus, but Jesus did not believe in them. His knowledge of the nature of man restrained an enthusiastic response to this expression of belief (v. 25).

There are two basic approaches to this text. Hodges affirms that those who, like Nicodemus (3:2; 7:47-52; 12:42-43; 19:39), witnessed the miracles were genuinely saved yet were untrustworthy because they had not the courage of their convictions.[10]

Tenney, on the other hand, suggests that John is referring to an "acceptance of the messianic mission" of Jesus and "does not indicate a wholehearted committal."[11]

According to Tenney, belief may be manifested in varying degrees as it develops in a normal relationship between an individual and Jesus. The initial belief is not to be despised and will often progress from belief in the signs to a genuine trust in the Person of Christ.

10. Zane C. Hodges, "Untrustworthy Believers—John 2:23-25," *Bibliotheca Sacra* 135 (April-June 1978): 139-52.
11. Merrill C. Tenney, "The Growth of Belief," *Bibliotheca Sacra* 132 (October-December 1975): 344.

Tenney's approach seems most consistent with the theological and thematic development of John's gospel (cf. Introduction, "That you may believe," pp. 20-22). Many who followed Jesus because of the signs He performed (John 6:2) had a mistaken or incomplete understanding of His true Person (6:15).

2:25   John reports that Jesus had no need to be told concerning the nature of man. He understood, as did Paul, that the natural man does not accept the things of the Spirit of God (cf. 1 Cor. 2:14). Jesus did not trust these people because He knew what was in their hearts. This is clear evidence of the omniscience of Jesus (cf. 1:47-48). As God, He knows all things—our attitudes as well as our actions. A knowledge of this doctrine may serve as a motivation for personal godliness.

HOMILETICAL SUGGESTIONS

The two main events of chapter 2 include the miracle at Cana (2:1-12) and the cleansing of the Temple (2:13-22). The first would fit well in a series on the seven miracles of the fourth gospel. Here we see that Christ, the master of creation, provides for man's needs. He is Lord over His creation and can be expected to meet a crisis with His provision. The fact that He provided about 120 gallons of wine suggests His ability and willingness to provide abundantly. The cleansing of the Temple points to the dangers of secularism and commercialism within Christianity. The Old Testament law guaranteed the Levite a living wage—but the Levites never lived above the standards of those to whom they ministered. May the Lord deliver us from the temptation to use the ministry for personal enrichment.

JOHN
CHAPTER
THREE

NICODEMUS AND NEW BIRTH

THE INTERVIEW WITH NICODEMUS, 3:1-21

Approximately 90 percent of what John records is not found in the other gospels. Jesus' interview with Nicodemus is among this unique material. The interview demonstrates the effect of miraculous signs (3:1) and illustrates how Jesus dealt with people to bring them to faith in His Person (cf. 19:39).

The word "Now" (*de*) ties chapters 2 and 3 together. The historical context of this interview is found in John 2:23-25. Jesus had attended the Passover (A.D. 30) and the seven days of Unleavened Bread that followed. During those days Jesus performed a number of miracles that stimulated significant interest in His Person. Here John records the encounter of one man who was moved by the signs to learn more about Jesus.

NICODEMUS AND NEW BIRTH, 3:1-15

3:1 John begins by telling something about the night visitor, Nicodemus. Religiously, he was a Pharisee, a member of that sect of Judaism that had a high regard for both the written law and oral traditions. Professionally, he was a prominent teacher of the law (3:10).

Nicodemus was also a member of the "Jewish ruling council," the Sanhedrin, a ruling body among the Jews consisting of scholarly scribes, elders, and the priestly aristocracy. According to the Mishna (*Sanhedrin* 1:6), there were seventy-one members in the Sanhedrin. It was empowered to preserve the Torah and served as the final court of appeal in matters of debated interpretation. The Sanhedrin was authorized to excommunicate any persons in violation of Jewish law and to conduct trials of false prophets and rebellious elders. This body retained power in religious and limited civil jurisdiction until the fall of Jerusalem to the Romans (A.D. 70).

3:2   John records that Nicodemus came to Jesus "at night." He must have regarded this as a significant detail because he mentions it again when Nicodemus reappears in 19:39. Why did Nicodemus come at night? Several factors may be involved. First, he apparently wanted a private interview with Jesus and that would be difficult during the busy daylight hours. Second, as a religious leader, he probably did not want to arouse the suspicion of his colleagues that he was seriously interested in what this miracle-working rabbi had to say. In keeping with his thematic contrasts between light and darkness, it may be that John recorded this detail to communicate something of the spiritual darkness in the heart of Nicodemus at the time (cf. 11:20; 13:30; 19:39).

Greeting Jesus respectfully (for "Rabbi," see 1:38), Nicodemus comments on the matter of His divine origin: "We know you are a teacher who has come from God." Now what would give Nicodemus that idea? Jesus' miracles, most definitely. Nicodemus had done what John the apostle wants the readers of the gospel to do. He had been convinced by the miracles of Jesus' divine origin (cf. 20:30-31). Nicodemus explains, "For no one could perform the miraculous signs you are doing if God were not with him." The signs had been effective in making an impact on Nicodemus. Responding with genuine interest, Nicodemus came with questions and personal needs.

Jesus welcomed this seeker and did not criticize him for coming at night or his association with a decadent religious establishment. Jesus, the friend of sinners, welcomed an opportunity to converse with a religious leader. He is an example to all who would seek to speak of their faith.

3:3   For Nicodemus, a committed Pharisee, the law and oral traditions marked the way of entrance into God's kingdom. It was hoped that by adhering to the commandments God would approve him as qualifying for eternal life. Jesus discerned Nicodemus's genuine interest and spiritual need. With startling abruptness, Jesus declared, "I tell you the truth, no one can see the kingdom of God unless he is born again."

The verb "see" (*oraō*) has the meaning "to experience," as is indicated by the parallel expression in v. 5. Only through new birth can one participate in God's kingdom.

The "kingdom of God" (*basileian tou theou*) is an expression used only twice in John (cf. 3:5), but it appears fifty times in the synoptic gospels. The parallel expression "kingdom of heaven" is used by Matthew out of sensitivity to the Jewish readers who, for fear of possible blasphemy (Lev. 24:10-23), avoided using the name of God. The kingdom of God refers to the rule of God over His creation and people. God's kingdom involves a king who rules, a people who are ruled, and a sphere where this rule is recognized. Essentially, the kingdom of God is God's people, in God's place, under God's rule.[1] It is a present spiritual reality (Col. 1:13) that will ultimately be realized in physical form (Matt. 25:34; 26:29; Luke 22:30; 1 Cor. 15:50; 2 Tim. 4:18; Rev. 20:1-6).

The deepest spiritual need of Nicodemus was to come under God's rule personally so that he might experience God's kingdom. This requires spiritual rebirth. The words "born again" (*gennēthe anothen*) may also be translated "born from above." Both ideas are probably intended, hence "born again from above."

3:4   Nicodemus was perplexed. How could this new birth issuing in kingdom life be accomplished? Physical rebirth is impossible. A spiritual change late in life may be no less difficult.

3:5   Jesus refused to back off from this most difficult requirement. He repeats Himself in verse 5, but He adds some clarification. One cannot "enter the kingdom of God unless he is born of water and the Spirit." The expression "enter the kingdom" is virtually the same as "see the kingdom" (3:3). Jesus is talking about entering and experiencing God's kingdom. To do so requires birth by water and by the Holy Spirit.

There is debate whether "water" refers to Christian baptism, natural birth, or the workings of the Spirit. Although it has been argued that Jesus refers to Christian baptism as a sacrament necessary for salvation, this view is out of step with both the immediate context and the theology of John (John 5:24). Hodges argues that "water and the

---

1. Graeme Goldsworthy, *Gospel and Kingdom* (Exeter: Paternoster, 1981), p. 47.

Spirit" should be translated "water and wind," a double metaphor for the work of the Holy Spirit (cf. Isa. 44:3-5; Ezek. 37:9-10).[2] Kent points out the similarity between the concept of being born "of water and of the spirit" and the New Covenant truths of Ezekiel 36:25-26. In Ezekiel's passage, the water symbolizes the cleansing aspect of the New Covenant experience, and the provision of the Spirit speaks of the impartation of the new (spiritual) life.[3]

Jesus' explanation in v. 6 suggests that He is referring to physical birth. He declares, "Flesh gives birth to flesh, but the Spirit gives birth to spirit." In other words, there are two kinds of births—natural ("flesh") and spiritual ("spirit"). Pamment points out that "the breaking of the water in natural birth makes sense of the double expression 'of water and spirit' as a description of birth and rebirth."[4] It has also been observed that, etymologically, the verb "to give birth" in Akkadian (*halum*) and Hebrew (*yalad*) denotes the rupture of the membranes.[5]

In Jesus' analogy, then, the fleshly, or natural, birth corresponds to being "born of water." During pregnancy the unborn child floats in the amniotic fluid within the mother's womb. During delivery, this water is expelled. The child is literally born "out of water" (*ek hudatos*). The expression "of water" is used here as a figure for physical birth.[6]

Being born of the Spirit alludes to the New Covenant provision of the Holy Spirit's ministry (Ezek. 36:27) and refers here to the Spirit's regenerating work (Titus 3:5).

3:6 Jesus is declaring that there can be no evolution from flesh to spirit. Just as physical birth is necessary for life on earth, so spiritual birth is necessary for life in heaven. Nicodemus of necessity had to be born again from above. His Pharisaical self-efforts would not bring him under God's rule and into God's kingdom. Many other people have attempted to enter God's kingdom through obeying the law, performing good works, or doing philanthropy. However, God's Word reveals that there is no other way except by spiritual birth. This is not an issue that can be conceded or compromised.

---

2. For discussion, see Zane C. Hodges, "Water and Spirit—John 3:5," *Bibliotheca Sacra* 135 (July-September 1978): 206-20.

3. Homer A. Kent, Jr., *Light in the Darkness* (Grand Rapids: Baker, 1974), p. 58.

4. Margaret Pamment, "Short Note," *Novum Testamentum* 25 (April 1983): 189-90.

5. Ibid., p. 190, n. 1.

6. Note Linda Belleville's excellent survey and evaluation of the views, "Born of Water and Spirit: John 3:5," *Trinity Journal* (1980): 125-41.

3:7   Verse 7 repeats the thought of vv. 3 and 5 for emphasis. It is impossible for fleshy, human nature "to evolve upwards into the kingdom of God."⁷ The word "must" (*dei*, subjunctive of *deo*) denotes the logical and absolute necessity of new birth.

3:8   Having set forth the necessity of spiritual birth, Jesus illustrates the mystery of this miraculous phenomenon. He presents an analogy between the "wind" and "everyone born of the Spirit." Jesus is making a play on words, for wind and Spirit are the same (*pneuma*) in the original. Even though wind gives evidence of its existence, visually and audibly, no one knows its origin or destination. Similarly, new birth gives evidence of itself, but the natural man knows neither the origin of this spiritual life nor the final destiny of those born again. God's work of regeneration cannot be explained by natural laws. Like the wind, it has evidences, but it cannot be explained.

3:9   Nicodemus was perplexed by Jesus' teaching. His question, "How can this be?" did not constitute a rejecting of the truth. Rather, he was seeking further understanding. "How can this new birth issuing in spiritual life be realized?" Jesus goes on in vv. 10-15 to explain.

3:10   Verse 10 contains a mild rebuke. Nicodemus was recognized as a prominent teacher (literally, "the teacher of Israel"). He may have held some official position. Jesus was simply discussing the provisions of the New Covenant (Jer. 31:31-34; Ezek. 36:25-27), a topic about which any knowledgable Jewish teacher should have been familiar. The New Covenant refers to God's promise to bring spiritual blessing to the nations through the work of Jesus Christ. The New Covenant amplifies and confirms the blessing and promises of the Abrahamic Covenant (Gen. 12:1-3) and is both unconditional and everlasting. The New Covenant promises regeneration and the forgiveness of sin through faith in Christ and His sacrificial death for sins (cf. 1 Cor. 11:25; Heb. 7:22; 8:6-13; 10:15-22).

3:11   Jesus states in v. 11 that His teaching can be relied upon. Identifying Himself with His disciples, and perhaps believers of John's day ("we"), Jesus declares that the teaching about new birth is based on "what we know" and "what we have seen." In spite of this reliable witness Jesus observes that Nicodemus and the Jews at large ("you people") did not "accept our testimony." In keeping with the theme of John 1:11, they were not believing in Jesus as Messiah and Son of God.

7. C. K. Barrett, *The Gospel According to St. John* (London: S.P.C.K., 1962), p. 175.

3:12   Returning to the first person singular, Jesus contrasts "earthly things" with "heavenly things." In the present context earthly things refer to what Jesus has been teaching—new birth and entrance into God's kingdom. These things are foundational, elementary, and must take place on earth. The heavenly things are those matters Jesus is about to address (3:13-15). If Nicodemus has failed to understand the simpler, earthly things, how can he expect to understand the more advanced heavenly realities? Nevertheless, Jesus proceeded with His teaching.

3:13   Jesus had authority to speak concerning those heavenly things because He came as a messenger from God. Certainly no man has ever ascended to heaven to bring back an authoritative word from God (cf. Prov. 30:4). Consequently, humanity is totally dependent upon the revelation God provides through Christ. The heavenly origin of Jesus points to His pre-existence and deity. For the expression "Son of Man," see comments on 1:51.

There is some debate about a final clause in v. 13, "who is in heaven," which is lacking in some important Greek manuscripts. Black argues rather convincingly that this longer reading has extensive external attestation and that transcriptional probabilities and John's style and theology lend strong support for the reading.[8] If taken as authentic, the phrase provides evidence for the omnipresence of Jesus (in heaven and on earth) during His earthly ministry.

3:14   Jesus uses an Old Testament analogy to illustrate the mode and purpose of His death. The illustration comes from Numbers 21:4-9 where Moses records how God judged the complaining Israelites with fiery snakes. When Moses interceded for the people, God directed him to fashion a bronze snake. The snake was set on a standard and lifted up so that the people could look on it and be healed. The Apocryphal book of Wisdom rightly acknowledges that it was not the snake but the Lord who brought deliverance (Wisdom 16:7).

There appear to be two major points in the analogy. As the snake was lifted up, so it would be necessary for Jesus to be "lifted up." This is an obvious reference to the mode of His execution—crucifixion (John 12:32). The verb may also have allusions to His exaltation to heaven (cf. Acts 2:33). Second, as looking upon the snake brought healing to the Israelites, so those who look with faith upon Jesus will

---

8. David Alan Black, "The Text of John 3:13," *Grace Theological Journal* 6 (1985): 49-66.

receive eternal life. The second point is not directly stated but is implied by the Old Testament analogy and by v. 15.

3:15 Verse 15 provides John's first statement regarding the purpose of Christ's death. It tells why Jesus must be lifted up. Jesus must die to give eternal life to all believers. Except for this text, John always uses the preposition *eis* ("in, into") after *pisteuein* ("to believe"). Here the preposition *en* ("in") indicates that "everyone who believes shall in him [i.e. resting upon Him as the cause] have eternal life."[9] Eternal life—what a special, blessed hope. Eternal life is essentially life pertaining to the age to come. It is the present possession of believers (John 5:24) and involves both a quality (10:10) and a quantity of life (10:28). Eternal life is life with Christ—now and forever (17:3).

It is not clear if this interview with Jesus led Nicodemus to place his personal faith in Christ. Nicodemus reappears in John 7:45-52 where he challenged the legitimacy of the legal proceedings against Jesus. Finally, he appears in John 19:38-42 in the company of Joseph of Arimathea at the burial of Jesus. In a provocative study of the spiritual status of Nicodemus, Bassler argues that he is a marginal and ambiguous figure "who moves through the narrative with one foot in each world, and in this Gospel that is just not good enough."[10]

REFLECTIONS ON THE SON OF GOD, 3:16-21

Opinion is divided as to whether this section contains Jesus' teachings or John's reflections. The original Greek provides no quotation marks to enable the reader to make such a determination. Although it does not make a great deal of difference one way or the other, it is probable that John is reflecting on the nature and mission of the Son of God as revealed by His teachings in 3:3-15.

3:16 Verses 16 and 17 state the purpose of Christ's coming, first positively and then negatively. Verse 16 reveals that Jesus came for the purpose of redeeming man. This redemptive work was motivated by the love (*agapē*) of God. God's sacrificial love for the unbelieving world (*kosmos*) is exhibited in the giving of His one-of-a-kind Son. For comments on the expression, "one and only" (*monogenēs*), see 1:14. The purpose (*hina*) of this gift is to provide eternal life to all who believe in God's Son. Those who believe will not perish eternally

---

9. Bruce M. Metzger, *A Textual Commentary on the New Testament* (London: United Bible Societies, 1971), p. 204.

10. Jouette M. Bassler, "Mixed Signals: Nicodemus in the Fourth Gospel," *JBL* 108 (1989): 646.

but will (by way of contrast) have life eternal. This key verse sets forth the sole basis for eternal life.

It is important that the word "believe" here not be regarded as casual intellectual agreement. Belief, or better "trust," involves a knowledge of, reliance upon, and a commitment to the truth that Jesus is God's divine Messiah. Belief is trusting your eternal destiny to the work of Christ and realizing that you have no other back-up (good works, sacrifices, sincerity) should that redemptive work fail. For example, after a lengthy period of investigation, a Buddhist woman turned to Christ. Her profession of faith in Jesus was a significant milestone in her spiritual life, marking her as a regenerate person. But she demonstrated her faith, showing her trust in Christ alone, only when she allowed her pastor to remove the Buddha and incense from her home.

3:17   John states from a negative viewpoint God's purpose in sending His Son. He did not send his Son into the world for the purpose of condemnatory judgment. Rather, He purposed to provide the unbelieving world with the opportunity of salvation through Christ.

John 9:39 ("For judgment I have come into this world") may appear to contradict the teaching of 3:17. The solution is to recognize that salvation for all who believe implies judgment for those who do not believe. For example, the purpose of the sun is to shed light, not darkness. But light thwarted produces a dark shadow. So, the purpose of Christ's coming was redemptive. Yet, when His saving work is rejected, judgment results. Even though judgment results from unbelief, condemnatory judgment was not the purpose of the incarnation.

3:18   Verses 18 and 19 clarify the issue of judgment mentioned in v. 17 and emphasize the contrasting results of belief and unbelief. John declares that belief in Jesus precludes judgment. Unbelief, however, means that one stands under a sentence of judgment. The perfect tense, "stands condemned already" (*ēdē kekritai*), emphasizes the present and ongoing effect of this judgment. As eternal life is a present reality with a future consummation, so also is God's judgment on unbelief. (For comments on "one and only," see 1:14.)

3:19   Verse 19 explains the basis of God's judicial verdict. He judges not in an arbitrary manner, but according to standard principles and expectations. Here John explains how God determines whether people are condemned or saved. Advancing his thematic contrast between light and darkness (cf. John 1:4-5, 7-9), he draws from a general observation about life. Few people are willing to carry on evil activity in the light of day. Pimps, prostitutes, and drug dealers do the bulk of their business at night. Characteristically, they seek the cover of darkness to cloak their evil deeds.

John points out that what is true on the street is true in the heart. Spiritual light has been revealed to the world in the Person of Christ. Mankind in general has rejected the light. Why? As criminals prefer darkness because it provides some cover for their evil activities, so unbelievers love spiritual darkness. The use of the word *agapaō* ("love") indicates that this love for spiritual darkness is not a passing fancy. It involves a deep, personal commitment. The hearts of unbelievers are perverse and evil beyond description. One needs to look no further than the morning paper to find this truth validated. Association with evil provides the conscience with a hedge against the penetrating conviction of God's revelation (e.g., "At least I'm not as bad as so-and-so").

3:20   Verse 20 confirms the truth of v. 19. Not only do unbelievers love darkness, they hate the light for fear of exposure. The Greek verb "will be exposed" (*elenchō*) means to expose something to be evil and wrong. The wicked do not want the light to shine on their evil actions.

3:21   John goes on in v. 21 to set forth the contrasting response of a believer to God's light.[11] The one who "lives by the truth" is in contrast with the "one who does evil" (v. 20). Here one's actions are reflective of one's spiritual state. The one who "lives by the truth" is the believer. Unlike the wicked, he has no fear of the light because he has nothing to hide. The believer exposes himself to the light so that his deeds may be shown to have been done by divine enablement ("through God"), in obedience to God.

THE TESTIMONY OF JOHN THE BAPTIST, 3:22-36

The rest of chapter 3 focuses on the testimony of John the Baptist (cf. 1:6-8) concerning the Person of Christ. This section also reveals something of the relationship between John and Jesus. It confirms the teaching of the previous section by showing that man's eternal destiny depends solely upon faith in Christ.

---

11. In his article, "Coming to the Light—Jn. 3:20-21," *Bibliotheca Sacra* 135 (1978): 314-22, Zane C. Hodges argues convincingly that this verse cannot describe an unsaved person.

THE QUESTION OF PURIFICATION, 3:22-26

3:22   After the feast of Passover (cf. 2:13) Jesus and His disciples left Jerusalem and ministered in other regions of Judea. Because most of the returning exiles were of the tribe of Judah, they came to be called "Jews" (*Yehudim*) and their land "Judah" (*Yehudah*). The term *Judea* is the Graeco-Latin form of *Judah*. In the time of Christ, Judea was a political-geographical term referring to one of the three districts of Palestine west of the Jordan, along with Galilee and Samaria (Josephus *Jewish Wars* 3.48).

Jesus was involved in two primary activities at this time. He was spending time with His disciples (cf. Mark 3:14) and baptizing. He was training a core of followers and reaching out to others who were responding to His message. Baptism involved immersion in water as a rite of identification (cf. comments on 1:15). Those being baptized were identified with Jesus as His followers. John 4:2 seems to indicate that Jesus Himself was not baptizing. That ministry was being performed on His behalf by the disciples.

3:23   It is important to observe that the ministries of John and Jesus overlapped. Both preached the same message (cf. Matt. 3:2; 4:17). Both ministered a baptism of repentance. The ministry inaugurated by John continued as Jesus commenced His work. John was now baptizing (cf. 1:18) and being enthusiastically received at Aenon near Salim. Eusebius and Jerome (*Onomasticon* 40) locate this site in the Jordan Valley at Tel Shalim, about eight miles south of Scythopolis, a place noted for an abundance of water. The place-name "Aenon" is probably derived from the Hebrew word for "spring" (*ayin*).

3:24   John the apostle notes in a parenthetical statement that this ministry at Aenon took place before John was arrested and imprisoned by Herod Antipas (cf. Matt. 4:12; 14:1-12; Josephus *Antiquities* 18. 116-20).

3:25   The apostle reports in v. 25 about an argument that took place between John's disciples and a certain Jew (some ancient manuscripts read "Jews") over the issue of ceremonial washing. The expression "ceremonial washing" translates the Greek word for "purification" (cf. 2:6). Although this may refer to any Jewish purification ritual, such as the washing of hands, cups, pitchers, and pots (cf. Mark 7:1-4), the context suggests that the issue may have been the relative merits of the baptisms of Jesus and John. What was the value of baptism for repentance? Whose baptism was to be preferred?

3:26   The relative success of Jesus' ministry appears to have surfaced in the argument. John's disciples were perplexed and perhaps slightly jealous. John had inaugurated the ministry of baptism for repentance. He had even baptized Jesus (Matt. 3:13-17). Now Jesus was experiencing a tremendous response to his baptism ministry, whereas John's influence among the populace of Judea was on the decline. The expression "everyone is going to him" is clearly an exaggeration. But John was losing part of his following to Jesus (cf. John 1:36-37). This provided an opportunity for jealousy to thrive. No Christian is immune to the subtle temptation to be jealous over the success of another's ministry. John's response in this situation provides believers with an excellent example.

THE HUMILITY OF JOHN THE BAPTIST, 3:27-30

John the Baptist understood the subordinate and temporary character of his ministry. He found his joy in attracting others to Jesus, even at the expense of losing his own following.

3:27   John's reply to his disciples reflects his humility, appreciation of God's sovereignty, and contentment in the ministry God had given him. His words "A man can receive only what is given him from heaven" were spoken about ministry. John viewed Jesus' success as divinely determined. People were coming to Jesus because God was bringing them. A Christian's ministry—whether great or small—is determined by the providence of God. Therefore, there is no basis for jealousy over another's opportunity or ministry.

3:28   John the Baptist appealed to his own teaching to emphasize that he was not the promised Messiah (cf. John 1:20, 23). The words "You yourselves" are emphatic in the Greek. John was the forerunner who prepared for Messiah's coming (Isa. 40:3; Mal. 4:5-6). Jesus' success was due, in part, to John's doing his job well.

3:29   John used a wedding illustration to instruct his disciples concerning his relationship with Jesus and his attitude toward Jesus' success. The marriage imagery was commonly used in the Hebrew Scriptures to picture the relationship between God and Israel (cf. Isa. 54:5; 62:4; Jer. 2:2; 3:20; Ezek. 16:8; Hos. 2:19). By way of analogy, the bride (believing Israel) belongs to the bridegroom (Christ). John the Baptist was likened to the "friend" or "best man" of the bridegroom, who rejoices at the success of the bridegroom. The friend was an important person but was not to take center stage. With this comparison in mind, John rejoiced fully in Jesus' success. A heart full of joy leaves no room for jealousy.

3:30   Verse 30 contains the last words of John the Baptist in this gospel. John was the forerunner, a servant of Messiah. It is expected of a servant to exalt not himself but the one he serves. So Jesus of necessity (*dei*) had to be exalted (literally, "go on growing"), whereas John's prominence had to decline (literally, "goes on decreasing"). John had introduced the Messiah. Now his ministry was fading as Jesus took over and carried on. (For Jesus' evaluation of John the Baptist, see Matt. 11:7-15.)

REFLECTIONS ON THE ISSUES OF LIFE, 3:31-36

As in John 3:16-21, so there is debate here over who spoke the words of vv. 31-36. They could be the words of John the Baptist or those of the apostle John. Tenny observes, however, that the phraseology accords better with the style of vv. 16-21 than that of John the Baptist.[12] It is probably that John the apostle is reflecting here on the Person of Christ and the crucial issues of life.

3:31   The apostle reflects on the contrast between Jesus and John the Baptist (cf. 3:30). The "one who comes from above" is the heaven-sent Messiah. He is "above all," preeminent over all His creation. The "one who is from the earth" refers to John the Baptist. His origins were earthly. His ministry was earthly. His very words give us evidence of his humanity. The first clause of v. 31 is repeated for emphasis.

3:32   Christ came from heaven with a message of what He "has seen and heard" (cf. 3:11-13). Because His message (literally, "witness") is based on first-hand observation and experience, it can be regarded as trustworthy. The words "no one accepts his testimony" advance the subtheme of unbelief (cf. 1:11). The statement should not be taken out of context (cf. 3:33). Exaggeration ("no one") is used here for the sake of emphasis.

3:33   By way of contrast with the unbeliever, the one who accepts God's revelation in Christ certifies by his faith that God is true. The words "God is true" mean that what God has said is true and reliable. A physician recently advocated in an interview that lying is both socially acceptable and a necessary part of socialization. It is encouraging to

12. Merrill C. Tenney, "The Gospel of John," in *The Expositor's Bible Commentary*, ed. Frank Gaebelein (Grand Rapids: Zondervan, 1981), 9:52.

know that in a world where truth is often twisted and perverted, God and His truth remain unchanging.

3:34   Verse 34 provides the basis for Christ's authority. He is "the one whom God has sent." As God's appointed messenger, He speaks the words of God—a divine and authoritative messenge. John further emphasizes the reliability of God's message communicated by Jesus with the words, "for God gives the Spirit without limit." God, who sends His Spirit (cf. 14:26), has provided the Messiah with an unlimited endowment (cf. Acts 10:38).

3:35   The ground for the plentiful endowment of the Spirit (3:34) is the love the Father has for the Son. The word "loves" is present tense, indicating that the Father continually loves the Son. Consequently, God has given Him all things: all authority, all knowledge, all truth, all of the Spirit.

3:36   John's reflections on Christ and the crucial issues of life conclude with a statement of the contrasting results of belief and unbelief. The one who believes (present tense, "continues to believe") in the Son has eternal life as a present possession. But the one who rejects the Son will not enjoy eternal life. The word translated "rejects" literally means "disobeys." To disbelieve Christ is to disobey Him. And logically, to believe in Christ is to obey Him. This text indicates clearly that belief is not a matter of passive opinion, but decisive and obedient action.

Rejection of God's Son leaves the sinner to continue under the wrath of God—a present wrath ("remains") that will culminate in eternal judgment (cf. 1 Thess. 5:9). The "wrath of God" is the response of God's holiness to sin. It refers to God's act of judging and punishing sin.

HOMILETICAL SUGGESTIONS

John 3, with its story of Nicodemus (3:1-15), is probably one of the most well-known chapters in the Bible. Jesus' interview with Nicodemus, taken together with later notices (7:51; 19:38-42), makes a wonderful biographical sermon. Here is an example of a very religious man who did not know the Lord. Whether Nicodemus actually came to faith through this encounter is uncertain. Listeners could be challenged to make their faith-encounter with Jesus certain and secure.

John 3:16-21 is more theological in orientation and lends itself to thematic development. Its truths are fundamental to the Christian faith—belief, eternal life, unbelief, and judgment.

The response of John the Baptist to a dwindling ministry (3:22-30) is a splendid example of Christian humility. This text, along with Matthew 3:1-12; 11:2-15; 14:1-12; Luke 1:5-25; John 1:6-8, 19-28, would provide material for a series on the life of John the Baptist. He is the kind of person God delights to use. Rather than seeking the limelight for himself, he was content to be an instrument to glorify Christ. John's joyful attitude in a time of diminishing ministry is worthy of emulation (3:29).

JOHN
CHAPTER
FOUR

SALVATION FOR SAMARITANS

THE INTERVIEW WITH THE SAMARITAN WOMAN, 4:1-42

A thorough consideration of the historical background is essential to a proper understanding of Jesus' interview with the Samaritan woman. It must be recognized that Jerusalem was the divinely designated worship center for the Israelites. It was there on Mt. Moriah that Abraham offered Isaac (Gen. 22:2). There David bought the threshing floor from Ornan the Jebusite and built an altar (2 Sam. 24:18-25). On that threshing floor Solomon later built the Temple (2 Chron. 3:1-2). God clearly intended for Jerusalem to be the place of worship (2 Chron. 6:6; 12:13), a fact well recognized by the prophets (Jer. 3:17; Zech. 14:16).

After the division of the kingdom (931 B.C.), Jeroboam feared that if the northern tribes went up to Jerusalem they would soon give their allegiance to his rival, Rehoboam of Judah (1 Kings 12:27). He solved the problem by establishing golden-calf worship centers in Dan and Bethel and instituting a feast to substitute for Jerusalem's Passover. This sin of false worship continued until the fall of the Northern Kingdom, when Samaria was destroyed by the Assyrians in 722 B.C.

It was the pattern of Assyria to exile the citizens of the nations they conquered to other regions where they would be less likely to rebel. This policy was applied to the northern tribes of Israel. Vast numbers of Israelites were forced from their homeland, and foreigners were brought in from Mesopotamia to occupy the land (2 Kings 17:24). The newcomers brought with them their foreign gods and customs. Yet they also recognized the importance of worshiping "the god of the land" (2 Kings 17:27). They soon developed a syncretistic religious system of idolatry and the worship of Yahweh that was eventually incorporated into the daily life of the Israelites remaining in the land (2 Kings 17:24-41). The Samaritan community of the first century had its roots in this religous syncretism.

The Samaritans in the time of Zerubbabel were not permitted to participate in the rebuilding of the Temple (Ezra 4:1-3). Perhaps as a result of being excluded from this opportunity they built their own temple in Samaria on Mt. Gerizim. They had their own Pentateuch, which some helpful scribe had emended to read that Mt. Gerizim was the proper place of worship. In 128 B.C. relations between the two groups worsened when Shechem was captured and the temple on Mt. Gerazim burned by a Jewish leader, John Hyrcanus (Josephus *Antiquities* 13.253-56). By New Testament times the Samaritans were regarded as apostate, unclean half-breeds. In traveling to Jerusalem from Galilee to attend a feast, Jews with religious scruples normally went through Perea to avoid the hostile and impure Samaritans. This is the background of Jesus' conversation with a Samaritan woman.

THE REASON FOR LEAVING JUDEA, 4:1-3

4:1 Encouraged by the selfless attitude of John the Baptist (3:30), Jesus was having a successful ministry in Judea. In fact, more were being baptized under His ministry than under John's. This soon came to the attention of the religious leaders, the Pharisees (cf. 3:1).

Verse 1 contains John's first use of the word *kurios* ("lord") to refer to Jesus. In its original sense, the word speaks of one who is the "owner." From this comes the concept *lord* or *master*, one who has full authority or dominion. The term is often used as a form of address to a respected person and may correspond to our word *sir* (cf. 4:11; 9:36). When John uses the term to refer to Jesus, His deity is implied (cf. 20:28).

4:2 The apostle points out in v. 2 that Jesus did not perform the baptisms that took place under His ministry. This may have been to avoid the possible claim that baptism administered by Him was somehow superior.

4:3 Upon hearing that the Pharisees knew of His increasing success in comparison with that of John's, Jesus left Judea and returned again to Galilee. There was the possibility that the Pharisees might (1) use this information to create rivalry between the disciples of Jesus and John, or (2) turn their attention to Jesus and precipitate a clash before the proper time.

THE DIVINE APPOINTMENT AT JACOB'S WELL, 4:4-6

There are no "accidents" in the world of a sovereign God. Jesus' encounter with the woman at the well was by divine design. Following the example of Jesus, believers ought to be open and sensitive to the possibility of divinely ordained witnessing encounters. God often uses such "chance" meetings to plant seeds for the kingdom.

4:4   The text indicates that Jesus "had to go" through Samaria. The name "Samaria" is taken from the name of the city built by King Omri as the capital of the Northern Kingdom (1 Kings 16:24). It became a designation for the northern territory stretching north from Jerusalem to the Valley of Jezreel.

Josephus reports that Galilean pilgrims did use this route (*Antiquities* 20.118; *Jewish Wars* 2.232), for it was the most direct and allowed for rapid travel. More scrupulous Jews, however, would cross the Jordan and travel through Perea (cf. Matt. 19:1; 20:29; 21:1). Jesus' route was determined by divine necessity, not physical geography. As the "Light of the world," he must bring His message to Samaria also.

4:5   Many have sought to identify Sychar with Shechem, a site identified with Tell Balatah and situated between Mt. Ebal and Mt. Gerazim. It is asserted that "Sychar" is a corruption of "Shechem." However, there is no textual evidence of this suggested emendation. Neither is there certain evidence of Roman occupation at Tell Balatah during the first century A.D.

'Askar, located one-half mile north of Shechem, is the more likely site for Sychar. Discovery of Roman tombs in the vicinity of the village indicates it was inhabited in the time of Christ. The Madaba mosaic map, which marks the site by a church just north of Jacob's well, and early pilgrim itineraries confirm the idenfitication of the site. Jacob and his family camped near Shechem (Gen. 33:18-20) before moving on to Bethel (Gen. 35:1).

4:6   There is no difficulty in identifying Jacob's well. Few sites in the Holy Land enjoy a better claim to antiquity and authenticity. The well is deep and noted for its delicious, cool water. Jacob's well can be seen today in the crypt of an unfinished Greek Orthodox church. Weary from travel, Jesus sat down by the well and waited for the disci-

THE VICINITY OF SYCHAR AND JACOB'S WELL
John 4:5-6

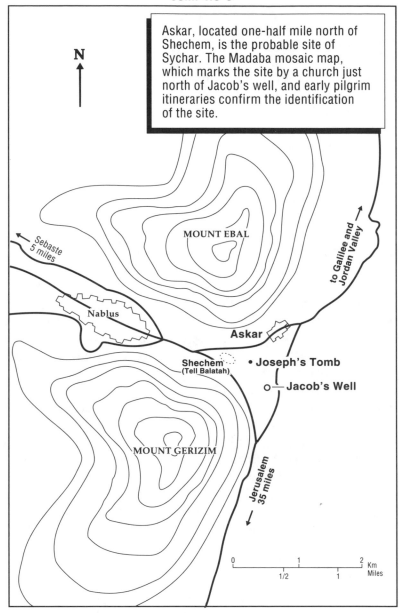

N

Askar, located one-half mile north of Shechem, is the probable site of Sychar. The Madaba mosaic map, which marks the site by a church just north of Jacob's well, and early pilgrim itineraries confirm the identification of the site.

MOUNT EBAL

Sebaste
5 miles

to Galilee and Jordan Valley

Nablus

Askar

Shechem
(Tell Balatah)

• Joseph's Tomb

○— Jacob's Well

MOUNT GERIZIM

Jerusalem
35 miles

0   1   2 Km
      1/2   1   Miles

ples to return from the village (4:8, 27). Jesus' weariness is a reflection of His humanity. Both His deity and humanity are emphasized in this chapter (cf. 4:26).

John reports that it was "the sixth hour." According to Jewish reckoning (a twelve-hour day from sunrise to sunset, the same as Roman sundials), "the sixth hour" refers to noon (cf. 1:39). It was the heat of the day, a most unusual time for someone to walk a half mile to draw water. Her lifestyle (cf. 4:18) may suggest that she wanted to avoid contact with other women at the well.

THE CONVERSATION WITH THE WOMAN, 4:7-26

4:7 In His interaction with the Samaritan woman, Jesus tactfully aroused her interest in spiritual things. He could have kept to Himself because of His weariness from walking and perhaps talking. However, He was so interested in people and their spiritual needs that He initiated the conversation by the simple request "Give me a drink." He then began carefully to direct the discussion to center eventually on her own spiritual needs.

4:8 John explains with a parenthetical aside that the disciples had gone to the nearby village (Sychar) to purchase food.

4:9 The Samaritan woman was startled by the request. She recognized Jesus as a Jew and was only too familiar with the history of ill feelings between Jews and Samaritans. John's explanation, "For Jews do not associate with Samaritans," is one of the classic understatements of the Bible. According to the Mishnah, "The daughters of the Samaritans are deemed unclean as menstruants from their cradle" (*Niddah* 4.1). According to popular opinion of the day, to receive food or drink from the hand or vessel of a Samaritan would be to share in this ritual impurity.

4:10 Jesus showed His disregard for traditional opinions by continuing the interaction. He was not bound by tradition or prejudice, which is an example today's church ought to consider and follow. In v. 10 He raises the conversation to a higher, spiritual plain. If the woman knew two things—(1) the "gift of God" (salvation) and (2) "who it is who asks you for a drink" (the Savior)—then she would ask and receive from Jesus "living water" (*hudōr zōn*).

"Living water" was a common designation for water that flowed from a spring, in contrast to the stagnant water taken from a cistern (cf. Jer. 2:13). Jesus was building on the metaphorical meaning of water—a meaning seen in the Hebrew Scriptures (Ps. 36:9; Isa. 55:1;

Ezek. 47:1-12). Using the term "living water," Jesus refers to the spiritual refreshment available in His own person. Later, the metaphor serves as a designation for the Holy Spirit (7:37-39).

4:11   The woman knew that the well was deep and that Jesus had nothing to draw with. Jacob's well is deep, about 120 to 200 feet. How was this man going to give her living water? She began to wonder if He might not be some extraordinary person.

4:12   The Samaritan woman asked Jesus, "Are you greater than our father Jacob?" The use of the negative particle *mē* in the Greek indicates that she expected a negative answer.

4:13   Jesus did not answer the woman directly. He was a master of the art of conversation. Sensitive to her spiritual needs, He continued to arouse her interest by comparing the water from Jacob's well with the living water He offered. Spring water relieves thirst only temporarily.

4:14   But the living water Jesus supplies provides eternal relief from spiritual thirst. It becomes a fountain (not just a cup) and provides a perpetual inner source of spiritual refreshment. This living water ultimately issues in eternal life.

The Greek language makes a significant contrast in the use of the word "drinks" (*pinō*). In v. 13 the word appears as a present participle and could be rendered "keeps on drinking." In v. 14 the word appears as a present participle and could be rendered "drinks at a point in time." Continual drinking of physical water leaves one continually thirsty. But one drink from the water of life (an individual act of faith) will quench thirst eternally.

4:15   Jesus masterfully directed the conversation to the subject of eternal life. Yet the woman was still focusing on physical things. She was apparently thinking, *Living water would be convenient. At least I would not have to lug my water pot to this well every day!* Jesus had raised the spiritual issue, but the woman's conscience had not yet responded.

4:16   Jesus' request "Go, call your husband" was intended to stir within the woman a conviction of sin and lead her to repentance. Just as a surgeon must treat an ugly cancer, so the Great Physician must deal with sin to bring spiritual healing. The issue of sin is often painful and difficult to address. But Christians who desire to be used as instruments of healing cannot ignore the matter.

4:17   Sensing that the conversation was getting a little too personal, the woman responded, "I have no husband." The word "husband" (*anēr*) can be translated "man" or "husband." As Robertson notes, "She had her 'man,' but he was not a legal 'husband.'"[1]

4:18　In v. 18 Jesus continues to press the issue of sin and the need for repentance. Although He was a stranger, Jesus displayed a knowledge of her intimate, personal life. This is another evidence of Jesus' omniscience (cf. 1:47), an attribute of deity. The Samaritan woman had been married five times and was now living in an adulterous relationship. The rabbis regarded two, or at the most three, marriages as the maximum number permissable for a woman.[2]

4:19　Jesus' insight into her personal life forced the woman to recognize that Jesus was no ordinary stranger. She concluded that He had to be a prophet (cf. Deut. 18:15, 18). Anxious to change the subject to something less personal, she immediately brought up an issue of major theological debate between Jews and Samaritans.

4:20　The Jews regarded Jerusalem, the site of Solomon's Temple, as the proper place for worship. The Samaritans worshiped on Mt. Gerizim where, according to the Samaritan Pentateuch, the altar was to be erected when Joshua came to Shechem (Deut. 27:4). The Samaritans believed that Abraham offered Isaac on Mt. Gerizim, and they continued to worship on the mountain even after the destruction of their temple by John Hyrcanus (Josephus *Antiquities* 13.255-56). A small community of Samaritans still observes an annual Passover sacrifice on Mt. Gerazim.

4:21　Rather than taking a position on this hotly debated issue, Jesus predicted a time when worship would not be limited by location. He was anticipating the dispensational change that would take place with the termination of the Old Covenant. Under the Old Covenant, worship was associated with the Temple, or sanctuary. The redemptive work of Christ has inaugurated a New Covenant relationship in which the Spirit of God indwells individual believers rather than a temple or holy place (1 Cor. 3:16; 6:19). Although a church building may be necessary for an effective ministry, it should never be the central attraction. Once when a worship center burned down the pastor was quick to explain that the church had not been destroyed. It would be meeting as usual on Sunday morning, but without the customary building.

---

1. A. T. Robertson, *Word Pictures in the New Testament* (Nashville: Broadman, 1932), 5:64.
2. Leon Morris, *The Gospel According to John*, NICNT (Grand Rapids: Eerdmans, 1971), p. 264, n. 43.

4:22   Jesus pointed out that Samaritan worship was based in ignorance. Because the Samaritans rejected all Scripture except the Pentateuch and regarded no prophet but Moses, their knowledge was limited. By way of contrast, the Jews accepted all of God's prophets and Scripture and worshiped with knowledge ("what we do know"). Jesus affirmed that God had revealed Himself in a unique way to the Jewish people and had worked His covenant purposes with them to bring salvation to the world (cf. Gen. 12:3).

4:23   Jesus proceeded to instruct the Samaritan woman regarding the nature of true worship. He acknowledged a future day of true worship that had, in fact, been inaugurated by His incarnation. The word "worship" (*proskuneō*) literally means "to kiss toward." It suggests reverence, adoration, and honor. To worship "in spirit" is to worship after the pattern of God's essential nature (cf. 4:24).

Jesus is pointing out that God the Father is actively seeking (present tense, "seeks") those who will worship Him in the manner he has prescribed. God has a rightful claim to worship and is daily seeking those who acknowledge His claim, will bow the knee, and ascribe Him worth.

4:24   Because "God is spirit" (without material being), worship must be bound up with spiritual realities, not physical formalities. Consequently, true worship is not limited by time, place, or ceremony. To worship in "truth" means to worship the true God, honestly, genuinely, and from the heart. It means to exalt God for who He is, not for what He gives. The repetition of the concepts "in spirit and in truth" serves to emphasize the point.

4:25   One cannot be sure why the Samaritan woman brought up the messianic issue. She may have once again attempted to turn the conversation away from her personal life to a less threatening matter. On the other hand, Jesus' knowledge and teaching may have stirred her messianic expectations. Could this stranger be the promised one?

Samaritans had a clearly defined messianic doctrine. The Samaritan messiah is referred to as *Taheb*, a term variously explained as "the restorer" or "he who returns."[3] According to Samaritan tradition, he would come as a teacher and restorer of true worship. The resurrection and final judgment would follow upon his death.

4:26   To this tainted Samaritan woman, an outcast of both Jewish and Samaritan society, Jesus disclosed the truth of His person. He did

3. C. K. Barrett, *The Gospel According to St. John* (London: S.P.C.K., 1962), p. 200.

not save this truth for the religious leaders or rabbis. He did not even save it for the disciples. The God-man reached out to a lowly sinner when He said, "I who speak to you am He." What an example for His followers of unbiased ministry to the outcast and unrecognized members of society.

"I who speak to you am He." Within this simple affirmation of His messiahship is an allusion to Jesus' oneness with God the Father. The Greek text literally reads, "I am, the one speaking to you." The words "I am" (*egō eimi*) are used in the Septuagint (Ex. 3:14) in connection with the revelation of God's personal name, Yahweh. The frequent use of the words "I am" by Jesus (cf. John 6:20, 35, 41, 48, 51; 8:12, 18, 24, 28, 58; 9:9; 13:19; 18:5, 6, 8) indicates His intentional identification with the God of Abraham, Isaac, and Jacob. This claim for deity becomes more apparent in later texts.

THE TESTIMONY IN SYCHAR, 4:27-30

The interview with the Samaritan woman took place while the disciples were visiting the nearby village to buy food. The conversation was interrupted by their return.

4:27   Upon their return, the disciples were surprised to find Jesus in conversation with a woman. It was the opinion of rabbis of Jesus' day that "he that talks much with womankind brings evil upon himself and neglects the study of the Law and at the last will inherit Gehenna" (Mishnah *Aboth* 1.5).

4:28   The Samaritan woman left Jesus and the disciples and went back to Sychar. The fact that she left her water jar at the well suggests she planned to return. There was more she wanted to learn from Jesus.

4:29   Her daring announcement, "Come, see a man who told me everything I ever did," must have stirred considerable interest (perhaps anxiety for some) among the people of Sychar. The words "everything I ever did" are hyperbole, exaggeration for emphasis. Although the conversation was too brief for a full biographical review, she was convinced that Jesus' knowledge of her was full and detailed.

The woman's question, "Could this be the Christ?" is phrased in the Greek in a way that expects a negative answer. Yet a positive answer was certainly hoped for. The manner of her question aroused interest instead of opposition.

4:30   The people of Sychar had heard the testimony of the Samaritan woman. With their curiosity aroused, they made their way to the well to meet Jesus.

THE PRIORITIES OF CHRIST, 4:31-38

In a world full of opportunity, decisions must be made on the basis of priority. Here Jesus reveals His own priorities.

4:31-32 The focus of the narrative now shifts from Jesus and the woman to Jesus and the disciples. Having returned from Sychar with food, the disciples were urging Jesus to eat. Jesus' response contains a riddle, "I have food to eat that you know nothing about."

4:33 The disciples' minds were on physical things, as was the Samaritan woman's. The disciples began discussing among themselves whether someone might have brought Him food during their absence. Their question in the original expects a negative answer (*mē*). Their speculation was not a reasonable possibility.

4:34 Jesus' response contains a great spiritual lesson. For Jesus, His ministry was as important and sustaining as food. Ministering to people ("doing the will of Him who sent me") was like vital nourishment to Jesus. This spiritual labor sustained Him even when it meant going without lunch. And Jesus would continue such small sacrifices "to finish His work" (cf. John 17:4). The Lord had a sense of priorities that made a significant impact on His ministry.

It is easy for people—even believers—to give themselves to the satisfaction of present physical needs, forgetting that these things are temporal, not eternal. There is no greater joy than seeing God work in one's life, providing spiritual resources where material ones are lacking. Fasting is a discipline that enables believers to express such dependence on God with a view to a focused period of prayer. God can sustain His people when they go without food for a time in order to worship and serve Him.

4:35 Jesus' priorities fell into the area of ministry and harvest. It is uncertain whether v. 35 alludes to an agricultural proverb, about which nothing is known, or simply refers to the harvest as being four months off. If the latter is the case, then Jesus' visit to Samaria took place sometime in January/February, with the harvest being in April/May.[4] From the farmer's perspective, the grain harvest was four months off. But from the viewpoint of God's kingdom purposes, the Samaritans of Sychar were ready for harvest ("ripe").

4:36 Although the harvest of grain was four months off, Jesus informed the disciples that the spiritual harvest in Samaria had begun.

4. Harold W. Hoehner, *Chronological Aspects of the Life of Christ* (Grand Rapids: Zondervan, 1970), p. 57.

As the reapers would cut and harvest grain, so the disciples would have the opportunity to harvest souls, telling Samaritans about the Messiah and His coming kingdom. And whereas a harvest of grain would provide physical nourishment, *this* harvest had eternal consequences. The words "for eternal life" refer to the results in the lives of those who believe, not the wages of the harvesters. The harvest unto eternal life gives both the sower (Jesus) and the reaper (the disciples) cause for rejoicing.

4:37   Verse 37 serves to link the proverb and explanation (4:35-36) with the application for the disciples (4:38). Jesus explains that as with farming "one sows and another reaps," so it is with the spiritual harvest.

4:38   Others—like Jesus, the prophets, and John the Baptist—have labored to prepare the soil and plant the seed. Now the disciples would reap the harvest of their labors. Note the emphatic contrast between the "others" and "you" (the disciples). Jesus was telling the disciples that He *expected* them to be reapers, gathering spiritual fruit into His kingdom.

THE BELIEF OF THE SAMARITANS, 4:39-42

The response of the Samaritans is reflective of the principle that where seed is sown, fruit can be expected.

4:39   John reports that a spiritual harvest was gathered among the Samaritans. Many from Sychar believed. What did they believe? Apparently, that Jesus was the promised Messiah (cf. 4:25-26, 29). "Believed in Him" is one of John's favorite expressions (7:31; 8:30; 10:42; 11:45; 12:42).

Belief is often initiated on the basis of another's testimony. Many believed at Sychar through the witness of the Samaritan woman. What heavenly reward is due her!

4:40   At the persistent urging of the Samaritans Jesus remained in Sychar two days ministering. This was most unexpected in view of the strong feelings between the Jews and Samaritans. Jesus, by personal example, was in the process of breaking down prejudice and ethnic barriers.

4:41   Although many believed through the witness of the Samaritan woman, many more believed as they heard Jesus' words. There is no other evidence of a large number of Samaritans coming to faith before Philip's ministry in Acts 8:4-25.

4:42   The belief among the Samaritans was initiated by the testimony of the woman at the well and validated by personal interaction. As a consequence, many of the Samaritans recognized that "this man really is the Savior of the world." It is amazing what God can do when believers take a step of faith, initiate a conversation, and show interest in the lives of others. God is able and willing to use our small gestures of kindness and expressions of interest to help bring people to faith. What a joy to look back and see how He has worked through a new and developing friendship.

The word "Savior" (*sōtēr*) speaks of one who saves, delivers, or preserves. The term was commonly used by the Greeks to refer to their gods, especially Asclepius, the god of healing. It is used of God in the Septuagint (Ps. 24[25]:5). The fact that this is the only occurrence of *sōtēr* in John's gospel makes its use here significant. John wants the world to know that the Samaritans, regarded by the Jews as spiritual outcasts, first called Jesus "Savior."

Verse 42 sums up the main theological point of this entire section. John wants the reader to appreciate that the gospel is universal in its application. Jesus is the "Savior of the world." Although He came to the Jews, He is "Savior" for the Samaritans—indeed the whole world (Gentiles)—as well.

Jesus' interviews with Nicodemus and the Samaritan woman provide a worthwhile study in comparison and contrast. Compare the spiritual backgrounds of the two—their spiritual interest, personal needs, questions, spiritual illustrations used by Jesus, His teaching, and their response.

THE HEALING OF THE NOBLEMAN'S SON, 4:43-54

The second miracle of John's gospel illustrates the progress or development of faith from belief based on signs, to belief based on the word of Jesus, culminating in belief based on the Person of Jesus.

THE DEPARTURE TO GALILEE, 4:43-45

4:43   After two days of ministry in Samaria, Jesus proceeded north to Galilee.

4:44   It is in connection with His move to Galilee that Jesus in this verse cites a proverb found also in Matthew 13:57; Mark 6:4; and Luke 4:24—"a prophet has no honor in his own country." The synoptic gospels use the proverb in connection with Jesus' rejection at Nazareth.

The fourth gospel uses the proverb in connection with Jesus' welcome in Galilee.

The key issue is the meaning of the phrase his "own country" or "fatherland" (*idia patris*).[5] Both the immediate context and John 7:41-42 make it unlikely that Nazareth or Galilee is in view. Nothing in the context commends the view that Jesus refers here to His rejection at Nazareth (Luke 4:14-30). Messiah is the descendant of David, of the tribe of Judah. Although accepted by many Samaritans (cf. 4:39-42), it was in His fatherland of Judea (Jerusalem) that Jesus had received less than an appropriate welcome. He did not entrust Himself to the Jews in Jerusalem (2:24), and there were usually conflicts associated with His visits (5:1-67; 7:1-52; 8:12-59).

4:45   Although rejected both in Judea and in Nazareth (Matt. 13:54-58), Jesus was welcomed by the Galileans. All His disciples except possibly Judas Iscariot came from Galilee, and it was there that Jesus found His greatest following. John notes that the positive response in Galilee was partly because many there had seen the miracles Jesus had performed at the Passover feast (cf. John 2:23; 3:2).

THE REQUEST OF THE NOBLEMAN, 4:46-47

4:46   Jesus returned to Cana of Galilee where He had performed His first miracle (cf. John 2:1-11). Eighteen miles northeast of Cana on the shore of Kinneret (the Sea of Galilee) was Capernaum, a place in which Jesus would later live and minister (cf. Matt. 4:13). Capernaum was an important tax collection station on the international highway (the Via Maris). Stationed there was a royal official, probably in the service of Herod Antipas (4 B.C.–A.D. 39), who ruled Galilee from Herod's capital at Tiberias, but perhaps in the service of Rome.[6] The official's son lay sick with fever in Capernaum. As a man of means and position, he had probably sought medical attention for the boy, but it had been to no avail. The son was "close to death" (4:47).

4:47   Learning that Jesus had come to Galilee, the royal official traveled from Capernaum to Cana to see Jesus. Possibly he had heard of Jesus' miracles at Passover and in a father's desperation appealed to Jesus to heal his dying son. The word "begged" reflects the imperfect tense of the verb and speaks of a persistent, repeated request. This is a

5. John W. Pryor, "John 4:44 and the *Patris* of Jesus," *Catholic Biblical Quarterly* 49 (1987): 254-63.

6. A. H. Mead, "The *Basilikos* in John 4:46-53," *Journal for the Study of the New Testament* 23 (1985): 69-72.

beautiful picture of prayer. The official obviously believed that Jesus could do something to help his son. His repeated request is reminiscent of Jesus' words in Matthew 7:7, "Keep on asking and it shall be given to you."

THE PROGRESS OF FAITH, 4:48-54

The nobleman, desperately seeking life for his son, found it himself in the person of Jesus.

4:48 Jesus' words in v. 48 seem at first harsh. But it is helpful to note that the remark was and is addressed to a wider audience than the royal official. The "you" is plural. Jesus is commenting on the tendency of people, Jews in particular, to seek signs (cf. Matt. 12:38; 1 Cor. 1:22). They look for something spectacular to validate and justify their faith.

The phrase "signs and wonders" (*sēmeia kai terata*) is a construction (called *hendiadys*, meaning "two for one") in which two nouns joined by *and* are used in place of the usual noun modified by an adjective.[7] Signs and wonders are not two different kinds of events. *Wonders* is simply a way of modifying and intensifying the noun *signs*. The phrase could be rendered "wonderful signs" or "marvelous miracles."

4:49 The royal official refused to be rebuffed by Jesus' comment. His faith had been tested and was seen to be based on something more significant than marvelous supernatural events. He persisted, "Sir, come down before my child dies." The words "come down" indicate that Capernaum was situated on the shore of Kinneret, 680 feet below sea level. It would be a downhill walk from Cana (approximately 2,000 feet above sea level).

4:50 Jesus encouraged the faith of the father by announcing good news. Although the NIV translates "will live," the Greek tense is present, not future. The son "is living" and will not die. Jesus was not merely predicting the outcome of the illness. He was announcing that a miracle had been accomplished through His powerful, healing word. Taking Jesus at His word, the royal official left Cana and began the eighteen-mile journey back to Capernaum.

4:51 On his way the official was met by messengers with the encouraging news that the fever had left the boy and that he was alive

7. Barclay M. Newman and Eugene A. Nida, *A Translator's Handbook on the Gospel of John* (London: United Bible Societies, 1980), p. 137

and well ("living"). In the original text the word "living" (*zaō*) appears in a place of emphasis at the end of the sentence.

4:52   The father saw the obvious link between Jesus' announcement and the boy's recovery. But he sought to confirm this by asking when the boy had become better. The fever had left him at the "seventh hour" (1:00 P.M.) the previous day.

4:53   The boy had been healed at the exact time Jesus had announced "Your son will live." The nobleman realized that a "long distance" miracle had taken place. The miracle confirmed the faith he had placed in Jesus' words. Subsequently he and his family ("all his household") trusted ("believed") in Christ.

John does not want the reader to miss a great message: Jesus gives life. Three times the Greek text repeats the words "he lives" (4:50, 51, 53). It is significant that both sickness and death will be absent in the future kingdom (cf. Isa. 35:5-6; 25:8; Rev. 21:4). There will be no feverish children and no anxious parents there—and no colds, measles, cancer, or any other disease. In His healing of the official's son He was giving a foretaste of kingdom glory.

The progress or development of the official's faith is significant. His faith first rested on the external testimony of others. Reports had come of Jesus' miracles in Jerusalem at Passover. Based on personal interaction with Jesus, he came to trust His words. That faith was confirmed by the recovery of his son and became fruitful in promoting like faith among his family members. The initial and hesitant faith that led him to Cana eventually culminated in an evangelistic faith. No step along the way is insignificant in the progress and maturing of a genuine and abiding faith.

It is rather exciting to see the ministry of Jesus expanding in John 3:1–4:53. In chapter 3 new life is offered to a Jewish religious teacher; in 4:1-42, to the despised Samaritans; and in 4:43-53, to a family of Gentiles. The Lord was teaching the disciples an important lesson in world missions. The blessings of His redemptive work extend not only to the Jews, but to the Samaritans and Gentile nations as well (cf. Gen. 12:3).

The question each believer must ask is, "What part am I having in God's plan to bring spiritual blessing to the world?" Are we sharing our faith? Supporting world missions? Praying for the nations? Participating in global outreach, either short term or career?

4:54   John concludes the record of this event by noting that this was the "second" miracle that Jesus performed in connection with His recent travels from Judea to Galilee. John is not saying that the second miracle of Jesus was done in Cana. The first miracle took place at Cana, after He left Judea (1:43; 2:1-11). Other miracles occurred during Jesus' Passover visit to Jerusalem (2:23; 3:2). The healing of the official's son was the "second" miracle that took place in connection with a later return to Galilee (4:3).

HOMILETICAL SUGGESTIONS

Jesus' dealings with various persons in John 4 provide a number of possibilities for sermonic development. His interview with the Samaritan woman provides a case study for making evangelistic contacts. The account also provides an opportunity for discussing God's essential character as spirit and for analyzing the nature of true worship (vv. 19-24). His discussion with His disciples after their return from Sychar provides an excellent opportunity to address the subject of ministry priorities (vv. 27-38). The healing of the nobleman's son (vv. 42-54) is the second of the seven signs intended to generate belief (cf. 20:30-31). One could develop the idea that Jesus has life in Himself and the ability to impart that life (spiritual as well as physical) to others.

JOHN
CHAPTER
FIVE

SABBATH BREAKER OR SAVIOR?

THE DEVELOPMENT OF UNBELIEF: CHAPS. 5-12

The early chapters of the fourth gospel present Christ's claims concerning Himself. He claimed to be the Messiah and demonstrated it with His miraculous signs. John the Baptist believed and so did some of his disciples. Many at Passover believed. Even a leading Pharisee, Nicodemus, showed interest in Jesus. Many Samaritans believed. And a royal officer in the administration of Herod Antipas came to faith.

Now the apostle describes the other response to the Person of Christ—rejection and unbelief (see 1:11). At first there was controversy over His Person claims (chaps. 5-6). The controversy centered on two miracles, each of which issued in a discourse. The controversy was followed by increased conflict with the Jewish religious establishment (chaps. 7-11). Chapter 12 brings the reader to the key crisis and turning point of the book.

THE HEALING OF THE LAME MAN, 5:1-18

Chapter 5 focuses on the theme of the life-giving power of the Son (vv. 21-26), as evidenced by a miracle (vv. 1-19) and reinforced by Jesus' own testimony (vv. 19-29). The healing of the man who had been lame for thirty-eight years serves as another illustration of Jesus' rolling back the effects of sin and His foreshadowing in a small but significant way the characteristics of the future messianic kingdom (cf. Isa. 35:5-6).

THE MIRACULOUS HEALING, 5:1-9

5:1 Although Jesus was ministering in Galilee, His ministry was by no means limited to the north. "A feast of the Jews" provided occasion for Him to travel south, ascend the hill, and visit Jerusalem.

There are many different opinions as to the identity of the Jewish "feast" to which John refers. The manuscript reading that adds the definite article ("the" feast) is doubtful. Wescott discusses the matter at length and concludes that Rosh Hashanah, the Feast of Trumpets, is in view.[1] Hoehner argues that it must refer to one of the three pilgrim feasts—Passover, Pentecost, or Tabernacles—and opts for the latter.[2] Others suggest Pesach (Passover)[3] or even the Feast of Purim. Ultimately, it must be said with Edersheim, "We must be content to call it 'the unknown feast.'"[4]

Some commentators believe that chapters 5 and 6 have been transposed and that the feast in 5:1 is the Passover of 6:4.[5] Yet there is no manuscript support for this view. If the feast is Passover, it must be the Passover of A.D. 31, between the Passovers of 2:13 and 6:4. If it refers to Tabernacles, in keeping with Hoehner's chronology, then the date would be October 21-28, A.D. 31.[6]

5:2 The miracle took place in Jerusalem at the pool near the "Sheep Gate." The Sheep Gate (Neh. 3:1, 32; 12:39) was located in the north wall of Jerusalem. The pool is referred to by Eusebius as the "Sheep Pool" (*Onomasticon*) and was apparently used for washing the sheep before they were brought into the Temple for sacrifice.

The Aramaic name for Sheep Gate appears in various manuscripts as *Bethsatha*, *Belzetha*, *Bethsaida*, and *Bethesda*. The name *Bethesda* (NIV) means "house of mercy," reflecting the tradition of healing associated with the place. Although the Jews read Hebrew,

---

1. B. F. Wescott, *The Gospel According to St. John* (Grand Rapids: Eerdmans, 1973), pp. 92-94.

2. Harold W. Hoehner, *Chronological Aspects of the Life of Christ* (Grand Rapids: Zondervan, 1970), p. 59.

3. William Hendriksen, *Exposition of the Gospel According to John* (Grand Rapids: Baker, 1953-54), 1:188.

4. Alfred Edersheim, *The Life and Times of Jesus the Messiah* (Grand Rapids: Eerdmans, 1971), 1:460.

5. Rudolf Bultmann, *The Gospel of John* (Philadelphia: Westminster, 1971), p. 240.

6. Hoehner, *Chronological Aspects of the Life of Christ*, pp. 61, 143.

Aramaic (a Semitic language very similar to Hebrew) was the common language spoken by the Jews in the first century A.D.

Archaeological excavation near the Church of St. Anne has uncovered a double pool that the Crusaders identified with the miracle. A large stone partition separated the northern and southern pools. Four colonnaded porches surrounded the two pools. The fifth porch was apparently situated over the stone partition.

5:3a John reports that the porches around the pool were gathering places for the sick—the blind, lame, and paralyzed.

5:3b-4 Some manuscripts add verses 3b-4: "And they waited for the moving of the waters. From time to time an angel of the Lord would come down and stir up the waters. The first one into the pool after each such disturbance would be cured of whatever disease he had."

It is argued by many scholars that these words were not originally part of John's gospel.[7] The text is lacking in the oldest and best manuscripts and contains what are thought to be non-Johannine words or expressions.[8] Morris regards this text as "a very ancient explanation which has somehow crept into the text."[9] Yet convincing argument has been presented in support of the authenticity of the passage.

Hodges provides a helpful summary of the arguments for the originality of the text.[10] (1) All known Greek manuscripts of John's gospel, with the exception of less than a dozen, include the verse. (2) The antiquity of the passage is vouched for from Tertullian in the third century. (3) The reading was widely diffused in both the East and West as evidenced in the versions and church Fathers. (4) In view of its unique content and probable connection with the traditions of Bethesda itself, the material is unobjectionable on stylistic grounds. (5) The deliberate omission can be explained as motivated by a falsely perceived "pagan tinge." (6) The statement about the assembled sick in v. 3 and the response of the invalid in v. 7 demand the presence of v. 4 in order to make John's text genuinely comprehensible.

---

7. Gordon D. Fee, "On the Authenticity of John 5:3b-4," *Evangelical Quarterly* 54 (October-December 1982): 207-18.

8. Bruce M. Metzger, *A Textual Commentary on the Greek New Testament* (London: United Bible Societies), p. 209.

9. Leon Morris, *The Gospel According to John*, NICNT (Grand Rapids: Eerdmans, 1971), p. 203.

10. Zane C. Hodges, "The Angel at Bethesda—John 5:4," *Bibliotheca Sacra* 136 (January-March 1979): 39.

Miraculous intervention into human life is clearly established in the Bible. God may have granted miraculous healings at the pool of Bethesda to enable some of the sick to find relief from their ailments.

5:5 There was at the pool a man who had been an invalid for thirty-eight years. The thirty-eight years is recorded to emphasize the wonder of the healing. His was a long-term illness. Humanly speaking, recovery was impossible.

5:6 It is not clear whether Jesus knew of the man's condition through His own omniscience (cf. 1:47; 2:24-25) or by overhearing the comments of others. The word "learned" (*gnous*) is the second aorist active participle of *ginosko*, "to know." Jesus' question, "Do you want to get well?" has an obvious answer. Perhaps Jesus was not so much seeking information as He was preparing the man to respond to His command.

5:7 The invalid tells Jesus of his inability to reach the pool (*kolumbēthra*, derived from the verb "to swim") and benefit from its healing properties. In addition to being an invalid, he lacked for anyone to assist him. Someone always reached the water before he could hobble to the pool. What frustration this poor man must have experienced! Healing was available, but he was too sick to benefit from it. And there was no one to help. What he needed was a friend. Little did he realize that Jesus had come to be that friend. Those who know and love our Lord are never without a friend (cf. 15:14-15).

5:8 Jesus commanded the impossible: "Get up! Pick up your mat and walk." These words can remind us of the challenges many present-day Christians face—the impossible task or the ministry that is just overwhelming. Realizing that something is impossible is often the first step in reaffirming our absolute dependence on God.

5:9 The healing occurred instantly, enabling the man to obey Christ's command. It is encouraging to know that Christ does not command the impossible without furnishing the enabling grace to accomplish it. God delights in using weak vessels to display the greatness and glory of His grace. The miracle demonstrated Christ's mercy and compassion, authenticated His messianic Person to His followers, and provided a preview of the health and physical blessing that will be experienced in the kingdom (cf. Isa. 35:5-6). It is significant that there is no mention of the man's faith in connection with this healing. Apparently this miracle was not dependent on his faith but on Christ's power.

John notes that this healing took place on a Sabbath. The absence of the definite article *the* suggests that this may not have been the weekly Sabbath but a feast day (cf. 5:1) when the Sabbath regulations applied (cf. Lev. 23:34-36).

God designed the Sabbath as a time of physical and spiritual refreshment (cf. Ex. 20:8-11; 23:12; Deut. 5:15; Isa. 58:13). It was not just a day off but a day to honor and delight in God. But by the time of the first century, the Sabbath had been perverted. Through the excessive and restrictive legislation of the rabbis, the Sabbath became a burden. The Mishnah devotes a tractate (*Shabbath*) to activities permitted and prohibited on the Sabbath. Thirty-nine classes of labor are forbidden (*Shabbath* 7.2).

Certain applications of medicine were permitted on the Sabbath; others were not. For example, a sick person could use medicines taken by those in good health, but remedies for specific ailments were often prohibited. One with pain in his loins was not permitted to anoint himself with wine or vinegar, but he could apply oil. Only rose oil was prohibited. A king's children, however, were permitted to anoint their wounds with rose oil on the Sabbath because it was their custom to do so on ordinary days (*Shabbath* 14.4).

THE RESPONSE TO THE MIRACLE, 5:10-18

5:10   Having been healed from his infirmity, the man began carrying his mat home in keeping with Jesus' instruction (v. 8). This brought charges by the Jews of a Sabbath violation. No specific law prohibited the carrying of a pallet on the Sabbath, but the Jews may have had in mind such passages as Jeremiah 17:21-27 and Nehemiah 13:15. The rabbis did forbid carrying a couch from one place to another on the Sabbath (*Shabbath* 7.2; 10.5).

5:11   The healed man explained that it was the one who made him well who gave him the instruction. He must have concluded that anyone who has authority to heal has the right to be obeyed.

5:12   The response elicited further inquiry: "Who is this fellow who told you to pick it up and walk?" These Jews had just learned of a great miracle. But instead of rejoicing they faulted the healed man over a trivial Sabbath violation. Is it not amazing how some people will see the work of God, whereas others will miss it altogether because of a critical and judgmental attitude?

5:13   The healed man was unable to provide the Jews with further identification. The pool of Bethesda was a crowded place, and Jesus had slipped away after the miracle.

5:14   Jesus later found the healed man at the Jerusalem Temple. Perhaps he had gone there to give thanks to God for his restoration to physical health. Jesus took the opportunity to instruct the man on how he could stay well: "Stop sinning or something worse may happen to you."

The negative adverb *mēketi* with the present imperative commands the cessation of some act in progress. Jesus associated this man's infirmity with present sin and warned against more grievous consequences of continued wrongdoing. The story of Job illustrates that sickness and suffering are not always the result of sin. Also, in John 9:1-3 Jesus corrects the disciples' mistaken assumption regarding the relationship of sin and suffering.

However, God may use physical suffering as a means of discipline (cf. 1 Cor. 11:29-30). In such cases, God's dealings are always quite apparent (cf. Acts 5:1-11). If sin is not fairly obvious, personal suffering should not be attributed to that cause.

5:15   As a result of this further contact, the healed man learned that it was Jesus who made him well. Perhaps fear of the authorities and concern for vindication (cf. 5:10) led him to identify Jesus as the one who made him well.

5:16   In v. 16 John marks the beginning of hostility against Jesus. Sabbath healings became a pattern for his ministry (cf. Mark 2:23; 3:2). The word "persecuted" (*ediōkon*) is an inchoative imperfect and means "began to persecute." They commenced persecution and kept it up.

5:17   Verses 17-18 are transitional, serving as the climax of the story of the healing and the introduction to the discourse on Christ's authority (5:19-47). In v. 17 Jesus links His Father's work with His own. As God the Father is always about His work of helping people and meeting needs, so Jesus is following that pattern. Both were "working" on the Sabbath. The Jews were mistaken in thinking that the Sabbath law prohibited the practical exercise of kindness and compassion (cf. Matt. 12:1-14).

Some Christians have sought to apply the Sabbath prohibition against labor to the Lord's day, Sunday. It should be pointed out that the Sabbath (the seventh day of the week) and Sunday (the first day of the week) are quite distinct. The Sabbath was the sign of God's covenant to the nation of Israel (Ex. 31:13-17). Sunday was the day observed by the church in Acts to worship and remember Christ's resurrection (Acts 20:7; 1 Cor. 16:2). Although believers under the

New Covenant are not obligated to observe the Sabbath, there are Sabbath principles that apply (Heb. 4:9), ones concerning rest from labor and spiritual rest and refreshment in Christ.

5:18   Jesus' teaching resulted in increased hostility against Him. The Jewish leaders were actually trying to kill Him. The imperfect tense ("tried," *zēteō*) indicates repeated attempts (cf. 7:19, 25; 8:37, 59). The charges were twofold: He was breaking the Sabbath (5:9) and making Himself equal with God. By calling God "His own Father" the Jews understood Jesus to be claiming that He shared God's divine nature. Had this been a mistaken inference, Jesus would have corrected His opponents at once. But He did not. Jesus was indeed claiming equality with God. Verse 18 is strong biblical evidence for the deity of Christ.

THE DISCOURSE ON CHRIST'S AUTHORITY, 5:19-47

The rest of chapter 5 is devoted to an explanation and defense of Jesus' claim of equality with God. This is a key discourse on the authority, deity, and messiahship of Christ.

THE BASIS OF CHRIST'S AUTHORITY, 5:19-23

Jesus begins the discourse by elaborating on His relationship with the Father. He is seen to be equal with God in five areas: work (5:19), knowledge (5:20), power (5:21), judgment (5:22), and honor (5:23).

5:19   Jesus declares in v. 19 that He does not act as an independent agent. Rather, He acts in dependence upon the Father and does His work. His words "I tell you the truth" signify a significant and solemn affirmation (cf. 1:51). Jesus is not able to do anything except what He sees the Father doing. And what the Father does, Jesus copies. In relationship to His healing of the lame man, Jesus was merely doing what the compassionate and merciful heavenly Father would have done.

5:20   Jesus affirms in v. 20 that He is loved by the Father and has a perfect knowledge of the Father's work. The words "loves" and "shows" are both present tense, which indicates that the Father's love and His revelation are continual. The revelation by the Father elaborates the reference in v. 19 to the fact that the Son "sees" what the Father is doing. The "greater things" to follow probably refer to the giving of life and execution of judgment (5:21-22).

111

5:21   Just as God the Father raises the dead as an exercise of His sovereignty over life (Deut. 32:39; 1 Sam. 2:6; 2 Kings 5:7), so the Son gives life to whom He wishes. Both the Father and the Son have authority to grant life—a divine prerogative. The words "to whom he is pleased to give it" suggest the concept of election. It is God the Son who chooses (cf. Eph. 1:5, 11). The doctrine of election, however, must always be balanced with the clear biblical teaching of human responsibility. God's elective purposes are accomplished by the appropriation of the gift of salvation through personal faith.

5:22   According to the rabbis, it is God who will judge the world. The Talmud declares, "God summons the soul from heaven and couples it again on earth with the body to bring man to judgment" (*Sanhedrin* 91b). Here Jesus reveals that God the Father judges no one but has delegated the exercise of all judgment to the Son. The exercise of Christ's judgment on the nations is elaborated in Matthew 25:31-46.

5:23   The prerogative of "judgment" (5:22) is given to Jesus to ensure (*hina* indicating purpose) that He will be honored just as the Father is honored. The word "honor" (*timaō*) means "to set a price on," "to value." In relationship to man, this is an attitude of respect. In relationship to God, this is reverence. Refusing to have reverence for Jesus, the Son, reflects an undervalued view of God, the Father.

THE EXTENT OF CHRIST'S AUTHORITY, 5:24-30

Jesus proceeds to disclose the extent of His authority. He has the right to give life (5:24-26) and to execute judgment (5:27-29).

5:24   Jesus declares that those who hear His message and heed it, because they believe that God authorized Him ("sent Me") have (present tense) eternal life. Eternal life is a present possession, not merely a future hope. The present tense "has" (*echei*) indicates that eternal life is a quality of present life on this earth that comes with knowing God (John 17:3). Eternal life has consequences for the future in that it precludes condemnatory divine judgment. The one who believes has left the state of spiritual death and come into spiritual life.

This is a key verse on the unity of the Father and the Son. Note that the one who "hears" Christ "believes" the Father. The verse also emphasizes that true believers are eternally secure. As Morris comments, "To have eternal life now is to be secure throughout eternity."[11]

---

11. Morris, *The Gospel According to John*, p. 316.

5:25 Most commentators interpret v. 25, which elaborates on the results of believing, as an extension of v. 24. The key phrase, "and has now come," suggests that Jesus refers here to spiritual regeneration rather than physical resurrection. The "dead" are the spiritually dead who enter into spiritual life ("will live") by responding to the voice of God's Son. Cook argues, however, that as with vv. 28 and 29, so here physical resurrection is in view.[12] He points to the words "I tell you the truth" as indicating a shift in subject matter. He understands Jesus as referring to the miraculous raising of Lazarus, Jairus's daughter, and the widow's son. Whether or not this was Jesus' intended meaning, His earthly resurrection ministry certainly foreshadows the resurrection power of the age to come.

5:26 Verses 26 and 27 explain how the truth of v. 25 is possible. The Hebrew Scriptures make clear that God gives life (Gen. 2:7; Job 33:4; Ps. 16:11; 36:9). As the Father has "life in Himself," implying that His self-existent life is a source of life to others, so Jesus shares this identical life and exercises its prerogative (cf. 1:3).

5:27 Again, the Old Testament makes clear that God alone exercises final judgment (Gen. 18:25; Judg. 11:27). Yet v. 27 reveals that this authority to execute judgment has been delegated to the Son. The explanation is given, "because He is the Son of Man." The expression Son of Man (*huios anthrōpou*) is the favorite self-designation of Jesus and appears ninety-four times in the New Testament. The expression links Jesus with "one like a son of man" in Daniel 7:13. He is given "dominion, glory and a kingdom" (NASB) by the "Ancient of Days" (compare 2 Sam. 7:12-16; Luke 1:32-33). As Messiah, Jesus has been delegated the task of judgment. It is reassuring to know that believers have been adopted (cf. Rom. 8:15) by the one assigned to world judgment.

5:28 The judgment of v. 27 will take place at the resurrection of the dead. Verse 28 affirms the doctrine of the universal resurrection—the righteous and the wicked (cf. Dan. 12:2). All those who have died ("are in their graves") will be included (Matt. 25:46; Acts 24:15; 2 Cor. 5:10).

5:29 Jesus speaks of two kinds of resurrections: a resurrection to life (cf. John 6:39; Rev. 20:4-5) and a resurrection to condemnation (Matt. 5:29; 10:28; Luke 11:32; Rev. 20:11-15). The determination will

---

12. W. Robert Cook, "Eschatology in John's Gospel," *Criswell Theological Review* 3 (1988): 89-91.

be based on the person's works, whether "good" or "evil." Many have wrestled with how this can be consistent with Paul's teaching that believers are saved by faith (Eph. 2:8-9).[13] It must be emphasized that the works are the distinguishing marks of belief or unbelief (cf. 3:36). The life lived either validates or refutes the faith professed (cf. Matt. 7:16-18; Titus 1:16).

5:30   Verse 30 is transitional, leading into the second half of the discourse. It continues the theme of judgment (5:27-29) but moves from indirect ("the Son") to first person ("I") narrative. Jesus again stresses His oneness with the Father. He does not act on His own initiative. He judges on the basis of what the Father reveals. His judgment is fair because His guiding principle is the will of the Father.

WITNESSES TO CHRIST'S AUTHORITY, 5:31-47

Jesus has presented a clear case for His divine authority and equality with the Father. Now, in what might be likened to a courtroom scene, He presents five witnesses before those who were opposing Him—Christ, the Father, John the Baptist, Jesus' works, and Scripture.[14] These witnesses were brought forth to substantiate His claims and authority and to drive His opponents to a true verdict.

5:31   The first witness to the truth of these claims is Christ Himself. Jewish tradition held, however, that self-testimony without supporting witnesses (Deut. 19:15) could not be regarded as legally valid. The Mishnah records the teaching of the rabbis that "none may be believed when he testifies of himself" (*Ketuboth* 2.9).

5:32   The second witness is God the Father who spoke from heaven at Jesus' baptism, "This is my Son, whom I love; with him I am well pleased" (Matt. 3:17). The voice of the Father continued to testify through the teaching of Jesus (John 3:34; 7:16; 18:8). The term "another" (*allos*) speaks of another of the same kind—one who shares his character and attributes. This testimony is legally valid because it serves as the second of the required "two or three" witnesses (Deut. 19:15). The Father's testimony is elaborated further in vv. 37-38.

5:33   John the Baptist is the third witness to the truth of Christ's Person. John was the messianic forerunner (Mal. 3:1; Matt. 11:10) who

---

13. Zane C. Hodges, "Those Who Have Done Good—John 5:28-29," *Bibliotheca Sacra* 136 (1979): 158-66.

14. Merrill C. Tenney, "Topics from the Gospel of John: The Meaning of 'Witness' in John," *Bibliotheca Sacra* 132 (1975): 232-39.

witnessed to Jesus' true identity when he declared, "Look, the Lamb of God" (John 1:29).

5:34   Jesus explains in verse 34 that He does not need the testimony of a human being like John. He simply mentions it so that those who doubt Him will believe John's testimony and be saved.

5:35   In v. 35 Jesus likens John to a brightly burning lamp that the Jews enjoyed and benefited from for a time. Josephus reports that the Jewish crowds were "aroused to the highest degree by His sermons" (*Antiquities* 18.18). Unfortunately, many did not follow through in believing in Jesus, the one whom John introduced. The past tense "was" implies that John's work is now over (cf. Matt. 14:1-12).

5:36   The fourth witness to which Jesus appeals to validate the truth of His Person is His "work" (*erga*, literally "works"). Although not all miracles are works, Jesus often uses this term to refer to His miraculous deeds (cf. John 10:37-38; 14:11; 15:24). These are God's works—miracles the Father has given Jesus to perform. His miraculous works authenticate the truth of His Person and His divine origin ("that the Father has sent Me").

5:37   Verses 37 and 38 elaborate on the witness of the Father, first mentioned in v. 31 ("another"). The Father, who sent the Son, has given testimony on Jesus' behalf. The word "testified" (*martureō*) is in the perfect tense, emphasizing the lasting effect of a past action. It is probable that Jesus has in mind God's testimony spoken from heaven at the time of His baptism (Matt. 3:17). The utterance at the Transfiguration (Matt. 17:5) and the royal entry (John 12:28) had not yet occurred. The weakness of this view is that the testimony given at His baptism is not recorded in John. Others take the Father's testimony to refer to the prophetic Scriptures or the witness in the heart of believers (1 John 5:9-10).

Jesus goes on to explain that because of their disbelief, the Jews had never heard God's voice or seen His form. This is a rather strong statement that would seem to be in contradiction to Israel's experience as recorded in the Hebrew Scriptures (cf. Ex. 19:16-19; 34:6-7). But what Jesus was emphasizing to those Jews present was that those who did not believe Him had never at any time (*pōpote*) had such personal contact with God as described in Exodus. Jesus alone has heard God's voice and seen His form. Yet as Von Wahlde points out, "Since Jesus has had direct experience of God and since he speaks what he heard and saw, the Jews do have the opportunity to be in contact with the word of God through Jesus" (cf. John 1:18; 3:34; 8:28, 38; 14:9).[15]

5:38   As the Jews had never experienced God as Jesus had, neither had they appropriated His Word. The reason is given: "for you do not believe the one he sent." Belief in Christ is the prerequisite to all spiritual illumination regarding the Person of God. Only through Jesus can people hear and see God (14:9).

5:39   The final witness Jesus offers in proof of His Person is Scripture. It is not that the Jews were neglecting the study of Scripture. Rather, they were studying Scripture to acquire a knowledge of it. They wrongly presumed that eternal life was found in one's sheer knowledge of the Word. In spite of their careful and detailed studies, the Jews failed to see how Scripture testified of Jesus.

Verse 39 demonstrates the futility of biblical studies that focus merely on academic attainment rather than on one's personal walk with God. Too many students of the Word have accomplished the former to the neglect of the latter. Such studies often result in increased pride instead of greater personal godliness.

5:40   Verse 40 reveals that the Jews were unwilling to follow where the light of the Word led. They were knowledgeable scholars, but they refused to come to Christ and receive His gift of life. Eternal life is not found *in* the Word as an end in itself (paper, ink, letters, and sentences) but *through* the Word as it points to Christ.

As the discourse draws to a conclusion, Jesus explains the reason for the unbelief of the Jews (5:41-44) and the result of rejecting Him (5:45-47).

5:41   Jesus explains that it is not His own "praise" (literally, "glory") that He seeks, but, by implication, the spiritual well-being of His listeners.

5:42   The problem He detected was the absence of God's love among His opponents. Although many Jews were "professionals" in the field of religion, they did not truly love God. How prone modern believers are to love books, love preaching, love writing, love the ministry—all without loving God.

5:43   Jesus contrasts His own rejection with the tendency of the Jews to accept other messianic claimants. Josephus tells of a number of false messiahs who led thousands of Jews astray (*Jewish Wars* 2.259-

15. Urban C. Von Wahlde, "The Witnesses to Jesus in John 5:31-40 and Belief in the Fourth Gospel," *The Catholic Biblical Quarterly* 43 (1981): 393-94.

63; cf. Matt. 24:23-24; Acts 5:36-37; 21:38). Even when Jerusalem was in the process of being destroyed by the Romans in A.D. 70, a deceiver announced that God commanded the Jews to come to the Temple to receive miraculous signs of their deliverance. Those who came, reports Josephus, perished in the flames (*Jewish Wars* 6.283-87). While accepting other leaders, the Jews at the same time refused Jesus, who came in His "Father's name." The name refers to the Father's character and reputation. He came with impeccable credentials.

5:44   Jesus makes another contrast in v. 44 by noting the tendency of the Jewish leaders to look for praise from one another instead of the praise that comes from God. Their scholarship and learning impressed each other but did not commend them to God for His approval. There is only one evaluation that ultimately counts—God's.

5:45   The Jews did not believe Jesus because they did not love God (vv. 41-44). Now Jesus explains the consequences of that decision. Jesus turns the tables in this courtroom scene. Whereas He has been the defendant, the Jews now take that role. They are accused, not by Jesus but by Moses. In rejecting the revelation of God, the opponents stood condemned by Moses—ironically, the one in whom they had set their hope.

5:46   Had the Jews really believed Moses, they would have believed Christ. Jesus explains, "for He wrote about me." This comment is a key to the interpretation of the entire Pentateuch. Jesus Himself had said, "Everything must be fulfilled that is written about me in the Law of Moses, the Prophets and the Psalms" (Luke 24:44; cf. Gen. 3:15; 12:1-3; 49:10; Num. 24:17; Deut. 18:15-18).

5:47   Jesus concludes the discourse with a rhetorical question: "Because you do not believe Moses, how are you going to believe Me?" Genuine belief in the revelation of Moses should lead to faith in Jesus. In spite of their professed allegiance to Moses, the Jews did not really believe the Mosaic message.

HOMILETICAL SUGGESTIONS

The healing of the lame man (5:1-18) fits nicely into the series of the seven miracles in John's gospel. The discourse on Christ's authority (5:19-47) is no doubt too lengthy for a single message. This section could be divided into three messages on the deity and authority of Christ. In 5:19-23, Jesus is seen to be equal with the Father in His work, knowledge, power, judgment, and honor. In 5:24-30, Jesus affirms His authority to give life (vv. 24-26) and to execute judgment (vv. 27-29). Finally, in 5:31-47, Jesus presents five witnesses to His authority: Himself, the Father, John the Baptist, His miracles, and Scripture.

JOHN
CHAPTER
SIX

BREAD FROM HEAVEN

THE FEEDING OF THE FIVE THOUSAND, 6:1-15

The importance of the miraculous feeding of the five thousand is seen in that it is reported by all four gospel writers. In John, the miracle sets the stage for Jesus' "bread of life" discourse.

THE OCCASION OF THE MIRACLE, 6:1-4

The first four verses of this chapter reveal the location and season of the miracle.

6:1 The miracle took place on the "far shore" of the Sea of Galilee. This fresh water lake is known also as "the Sea of Tiberias" (21:1) after the regional capital built by Herod Antipas and named in honor of the Roman emperor. The location of the miracle is described in the synoptic gospels as in a deserted place (Mark 6:35) near Bethsaida (Luke 9:10), a reference to Bethsaida-Julias located on the northeast shore of the sea (cf. John 1:44).

6:2 John records that a great crowd of people followed Jesus because of the miracles He had been performing on the sick. Jesus and His disciples had been so busy ministering to the multitudes that they did not even have time to eat (Mark 6:31).

6:3 Jesus knew that His disciples needed some time alone with Him, and they withdrew to a secluded place for rest and refreshment—a hillside overlooking the sea. But a period of seclusion for

THE LOCATION OF THE FEEDING OF THE 5,000
John 6:1

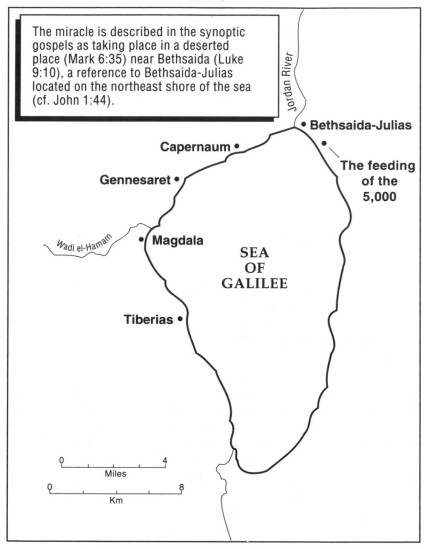

The miracle is described in the synoptic gospels as taking place in a deserted place (Mark 6:35) near Bethsaida (Luke 9:10), a reference to Bethsaida-Julias located on the northeast shore of the sea (cf. John 1:44).

Jordan River

• Bethsaida-Julias

Capernaum •

The feeding of the 5,000

Gennesaret •

Wadi el-Hamam

• Magdala

SEA OF GALILEE

Tiberias •

0   4
Miles

0   8
Km

Him and His disciples was not to be. The sign-seeking multitudes followed. And Jesus was compelled to minister to them.

6:4   John notes that it was the season of Passover (Ex. 12:1-14). Hoehner has determined that the year was A.D. 32, just one full year before Christ's crucifixion.[1] The reference to Passover provides more than a mere chronological note. The two primary foods of Passover were lamb and unleavened bread (*matzah*). In the discourse that follows, Jesus presents Himself as the "bread" of heaven, which gives life to those who eat it. There is a definite theological and thematic link with the season in which the miracle took place. Eating unleavened bread served as a reminder of Israel's separation from Egypt and the fellowship made possible with God because of Passover. Jesus is the fulfillment of all that was symbolized in the Passover *matzah* (cf. 1 Cor. 5:7-8).

THE TEST OF FAITH, 6:5-9

Although the feeding of the five thousand provided the needs of the multitude, the miracle should also be understood in light of what it meant to the twelve. Jesus was teaching the disciples that, although they were inadequate in themselves to meet human needs, they would find their sufficiency in Christ.

6:5   Jesus saw the crowd and knew the people were hungry. It was His pattern to see people in light of their needs. He approached the subject asking Philip the question, "Where shall we buy bread for these people to eat?"

6:6   John explains that Jesus was not really asking Philip to solve the problem, for Jesus had already decided what to do. Rather, He was "testing" (*peirazō*) Philip and his faith, and in so doing Jesus was "trying" or "proving" Philip's spiritual character.

This verse reflects both Jesus' omniscience and omnipotence. He had a complete knowledge of the situation and the power and authority to meet the need. God may place believers in seemingly impossible situations to teach them something about the greatness of His Person.

6:7   Philip saw no need to discuss the matter of where to buy food. The suggestion was simply out of the range of economic possibility. The words "eight months' wages" literally reads "two-hundred den-

1. Harold W. Hoehner, *Chronological Aspects of the Life of Christ* (Grand Rapids: Zondervan, 1970), p. 143.

arii." The denarius was a Roman coin that amounted to the daily wage of a rural worker.

6:8   Peter's brother Andrew was a bit more optimistic about feeding the crowd and had begun taking food donations. He brought a boy who was willing to share his lunch.

6:9   But even Andrew recognized that there simply was not enough to go around. Jesus had the disciples exactly where He wanted them. They recognized their own insufficiency and need to depend on Him.

The boy's lunch consisted of "five small barley loaves and two small fish." Barley was one of the main cereal crops in ancient Palestine and was used for feeding horses, donkeys, and cattle. It was sometimes mixed with wheat to prepare flour for human consumption. Because barley was cheaper than wheat, barley bread was the food of the poor. It is evident that the boy did not come from a wealthy family. The word translated "fish" (*opsarion*) can also be rendered "tidbit," referring to a small bit of meat eaten with bread. However, the synoptic parallels use the term *ichthus* for "fish," which lends support to the traditional rendering in John 6:9.

It has been said that God cannot use us in a ministry until we recognize our own inability to accomplish the task. This concept turns human thinking and planning around and upside down. If we think we can, we can't. If we can't, God can. God loves to take our inability and demonstrate the matchless wonder of His greatness and grace.

THE MIRACULOUS FEEDING, 6:10-13

6:10   It was the spring of the year and there was plenty of green grass on which to "sit down," literally "lie down" or "recline" (aorist active infinitive of *anapiptō*). The group numbered about five thousand "men" (*anēr*), a Greek word that distinguishes the male gender. Counting women and children, the group would number considerably more than five thousand.

6:11   Setting an example for His followers, Jesus was careful to give thanks to God for His provision (Deut. 8:10). The words "gave thanks" translate the Greek word on which the word *eucharist* is based. According to the synoptic accounts, the disciples distributed the food to the multitude (Matt. 14:19; Mark 6:41; Luke 9:16).

6:12   The words "had enough" would be better rendered "completely filled" (aorist passive indicative of *empiplemi*). No one was left thinking, *Another piece of bread would be nice.* They were all satisfied. Jesus was careful that His abundant provision did not encourage waste. He instructed His disciples to gather up the bread that was broken but not consumed.

6:13   Twelve full baskets were collected—a witness to the abundance of the provision. Jesus had shown the disciples that in difficult or impossible situations they must find their adequacy in Him. He is a faithful God and will not fail those who put their trust in Him.

THE RESPONSE TO THE MIRACLE, 6:14-15

6:14   Realizing that a miraculous sign (*sēmeia*) had taken place, the people made a connection between Jesus and the prophet promised in Deuteronomy 18:15. The Pharisees distinguished between the prophet of Deuteronomy 18:15 and the Messiah (cf. John 1:21), but the Galileans may not have held such a distinction. The multitude was correct in its identification (cf. Acts 3:20-22; 7:37), but its motivating interests were physical and superficial.

There was a first-century Jewish expectation, based on noncanonical writings, that the Messiah would renew the miracle of manna (2 Baruch 29:8).[2] This expectancy may also find support from Psalm 132:15, which promises to "provide the needy with bread" (NASB) when the Messiah rules in fulfillment of the Davidic covenant (2 Sam. 7:12-16).

6:15   The Roman domination of Palestine in the first century kindled strong nationalistic hopes among the Jews. Although there was no consistent concept of "the anointed one" at the time of Jesus,[3] the Jews of His day longed for a dynamic and powerful figure who could lead them in their political struggle against Rome. Suffering so long under Roman rule, the Jewish people must have been eager for an anointed king from among their own ranks. Jesus had the qualities and credentials that commended Him to leadership, and the people decided to "make Him king by force." By popular demand they intended to force kingship upon Him.

This was the high point of Jesus' popularity in Galilee. As sincere as it might have appeared to the disciples, Jesus knew that the crowds were more interested in being fed (6:26-27). He rejected this superfi-

---

2. Second Baruch dates from around A.D. 50-90. The text reads, "And it shall come to pass at that self-same time that the treasury of manna shall again descend from on high, and they will eat of it in those years, because these are they who have come to the consummation of time" [i.e., the Messianic age]. The Sibylline Oracles (160 B.C.–5th century A.D.) also teach that manna is food for members of the messianic kingdom (Sibyll. Or. 2.49).

3. Richard A. Horsley, "Popular Messianic Movements Around the Time of Jesus," *The Catholic Biblical Quarterly* 46 (1984): 471.

cial offer of kingship and immediately sent His disciples away by boat and withdrew to a mountain to pray (Matt. 14:22; Mark 6:45). Jesus would one day rule His people as king, but they must first come to Him in genuine faith.

WALKING ON THE SEA, 6:16-21

The miracle of Jesus walking on the Sea of Galilee was intended as an encouragement to the disciples, who had just seen Jesus reject an offer of kingship. A recognition of His royal, messianic Person by the Jews was what they had been working for. But Jesus had refused the offer. The twelve may have been wondering, *Have we been mistaken? Have we put our faith in the wrong person?* Jesus answered such questions and strengthened their faith through the miraculous sign that followed. John omits the detail of Peter's attempt to walk on the water (Matt. 14:28-32).

THE DELAYED CROSSING, 6:16-17

6:16 Before sending the disciples away Jesus had apparently explained that He would meet them at a designated location but that they should go on if He did not arrive by a certain time.[4] Their waiting for Jesus' arrival delayed the crossing of the sea until dusk ("evening").

6:17 The disciples needed to cross the northern section of the Sea of Galilee to get to Capernaum.[5] That city, identified with Tel Hum, is located on the northwest shore of the sea of Galilee. The city boasts a lovely second-century synagogue that is in a remarkable state of preservation.

John reports that it was dark and Jesus had not come. The disciples were alone in what could turn out to be a dangerous situation. God's people sometimes find themselves in similar circumstances. The miracle that follows may give believers a renewed sense of confidence in the face of danger and uncertainty.

THE COMING OF JESUS, 6:18-21

6:18 The Sea of Galilee is usually a very calm body of water during the morning hours. In the afternoon, however, the lake is often stirred

4. B. F. Westcott, *The Gospel According to St. John* (Grand Rapids: Eerdmans, 1973), p. 98.
5. Although their ultimate destination was Capernaum, they set off in the direction of Bethsaida (Mark 6:45). The words of Mark 6:45 are best rendered "toward [*pros*] Bethsaida."

up by the Mediterranean winds that funnel through the valleys of Galilee and swoop down upon the placid water. Particularly stormy weather can make the Sea of Galilee look like a boiling cauldron. Such were the conditions as the disciples rowed against the wind toward Capernaum.

6:19   Although the disciples had been rowing most of the night (cf. Mark 6:48), they had only traveled 3 to 3.5 miles (literally, "twenty-five to thirty stadia"). A stadia is the equivalent of 607 feet or 192 meters. Then Jesus appeared walking on the water. The word translated "saw" is actually present tense, emphasizing and preserving the drama of the moment. The disciples literally "became terrified" (ingressive aorist passive indicative of *phobeōmai*). The disciples' fear is understandable in light of the storm, the darkness, and the weariness of their own minds and bodies.

6:20   At first the disciples thought they were seeing a ghost (cf. Matt. 14:26). Then Jesus spoke. "It is I" (literally, "I am"). This self-identification hints at His deity (cf. John 8:58). Then He instructed them in the present imperative, "Stop being afraid."

6:21   After taking Jesus into the boat, they immediately found themselves at their destination. The word "immediately" (*eutheōs*) may suggest an additional miracle. But the text does not demand this. John may be simply stating that, without further hindrance from the wind (Mark 6:51), they arrived quickly at their destination.

THE DISCOURSE ON THE BREAD OF LIFE, 6:22-71

The Bread of Life discourse is a sequel to the feeding of the five thousand. The discourse was intended to force the materialistic multitudes to face the crucial issue of faith in the Messiah, Jesus. He is more than a provider of bread. He is the life-giving Son of God. His words call for a decision to trust in His Person.

The discourse divides into three sections. Jesus began by addressing the multitudes (6:22-40), then the Jews in the synagogue at Capernaum (6:41-59), and finally, He spoke to His disciples (6:60-71).

TO THE MULTITUDE, 6:22-40

The first part of the discourse was addressed to crowds that had participated in the miraculous feeding and were looking for more of the same. To those He presented Himself as the Bread of Life (6:35).

The Arrival of the Crowds, 6:22-24

6:22   The day following the miraculous feeding the crowds did not find Jesus on the lakeshore. The people were confused because only one boat had departed and Jesus had not gone with His disciples.

6:23   By the time the crowds realized that Jesus was gone, some boatmen had arrived from Tiberias, the capital of Galilee, from which Herod Antipas ruled. Tiberias was located along the southwest shore of the lake, about a seven-mile boat ride from Capernaum. The boatmen came either with the hope of seeing Jesus or the prospect of finding customers to ferry back to town.

6:24   When the people realized Jesus had left the site of the miraculous feeding, the boats were hired and they set out for Capernaum in search of Him.

The Work of Faith, 6:25-29

6:25   Finding Jesus on the other side of the lake at Capernaum, the crowds came to Him with a question. We would expect them to ask, "How did you get here?" Instead they asked, "Rabbi, when did you get here?" The term *rabbi* (from the Aramaic for "great") was a term of honor used for a Jewish teacher.

6:26   Jesus did not answer their question. Instead, He rebuked their materialistic desires. They sought Him not because of the signs of His messiahship, but because of the bread they had received. Sadly, they were more concerned with their stomachs than their souls. This is characteristic of unbelieving people. They focus on what is material and passing, neglecting what is spiritual and enduring. Even believers can have their values turned around.

6:27   Jesus at this point began to develop a contrast that would be amplified throughout the discourse. Physical food quickly spoils. The spiritual food, which the Messiah ("Son of Man") has authority to provide, issues in eternal life.

The "seal" (from *sphragizō*, "to seal") suggests God's approval. In antiquity, a seal was a mark of ownership and sign of approval. God the Father has set His "seal of approval" on Jesus.

6:28   Jesus' mention of "work" in v. 27 may have led the crowds to ask their next question. They wanted to know what kind of religious duty was necessary to meet God's approval.

6:29   Rather than rebuking their desire to work for God's approval, Jesus defined the necessary work in terms of belief. There is essentially just one work that God requires—belief in the One He has sent.

Paul refers to this as "your work of faith" (1 Thess. 1:3). Verse 29 serves to answer those who seek salvation by good works. The only work that pleases God is the labor of faith.

The Bread of Life, 6:30-40

6:30   The crowds had already seen one sign (6:14), but they either failed to grasp its significance or simply wanted further confirmation. They demanded another miraculous sign before they would believe Jesus. The words "believe you" (*pisteusōmen soi*) do not reflect John's normal Greek construction for believing in Jesus. At this point, the people were simply considering whether or not Jesus' words were true.

6:31   Referring to the events of Exodus 16:13-21, the crowds recalled the miraculous provision of manna in the wilderness. Although the source of the quotation "He gave them bread from heaven to eat" is disputed, it appears to be taken from the Septuagint's rendering of Psalm 78:24.[6] The comment may reflect a minimizing of Christ's miracle. Moses provided bread for a nation; Christ provided for a multitude. Moses provided bread for forty years; Christ for one day. Moses provided "bread from heaven"; Jesus gave them bread from earth.

6:32   Jesus responded by correcting their mistaken opinion. First, it was not Moses but God the Father who provided manna in the wilderness. Jesus once again identified God as "my Father" (cf. John 5:18).

6:33   Second, the "true bread from heaven" (6:32), "the bread of God," is none other than Jesus Himself. The manna in the wilderness sustained the life of the nation; the "true bread," Christ, "gives life to the world." The words "comes down" (*katabainō*), repeated seven times in various forms (6:33, 38, 41, 42, 50, 51, 58), stress the incarnation of Christ.

6:34   Like the woman at the well, members of the crowd were focusing on physical rather than on spiritual realities. Hopeful for another meal they asked Jesus ("Sir") for this heavenly bread.

6:35   Jesus responded by identifying Himself as "the bread of life." The metaphor suggests that as bread is necessary for physical life, so Christ is the necessary sustenance for spiritual life. Those who come to Christ with personal faith (trust) will never, never be spiritually hungry or thirsty again. The Greek uses double negatives (*ou mē*) to

6. M. J. J. Menken, "The Provenance and Meaning of the Old Testament Quotation in John 6:31," *Novum Testamentum* 30 (1988): 39-56.

negate absolutely the possibility. To know Christ is to be spiritually filled and eternally refreshed.

6:36   The true bread, Christ, can only be assimilated by personal faith—a point at which the curious crowd had not yet arrived. Morris comments that the "But" (*all*) introduces a strong contrast with what Jesus would have wished to see.[7]

6:37   Verse 37 presents a delicate balance between divine sovereignty and man's response with regard to salvation. Divine sovereignty is reflected in the first phrase, "All that the Father gives Me will come to Me." Believers are given to Christ by the Father's sovereign determination. Human response is reflected in the second phrase, "Whoever comes to Me I will never drive away." These statements strongly affirm the two great truths of divine sovereignty and human responsibility. Believers, however, tend to embrace one to the neglect of the other, and theologians rarely embrace the seemingly contradictory concepts with equal enthusiasm.

The expression "drive away" (*ekballō*) is a strong one and could be translated "cast out" (Matt. 8:12; 22:13; 25:30). Ultimately, those who "come" and those who are "given" are one and the same (Eph. 1:4-5).

6:38   Verses 38-40 focus on the theme of the Father's will. The purpose of Jesus in His incarnation ("come down from heaven") is to do the will of the Father.

6:39   The will of the Father is revealed in v. 39. God's will is that none of those given to Christ will be lost. The word "lose" (*apollumi*) can be translated "destroy" or "perish" and refers to the loss of eternal life (John 3:16). It is not the Father's will that any believer perish. He wills their security in Christ. The promise to "raise them up at the last day," repeated in vv. 40 and 44, speaks of the believer's resurrection (5:28-29). The "last day" refers here to a time just before the inauguration of the age to come, the messianic kingdom.

6:40   Verse 40 continues the theme of the Father's will but adds the dimension of the human response—belief issuing in eternal life. The words "looks to the Son" and "believes in Him" are parallel concepts, although the former suggests the gaze of contemplation and reflection.

TO THE JEWS, 6:41-59

Jesus' teaching brought opposition from "the Jews," apparently the leading Jews or religious authorities. Their concerns focus on two

---

7. Leon Morris, *The Gospel According to John*, NICNT (Grand Rapids: Eerdmans, 1971), p. 366.

main issues: the matter of Christ's divine origin and the problem of eating His flesh.

Christ's Divine Origin, 6:41-51

6:41   Jesus' claim to be of heavenly origin caused murmuring among the Jews. The imperfect tense of the verb "murmur" (*gog-guzō*) indicates that they began grumbling and persisted in it.

6:42   They were saying, "How can this be true of someone we have known all these years?" They knew Jesus' family background. Identifying Him as "the son of Joseph" reflects either their ignorance or denial of the supernatural circumstances of His birth (cf. Matt. 1:18-25; Luke 1:31-35).

6:43   Jesus commanded that they "stop grumbling" (*mē* with the present imperative). This is such a simple and practical command. God takes no pleasure in grumblers. It was grumbling and complaining that got the Israelites into such serious trouble in the wilderness (cf. Num. 11:1; 12:1; 14:2). Paul uses Israel's experience as the basis for a warning to the church (1 Cor. 10:10). After dealing with the grumbling of the people, Jesus explained their unbelief.

6:44   The crowd had not been drawn by the Father nor had it been listening to His words through the prophets. Consequently, the crowd was not believing in Jesus. The word "draws" (*elkuō*) is a strong verb. It is used of dragging a fishing net (John 21:6, 11) and dragging Paul from the Temple area (Acts 21:30). The verb contains the idea of resistance—but resistance that is unsuccessful. The drawing power of God is always triumphant (John 12:32).

Verse 44 clearly indicates that God must initiate an individual's salvation. God elects and draws. Man must respond by personal faith. Believers often pray that a person will respond. We should pray with equal fervor that God will draw.

6:45   The source of the quotation from the "Prophets" is difficult to pinpoint with certainty. The Greek text is quite close to the Septuagint's translation of Isaiah 54:13. The plural "prophets" may indicate that John has more than one source in mind (cf. Jer. 31:34). Jesus is saying that the Father will teach the truth about His Son. Those who heed God's instruction ("listens" and "learns") will come to Christ.

6:46   Lest anyone suggest that hearing God (v. 45) implies seeing Him, Jesus declared that no one has seen (present active indicative of *horaō*) the Father except the Son (cf. 1:18). The only way for others to "see" God is through Jesus Christ.

6:47   Whereas the sovereignty of God was emphasized in v. 44, v. 47 points to the necessity of an individual response. For the third time in this discourse Jesus used the solemn phrase "I tell you the truth" (cf. 1:51). Those who trust in the truth of Christ's Person have the gift of eternal life.

6:48   The words of v. 35 are repeated to introduce an analogy between Jesus, "the bread of life," and the manna that God provided in the wilderness.

6:49   The forefathers of the Jews ate manna in the wilderness, yet they died. The manna merely sustained their lives temporarily.

6:50   The bread of Christ, on the other hand, gives and sustains life eternally. Those who "eat" (*esthiō*) the bread of heaven are not subject to spiritual death ("and not die"). Eating is a metaphor for appropriation and assimilation (cf. Ezek. 3:1-4; Rev. 10:8-11). Food that is eaten must be chewed and digested. It then nourishes and invigorates the body. The aorist tense suggests a point in time when the individual believes and appropriates the gift of salvation.

6:51   Jesus has referred to Himself as the "bread of life" (6:35, 48), but now He uses the words "living bread." The phrases are near synonyms meaning "bread which gives life." Here He identifies the bread as His "flesh," which people must eat to live eternally. The words "which I give for the life of the world" express something of the extent of His atonement. Christ's redemptive work was with a view to providing eternal life for the unbelieving world.

Eating Christ's Flesh, 6:52-59

6:52   The listeners apparently understood Jesus' self-identification as "bread." But the concept of eating His flesh troubled them. It sounded a lot like the horror of cannabalism (Deut. 28:53-57; Lam. 2:20). The Jews debated this repugnant suggestion among themselves.

6:53   Verses 53-58 have been interpreted by some as Christ's teaching regarding Communion (the Eucharist). There are several objections against this view. First, these words were spoken one full year before the Lord's Table was instituted by Jesus in the upper room (cf. Matt. 26:26-29). It is an inversion of the chronology to impose that teaching here. Second, John does not record the institution of the Lord's Table. The larger context of the book would provide no basis for finding eucharistic teaching here. Third, the word "flesh" is not used in 1 Corinthians 10:14-22; 11:17-34 or in the synoptic gospels with reference to the Communion table.

In v. 53 Jesus uses a difficult metaphor. He declares that in order to possess "life" (i.e., eternal life), it is necessary to "eat the flesh of the Son of Man and drink His blood." Like a riddle or a parable, this metaphor was designed to cause the responsive to reflect and inquire further. Those with a superficial interest in the teachings of Jesus would be offended and turned away by such difficult teaching.

Bible teachers should note that Jesus did not always make the truth clear and simple. Sometimes He couched the truth in a riddle or enigma to stimulate the thinking of His listeners and encourage their participating in the process of discovery.

Bullinger points out that the Hebrews used the verbs *eating* and *drinking* to denote the operation of the mind in receiving, understanding, and applying doctrine or instruction of any kind.[8] In Ecclesiasticus 24:21, Wisdom speaks her own praises and declares, "They who eat me will hunger for more, and they who drink me will thirst for more." In more common usage today is the term *digest.* Someone is asked, "Have you digested that recent article on the Holy Spirit?"

The "flesh" (*sarx*) of Christ refers to His true Person. The "blood" (*haima*) refers to His life (cf. Lev. 17:14). Jesus is saying, "My true Person and life must be personally appropriated and assimilated in order to have eternal life."

6:54   Verse 54 provides a simple cause-and-result formula for eternal life: "Whoever eats My flesh and drinks My blood has eternal life." The formula is illuminated by the parallel thought in v. 40, "Everyone who looks to the Son and believes in Him shall have eternal life." The following chart summarizes the relationship:

verse	*action*	*object*		*result*
v. 40	Looking and believing	Christ	=	eternal life
v. 54	Eating and drinking	Christ	=	eternal life

If the results are the same (eternal life), then the actions leading to this result must be theologically equivalent. "Eating and drinking Christ" is another way of saying, "looking to and believing in Christ."

When communicating the gospel it is helpful to use a variety of terms to describe how an individual appopriates Christ's provision of salvation. We must *believe* in Christ, *receive* Him as our Savior, put our

---

8. E. W. Bullinger, *Figures of Speech Used in the Bible* (Grand Rapids: Baker, 1968), p. 826.

trust in Him, *welcome* Him into our lives, *open* the doors of our hearts. The use of a variety of terms may help a person understand more clearly what he must do in response to the gospel message.

6:55   These words are the basis for the Roman Catholic teaching that the Communion elements miraculously become the physical flesh and blood of Jesus in the sacrifice of the mass. It is better to understand Jesus as emphasizing the spiritual significance of His Person—flesh and blood. As He says in v. 63, "the flesh counts for nothing." There is a higher level of reality than that of physical flesh and blood. Jesus is saying that true spiritual food and drink, nourishment for the soul, must be found in Him.

6:56   Verse 56 repeats the thought of vv. 53-54. Those who appropriate the spiritual provision of His Person ("eats My flesh and drinks My blood") remain or abide in Christ. The present tense of verbs "eat" and "drink" point to a continuing appropriation. The present tense of "remains" (*menō*) suggests a continuous relationship (cf. John 1:32-33; 14:10). The focus of this term is on the union of the believer with Christ. The relationship between Christ and the believer is depicted as a spiritual union involving a continuous, mutual indwelling. The concept of abiding is further developed in 15:4-6.

6:57   Jesus presents an analogy of life and relationship. As the Son has no life apart from the Father, so people have no spiritual life apart from Christ. The one who "feeds" on Christ "will live" eternally. Spiritual life is bound up with one's relationship with Christ. Jesus and His relationship with the Father is the basis for the believer's immortality. The expression "the living Father," occurring nowhere else in Scripture, builds on the image of Christ as the "living bread" (6:51).

The words "because of" (*dia*) can also be translated "for the sake of" or "on account of." The first alternative suggests an obligation to the life-giver (i.e., obedience); the second simply indicates the source of life. The context seems to support the second view. As the Son has life in the Father, so believers have life in Christ. Both the Father and Son have life and the capacity to extend life to others.

6:58   Here Jesus repeats and develops the thought introduced in v. 49. The manna eaten by the Israelites in the wilderness did not prevent them from experiencing death just as all peoples do. But those who feed on the true bread, Christ, will live eternally. Eternal life results from assimilating Christ—appropriating His work by believing in Him.

132

6:59   John notes that Jesus delivered this discourse in the "synagogue" at Capernaum. The word *synagogue* is derived from a Greek word that means "together" or "bring together." A synagogue, therefore, is a gathering or an assembly. A Jewish synagogue was a building set aside for the purpose of teaching the law and observing Sabbath services. The synagogue at Capernaum has been excavated and partially restored. Excavations in 1981 uncovered a basalt floor dating to the first century A.D. or earlier.[9] This may well be the floor of the synagogue in which Jesus preached.

TO THE DISCIPLES, 6:60-71

The last section of the discourse was addressed to "His disciples" (6:61). The term "disciple" literally means "learner." It is a term used of the twelve (Matt. 10:1; cf. John 4:31; 11:7), the early Christians (Acts 9:1), and of the large crowds of interested listeners (Luke 6:17; 19:37), which included both believers (6:68-69) and unbelievers (John 6:66). It is the latter sense in which John uses the term here.

6:60   Many of the disciples who heard Jesus' discourse on the Bread of Life struggled with the teaching. The concept of eating His flesh and drinking His blood (6:56) was difficult indeed. The word "hard" (*skleros*) is used of physical objects that are stiff or rough. Metaphorically, it refers to what is austere or severe. They simply could not accept this teaching.

6:61   Earlier the Jews had grumbled. Now His "disciples" were grumbling. Jesus responded with the question, "Does this offend you?" He knew the answer. They were stumbling over His teaching. The difficult teaching was turning them away from Jesus.

6:62   In the Greek, v. 62 is grammatically incomplete. It states a condition but omits the conclusion. Jesus calls attention to His future return to heaven (cf. 13:33; 14:2). "Imagine," says Jesus, "if you should see the Messiah [Son of Man] ascending to heaven?" What would be the result? Jesus does not say. Perhaps He is implying, "If you stumble over this teaching, you will stumble later." Or maybe, "You wouldn't stumble over this if you understood My future ascension."

6:63   In v. 63 Jesus illuminates the concept He was teaching in vv. 53-58. The Spirit of God gives life (cf. 3:5, 8; 7:38-39), not the "flesh"

9. James F. Strange and Hershel Shanks, "Synagogue Where Jesus Preached Found at Capernaum," *Biblical Archaeology Review* (November/December 1983): 24-31.

of man. Jesus further explains that His words are "spirit" and "life." That is, they are to be understood as communicating a spiritual message ("spirit") that would issue in "life."

6:64   Jesus acknowledges that among His followers there are those who do not believe. They were not yet trusting in His messianic Person. John explains that the desertion of some of the disciples was not unexpected. Jesus had known from the beginning of His ministry those who did not believe. Once again His omniscience was demonstrated (cf. 1:47). Jesus even knew that Judas Iscariot would betray Him (cf. 6:16; 13:2, 21-30).

6:65   Verse 65 traces the initiative for believing in Christ to God. No one is able to come to Christ apart from the workings of God. Jesus did not expect all to believe. Faith is a gift that comes from God (Eph. 2:8-9). But this wonderful truth should not make believers any less obligated to witness. As Paul says, "And how can they believe in the one of whom they have not heard? And how can they hear without someone preaching to them?" (Rom. 10:14).

6:66   Jesus' teaching in the Bread of Life discourse resulted in a thinning of the ranks of His followers. Many supposed disciples abandoned Jesus. He was not the kind of messiah they were looking for. It was this same group that had sought to make Him king (6:15). By leaving Jesus, they demonstrated their lack of genuine faith.

Although it is sad when once-interested listeners turn away from Christ, it should not surprise us. Many of those who look into spiritual matters are only interested in "loaves and fishes." Only the true sheep will hear the Shepherd's voice and respond in earnest to the gospel.

6:67   Jesus here turns His attention to the twelve. This is the only passage in John where He speaks with the twelve alone. Where were they in the progress of their faith? Were they ready to abandon Christ too?

6:68   Peter spoke for the twelve to affirm their faith in Christ. He addressed Jesus as "Lord" (*kurie*), an indication of his faith in Christ's deity. If they turn from Christ, there is none other to whom they can go. The message that repelled the multitude was embraced by Peter as "the words of eternal life."

6:69   Peter here makes a strong affirmation of faith in behalf of the apostles. The words "believe" and "know" are in the perfect tense, indicating that the twelve had come to believe and were convinced of the truth of Christ's Person. The designation "Holy one of God" serves as a messianic title (cf. Mark 1:14; Luke 4:34; Acts 3:14). The term may have been derived from Isaiah's favorite designation of God, "the Holy One of Israel" (Isa. 1:4).

6:70 The strong affirmation of faith by Peter in behalf of the twelve reflects the progress of belief emphasized throughout the gospel. But Jesus knew the hearts of His disciples and did not allow Himself to be carried away with enthusiasm over Peter's confession. One of the chosen twelve was doing the devil's work (13:2, 27).

6:71 The apostle John explains Jesus' remark as referring to Judas Iscariot, who was later to betray Christ. Judas was among those "chosen" (6:70) by Jesus, but he did not follow through with personal faith. Once again John presents the reader with the delicate balance between divine sovereignty and human responsibility. The reference to Judas marks a significant development in unbelief as opposed to belief.

HOMILETICAL SUGGESTIONS

The feeding of the five thousand (6:1-15) fits nicely into a preaching series on the seven signs of John's gospel. The miracle of Jesus walking on the Sea of Galilee (6:16-21) provides the text for the fifth message in such a series.

The Bread of Life discourse (6:22-71) is much too long for a single message. It divides into three sections: Christ's words to the multitude (6:22-40), to the Jews in the synagogue (6:41-59), and finally to the disciples (6:60-71). Serving the congregation loaves of warm bread during one of these messages would enhance the metaphor of bread and make for a memorable message.

JOHN
CHAPTER
SEVEN

TEACHING IN THE TEMPLE

CONFLICT AT THE FEAST OF TABERNACLES, 7:1-52

Chapters 7-11 record how the hostility against Jesus in Jerusalem and Judea advanced from hatred to murder. Here John records the clash between belief and unbelief. As the scene of conflict moves from Galilee to Jerusalem, the conflict becomes more heated. Six times in this section it is said that the Jewish officials sought to "seize" or arrest Jesus (7:30, 32, 44; 8:20; 10:39; 11:57). Five times it is said they sought to take His life (7:1, 19, 25; 8:37; 11:53). This murderous hatred manifested itself in the autumn of A.D. 32, about six months before Christ's crucifixion.

JESUS AND HIS BROTHERS, 7:1-13

Verses 1-9 set the stage for the misunderstanding and hostility Jesus would face in Jerusalem.[1] Just as Jesus' own brothers misunderstood Him, so the Jewish authorities would misunderstand Him and seek to kill Him.

7:1 The words "after this" refer to the events surrounding the Bread of Life discourse that Jesus delivered in Capernaum. Comparing 6:4 with 7:2, one discovers that about five months had passed. During

---

1. Barclay M. Newman and Eugene A. Nida, *A Translator's Handbook on the Gospel of John* (London: United Bible Societies, 1980), p. 219.

that period Jesus ministered in Galilee and avoided Judea. John explains why. The Jewish authorities[2] were seeking to kill Jesus (cf. 5:18). The imperfect tense of *zēteō* ("seeking"; NIV "waiting") indicates that this treachery was progressive and continual.

7:2   The Feast of Tabernacles (*Sukkoth*) was a fall harvest festival and one of the three feasts Jews were required to attend in Jerusalem (Deut. 16:16). Josephus notes that this feast was "kept with greatest care" (*Antiquities* 15.50). Most of the first-century Jews were farmers and their lives depended on their crops. Their work prevented many farmers from attending the spring festivals of Passover and Pentecost. But once the harvest was over and the crops were stored, they could stop laboring and enjoy themselves for a while. Thus Sukkoth became the most popular and well-attended feast.

The celebration looks back to the wilderness wanderings when the people lived in temporary shelters (Lev. 23:39, 42-43), and looks ahead prophetically to Israel's kingdom joy when the nation is regathered in the land (Zech. 14:16). The distinctive event of the feast involved the building of the *sukkah*, or tabernacle, where the family would sleep and take its meals during the seven-day celebration (*Sukkah* 1:1; 2:6).

7:3   Jesus' "brothers" (actually half-brothers) were the children of Joseph and Mary. They are identified in Matthew 13:55 as James, Joseph, Simon, and Judas. Inasmuch as Jesus was gathering disciples and presenting messianic credentials ("miracles"), His brothers suggested that He ought to leave Galilee and go to Judea (i.e., Jerusalem) where there was great interest in such things. Verse 5 reveals that their recommendation was not made with sincere interest in the success of Jesus' ministry. A note of sarcasm may be detected in their comment. They were hostile toward His messianic claims.

7:4   Verse 4 explains the brothers' thinking. The general principle is stated first. "No one who wants to become a public figure acts in secret." The implication is then drawn, "Since you are doing these things [the miracles], show yourself to the world." The words "in secret" (*en kruptō*) are an apparent reference to Galilee. From the viewpoint of Judaism, Jerusalem is "the world." The brothers were saying in effect, "If you are serious about being accepted as Israel's Messiah,

2. In a helpful study, "'The Jews' in the Gospel of John," by R. G. Bratcher, in Newman and Nida's *A Translator's Handbook on the Gospel of John*, pp. 641-49, it is shown that "the Jews" can refer to (1) the Jewish people, (2) Judeans, (3) people hostile to Jesus, or (4) Jewish authorities in Jerusalem.

you had better make your claims in Jerusalem rather than in obscure parts of Galilee."

Perhaps they recognized the eschatological implications of the feast (Zech. 14:16) and were suggesting that this would be a good time to make His kingdom claims. This would not happen, of course, because the King had already been rejected by the nation's leaders (cf. John 5:18).

7:5   John interrupts the flow of the narrative to explain that Jesus' own brothers were not believing in Him. The emphasis in the original is that their unbelief is contrary to expectation. The words "did not believe" (imperfect tense) denote a continuing attitude. They persistently refused to believe. But this would change later (cf. Acts 1:14; 1 Cor. 9:5; 15:7; Gal. 1:19). According to the early church, James and Jude ("Judas") eventually wrote New Testament epistles.

Many Christians are troubled by unbelief within their own households. There may be parents, siblings, or children who do not believe. There is some comfort in knowing that Jesus experienced the same difficulty in His earthly family.

7:6   In response to His half-brothers, Jesus explained that the "right time" (*kairos*) had not yet come. The word translated "right time" refers to the suitable time, the favorable opportunity. It was an appropriate and suitable time for His brothers to go to the feast. But Jesus was operating on a divine timetable and the "right time" for His public manifestation to Israel had not yet come.

7:7   Jesus continues the contrast between Himself and His brothers. The "world" (*kosmos*) of unbelievers accepts its own but hates Christ. The reason given is because of Christ's continual testimony (present tense) that their deeds are evil. Jesus develops the world's hatred and hostility further in the Upper Room discourse (John 15:18-23).

Christ was not unwilling to stand up and denounce the sin of the world. Sometimes Christians are afraid that if they speak out against sin they will alienate sinners. Jesus was able to hate the sin and yet love the sinner.

7:8   Jesus encourages His brothers to go on up to Jerusalem to attend the Feast of Tabernacles and repeats that it is not yet the appropriate time to present Himself publicly as they had suggested.

The word "yet" (*oupō*) is absent in some early manuscripts and appears to have been introduced into the text in order to alleviate the apparent inconsistency between v. 8 and v. 10, where it is recorded that Jesus went to the feast.[3] As the harder reading is usually preferrable, it is probable that the original text was "not" (*ouk*) instead of "not yet" (*oupō*).

The reader is left with an apparent contradiction. How could Jesus reject His brother's request and then attend the feast anyway? Jesus, it seems, negated the request of His brothers, but not the possibility of attending the feast in a different manner later. This is suggested by John's words in v. 10, "He went also, not publicly, but in secret." He would attend the feast, but not in the way His brothers had suggested. There would be no great, public display of messianic credentials.

7:9 Jesus remained for a time in Galilee, allowing his brothers and the other pilgrim travelers to make their way to the feast.

7:10 After some delay, Jesus also went up to Jerusalem for the feast. The words, "not publicly, but in secret," indicate that He did not want to draw attention to Himself. The contrast is with His final entry as recorded in 12:12 ff.

7:11 The Jewish authorities at the feast remembered the healing of the lame man a year or so before (cf. 5:1ff.) and were undoubtedly wondering if Jesus was going to cause a stir again. They were continually "watching" (imperfect tense of *zēteō*, "to seek") for Him and asking pilgrim visitors, "Where is that man?"

7:12 There was quite a variety of opinion circulating in Jerusalem regarding Jesus. Some were convinced that He was a "good [*agathos*] man." His motives were pure. He had healed people and miraculously provided food. His words reflected truth and integrity. Others rejected these evidences and argued, "No, He deceives the people." The debate was right on target. The central issue, then and now, is the Person of Christ.

7:13 Fear of the Jewish authorities intent on murdering Jesus made the pilgrim visitors at the Feast of Tabernacles cautious in expressing themselves. Experience taught them it was dangerous to take a viewpoint that was not officially sanctioned by the religious authorities (cf. 9:22, 34).

TEACHING IN THE TEMPLE, 7:14-24

7:14 John reports that it was in the middle of the seven-day feast that Jesus arrived in Jerusalem. There in the Temple precincts He be-

---

3. Bruce M. Metzger, *A Textual Commentary on the Greek New Testament* (London: United Bible Societies, 1971), p. 216.

gan to teach the people. The content of what He taught on this occasion is not indicated, but the dialogue that follows indicates the discourse focused on His divine Person and origin (cf. 7:28-29).

7:15   The Jewish authorities who heard Jesus speak had to admit He was a knowledgeable teacher. This greatly surprised them. Normally, before becoming a rabbi, an aspiring student would study under leading rabbis, memorizing what former Jewish teachers had taught about the law. Jesus had no such formal rabbinical training, yet He was a fountain of knowledge and wisdom.

7:16   Jesus responded to the question of v. 15 by explaining that His teaching was not His own origination. Rather, it came from "Him who sent me" (*tou pempsantos me*), a clear reference to the Father (cf. 5:23-24; 6:44). Whereas the rabbis quoted one another and appealed to earthly authorities, Jesus taught the message that God the Father had given Him.

7:17   Jesus states that a willingness to *obey* the truth is a prerequisite to an *understanding* of His message. If anyone purposes to do God's will, he will come to recognize (*ginōskō*) the divine origin of Jesus' teaching. Plummer remarks, "The mere mechanical performance of God's will is not enough; there must be an inclination towards Him, a wish to make our conduct agree with His will; and without this agreement Divine doctrine cannot be recognized as such."[4] Experiential knowledge of God comes with a willingness to do His will.

7:18   Jesus contrasts two kinds of teachers: the self-taught teacher who promotes his own ideas and seeks his own honor, and the teacher who desires to honor the one who sent him. Jesus is the latter kind. This quality of humility is indicative of the truth He presents. Elsewhere in John the term "truth" is used of God (cf. 3:33; 8:26). Jesus shares this quality with the Father. The word "false" (*adikos*) may be better translated "unrighteous."

7:19   Jesus proceeds to point out the hypocrisy of Jewish law keeping. He uses a rhetorical question to show that although they had the law of Moses, they were not obeying it. In fact, they were violating the law by continually seeking (present tense of *zēteō*) to put Him to death (cf. 7:1).

7:20   The people in the multitude attending the feast apparently knew nothing of the plot of the religious leaders. They suggested that

---

4. A. Plummer, *The Gospel According to St. John* (Cambridge: At the University Press, 1899), p. 165.

Jesus must have had a demon (cf. Matt. 12:22-32; Mark 3:22-30; Luke 11:14-23). Only demon possession could account for such demented comments about plots on His life. It is amazing what wild theories unbelievers will resort to in their attempt to avoid the truth. The evolutionary hypothesis regarding the creation of the universe is full of holes, for example, but what else could an unsaved person believe?

7:21 Jesus answers the question "Who is trying to kill you?" by referring the crowd back to an earlier miracle, apparently the healing of the man at the pool of Bethesda, which had caused such an uproar about keeping the Sabbath (John 5:1-18).

7:22 The controversial Sabbath miracle was set in contrast with the Jewish practice of circumcising on the Sabbath. Jesus notes parenthetically that circumcision did not originate with Moses, but with the patriarchs. Circumcision, the removal of the male foreskin, was the sign of God's covenant with Abraham (cf. Gen. 17:9-14).

7:23 The hypocrisy of the Jewish Sabbath regulations is highlighted in v. 23. They saw no wrong in circumcision on a holy day. So binding was the law of circumcision (Lev. 12:3) that the rite was observed even if the eighth day fell on the Sabbath. As the Mishnah states, "And they may perform on the Sabbath all things that are needful for circumcision" (*Shabbath* 18:3; 19:1, 2). Yet the Jews faulted Jesus for making a lame man well on the Sabbath. They should have seen that a practice that overrode the Sabbath for ceremonial purposes justified the overriding of the Sabbath to provide bodily healing.[5]

7:24 Having pointed out their hypocrisy, Jesus challenges the crowd to "stop judging" (*mē* with the present imperative) superficially (literally, "according to sight"), but on the basis of what is right. The contrast is between external and true standards. Appearances can be deceiving. Jesus is calling for judgment on the basis of principle, not surface issues (cf. Matt. 7:1-5).

THE RESPONSE OF THE CROWD, 7:25-31

This section centers on the questions some people were asking themselves about Jesus. As in the Bread of Life discourse, the main issue is Christ's divine origin (cf. 6:41-51). Here He focuses on that issue again.

5. Leon Morris, *The Gospel According to John*, NICNT (Grand Rapids: Eerdmans, 1971), p. 408.

7:25   Some of the residents of Jerusalem had heard a nasty rumor about the Jewish authorities' plan to kill Jesus. "Isn't this the man they are trying to kill?" they asked.

7:26   In spite of the death threat, Jesus continued to speak publicly, and no one was making any attempt to arrest Him. "Could it be," they wondered again, "that the authorities have recognized Him as Messiah?" Their question reflects a degree of doubt or hesitation. The negative particle *mēpote* indicates that a negative answer is expected. Certainly they could not be planning to kill someone they were recognizing as the Messiah.

7:27   Although contrary to Scripture (2 Sam. 7:12-16; Isa. 9:7; Mic. 5:2), some of the people of Jerusalem held to a tradition that the Messiah's place of origin would be unknown and that He would be an unknown individual until anointed by Elijah.[6] Plummer suggests, on the basis of 6:42, that it was not the birthplace or remote descent, but the immediate and actual parentage of the Messiah that would be unknown.[7]

7:28   In response to the debate taking place in the Temple courts, Jesus "cried out" a statement designed to help the people discover the truth of His Person. The expression "cried out" (*ekrazen*) suggests a loud expression of strong emotion. His words may be taken as a statement, "Yes, you know me, and you know where I am from," or as a question, "Do you really know me and know where I am from?" There was no punctuation in the original Greek manuscripts. Because the response of the people indicates they did not really know where Jesus came from, it seems best to translate these words as a question. This contrasts with their professed knowledge in v. 27.

When Jesus explained to the people that He was not on His own but had been sent on a mission by one who was (and is) "true" (*alēthinos*), He was referring to the Father (cf. 6:44), one whom they did not know.

7:29   Jesus sets himself in contrast to the crowds in the Temple court. The pronoun "I" in the emphatic position serves to highlight this contrast. Jesus declares His personal knowledge of God, His divine origin, and His unique mission. The word translated "from"

---

6. Justin Martyr's (c. 100-165) dialogue with a learned Jew, Trypho, writes, "But Christ—if He has indeed been born, and exists anywhere—is unknown, and does not even know Himself, and has no power until Elias [Elijah] came to anoint Him, and make Him manifest to all" (*Dialogue with Trypho VIII, Anti-Nicene Fathers*, vol. 1, p. 199).

7. Plummer, *The Gospel According to St. John*, p. 408.

(*para*) has the sense of "from alongside," indicating that Jesus came from the Father's presence.

7:30   There were basically two ways people responded to the Person of Christ: with belief or unbelief. So it was in this situation. There was no doubt among His listeners that Jesus was claiming divine origin and mission. Having heard His claims, some of the people of Jerusalem (cf. 7:25) concurred with the Jewish authorities that Jesus was a deceiver and ought to be killed. They tried to seize Him, but the time appointed for His Passion had not yet come (cf. 12:23; 13:1).

7:31   Others among the crowd are said to have "put their faith in" Jesus. The aorist tense of *pisteuō* indicates that those persons came to believe at this point. It was the miracles that convinced them. They could not imagine that the prophesied Messiah would do more miracles than Jesus. Their question implies that Jesus must be the Christ.

THE RETURN TO THE FATHER, 7:32-36

7:32   The crowd's interest in the Person of Christ stirred the religious leaders to move ahead with their plan to do away with Jesus (cf. 7:1, 19).

There is some debate as to the identity of the "chief priests." According to Jewish law there was only one high priest at any time in Israel. At the death of the high priest, his office passed to his eldest son (cf. Num. 20:25-28). However, the Romans were in the habit of replacing high priests at their own discretion. Consequently, there were a number of former high priests living during the first century. Annas (John 18:13), high priest from A.D. 6-15, was deposed and replaced, but he remained active during the rule of his son-in-law, Caiaphas (A.D. 18-37). These ex-high priests, and other adult male members of prominent priestly families, may have been the "chief priests." Jeremias, on the other hand, argues that the "chief priests" were holders of such priestly offices as treasurer, captain of police, Temple overseers, who had jurisdiction over the priesthood and were members of the Sanhedrin.[8]

The chief priests, who would have held to the Sadducean doctrines, joined forces with the Pharisees in sending Temple guards to arrest Jesus. The word translated "temple guards" (*hupērētes*) literally means "servants" and refers here to officers under the authority of the Sanhedrin.

8. Joachim Jeremias, *Jerusalem in the Time of Jesus* (Philadelphia: Fortress, 1969), p. 160-81.

7:33   Jesus introduces in vv. 33-34 the subject of His return to the
Father, a matter to be developed further with the disciples (cf. 13:33;
14:2-4; 16:5-7, 28). Jesus announced that He would be with His disciples
for "only a short time"—it was only six months before His last Passover.
7:34   Verse 34 contains an enigmatic announcement of Jesus' death.
Jesus anticipated a time after His death when the people of Jerusalem
would seek Him, but it would be too late. He would have already died
and ascended to the Father. They would not be able to join Him there
because of their unbelief.
7:35   The statement of His departure puzzled the Jewish authorities. They wondered where He could go that they would not find Him.
They wondered if He was possibly planning a trip to visit the Jews
("our people") dispersed among the Gentile nations. The term
"Greeks" (*hellēn*) refers to Gentile or heathen people. The Greek culture had so influenced the Roman world that the people could be
loosely referred to as "Greeks."
7:36   The Jewish authorities could not understand Jesus' cryptic announcement of His depature (v. 34). They continued discussing the
matter, asking themselves, "What did He mean?"

THE PROPHECY OF THE HOLY SPIRIT, 7:37-44
     A bit of extrabiblical cultural background is necessary for a full
appreciation of the teaching of Jesus in this section. The Mishnah, con-
taining the oral teachings of Judaism around the time of Jesus, records
that during the celebration of the Feast of Tabernacles a water libation
was poured out each day before the morning sacrifices (*Sukkah* 4:9-
10). A priest would lead a procession from the Temple area down to
the pool of Siloam where a golden pitcher would be filled with water.
The priests, leading the procession, would then return to the Temple
altar. There he would pour out the water, along with a wine libation,
as the Temple music began and the Hallel psalms (Pss. 113-118) were
sung as the worshipers shook their *lulavs* (leafy branches, cf. Lev.
23:40) toward the altar.[9]
     The ritual pouring of water served as a confession of thirst and
an expression of prayer for autumn rains after the long, dry season.
7:37   The festivities of the week of Tabernacles were drawing to a
close. It was on the "last day" of the feast—after the priest had re-

9. Alfred Edersheim, *The Temple: Its Ministry and Services* (Grand Rapids: Eerdmans, 1958), pp.
   277-79.

turned from Siloam with his golden pitcher and for the last time had poured out its contents at the base of the altar, after the "hallel" had been sung and the people were waving their leafy branches (*lulavs*) toward the altar—that a voice was raised above the din of Temple ritual. It was Jesus, who cried out in a loud voice, "If anyone is thirsty, let him come to me and drink."

Jesus elevated the ritual expression of prayer for rain to a spiritual plane. The people were thinking of their physical need for rain. Jesus focused their attention on the spiritual thirst of the soul (cf. Isa. 12:3; 55:1). He was saying, "Have your spiritual thirst quenched in Me."

7:38   Continuing the theme of "water," so dominant in the Feast of Tabernacles, Jesus declares in v. 38 that those who believe in Him will have "streams of living water" flow from within. Some scholars have argued that the traditional punctuation of the verse is incorrect and that Christ, not the believer, is the one from whom the living waters flow. However, Cortes and Hodges have shown the inadequacy of those suggestions.[10] The believer is clearly the source of the rivers of living water.

The spiritually needy cannot satisfy their own thirst, but when they believe in Christ they receive an inner source of spiritual refreshment (cf. 4:14). "Streams," rather than cisterns or jugs, suggests a continual source and abundant provision. The appropriation of this refreshing provision is only by faith.

The major difficulty with this verse is the words, "As the Scripture has said." What Scripture is being referred to? Among suggestions that have been made are such Old Testament references as Exodus 17:5-6; Numbers 20:7-11; Psalm 78:15-16; Proverbs 5:15; 18:4; Isaiah 12:3; 44:3; 55:1; 58:11; Ezekiel 47:1-11; Zech. 13:1, and others.[11]

Although Hodges argues that Ezekiel's vision of a future Temple serves as a fitting image for the believer in Christ (Ezek. 47:1-11),[12] Isaiah 44:3 seems to have more direct thematic and theological links ("water," "thirsty," "Spirit") with what Jesus is discussing in this passage. Because there is no explicit Scripture citation given by John, it

---

10. J. B. Cortes, "Yet Another Look at John 7:37-38," *The Catholic Biblical Quarterly* 29 (1967): 75-86; Zane C. Hodges, "Rivers of Living Water—John 7:37-39," *Bibliotheca Sacra* 136 (1979): 239-43.

11. For a full discussion of alternatives, see Raymond E. Brown, *The Gospel According to John (i-xiii)*, The Anchor Bible (Garden City, N.Y.: Doubleday, 1966), pp. 321-23.

12. Hodges, "Rivers of Living Water—John 7:37-39," pp. 243-48.

may be best to understand the reference as an allusion rather than a quotation.

7:39   John here provides the reader with his divinely inspired interpretation of Jesus' teaching. The "streams of living water" (v. 38) is an allusion to the Spirit of God. As was promised through Isaiah, "I will pour water on the thirsty land, and streams on the dry ground; I will pour out my Spirit on your offspring" (Isa. 44:3). Those at the feast who put their trust in Jesus would later receive this Spirit (cf. John 14:16-17, 26; 15:26; 16:7; 20:22). It was not until Christ had been "glorified" (i.e., lifted to the cross and then to heaven) that the Spirit was bestowed in full New Covenant measure (Ezek. 36:27; cf. Acts 1:5; 2:4).

7:40   Jesus' teaching in the Temple on the last day of the Feast of Tabernacles resulted in differing interpretations of his Person. Some of the people were convinced that he was the long awaited "Prophet" promised by Moses in Deuteronomy 18:15.

7:41   Others concluded that Jesus must be the "Christ," the prophesied Messiah (cf. Isa. 2:2-4; 9:6-7; 11:1-5). Some, however, objected to His coming from "Galilee."

7:42   Scripture clearly indicates that the Messiah was to come from David's family (cf. 2 Sam. 7:12-16; Mic. 5:2). If the Messiah was to be the descendent of David, one would expect him to be from David's hometown, Bethlehem of Judea.

7:43   John reports that the differing opinions regarding Jesus resulted in division among the people. The word "divided" (*schisma*) means a clear split. No one view prevailed.

7:44   Some of the crowd, provoked by His teaching, wanted to seize Jesus, apparently to drag Him before the Sanhedrin. But, as in v. 30, nothing came of this. Jesus would not be arrested before His divinely determined hour.

As God protected Jesus from untimely harm, so God will protect His children. A missionary serving in a war-torn country was once asked about her personal safety. She responded, "It is God's will for me to be there, and the safest place for any Christian is to be in the will of God."

THE UNBELIEF OF THE JEWISH LEADERS, 7:45-53

7:45   Verse 32 records how the chief priests and Pharisees commissioned officers to arrest Jesus. Returning empty handed, the religious authorities asked, "Why didn't you bring Him in?"

7:46   The officers responded, "No one ever spoke the way this man does." Although intending to make an arrest, they were themselves arrested by Jesus' words. He spoke with an intrinsic authority and persuasive power that the Sanhedrin officials could not match.

7:47   The Pharisees (cf. 3:1) responded in such a way as to suggest that only a fool would be deceived by the teaching of Jesus. Their question, "Were you also led astray?" expects a negative answer. The sense is, "Surely you have not been deceived!"

7:48   The Pharisees set themselves apart from the subordinate officers sent to arrest Jesus. The question in v. 48 expects a negative answer. Certainly none of the members of the Sanhedrin ("rulers") or the Pharisees had been persuaded to believe in Him. As the educated elite, they knew better than to believe on Jesus. Nicodemus (vv. 50-51) may have already believed, but had not yet made his faith public (cf. 19:38-39).

7:49   The Pharisees added by way of theological outburst that "this mob" (the people responsive to Jesus' teaching) was cursed. What right had they to hold opinions contrary to the Sanhedrin and the Pharisees? Their "curse" may have been based on Deuteronomy 27:26, "Cursed is the man who does not uphold the words of this law by carrying them out."

7:50   There was one religious leader who objected to these proceedings: Nicodemus, who came to Jesus by night (3:1) and was a member of the Sanhedrin.

7:51   Nicodemus objected to what he regarded as an injustice. While the Sanhedrin was condemning the multitude for its ignorance of the law, Nicodemus pointed out the Sanhedrin's disregard for the law. Appealing to the elementary principles of justice found in Jewish law (cf. Deut. 1:16, 17; 17:8; 19:15), he questioned the legitimacy of condemning a man without first hearing him. Morris quotes Rabbi Eleazar ben Pedath as saying, "Unless a mortal hears the pleas that a man can put forward, he is not able to give judgment."[13]

Whatever the spiritual status of Nicodemus at this time, He must be acknowledged as a man who sought justice and fairness in dealing with Jesus. It is encouraging to find a person of any age who stands up for what is right.

7:52   The reply of the religious leaders, "Are you from Galilee, too?" suggests that they thought only pride for one's home region

13. Morris, *The Gospel According to John*, p. 434, n. 107.

could account for a sympathetic view of Jesus. They asked Nicodemus to do some research and he would discover that no prophet came out of Galilee. They apparently forgot about Jonah, who came from Gath-hepher (2 Kings 14:25), located about three miles north of Nazareth at Tel Gat Hefer. Nevertheless, their statement was only a slight exaggeration. One would not *expect* Galilee to produce a prophet, much less the Messiah.

7:53   This verse is part of the pericope of the adulterous woman (7:53–8:11) and will be treated in the context of that discussion.

HOMILETICAL SUGGESTIONS

In His teaching in the Temple (7:14-24) Jesus emphasized the importance of making decisions based on reality, not appearance. We so often judge ideas and people on first impressions, which are often wrong. We think too highly of some and have too little regard for others.

John 7:37-44 would serve as an excellent message for a hot, dry summer Sunday. Here Jesus deals with spiritual thirst. This thirst will never be quenched by ice water, lemonade, or a cold soft drink. Jesus alone can quench this thirst. He does this by providing believers with the New Covenant ministry of the Holy Spirit (7:39; Isa. 44:3).

JOHN
CHAPTER
EIGHT

LIGHT FOR THE WORLD

THE PARENTHESIS ON THE ADULTEROUS WOMAN, 7:53–8:11

Before commenting on this passage, it is necessary to give consideration to the text and the context.

Serious questions have been raised as to the authenticity of the passage about Jesus and the adulterous woman. It has been argued that this pericope is (1) absent in the oldest and best manuscripts, versions, and patristic citations; (2) foreign to the context; and (3) linguistically incompatible with the vocabulary and style of the fourth gospel. Metzger concludes, "The evidence for the non-Johannine origin of the pericope of the adulteress is overwhelming."[1] Yet with others of a similar opinion he concedes that the account "has all the earmarks of historical veracity."[2] Similarly, Morris, who states that this section is not an authentic part of the gospel, believes that "the story is true to the character of Jesus."[3] These opinions reflect something of the difficulty commentators have had in analyzing this most interesting text.

---

1. Bruce M. Metzger, *A Textual Commentary on the Greek New Testament* (London: United Bible Societies, 1971), p. 219. For detailed arguments, see Gary M. Burge, "A Specific Problem in the New Testament Text and Canon: The Woman Caught in Adultery (John 7:53–8:11)," *JETS* 27 (1984): 141-48.

2. Metzger, *A Textual Commentary in the Greek New Testament*, p. 220.

3. Leon Morris, *The Gospel According to John*, NICNT (Grand Rapids: Eerdmans, 1971), p. 883.

In spite of the questions, doubts, and denials regarding John 7:53–8:11, several insightful arguments have been set forth in favor of its authenticity.

THE STYLISTIC TRAIT

Alan Johnson has observed a stylistic trait in the fourth gospel of introducing short explanatory phrases to interpret the significance of words just spoken.[4] Note the following:

> 6:6   And this He was saying to test him . . . .
> 6:71   Now He meant Judas . . . .
> 11:13 Now Jesus had spoken of his death . . . .
> 11:51 Now he did not say this on his own initiative . . .
> 13:11 For He knew the one who was betraying him . . . .
> 13:28 Now no one of those reclining knew for what
>   purpose He had said this to him.

This very stylistic trait is observable within the questionable passage. "And they were saying this, testing Him" (John 8:6, NASB). Because this interjectory statement is a part of the whole narrative, it can be argued that the passage is an integral and authentic part of the whole gospel.

THE CONTROVERSY PATTERN

Trites works along different lines but comes to the same conclusion as Johnson. He has demonstrated that the same kind of controversy language, imagery, and terminology that is observed in John 1-12 is also evident in 7:53–8:11.[5]

Tracing this controversy pattern through chapters 1-12, Johnson points out that the forensic language used in John depicts a cosmic lawsuit between God and the world. The Jews appealed to their law, and Jesus appealed to His witnesses (John the Baptist, Scripture, His works, and the Father). All this is presented to achieve the purpose the author has stated in John 20:30-31. It is quite significant that this controversy pattern, evidenced throughout the book, is displayed in 7:53–8:11. Note the forensic language and imagery:

4. Alan F. Johnson, "A Stylistic Trait of the Fourth Gospel in the Pericope Adulterae?" *Bulletin of the Evangelical Theological Society* 9 (Spring 1966): 91-96.
5. Allison A. Trites, "The Woman Taken in Adultery," *Bibliotheca Sacra* 131 (April-June 1974): 137-46.

8:3	Judicial examination
8:4	Accusers involved
8:6	Challenge presented
8:6, 10	Legal words
8:9	Case collapses
8:10-11	Verdict pronounced

Whatever textual problems may be associated with the passage, Trites argues that there is no overriding contextual problem.[6] The case of the adulterous woman fits admirably into the controversy developed in John 1-12.

THE TEXTUAL EVIDENCE FOR INCLUSION

Hodges presents textual evidence in favor of the pericope.[7] He points out that evidence for the inclusion of this story is very early and that the passage is found in a large majority of the surviving Greek manuscripts. There are about 450 Greek texts that include the pericope.

Hodges also appeals to evidence from the church Fathers to argue for the authenticity of the text. He cites Jerome (c. 420), who writes, "In the Gospel according to John in many manuscripts, both Greek and Latin, is found the story of the adulterous woman who was accused before the Lord" ("The Dialogue Against the Pelagians," 2.27).[8] He also quotes the explanation of Augustine (c. 430) for the absence of the passage in some manuscripts: "Certain persons of little faith, or rather enemies of the true faith, fearing, I suppose, lest their wives should be given impunity in sinning, removed from their manuscripts the Lord's act of forgiveness toward the adulteress, as if He who had said, 'sin no more' had granted permission to sin" ("Adulterous Marriages," 2.7).[9]

Hodges presents convincing evidence from Greek manuscripts, early translations, and the church Fathers for regarding the text as authentic. The vast majority of the surviving Greek manuscripts of John's gospel contain the story, and it is likely to have always been found in the majority of the extant Greek texts of every period.

6. Ibid., p. 146.
7. Zane Hodges, "The Woman Taken in Adultery (John 7:53–8:11): The Text," *Bibliotheca Sacra* 136 (October-December 1979): 318-32.
8. Ibid., p. 330.
9. Ibid., pp. 330-31.

It is quite clear from this brief survey that the evidence against the pericope of the adulterous woman is not as overwhelming as it is sometimes made out to be. As it has been noted, even those who deny the authenticity of the text support the historicity of the incident. Commentators and expositors should exercise considerable caution before excising John 7:53–8:11 from Scripture. At the same time, care should be taken to avoid building any distinctive doctrines on a questionable text.

Charles Baylis has presented an insightful analysis of the pericope in the context of John's presentation of Jesus as a prophet like Moses (Deut. 18:15).[10] He shows how the first seven chapters of the gospel contrast Jesus, the "Greater Prophet" of the New Covenant, with Moses, the prophet of the Old Covenant. In those chapters Jesus identifies Himself as the prophet of whom Moses wrote (John 5:46) and is recognized as such by some of the people (7:40). Yet the religious leaders object, arguing that no prophet arises out of Galilee (7:52).

The religious leaders were facing a crisis. Many of the people were beginning to believe in Jesus. Yet if the leaders could show that Jesus opposed Moses, the people might be persuaded to abandon Him. And so the religious leaders arranged the "test case" of the woman caught in adultery. It was their purpose to trap Jesus into speaking against Moses and the law and thus provide the basis for an indictment against Him.

THE MINISTRY IN THE TEMPLE, 7:53–8:2

7:53   The Feast of Tabernacles was over (cf. 7:37), and the celebrants returned to their own homes.

8:1   By contrast, Jesus went to the Mount of Olives, the long, north-south ridge overlooking the Temple mount east of Jerusalem. The Mount of Olives is the place to which the Messiah will return at His second advent (Zech. 14:4).

8:2   It was early in the morning when Jesus appeared again in the colonnaded Temple courts. As people gathered, Jesus began to teach. This was in fulfillment of the prophetic word given through Moses "I

10. Charles P. Baylis, "The Woman Caught in Adultery: A Test of Jesus as the Greater Prophet," *Bibliotheca Sacra* 146 (April-June 1989): 171-84.

will raise up for them a prophet like you from among their brothers; I will put my words in his mouth, and he will tell them everything I command him" (Deut. 18:18). In accordance with the usual rabbinic practice, Jesus "sat down" to teach them.[11]

THE TESTING OF THE PROPHET, 8:3-6

8:3   The scribes ("teachers of the law") and the Pharisees (cf. John 3:1) worked together to set up a trap for Jesus. While Jesus was teaching in the Temple they brought before Him a woman accused of breaking the seventh commandment, "You shall not commit adultery" (cf. Ex. 20:14; Deut. 22:22-27).

8:4   As she stood before Jesus and the people gathered around Him, the woman was publicly accused: "Teacher, this woman was caught in the act of adultery." The expression "caught in the act of adultery" indicates that there were verifying witnesses. The text leaves no doubt that the woman was guilty of the sin. It may be that she was deliberately entrapped for the purpose of bringing this case before Jesus.

It is sad but true that many people take more delight in investigating the faults of others than in scrutinizing their own lives and conduct. The religious leaders epitomized this perversity—something against which we all need to guard ourselves.

8:5   Jesus was then confronted by the woman's accusers. They cited the law of Moses, which commanded the stoning of an adulteress (Deut. 22:24). Would Jesus, as a teacher of the law and recognized "prophet," affirm the Mosaic commandment? As Stephen James points out, although the propriety of capital punishment in a case of adultery was the bait in this trap set for Jesus, the real issue here was whether or not He was in strict compliance with the Mosaic law.[12]

The religious leaders believed they had finally trapped Jesus. If He advocated stoning the adulteress He would be going against the policy of Rome, which did not permit the Jews to execute the death sentence (cf. John 18:31). If He advocated her release, Jesus could be accused of contradicting Mosaic law (Lev. 20:10; Deut. 22:23-24) and

---

11. Zane C. Hodges, "The Woman Taken in Adultery (John 7:53–8:11): Exposition," *Bibliotheca Sacra* 137 (January-March 1980): 43.

12. Stephen A. James, "The Adulteress and the Death Penalty," *JETS* 22 (1979): 52-53.

disqualified from being the great prophet (Deut. 18:15-19). Either way, Jesus was going to face charges under Roman or Mosaic law.[13]

8:6 John explains in this verse that the religious leaders raised the question to trap Jesus. They wanted to pit Him against Moses. The scribes and Pharisees were not interested in learning from Jesus. They were simply seeking a basis for an indictment against Him.

Jesus here provides a good example of how teachers might deal with proud and arrogant students. He did not argue with them. Rather, He gave them time to think about the implications of their own question.

Instead of answering the question, Jesus bent down and began writing in the ground with His finger. There are many different opinions as to what Jesus wrote. Apparently John did not believe it was necessary for his readers to know what Jesus wrote. As Baylis correctly observes, "The importance is in what Jesus did and what He said, not what He wrote."[14] As Jesus wrote with His finger on the ground, so the law was written by the "finger of God" (Deut. 9:10). Jesus' action may suggest that He was claiming authorship of the law.

THE APPLICATION OF THE LAW, 8:7-8

8:7 After presistent questioning by the religious leaders, Jesus stood up and made careful application of the Mosaic law. Yes, the woman was guilty. Indeed, her sentence should be carried out according to the Mosaic law. Yet, the law that required death for the adulteress also demanded that qualified witnesses be the first to begin the stoning (Deut. 17:7). Were these witnesses qualified according to the requirements of the Mosaic law?

Jesus' words "If any one of you is without sin" refer to the key qualification according to Mosaic law, namely that the witnesses be nonmalicious (Deut. 19:16-19, 21; cf. Ex. 23:1-8). A malicious witness promotes violence, perverts justice, and misuses the law for selfish purposes, precisely what the religious leaders were doing in this case. Jesus knew that those testifying against the woman were not doing so out of pure hearts and a concern for right. Their conspiracy, inequity, and selfish purposes disqualified them from participation in the execution called for by Mosaic law.

---

13. For valuable legal background on this text, see J. D. M. Derrett, "Law in the New Testament: The Story of the Woman Taken in Adultery," *New Testament Studies* 10 (1963-1964): 1-26.
14. Baylis, "The Woman Caught in Adultery," p. 180.

8:8   Jesus did not set aside or modify the Mosaic law. Having faithfully and accurately applied it, Jesus stooped down and once again wrote on the ground.

THE MINISTRY OF JESUS, 8:9-11

8:9   The scribes and Pharisees had sought to trap Jesus, but now they had become trapped by the Mosaic law. Disqualified as witnesses by the Mosaic law, they left, one-by-one, until only the woman was left standing there with Jesus. John notes that the oldest were the first to leave. Perhaps their greater familiarity with the Scriptures made them realize more quickly their disqualification under the law.

8:10   When Jesus straightened up, the accusers were gone. He asked the woman where were the witnesses who had accused her. "Has no one condemned you?" asked Jesus.

8:11   The woman responded simply, "No one, sir." The term "sir" (*kurios*) is sometimes translated "lord" or "master," but the context here does not suggest that anything more than a respectful address is intended. It is not known whether the woman came to faith in Christ.

Jesus' words "Then neither do I condemn you" have often been misapplied. They have been used to justify leniency in criminal cases, to oppose capital punishment, to argue against church discipline, and to relax moral standards. Jesus intended none of these things. He was simply being faithful to the Mosaic law. A sentence of condemnation required two or three witnesses (Deut. 19:15). Lacking credible witnesses, the law of stoning could not be applied. Jesus was not modifying the law or demonstrating the overly gracious condoning of sinful behavior. He was simply upholding the law that demanded credible witnesses.

Jesus concluded the incident by instructing the woman to make a clean break from sin and obey the law. The present imperative, "Leave your life of sin," could be translated, "Stop your sinful habit."

Jesus was not applying "situation ethics." He called adultery sin and commanded the woman to cease sinning. Jesus was not relaxing the moral standards of God. Rather He was carefully applying the law. The law called for stoning, but it also required that the witnesses be qualified. By His careful application of the law, Jesus proved that He was indeed the prophet of whom Moses wrote. This passage may not legitimately be used as a proof text against capital punishment for adultery or any other crime, because Jesus actually commanded qualified witnesses to begin the execution by casting the first stone.

THE CONFLICT AFTER THE FEAST, 8:12-59

Although the Feast of Tabernacles was over (cf. 7:37, 53), a number of His disciples stayed on in Jerusalem after the feast to hear Jesus teach (8:2). While teaching in the Temple, He was once again challenged by the religious leaders (8:13). The discourse recorded here is Jesus' explanation of His Person and work to those who opposed Him.

JESUS, THE LIGHT OF THE WORLD, 8:12-20

The traditional observance of the Feast of Tabernacles as set forth in the Mishnah provides rich cultural background for Jesus' claim to be the light of the world. In the court of the women in the Temple were four golden candelabra that were lit in the evening during the Feast of Tabernacles (*Sukkah* 5.2). According to the Talmud, these candlesticks were 50 cubits (75 feet) high. It was said there was not a courtyard in Jerusalem that did not reflect the light (*Sukkah* 5:3). As the Levites played their instruments, the pious would dance around the candles with burning torches in their hands, singing songs and praises (*Sukkah* 5:4). During these festivities, two priests would stand at the east gate of the Temple facing west and declare, "Our fathers when they were in this place turned with their backs toward the Temple of the Lord and their faces toward the east, and they worshipped the sun toward the east [Ezek. 8:16]; but as for us, our eyes are turned toward the Lord" (*Sukkah* 5:4).

The illumination of the court of the women by the candelabra was reminiscent of the Shekinah glory that once filled the Temple (cf. 1 Kings 8:10-11).

8:12 The Feast of Tabernacles was over, but the memories of the celebration were fresh. Jesus was in the treasury (8:20), part of the court of the women where the great candelabra stood darkened. There He made the impressive claim "I am the light of the world." This is the climax of John's development of the theme of "light." Light dispels darkness and enables one to see along a dark path. Jesus is the light. There is no spiritual light apart from right relationship with Him. Edersheim points out that in Jewish literature the term *light* is often applied to the Messiah (cf. Isa. 9:2; Luke 2:32).[15] The Jews could

---

15. Alfred Edersheim, *The Life and Times of Jesus the Messiah* (Grand Rapids: Eerdmans, 1971), 2:165-66.

not have mistaken the messianic significance of Jesus' words. The fact that Jesus is the light "of the world," not just the Jewish people, is in keeping with John's thesis of the universal provision of Christ's saving work (John 3:16; 4:42). As with the other "I am" statements in chapter 8 (cf. vv. 24, 28, 58), Jesus is here making a strong allusion to His deity.

Jesus adds that those who follow Him as disciples will never live in spiritual darkness but will have "the light of life." It is debated whether Jesus means "the light that gives life" (subjective genitive), "the light that is life" (genitive of apposition), or "is characterized by life" (genitive of description). It may be that Jesus did not intend to limit the meaning of this rich expression.

8:13 The Pharisees challenged Jesus' teaching on the matter of a legal technicality. A single testimony without supporting witnesses (Deut. 19:15) was not regarded by the Jews as legally valid (cf. comments on 5:31). The words "not valid" (*ouk alēthēs*) mean that the testimony would not be accepted in a court of law.

8:14 In v. 14 Jesus defends His claim (8:12), arguing that He is qualified to bear valid testimony because He knows His divine origin ("where I came from") and heavenly destiny ("where I am going"). The Pharisees, on the other hand, were ignorant of these essential truths concerning His Person. John V. Dahms traces John's "proceeding from/ returning to God" motif (cf. 13:3; 16:27-30; 17:8, 11, 13) to Isaiah 55:11, "My word that goes out from my mouth; it will not return to me empty."[16]

8:15 Jesus points out that the Pharisees judged on the basis of outward appearances (cf. 7:24), literally "according to the flesh." Christ, on the other hand, judges no one. He did not come to judge but to save (3:17).

8:16 Yet when it is necessary for Christ to exercise judgment (5:27-29), His decisions will be right. Jesus explains how this is assured. He does not act alone but in union with the Father. His oneness with the Father guarantees the validity of His judgment.

8:17 Jesus now appeals to the law (*nomos*) to support the validity of His claims. According to Deuteronomy 17:6 and 19:15, the testimony of two (or three) witnesses was regarded as legally valid in a court of law. (This requirement of two or three witnesses in the Mosaic law served to prevent false incrimination and uphold justice.)

---

16. John V. Dahms, "Isaiah 55:11 and the Gospel of John," *The Evangelical Quarterly* 53 (April-June 1981): 78-88.

8:18   Jesus points out here that there are two who bear witness to the truth of His Person—Jesus Himself and God the Father. If the witness of two men is legally valid, how much more is the testimony of God the Father and the Son.

8:19   The question, "Where is your father?" was probably asked with a mocking sneer. Jesus had already made clear enough that God was His Father (7:16, 28-30, 33). Jesus responded not by answering the question but by pointing out their ignorance of both the Father and the Son. The last statement of v. 19 advances a great truth first introduced in the prologue: God the Father is known through Christ (cf. 1:18). Knowing Christ means knowing the Father. The Jews prided themselves in their knowledge of God. But Jesus says, "Unless you know Me, you are ignorant of God!" Their ignorance of Jesus proved that they did not know God the Father.

8:20   John explains that this confrontation with the Pharisees took place in the Temple area near the place where offerings were put (literally, "in the treasury"). The "treasury" was part of the court of the women where thirteen trumpet-shaped collection boxes were kept for receiving the half-shekel Temple dues (Ex. 30:13-16; *Shekalim* 2:1).

CHRIST, THE TRUE OBJECT OF FAITH, 8:21-30

In v. 21 Jesus resumes His dialogue with the Jewish leaders. Through this interaction He presents some profound truths concerning the result of unbelief (8:21-24) and personal identity.

The Result of Unbelief, 8:21-24

8:21   Jesus turns once again (cf. 7:33-34) to the subject of His return to the Father. Once again He announces His departure. The expression "going away" (*hupagō*) is generally used by John to refer to the death of Jesus, by which He would return to the Father. Because the Father is in heaven (cf. Matt. 6:9), the unbelieving Jews would not be able to join Him there. Although they would look for Him after His departure, their unbelief would prevent their finding Him. Jesus was addressing the same group of religious leaders who had committed the unpardonable sin, attributing the work of the Holy Spirit, through whom Christ did His miracles, to Satan (cf. Matt. 12:22-32). Consequently, Jesus announced to them, "You will die in your sin."

To die unrepentant, with the guilt and stain of sin, is the ultimate, unnecessary tragedy. This seems to be the central concern of vv. 21-24, for here Jesus repeats this phrase three times.

8:22   As the Jews misunderstood His meaning in 7:35-36, so they misunderstand Him here. They detect an allusion to His death but think that Jesus might be referring to suicide, an act generally abhorrent to Jews (cf. Josephus *Jewish Wars* 3.375). The untranslated interogative particle *meti* suggests hesitancy—the question is raised but the idea's validity is doubted.

8:23   Jesus contrasts Himself with the Jewish antagonists. The Jews are "from below," an expression Jesus defines as belonging to this world (i.e., "earthly"). Jesus is "from above," that is, not belonging to this world (i.e., "heavenly"). A similar contrast appears in 3:31.

8:24   Jesus makes a strong and emphatic statement here that refusal to believe in the truth of Christ's Person has eternal consequences. Rejecting Jesus means death with sins unatoned for.

The expression "believe that I am [*egō eimi*] the one I claim to be" means more than belief in Jesus' messiahship. There is an allusion to Jesus as the "I AM" of Exodus 3:14. The allusion is stronger and more direct in 8:58.

The Proofs of His Person, 8:25-30

8:25   The religious leaders asked Jesus a more specific question, "Who are you?" They wanted Him to complete the statement "I am so-and-so." The precise meaning of Jesus' answer is not clear. Because the original Greek manuscripts lacked punctuation and were written without division between words, it is possible to interpret His words several ways:[17] (1) as an affirmation: "What I have told you from the very beginning" (NASB margin, RSV, NIV); (2) as a question: "Why should I speak to you at all?" (Moffat, RSV alternative rendering); and (3) as an exclamation: "That I should speak to you at all!" (Greek Fathers). The Bodmer Papyrus II (p[66]), a second- or third-century manuscript, reads, "I told you in the beginning that which also I am telling you."

Although the text is far from clear, the context would lead the reader to anticipate some answer or affirmation. In His response Jesus

---

17. Metzger, *A Textual Commentary On the Greek New Testament*, pp. 223-24; Barclay M. Newman and Eugene A. Nida, *A Translator's Handbook on the Gospel of John* (London: United Bible Societies, 1980), p. 273.

points the Jews to His previous teaching and the term *Messiah* with its political connotations.

8:26　Jesus acknowledged that there was much He could say in judgment of the unbelieving Jews. But that was not going to be His focus. Jesus stuck to His priorities. He would not stop speaking the Father's truth in order to condemn the Jews.

Often believers get sidetracked from the central issues of the gospel to gather information to bombard a false teacher or growing cult. Although there is a place for the study of false religions, the best way to identify what is false is by the straight-edge of truth.

The logical link between the two halves of this verse is not quite clear. But in keeping with the thought of v. 25, Jesus proceeds to present evidence for the truth of His divine claims. The first proof of His Person is His identity with the Father—Jesus was sent by the Father and spoke the Father's words. His message is to the "world" (*kosmos*), the unbelieving world of mankind.

8:27　John's comment in v. 27 may seem inconsistent with Jesus' clear statement in 8:18. This suggests that there may have been a break in the conversation, probably between v. 20 and v. 21. If that is the case, then the audience has perhaps changed.

8:28　The second proof of His Person is His resurrection following crucifixion. The expression "lifted up" is used in John 3:14 and 12:32 to refer to Christ's crucifixion. Jesus repeats the thought of v. 26 that His message is not His own but God the Father's. As with vv. 24 and 58, the words "I am" (*egō eimi*) demonstrate Christ's claim to deity.

8:29　Jesus repeats the thought of His having been "sent" (*pempō*) from the Father (8:26). But being sent does not mean that Jesus was alone. God was with Him (8:16; 17:21-26). The third proof of His person is His perfect obedience to the Father's desire. The "I" and "always" are in the place of emphasis. Jesus is not only sinless (Heb. 4:15), but on every occasion He is active in doing what pleases God.

8:30　John records that as a result of this interaction Jesus won some adherents. Whereas the statement is rather straightforward, the concept of "belief" is more complex. Did the adherents really come to trust in His Person as Messiah and Son of God. Were they saved? Regenerated?

It is suggested that those people had an intellectual understanding rather than personal trust. They had begun believing but did not continue in the faith. Those same Jews would later seek to kill Him.

Their "belief" seems to have come short of regenerating faith (cf. Introduction, under Purpose).

This verse reflects the crucial need for follow-up after an evangelistic encounter and profession of faith. Some who profess Christ may not truly embrace Jesus and experience the regenerating work of the Holy Spirit apart from continued nurture, teaching, and support. The idea of "winning" the lost and then merely committing them to the Lord is not a biblical concept. Follow-up and discipleship are essential aspects of the Great Commission (cf. Matt. 28:18-20).

CHRIST, THE FULFILLMENT OF OLD TESTAMENT HOPES, 8:31-59

Challenging and clarifying the issues of faith, Jesus continues His interaction with the Jews who "believed" in Him. Here Jesus lays down key criteria for identifying the true descendants of Abraham (or "children of God"). They continue in His word (v. 38) and do the works of their Father (vv. 39-41).

The Source of Spiritual Freedom, 8:31-36

8:31 To the Jews who had "believed Him," a weaker statement than "put their faith in Him" (8:30), Jesus offered a challenge. The NIV's "hold to My teaching" seems to suggests that orthodoxy is evidence of true faith. The Greek expression is stronger. "If you continue in my word [i.e., teaching], truly my disciples you are." The word for "if" is *ean* with the subjunctive, indicating some doubt. The sense is, "If you continue (and it is doubtful that you will)." Jesus is saying, "Your persistent loyalty to the truth I have taught will prove the reality of your present profession."

Jesus is teaching a profound truth. Evangelicals put great weight on professions of faith. And rightly so. But equally as significant is adherence to the faith. Continuance in the teaching of Christ is the acid test of genuine, regenerating faith.

8:32 Jesus acknowledges here that a personal knowledge of the truth, the teachings of Christ (8:31), will have an effect in the life of a true disciple: "The truth will set you free." Jesus uses the word ("set you free," *eleutheroō*) that was used regularly in the first century for the release of slaves. Here it is used of spiritual or moral slavery. Apart from the truth of Christ, all mankind is enslaved to sin. But with His truth comes freedom—not freedom *to* sin (the world's perspective) but freedom *from* sin (the grace of God).

8:33   The Jews objected to Jesus' suggestion that they were en-slaved. By virtue of their heritage and relationship with Abraham they professed to have never been in bondage. Their pride seemed to have dulled their memories of the Egyptian sojourn, oppressions in the time of the judges, and Babylonian captivity. Yet, even while under the Roman yoke they claimed not to serve Rome, but God (Josephus *Jewish Wars* 7.323).

8:34   Jesus in this verse clarifies the matter of slavery. The solemn affirmation "I tell you the truth" (literally, "Amen, Amen") serves as a preface to His remarks. Jesus is talking about spiritual, not personal, bondage. Sin causes spiritual enslavement. Everyone who practices sin is enslaved spiritually. People sin not because it is fun and satisfying but because they cannot help it. They are addicted to sin.

8:35   Jesus explains what it meant to be a slave. In contrast to the son (*ho huios*), the slave (*ho doulos*) had no permanent place in the family. A slave could be bought and sold. The slave had no rights, no security, no inheritance. By their rejection of God's son, the unbelieving Jews were not part of God's spiritual family. They thought they were sons, but in fact they were slaves.

8:36   Although the Jews considered themselves free (8:34), they were not really free. True spiritual freedom can be found only in the Son. The word translated "indeed" (*ontōs*) occurs only here in John. It appears to express a reality of essence (from within), distinguished from reality as seen and known.[18] It is used in 1 Timothy 5:5 of the "real" widow, in contrast to the one who has relatives or is still of marriageable age.

The Jews' True Identity, 8:37-47

The Jews based their relationship with God on their physical descent from Abraham (cf. 8:33). In this passage Jesus denies their relationship with God and reveals their true spiritual father.

8:37   Jesus acknowledges that the Jews were physical descendants from Abraham. Yet, as Paul says, physical descent from Abraham did not necessarily make them God's children (cf. Rom. 9:8). Indeed, those professed "believers" (John 8:31) were ready to "kill" (7:20, 25) Jesus because they had rejected His claims.

8:38   Jesus contrasts His "Father" with the "father" of the Jews. He speaks the truths He has heard in the presence of His heavenly Father.

18. B. F. Westcott, *The Gospel According to St. John* (Grand Rapids: Eerdmans, 1973), p. 134.

The Jews practiced what they had heard from their father. At this point, Jesus had not yet said who their father was (cf. 8:44).

8:39   The Jews once again laid claim to their physical descent from Abraham (cf. 8:33). But Jesus raised a major objection to that claim. Children characteristically emulate their father. This was true of those Jews who had professed faith.

8:40   Yet those unbelieving Jews were not doing the works of faith characteristic of Abraham. Instead, they had determined to kill the divine Messiah, who had revealed the truth of God. This was utterly unlike Abraham, who was known as "God's friend" (James 2:23).

8:41   Jesus acknowledged that the maxim "Like father, like son" was true in their case. The actions of the Jews were patterned after their spiritual father.

The Jews then seemed to pick up on the issue Jesus was bringing to their attention. They dropped the issue of literal parentage and focused on spiritual heritage. They denied illegitimacy and asserted, "The only Father we have is God Himself."

The words "We are not illegitimate children" may be a slam against Jesus in view of the unusual circumstances of His birth. Yet there is no evidence that these circumstances were generally known, and because Joseph and Mary were married at the time of His birth, it could not be said that Jesus was an illegitimate child. Plummer argues that the Jews were referring to their spiritual heritage as uncontaminated by idolatry.[19] Throughout the Hebrew Scriptures idolatry is spoken of as harlotry and fornication (cf. Ex. 34:15-16; Lev. 17:7; Judg. 2:17; 2 Kings 9:22; Isa. 1:21; Jer. 3:1, 9; Ezek. 16:15). It would not be unexpected, then, in a discussion of spiritual heritage, for a Jew to make the claim "We are not idolaters; God is our spiritual Father."

8:42   Jesus challenged their claim to spiritual legitimacy. If God were their spiritual Father, they would share the Father's love for His Messiah. Love for God's Son is the proof of a family relationship with the Father.

Verse 42 contains a rather complete statement of Jesus' origin. He "came from God" and was "sent" by Him. His coming was by divine determination, not self-appointment.

8:43   Jesus explains in v. 43 why the Jews were having a difficult time with His message. His "language" or "speech" (*lalia*) was not

19. A. Plummer, *The Gospel According to St. John* (Cambridge: At the University Press, 1899), p. 190.

clear because the Jews were unable to "hear" or "obey" (*akouō*) His teaching. They could not understand His words because they had rejected His message. They were "of this world" (8:23), and He was speaking to them of "heavenly things." There is a strong statement of man's depravity here. Understanding Christ's words is an impossibility apart from enabling grace.

8:44   Finally, Jesus identifies His Jewish antagonists in terms of their spiritual heritage. "You belong to your father, the devil, and you want to carry out your father's desire." Their hostility and murderous intentions proved that their spiritual kinship was with Satan, not Abraham or God the Father. They were eager to gratify his evil desires.

Jesus proceeds to describe the devil in terms of his character and activities. First, "he was a murderer." The word for "murderer" (*anthrōpoktonos*) means "man-slayer." The words "from the beginning" may refer to Satan's part in the murder of Abel (Gen. 4:1-8; 1 John 3:12) or the fact that death came to the world through Satan's deception (Gen. 3:1-6, 14; Rom. 5:12-14). The conduct of the Jews in seeking to kill Jesus (John 8:40) reflects their spiritual kinship with Satan. Second, the devil is "a liar and the father of lies." The first lie recorded in the Bible is found in the mouth of Satan (Gen. 3:4).

The phrase "father of lies" literally reads "father of it (neuter)," referring to the lie; or "father of him" (masculine), referring to the liar. Although both are probably true, most translators take *autou* as neuter. Satan is the propagator of lies and the spiritual father of liars.

8:45   Jesus next points out that, consistant with their spiritual heritage, the Jews would believe a lie. But because (causal *hoti*) Jesus spoke the truth, they would not believe Him. Here lies the battle: truth vs. falsehood.

8:46   Jesus raises the question of His credibility. People with a history of sin and deception cannot be trusted. But Jesus had no such history. He raised to the Jews the rhetorical question, "Can any of you prove Me guilty of sin?" No one responded. No charge was able to be laid against Him (Heb. 4:15). He raised the next question, "If I am telling the truth, why don't you believe Me?" To paraphrase Jesus, "If I am free from falsehood and speak the truth, why do you refuse to believe me?"

8:47   Here Jesus answers the second question raised in v. 46. He sets forth a principle, "He who belongs to God hears what God says." Only those who are truly God's sons recognize His voice speaking in Jesus. He then makes an application. Because they did not belong to

God, the Jews were not responding to Jesus. The word "hear" (*akouō*) implies more than mere audible perception. Hearing leads to comprehension and response.

The Accusation of Demon Possession, 8:48-53

The Jews did not appreciate Jesus' declaring their spiritual kinship with Satan rather than Abraham. Their accusation is similar to that made by the religious leaders in Matthew 12:22-32.

8:48 The Jews accused Jesus of being "a Samaritan" and "demon-possessed." Unable to answer His arguments, they resorted to name calling. In the first century, to refer to a Jew as a "Samaritan" was a form of slander. The Samaritans (cf. introductory comments on 4:1-42 and 4:9) were regarded as syncretistic half-breeds noted for their uncleanness and deviations from the Mosaic law. Perhaps His association with the people of Samaria (4:40-42) led the Jews to call Jesus a "Samaritan."

This was not the first or last time Jesus was accused of demon possession (7:20; 8:52; 10:20). In the synoptic gospels a similar accusation is identified as the unpardonable sin (cf. Matt. 12:22-32; Mark 3:22-30).

8:49 Jesus did not refute the charge of being a Samaritan. It was an ethnic slur that did not merit His attention. He did refute the charge of demon possession. The charge could not be true because Jesus honored the Father. The Jews, on the other hand, had dishonored God by their insulting remarks concerning Jesus.

8:50 Although Jesus does not seek His own glory, there is one literally "seeking and judging." The obvious reference is to God the Father. He seeks the glory of Christ and passes judgment in His favor. In contrast with the unbelieving Jews, God's judgment is correct in assigning honor to the Son.

8:51 The words of v. 51 turn to a new thought. Belief in Jesus results in eternal life (John 3:16), but belief in Jesus is more than mere intellectual assent. Jesus declares, "If anyone keeps My word, he will never see death." The phrase "keeps My word" is an expression of obedience (cf. 8:55; 14:23; 15:20; 17:6; cf. 1 John 1:3, 5). The Greek term *tēreō* means "to guard, keep, or preserve." The thought here is quite similar to Jesus' words in John 8:31 ("If you hold fast My teaching"). The words "shall never see death" do not preclude physical death. But for the believer, death is not eternal (cf. 5:24). Physical death will not affect the believer's eternal life.

8:52   The Jews returned to the charge made in v. 48. What was con-
jecture was now evidenced as fact. It was His words "shall never see
death" that riled them. They immediately began to mount the evidence against what was to them a ridiculous claim. Death comes to all
men. Abraham and the prophets had kept God's word. If those holy
men died, how could Jesus' word be true?

Jesus used the words "will never see death," whereas the Jewish
opponents used the words "will never taste death." The expressions
are synonyms, but the latter is a bit stronger. To "taste" death is to
experience it (cf. Heb. 2:9). The Jewish opponents were thinking of
physical death, whereas Jesus was focusing on a much more final
event—spiritual death.

8:53   Verse 53 repeats the thought of v. 52, but states the issue in
the form of a question. The Greek construction of the rhetorical question, "Are you greater than our father Abraham?" expects the answer
"No." To be "greater than" Abraham means to surpass him in importance. Abraham died; the prophets died. What was Jesus claiming
about Himself?

The "I AM" Antedating Abraham, 8:54-59

Jesus concludes His interaction with the religious leaders with a
final and climactic claim linking Him with Abraham's prophetic hope.

8:54   Self-praise is worthless. That is why someone invented the
"reference" letter. Jesus applies this concept in v. 54. To glorify Himself would mean nothing in the eyes of the Jews. But to be glorified by
the Father, whom the Jews acknowledge as God, is quite another matter. The word "glorify" (*doxazō*, from which "doxology" is derived)
means to magnify, extol, or praise.

8:55   Jesus rested His claim on His relationship with the Father. In
contrast to His opponents, Jesus knew and obeyed God the Father. To
deny His personal and intimate relationship with God would be no
less a falsehood than to tell an outright lie. Two different Greek words
are translated "know" (*oida* and *ginōskō*), but they are used synonymously here.

8:56   Jesus declared that Abraham, through the eyes of faith, saw
the truth of God's provision of the Messiah/Redeemer and joyously
anticipated His coming (cf. Gen. 22:8, 14; Heb. 11:8-13). The word
translated "rejoiced" (*agalliaō*) is a strong verb that speaks of joyous

exultation. What Abraham "saw" was the "day" of the Redeemer's coming, the event. Although He struggled with the "hows" and "whens," Abraham maintained faith in God and the fulfillment of His promise (Rom. 4:20-21).

8:57   The Jewish opponents saw the logical and necessary implications of Jesus' claim. To say that Abraham saw the coming of Jesus implied that Jesus saw Abraham. From a human perspective this was absolutely impossible. The words "You are not yet fifty years old" serve to underscore the absurdity of the claim. It should not be concluded that Jesus was nearly fifty years old in light of Luke 3:23. The Jews were using a round number to contrast the great antiquity of Abraham with the relatively short lifetime of Jesus.[20]

8:58   Jesus introduces His stupendous claim in v. 58 with the solemn words "I tell you the truth" (literally, "amen, amen"). Before Abraham was born, Jesus existed ("I am" [*egō eimi*]). This expression conveys the idea of existence prior to Abraham. The fact that the words are present tense suggests Jesus' eternal existence as well.

In Exodus 3:14 where God reveals His name to Moses, the Septuagint translates *egō eimi ho ōn* ("I am who continuously is"). The words "I am" (*egō eimi*) are used by the Septuagint in Deuteronomy 32:39 and Isaiah 41:4; 43:10 to translate God's self-identification, "I am He." By His use of the words "I am," Jesus was making a strong statement of His relationship with the I AM (Yahweh) revealed in the Hebrew Scriptures. He was virtually identifying Himself as Yahweh, Israel's covenant God.

8:59   The Jews were quick to recognize Jesus' claim to preexistence and deity. They immediately picked up stones intending to execute Jesus for blasphemy (cf. Lev. 24:16). The stones were probably taken from the materials being used to refurbish the Temple, a project that was not completed until around A.D. 62 (cf. comments on John 2:20; Josephus *Antiquities* 20.219).

It need not be concluded that Jesus "hid Himself" through miraculous means. The same expression is used in 12:36 where an avoidance of the crowds is in view. His "hour" had not yet come (12:23). Jesus quietly slipped away from the crowd and left the Temple area (cf. 10:39).

---

20. Homer A. Kent, Jr., *Light in the Darkness* (Grand Rapids: Baker, 1974), p. 128, n. 30.

HOMILETICAL SUGGESTIONS

John 8 is a rich resource for expositors. The case of the adulterous woman (8:1-11) has often been used to teach grace, forgiveness, and a relaxed moral standard. Actually, the incident serves as a warning against the moral and religious hypocrisy in the religious leaders of the time. Jesus' words "Go now and leave your life of sin" teach a lesson regarding the nature of repentance.

John 8:21-30 contains dialogue with the Jewish leaders. This would be a difficult section to preach. Here Jesus presents several proofs of His Person—His identity with His Father (8:26) and His future resurrection (8:28).

John 8:31-36 provides the text for a powerful Independence Day message. True freedom does not come through wars or military operations but through individual faith in Christ.

Verses 37-47 have possibilities as a Father's Day message. In v. 41, Jesus acknowledges the maxim, "like father, like son." The passage could be used to illustrate that being reared in a Christian home does not make one a Christian. The Jewish leaders were descendants of Abraham, but they did not share his spiritual life. Kinship is proved by actions, not merely by ancestry.

JOHN
CHAPTER
NINE

FROM DARKNESS TO LIGHT

THE CONFLICT OVER HEALING THE BLIND MAN, CHAP. 9

John 9 advances the "light/darkness" motif begun in the pro-logue (1:4-5) by contrasting the spiritual light enjoyed by the man born blind with the spiritual darkness of the unbelieving Pharisees. Ironically, the Pharisees were found to be "blind," whereas the blind man was able to see.

This chapter also serves to validate several of the claims Jesus made in chapter 8:

8:12	Jesus claims to be "light"	→	9:7	Jesus brings light to the blind
8:36	Jesus claims to be liberator	→	9:38	Jesus liberates a sinner
8:58	Jesus claims to be pre-existent	→	9:38	Jesus accepts worship

The encounter with the blind man and the conflict that followed illustrate the conflict between belief and unbelief. These incidents took place in Jerusalem on the Sabbath (9:14) during the year A.D. 32, sometime between the Feast of Tabernacles (7:2) and the Feast of Dedication (10:22).

THE RESTORATION OF SIGHT, 9:1-12

The healing of a man blind from birth illustrates one of the characteristics of the messianic kingdom when "the eyes of the blind will be opened" (Isa. 35:5). Jesus used the miracle to confirm His messianic credentials before His disciples and bring the blind man to physical and spiritual sight.

9:1 The words "As he went along" (*paragōn*) are quite general and do not provide an exact time frame for the miracle. It could have taken place as He left the Temple or on another occasion. The man was afflicted with congenital blindness, an affliction from which one would not expect to be healed. The words "blind from birth" occur nowhere else in the New Testament but are common among other Greek writings to describe congenital blindness.

9:2 Seeing the blind man stimulated a question from Jesus' disciples regarding the relationship between sin and misfortune. It was widely held by the Jews that physical suffering was due to sin. This was the unanimous opinion of Job's three friends (Job 4:8; 8:13, 20; 11:11, 13-15). Even Jesus had associated sin and suffering (John 5:14). The question in the minds of the disciples was, "Who sinned?" The word "sinned" (aorist active indicative of *hamartanō*) means "to miss the mark" or "to do wrong."

It was held in antiquity, though not widely, that the soul of a man could sin in a preexistent state (Wisdom 8:20). Jewish opinion also held that it was possible for an unborn baby to have feelings that might be sinful (cf. Gen. 25:22; Luke 1:41-44). A popular misunderstanding of Exodus 20:5 and 34:6-7 held that offspring would be punished for the sins of their parents. The disciples merely wondered which was the case in the example of the blind man.

9:3 Jesus rejected both alternatives suggested by the disciples. No particular sin had produced the blindness. The next clause literally reads, "That the works of God might be revealed in him." The Greek word for "that" (*hina*) frequently indicates purpose, and most translations take it in that sense here (NIV, NASB). But *hina* can also indicate result, as seen by its use in 9:2 ("Who sinned . . . with the result that he was born blind?"). If the *hina* expresses purpose, then Jesus was commenting on the divine intent of the blindness (cf. Rom. 9:17). If the *hina* expresses result, Jesus was focusing on the opportunity that resulted from the blindness.

Newman and Nida propose a third alternative based on the fact that the original text had no punctuation.[1] Replacing the period at the end of v. 3 with a comma, it is possible to link the last part of v. 3 with the first part of v. 4. The following translation then results: [3]"'Neither this man nor his parents sinned,' said Jesus. 'But that the works of God might be displayed in his life, [4]we must keep on doing the works of him who sent Me as long as it is day.'" The translation is grammatically possible and suits the context well.

Accordingly, Jesus made no judgment as to the reason the man was born blind. He simply declared that the man's blindness provided an opportunity to show the power of God at work. And Jesus Himself had come to reveal that power. The comment was the prelude to a great miracle.

Believers today sometimes encounter tragedies and misfortunes that are difficult to explain. Like Job we wonder, "Why?" Often the best explanation available is that the trial may be a means of displaying the glorious works of God.

9:4   The phrase "As long as it is day" must be interpreted figuratively. "Day" is the time for labor. The opportunity for labor ends as night falls. As the verse concludes, "Night is coming, when no one can work." Jesus is acknowledging that the period of opportunity is limited. Because the passage of time removes present opportunity, there is motivation to make the most of every occasion to do God's work. For disciples, sharing in God's work is an intrinsic necessity ("we must"). And so it is for modern believers. God will accomplish His work on earth through the church as we redeem the time and put our shoulders to the plow for His kingdom. Realizing that our time for ministry is growing shorter every day, Christians should take advantage of every opportunity.

There is some debate whether the text reads (1) "We must do the work of Him who sent us," (2) "I must do the work of Him who sent Me," or (3) "We must do the work of Him who sent Me." The third is probably correct. It is the more difficult reading (mixing "we" and "me") and avoids the non-Johannine expression "Him who sent us."[2] Some copyists apparently altered "we" to "I" to bring agreement with "me," and others altered "me" to "us" in conformity with "we."[3]

1. Barclay M. Newman and Eugene A. Nida, *A Translator's Handbook on the Gospel of John* (London: United Bible Societies, 1980), p. 299.

2. Bruce M. Metzger, *A Textual Commentary on the Greek New Testament* (London: United Bible Societies, 1971), p. 227.

3. A. Plummer, *The Gospel According to St. John* (Cambridge: At the University Press, 1899), p. 198.

9:5 Jesus here repeats the claim He made in 8:12, "I am the light of the world" (*phōs eimi tou kosmou*). The words "While I am in the world" refer to His incarnation (1:14). Jesus is always the "light of the world" (1:4, 10; 8:12). But here the absence of the definite article (*to phōs* in 8:12) focuses on His manifestation "in the world."[4] The text could be rendered "I am light of the world, whenever I am in the world." While in the world Jesus will function as the "light" (*phōs*) illuminating the darkness—both physical and spiritual.

9:6 Jesus could have healed the blind man with a mere touch of His hand (cf. Matt. 20:29-34), but in this case He made some mud with His saliva and applied that mixture to the man's "eyes" (apparently a reference to his eyelids rather than the delicate eyeballs). Spittle was believed in antiquity to be a remedy for diseased eyes. The Roman historian Tacitus (A.D. 55-117) reports that a blind man once sought healing from the Emperor Vespasian by means of his spittle (*The Histories* 4.81).

One wonders why Jesus chose this particular method. It may be that He chose to violate several of the Jewish traditions regarding the Sabbath law to stimulate thinking and elicit a decision concerning His Person (9:16). According to the Mishnah, the application of any healing remedy was strictly forbidden on the Sabbath unless a life was in danger. In ministering to the blind man, Jesus violated Sabbath injunctions against kneading (*Shabbath* 7.2) and anointing (*Sabbath* 14:4).

9:7 After anointing his eyes, Jesus directed the blind man to wash in the Pool of Siloam (cf. Neh. 3:15; Isa. 8:6). The pool, located in the Tyropoeon or central valley, was originally built by King Hezekiah to serve as a reservoir for the water flowing through the Siloam Tunnel from the Gihon Spring (cf. 2 Kings 20:20; 2 Chron. 32:2-4). Rabbinic discussion on the Pool of Siloam associated the free-flowing fountain with God's fountain—especially in the messianic age.[5] The "tower in Siloam" (Luke 13:4) may have been a building near the pool or aqueduct. John explains the meaning of the Hebrew word ("*Siloam*" or "*Shiloah*" as in Isa. 8:6) with the Greek translation ("sent"), reflecting that the water from the spring was "sent" to the pool.

John reports the miracle as simply as possible. "So the man went and washed, and came home seeing." His obedience to Christ's command enabled him to enjoy the blessing of full vision.

---

4. A. T. Robertson, *Word Pictures in the New Testament* (Nashville: Broadman, 1932), 4:161.

5. Bruce Grigsby, "Washing in the Pool of Siloam—A Thematic Anticipation of the Johannine Cross," *Novum Testamentum* 27 (1985): 229.

There is an important lesson here. Obedience is the prerequisite to much of the blessing of God for any believer. Disobedience to the clear command of Jesus would have left the blind man in darkness.

The healing of the blind man serves to illustrate the spiritual condition of the Jewish people whose eyes were literally "besmeared" (Isa. 6:10) because of their unbelief. Yet the "washing" of regeneration (Titus 3:5) would bring them to spiritual sight. The miracle also provides a foretaste of the blessings to be realized in the messianic kingdom when "the eyes of the blind will see" (Isa. 29:18; cf. Isa. 35:5; 42:7, 16).

9:8   The healing of the blind man quickly attracted the attention of his neighbors and those who had formerly seen him begging. The question "Isn't this the same man who used to sit and beg?" expects the answer "Yes."

9:9   Public opinion was divided. Some agreed that it was the man. Others thought he was merely a "look-a-like." But the man who had been healed insisted, "I am the man." The expression "I am the man" (*egō eimi*) is the same expression that Jesus used to identify Himself with God the Father (John 8:59). Here it is a simple affirmation of identity. No such suggestion of deity is implied.

9:10   Identifying himself as the formerly blind man did not satisfy the neighbors and acquaintances. The next natural and logical question was, "How then were your eyes opened?"

9:11   The man went on to explain how he had received his sight. He referred to "The man they call Jesus," not yet knowing that Jesus was the Messiah and Son of God. The words "I could see" (*aneblepsa*) may be translated "I looked up," as in Mark 6:41, or "gain sight," as in Matthew 11:5. The latter is preferred on the basis of context and analogy with v. 7.

9:12   When the neighbors and acquaintances heard that Jesus was involved in this healing, they apparently concluded that an official investigation was warranted. They asked, "Where is this man?" But the healed man could not help them.

THE FIRST INTERROGATION, 9:13-23

The Sabbath miracle sparked considerable opposition from the religious leaders who interrogated the blind man twice, seeking to detect fraud in the miracle.

9:13   Concerned about a healing done on the Sabbath, the friends and neighbors took the man who had been blind to the Pharisees, the

Jewish authorities on the technical matters of law and orthodoxy (cf. comments on John 3:1). In view of the authority they exercised (9:34), it seems that they were probably official representatives of the Jews' highest religious body, the Sanhedrin.

9:14   John now explains for the reader that the day when Jesus performed this miracle was a Sabbath. The Mishnah devotes a tractate, *Shabbath*, to the Sabbath regulations observed by the Jews in the time of Jesus.

This miracle was one of seven healings Jesus worked on the Sabbath: the withered hand (Matt. 12:9), the demoniac at Capernaum (Mark 1:21), Peter's mother-in-law (Mark 1:29), the bent woman (Luke 13:14), the man with dropsy (Luke 14:1), the paralytic at Bethesda (John 5:10), and the man born blind.

9:15   The Pharisees questioned the man. The imperfect form of the verb "asked" (*ērōtaō*) indicates that the questioning was persistent. They continued to question him. As he had explained to the neighbors and acquaintances, so he also related to the religious leaders how he came to see.

9:16   It did not take the Pharisees long to formulate an opinion on this case. "Jesus was a Sabbath breaker and could not, therefore, be from God." Indeed, the evidence indicated that He was more of a sinner than a saint.

Others were more persuaded by the evidence of the miracle. "How can a sinner do such miraculous signs?" The evidence said He was a miracle worker and therefore from God. The "miraculous signs" (*sēmeia*) were significant for Nicodemus (3:2) and made an impact on Jewish opinion here as well.

There was a clear division, and the division over Jesus remains until this day. Jesus was either a Sabbath breaker and therefore a *sinner*, or He was a miracle worker and therefore *from God*. From the viewpoint of the Pharisees, or any rational thinker, He could not be both.

9:17   Unable to come to a consensus of opinion, the Pharisees turned once again to the man who had been healed. Because he was the one who benefited from the miracle, he must have an opinion about Jesus, they reasoned.

When pressed for a decision about Jesus, the man replied, "He is a prophet." This was not an acknowledgement that Jesus was "the" prophet of Deuteronomy 18:15 (cf. John 6:14; 7:40). The basic meaning of the word "prophet" (*prophētēs*) is "one who speaks for another" (cf. Ex. 7:1-2). The term is used in the Bible of those called to speak for God. The man was simply saying that Jesus was someone sent by God to proclaim His message.

9:18   In spite of the evidence, many were unwilling to believe that a miracle had actually taken place. Rejecting the testimony of the healed man, the Jewish authorities demanded that his parents testify.

9:19   The Jewish investigators were seeking some evidence of fraud. Although the NIV records three questions, there are only two in the original. The investigators first sought to confirm the identity and original condition of the healed man. They asked, "Is this your son, who you say was born blind?" Their second question called for an explanation of how he came to see.

9:20   The parents were quick to confirm the identity of their son and the fact of his congenital blindness. By so doing, they removed all basis for doubting the reality of the miracle.

9:21   But the parents seemed to be hesitant to involve themselves in the controversy over the miracle. They did not know "how" their son was cured or "who" did it. Because he was old enough to have legal standing in the community, he could speak for himself. They deferred to him for any further explanation.

9:22-23   John offers an explanation of the parents' comment, "He is of age; ask him" (9:21, 23). The parents were afraid of what the Jewish authorities might do to them. John reports they had already decided that anyone who acknowledged Jesus as the Messiah would be expelled from the synagogue.

The expression "put out of the synagogue" (*aposunagōgos*) is peculiar to John (cf. 12:42 and 16:2) and appears nowhere else in the New Testament. It refers to some form of excommunication.

According to the Talmud, twenty-four offenses were punishable by excommunication (Babylonian Talmud *Mo'ed Katan* 15a, 16a; *Berakot* 19a; Jerusalem Talmud *Mo'ed Katan* iii.1), including "refusing to abide by the decision of the court," an offense that seems to coincide with the concern expressed in v. 24. The Mishnah refers to excommunication, but it provides no details. Apparently the judgment did not prevent one from entering the Temple area (*Middoth* 2.2).

Three forms of excommunication are described in the Talmud.[6] Each form involved the person's or persons' being cut off from all normal dealings with Jewish society. The mildest form, the *nezifah* (a

6. *The Jewish Encyclopedia*, 1903 ed., s.v. "excommunication," 5:285-87.

"snub" or "reproof"), was applied when someone had insulted a prominent or learned person. For a period of seven days the offender dare not appear before the one he displeased. He had to retire to his house, speak little, refrain from business and pleasure, and manifest his remorse. To impose the more serious *niddui* ("separation") the offender was first publicly warned three times at the regular service in the synagogue. During the period of discipline (seven days according to the Babylonian Talmud, thirty days according to the Jerusalem Talmud) no one except the members of his immediate household were permitted to associate with the offender, or sit within four cubits of him, or eat in his company. He had to observe all the laws that pertained to a mourner and could not be counted among the number necessary for the performance of a public religious function. The *herem* ("ban") was the most rigorous form of excommunication. This extended for an indefinite period during which no one was permitted to teach the offender, work for him, or benefit him in any way. It meant exclusion from the religious community and intercourse with Jewish society.

It is uncertain whether these Talmudic categories of excommunication were in force in Jesus' day. Whatever the type of suspension referred to by John, the threat was serious enough to keep the man's parents from becoming involved in the controversy.

THE SECOND INTERROGATION, 9:24-34

9:24 The man who had been born blind was summoned a second time before the religious leaders. Citing their opinion, "We know this man is a sinner," may have been an attempt to force the man into modifying his testimony. The expression "give glory to God" is illuminated by Joshua 7:19 where Achan is similarly challenged, "My son, give glory to the Lord, ...Tell me what you have done; do not hide it from me." The meaning is "Give God glory by telling the truth."

9:25 The healed man refused to disavow the miracle. He was not prepared to debate with the learned Pharisees whether Jesus was a sinner or not. But he was sure of one thing. "I was blind but now I see!" This simple answer was based on the reality of his experience with Jesus.

Often the best explanation of the gospel to an unbeliever is simply one's personal testimony. Philosophical arguments for the existence of God and Christian apologetics have their place. But no defense of the gospel is quite as powerful as a personal testimony of how God has worked in one's life. The blind man would not argue. He simply affirmed that something marvelous had happened in his life.

9:26   The religious authorities pressed the man further. Returning to the subject of the healing, they sought further details. Perhaps they sought to find some discrepancy in his earlier testimony.

9:27   At this point, the healed man appears to have lost his patience with the Jewish authorities. They did not seem to listen to what he said. Why did they want to go over it again? He questioned them, "Do you want to become his disciples, too?" In the original Greek, the rhetorical question expects a negative answer (*me* with the indicative).

The significance of the word "too" (*kai*) is debated. Morris holds that the man is "now counting himself among Jesus' disciples."[7] He appeals to the response of the Jews in v. 28 in support of his interpretation. Plummer argues that the man was not so advanced in faith as to count himself a disciple of Jesus. Plummer takes the "too" (or "also") to refer to Jesus' well-known disciples.[8]

9:28   At this point in the interrogation, the religious authorities became verbally abusive. They rebuked the healed man and contrasted their position with his. The contrast in the original is emphatic, "You are his disciple, but we are disciples of Moses."

The words "You are this fellow's disciple" were spoken with anger by hostile Jewish authorities and should not be taken as an accurate description of the healed man's relationship with Jesus. The religious leaders called themselves "disciples of Moses," a phrase that expresses their allegiance to Moses and the law.

9:29   The contrast between Jesus and Moses continues in v. 29. Here the Jews affirm that "God spoke to Moses." The perfect tense (expressing present results of past action) of the verb "speak" (*laleō*) indicates that his words are still on record.

In contrast with their knowledge of Moses, the Jews did not know "where" Jesus came from. They were not just saying, "We don't know his hometown" (cf. 7:27). Whereas Moses was commissioned and sent by God, they did not know who commissioned or sent Jesus.

9:30   The healed man was struck by the Jews' inability to come to an accurate conclusion regarding Jesus. The words "Now that is remarkable!" express a high degree of amazement. A great miracle had

7. Leon Morris, *The Gospel According to John*, NICNT (Grand Rapids: Eerdmans, 1971), p. 491.
8. Plummer, *The Gospel According to St. John*, p. 205.

been accomplished, but the religious leaders failed to realize its significance. It is amazing how people can be blind in their fallenness.

9:31   The healed man proceeded to give the Jewish leaders a concise lesson in logic (9:31-33). His argument may be summarized as follows:

1. Only God could heal congenital blindness.
2. Jesus healed congenital blindness.
3. Jesus must be from God.

The statement "We know that God does not listen to sinners" is the straightforward teaching of the Old Testament (cf. Ps. 66:18; Prov. 15:29; Isa. 1:15; Mic. 3:4). But God hears and responds to the repentant, "the godly man who does his will." The New Testament teaches as well that sin in the life of a believer can be a hindrance to prayer (cf. 1 Pet. 3:7).

9:32   The healed man acknowledged that there was no previous record of anyone being healed of congenital blindness. The Old Testament records no miracles of this nature, although such were anticipated in the messianic era (Isa. 35:5).

9:33   Convinced that Jesus must be from God, the healed man drove home his conclusion. "If this man were not from God, he could do nothing." As in the case of Nicodemus (cf. John 3:2), the miracle had pointed the way to the truth of Jesus' divine origin. It is also amazing how this healed man was able to see things so clearly in contrast to the religious leaders who were so prejudiced against Jesus.

9:34   The religious leaders were not about to be lectured by a man who had only recently been a blind beggar. Their words "You were steeped in sin at birth" reflect their opinion on the question raised earlier by the disciples (9:2). Concluding that he was a sinner from birth, they refused to listen to him any further.

The significance of the words "And they threw him out" are debated. Was this a fulfillment of the threat of excommunication mentioned in 9:22? If so, it seems to be premature because the healed man had not yet confessed Jesus to be the Messiah. In addition, the procedures for excommunication do not seem to have been followed. Most likely the man was forcibly driven from the presence of the Jewish authorities. Perhaps John is simply saying, "They kicked him out of there."

180

THE CONSEQUENCE OF THE MIRACLE, 9:35-41

The rest of chapter 9 records the consequences of the miracle in terms of belief (9:35-38) and unbelief (9:39-41).

9:35   Having heard that the healed man had been ignominiously dismissed from the assembly of the Pharisees, Jesus sought him out to offer him spiritual healing as well. The question, "Do you believe in the Son of Man?" reflects the key issue with which John is seeking to challenge his readers (cf. 20:30-31). In the original, the word "you" is in the emphatic position. Jesus was interested in a personal decision. The word "believe" (*pisteuō*), John's favorite, speaks of "trust" and suggests reliance upon a truth, not merely intellectual acceptance of facts.

Jesus used His favorite self-designation, "Son of Man," to introduce His messianic Person to the healed man. For further discussion on the meaning and significance of this term, see comments on 1:51.

9:36   The healing of the blind man seems to have prepared him to be spiritually responsive. He seems to have understood the meaning of the expression "Son of Man." All he sought was His identity. "Who is he, sir?" The term "sir" (*kurie*) is sometimes translated "Lord" (cf. 9:38), but at this point the healed man was using it only as a term of respect, as in 4:11, 15, 19, 49. He wanted to know whom to place his faith in. He was already trusting Jesus to provide this information.

9:37   Jesus identified Himself as the object of true faith. The words "You have now seen him" may be translated "You have even seen him." Prior to the man's healing, vision would not have been even a remote possibility. But now things were different. The latter half of the sentence is similiar to Jesus' self-identification in 4:26.

9:38   The healed man responded with a declaration of personal faith, "Lord, I believe." The Greek word order is "I believe, Lord." Here the term *kurie* (cf. 9:36) is no longer a mere term of respect. It is an acknowledgement of Jesus' deity and lordship.

The development of the man's faith is significant. At first he knew only that the one who healed him was named "Jesus" (9:11). Then, he concluded that Jesus was "a prophet" (9:18). Next, he concluded that Jesus must be "from God" (9:33). Finally, he called Jesus "Lord" and worshiped Him (9:38). The belief expressed by the healed man was simple, childlike faith that would continue to progress and deepen as he went on to follow Jesus (cf. 8:31).

His confession by word was followed by deed. This is a logical and biblical step. Although the term for worship (*proscuneō*) is sometimes used of men to express respect (cf. Matt. 18:26), it is always used in John to express divine worship (cf. John 4:20-24; 12:20). The fact that Jesus made no protest against this act (cf. Acts 10:25-26; 14:18) indicates that He was worthy of worship by this new believer.

9:39   The words of v. 39 were apparently spoken while the healed man prostrated himself at the feet of Jesus. One can imagine people stopping to stare at this unusual spectacle. The words were addressed to the bystanders, which included some Pharisees.

The words "For judgment I have come into this world" may appear to contradict the statement in 3:17, "For God did not send the Son into the world to judge the world." But the difference here is between purpose and result. Jesus did not come for the purpose of condemnatory judgment, but His coming results in sifting or separation as people are divided according to their response to Him. The word for "judgment" (*krima*) in 9:39 is used only here in John and signifies not the act of judging, but speaks of the result.

The inevitable result of Christ's coming is that men must make a decision for or against Him, and this decision determines their destiny. The twofold result of the judgment is reflected in the words "so that the blind will see and those who see will become blind." In keeping with John's emphasis on "light," the issue here is spiritual sight or blindness. Jesus is saying that the spiritually blind "will see" when they believe in Jesus, as the healed man did. By contrast, those who falsely profess spiritual sight "will become blind." They will pass from perceived light into deep, spiritual darkness as a result of their refusal to trust Jesus.

9:40   There were some Pharisees who were with Jesus. Perhaps they were looking for further evidence to indict Him of a Sabbath violation. They understood that Jesus was speaking figuratively and concluded, rightly, that He was speaking about them. "What?" they asked, "Are we blind too?" Surely Jesus could not be implying that they, the most enlightened of the Jewish leaders, were spiritually blind, or so their reasoning went.

9:41   Jesus left the Pharisees with a paradox. He explained that the handicap of physical blindness would have limited the Pharisees' accountability before God. They would not be held accountable for their inability to read, study, and apply the law. The words "not guilty of sin" should not be understood as a general description of a blind person's spiritual state (cf. Rom. 3:23; 5:12). The "sin" refers to an act of sin—failure to obey the law at a particular point. Jesus is saying that people are accountable to the degree that God has provided them with light. The greater the light, the greater the accountability (Matt. 11:20-24).

But the Pharisees were not blind. Indeed, they boasted of great spiritual insight ("you claim you can see"). They were unwilling to acknowledge their own spiritual darkness and come to the light (John 8:12; 9:4). To these Pharisees Jesus declared, "Your guilt remains." There is no freedom from sin to those who refuse to acknowledge their spiritual need.

Verse 41 might be paraphrased, "Blindness would have been an excuse for your ignorance in spiritual matters, but by claiming spiritual sight (i.e., refusing to admit your need), you are blind to your true condition and are left in your sinful state." Tenney remarks, "While the blind man gained physical and spiritual sight through faith, the Pharisees lost the light they had and lapsed into complete spiritual darkness."[9]

HOMILETICAL SUGGESTIONS

The healing of the blind man (9:1-12) is the sixth of the seven signs of John's gospel and fits well into that sermon series. By way of application, the miracle presents Jesus as the great illuminator, bringing light to those cloaked in spiritual darkness.

This whole chapter could be considered from the standpoint of the blind man as a witness to the powerful impact of a personal encounter with Christ. A friend of mine who is an eye surgeon went to Mexico to work for several weeks in a mission hospital. There he performed numerous cataract surgeries. He tells of the joy of introducing a man to his children whom he had never before seen. In chapter 9, the blind man gains not only physical but also spiritual sight—an even more joyous event.

A sermon on the interrogations of the blind man (9:13-34) could focus on the theme of spiritual blindness and unbelief in the face of the clear evidence for the truth of Christ's claims. It is amazing how blind mankind is apart from enabling grace, which is a clear illustration of humanity's depravity.

9. Merrill C. Tenney, *John: The Gospel of Belief* (Grand Rapids: Eerdmans, 1948), p. 161.

The last section (9:35-41) focuses on the consequences of the miracle of the blind man in terms of belief (vv. 35-38) and unbelief (vv. 39-41). A sermon could be entitled "The Great Reversal." Those with sound physical vision were spiritually blind, and the man who was physically blind gained spiritual sight.

JOHN
CHAPTER
TEN

SHEPHERD OF SOULS

THE CONFLICT OVER THE SHEPHERD, CHAP. 10

John 10 records the last public discourse of Jesus in the fourth gospel. Here Jesus is presented as the Good Shepherd who cares for His flock. The familiar shepherd metaphor was not original with Jesus. It was deeply rooted in ancient literature and culture. The metaphor was used widely throughout the ancient Near East as a designation for leadership, both divine and human.[1] For example, in an ancient Sumerian hymn the god Enlil is addressed as the "faithful shepherd" of all living creatures; and in the prologue of his famous law code, the Babylonian king Hammurabi describes himself as a shepherd appointed by Enlil for his people.[2] This shepherd imagery also appears in the Old Testament prophetic books and Psalms. The prophets rebuke the leaders of Israel who failed in their duty as shepherds of God's people (cf. Isa. 56:9-12; Jer. 23:1-4; 25:32-38; Ezekiel 34; Zechariah 11). God is seen to be the faithful shepherd of His people (Gen. 49:24; Ps. 23:1; 80:1; Isa. 40:10-11).

Ezekiel 34 is especially significant in providing the theological background for John 10. There Yahweh indicts the shepherd-leaders

1. Werner E. Lemke, "Life in the Present and Hope for the Future," *Interpretation* 38 (April 1984): 173, n. 9.
2. James B. Pritchard, ed., *Ancient Near Eastern Texts*, 3d ed. (Princeton, N.J.: Princeton U., 1969), pp. 164, 574.

of Israel for their failure to care for the flock of Israel. The Lord declares, "Woe to the shepherds of Israel who only take care of themselves! Should not shepherds take care of the flock?" (Ezek. 34:2). Israel's leaders had exploited the sheep rather than meeting their needs (Ezek. 34:4). As a result, the flock (God's people) had strayed from God's ways and become food for "all the wild animals," that is, the nations (Ezek. 34:4-6).

In the face of this leadership failure, the Lord goes on to declare that He would become Israel's shepherd, gathering and caring for the scattered flock of His people (Ezek. 34:11-16). After regathering His people, the Lord announces, He will place over them "one shepherd, my servant David" (Ezek. 34:23-24; cf. Isa. 55:3-4; Jer. 23:5-6). The name "David" is used because King David was the prototype and chief ancestor of the messianic shepherd (cf. 2 Sam. 7:12-16; Luke 1:31-33).

John 10 brings the promise of a coming messianic shepherd to historic realization as Jesus declares, "I am the good shepherd" (v. 11). In contrast to the shepherd-leaders of Israel's past, the shepherd Jesus "lays down his life for the sheep." Although this discourse is unique to John's gospel, the figure of Christ as shepherd is found also in the synoptics (cf. Matt. 9:36; 15:24; 18:12-13; Luke 15:4-7).

CHRIST, THE DOOR, 10:1-10

There is some debate whether the literature of vv. 1-6 should be regarded as a parable or an allegory. The fact is, it does not precisely fit either category. The word used in v. 6, *paroimia* ("figure of speech") literally means "by the way." Like its Old Testament counterpart, *mashal*, it is a general term for a figurative discourse. The word emphasizes that a comparison is made whereby a known concept is used to illustrate a new idea or truth. Jesus uses the familiar shepherd imagery in this extended metaphor to teach truth about His relationship with believers.

The metaphor is twofold. In the first part (10:1-9), Christ is the "gate" (NIV; NASB reads "door") of the sheep pen; in the second part (10:11-18), He is the "shepherd." Verse 10 forms a link between the two parts.[3]

10:1   John records the discourse without any indication of a new audience or occasion. Because there was no chapter break in the orig-

3. A. Plummer, *The Gospel According to St. John* (Cambridge: At the University Press, 1899), p. 221.

inal, it is likely this passage has a close connection with Jesus' discussion with the blind man and the Pharisees (cf. 9:35-41). This agrees with the opening "I tell you the truth" (cf. 1:51), for this expression always follows up some previous teaching.[4] Chapter 10 provides an excellent analysis of why some gain spiritual sight and others do not.

The "sheep pen" or "sheepfold" was a walled enclosure where the sheep were gathered for protection at night.[5] The word *aulē* is used elsewhere to refer to the open courtyard of a house (Matt. 26:58). In the limestone of the land of Israel are many natural caves that served well as sheepfolds. Other enclosures were made of a circular wall with thorns piled on top to keep out intruders.

Jesus identifies the one who climbs over the wall instead of using the proper entrance as a "thief and a robber." The thief is cunning and seeks to avoid detection, whereas the robber is more aggressive and may use force or violence.

10:2 In contrast to the thief and robber is the shepherd, who "enters by the gate." He enters the sheepfold in the proper and legitimate way. The word "shepherd" (*poimēn*) is derived from a root that means "to protect." Jesus interprets the "gate" or "door" (*thura*) metaphor in v. 7.

10:3 Four observations are made here about the shepherd. First, the "watchman" opens the gate for him. The watchman (*thurōros*), literally "door-keeper," would stand guard at the sheepfold where several flocks would be sheltered. Some have identified the door-keeper with John the Baptist or the Holy Spirit, but this is mere speculation. Jesus Himself explains the figure and makes no identification of the door-keeper.

Second, the sheep "listen" (*akouō*) to the shepherd's voice. In this context, the word means more than mere hearing. Attentive appreciation is implied. Third, the shepherd calls his sheep by name. The shepherd would often name the sheep on the basis of individual characteristics. His level of personal knowledge was beyond that of casual familiarity. Calling the sheep "by name" suggests a personal and intimate relationship. Fourth, the shepherd "leads" his sheep. They respond to the shepherd as he gives them leadership and direction.

---

4. Leon Morris, *The Gospel According to John*, NICNT (Grand Rapids: Eerdmans, 1971), p. 501.

5. Ralph Gower, *The New Manners and Customs of Bible Times* (Chicago: Moody, 1987), pp. 139-40.

10:4   After bringing the sheep out of the sheepfold, the shepherd goes ahead of them, leading them along the way. The shepherd does not drive the sheep as one would cattle. Rather, the sheep follow because they recognize the voice of their shepherd. I once heard a shepherd in Israel speaking to his flock of sheep in low, guttural tones. As the shepherd spoke, the sheep followed and paid no attention to others who were speaking nearby.

10:5   Jesus contrasts the shepherd and the stranger. Although it is the nature of sheep to follow the shepherd, they will not follow a stranger whose voice they do not recognize. Being timid with unfamiliar persons, the sheep will run away. The words "will not" include the double negative (*ou mē*), making this an especially strong statement.

10:6   John explains in v. 6 that Jesus was making use of an extended metaphor (cf. introductory comments on 10:1-6). But as with the parables (Matt. 13; also John 16:25, 29), the listeners did not understand the truth Jesus was teaching.

10:7   Because they did not understand the metaphor, Jesus proceeds in 10:7-9 to provide his own interpretation. After the opening "I tell you the truth" (cf. 1:51), Jesus declares, "I am the gate of the sheep." Jesus is using the term "gate" or "door" figuratively. A door provides entrance or access. So Jesus is one way of entrance or access into the sheepfold. No one enters into God's family but through Him (cf. 14:6).

10:8   Jesus contrasts Himself with His predecessors. He is not referring to the patriarchs and prophets, but to those among the Jewish religious establishment. Like "thieves and robbers" they were seeking to take advantage of the flock by deception and force. Yet they spoke with no divine authority (cf. Matt. 7:29), and the sheep did not respond. There were those who followed the religious authorities and accepted their teaching, but they were not the sheep of God's fold.

10:9   Jesus repeats the claim of v. 7, "I am the gate." With brevity and simplicity He explains, "Whoever enters through me will be saved." The word "saved" (future passive indicative of *sōzō*) can refer to physical deliverance or spiritual salvation. As the shepherd provides physical protection, so Jesus provides spiritual salvation. Once again (cf. John 3:17; 5:34; 11:12; 12:27, 47) Jesus has touched on the redemptive purpose of His incarnation.

But Christ's work as the "gate" means more than salvation, as important as that is. Those who enter God's family through Jesus will "go in and go out, and find pasture." The phrase "go in and go out" is a figurative expression for living one's life and carrying on one's affairs (cf. Acts 1:21). The word "pasture" speaks of provision. The sheep entering God's flock through Jesus will receive salvation, life, and blessing. There is joy for the sheep in the pasture provided by the shepherd.

10:10   Sheep do not have any means of self-protection and are vulnerable to thieves and attack by predatory animals. Xenophon (430-354 B.C.), a Greek historian and soldier, pictures a sheep dog as saying to the sheep, "Do not I keep you from being stolen by thieves and carried off by wolves?" (*Memorabilia* 2.7, 14). Verse 10 returns to the thought of v. 1 regarding the "thief." The thief has no interest in the well-being of the flock. He comes only "to steal and kill and destroy." His main purpose is to steal. But he will "kill and destroy" if necessary. The word translated "kill" (*thuō*) can mean "to sacrifice," but the context here suggests a general meaning, "to kill for food."

In contrast to the "thief," Jesus declares He has come to benefit the sheep. He has come to bring "life," not death. And the life He provides is "full" (NIV) or "abundant" (NASB). The expression "have it to the full" (*perisson echein*) was used in classical Greek of what was more than sufficient. It means "to have a surplus." It was often used in military contexts for the reserve horse or the spare tents.[6] Jesus is speaking of "life in full measure." This is much more than a fulfilling life on earth. Jesus came to provide abundant life now and something more—spiritual life forever.

CHRIST, THE SHEPHERD, 10:11-18

As the door gives entrance, so the shepherd gives guidance and protection. Some have wondered how Jesus can be both the door and the shepherd. This was no problem for the Oriental mind, which is not inclined to operate in such mutually exclusive categories as is the Western mind. Jesus reveals three great truths concerning His relationship with the sheep: He dies for the sheep (vv. 11-13), He knows His sheep (vv. 14-15), and He gathers His sheep (v. 16).

10:11   In contrast to hired hands and false shepherds, who have little personal concern for the sheep, Jesus presents Himself as the "good shepherd." The original reads, "I am the shepherd, the good

6. H. G. Liddell and R. Scott, *An Intermediate Greek-English Lexicon*, 7th ed., s.v. "*perissos*" (New York: Oxford U., 1959), p. 632.

one," which emphasizes the character of the shepherd. The term "good" (*kalos*) speaks of what is morally good, noble, praiseworthy. It sums up the attributes of the ideal, messianic shepherd anticipated in the Old Testament (Ps. 23; Isa. 40:11; Ezek. 34:23-24; 37:24; Zech. 13:7).

The personal sacrifice of the shepherd is seen evident in the words "The good shepherd lays down his life for the sheep." This phrase is repeated in 10:15, 18; 13:37, 38; and 15:13 (also 1 John 3:16). The expression "lays down his life" speaks of the shepherd's willingness to die for his sheep (cf. David's example in 1 Sam. 17:33-34). The word "for" (*huper*) is a preposition of substitution and anticipates the substitutionary atonement of Christ (cf. John 1:29; 1 John 2:22).

10:12   Christ, the Good Shepherd, is contrasted with the hired hand who does not share the shepherd's concern for the flock. He tends the flock only because he is paid to do so. When danger comes ("the wolf"), the hired hand simply abandons the sheep and runs away. Jesus paints a vivid picture of the certain result: "Then the wolf attacks the flock and scatters it" (cf. Ezek. 34:5).

Jesus is teaching an important lesson. The hired man looks like a shepherd and sometimes even acts like a shepherd. But in times of danger, he cannot be relied upon. There is no protection or security for God's flock apart from the protective presence of Jesus, the Good Shepherd, who loves the sheep.

10:13   Verse 13 simply offers two explanations of why the hired man runs away. The first has to do with his position. Because he is a hired man, and not the owner, he has no committment to the flock. The second has to do with his affection. Being a hired hand, and not the shepherd, he has no personal affection for the flock. What a contrast with Jesus, who has purchased His sheep with His own blood and loves them even to the point of giving His life.

10:14   Jesus here repeats the claim of v. 11 but adds a new dimension—His personal knowledge of the sheep. It is extremely important that the shepherd "know" his sheep (cf. 10:3). He must know their needs, their weaknesses, and their problems. Without such knowledge he could not adequately care for their needs. Likewise, Jesus, the Good Shepherd, "knows" (*ginōskō*) in a personal, experiential way the needs of His people. And it is important for the sheep to know their shepherd. They must know His voice so they can respond when He calls (cf. 10:4). They must be able to trust Him to lead the way and provide for their needs. So, God's flock must know the shepherd, Jesus.

The mutual knowledge Jesus is speaking of here is more than that of a superficial knowledge about someone. The word "know" translates *ginōskō*, which speaks of a personal, intimate knowledge. Jesus is speaking of an intimate, personal relationship between the sheep and the shepherd.

10:15   The relationship of mutual knowledge between the sheep and the shepherd is compared with that between the Father and the Son. God the Father and God the Son have a perfect, mutual knowledge because they are one in their relationship. This is the kind of relationship the shepherd desires with His sheep. How often the flock of God's people settle for so much less.

In v. 11 Jesus said the "good shepherd lays down his life for the sheep." Now He personalizes the promise, switching from the third to the first person, "And I lay down my life for the sheep."

10:16   Jesus reveals in v. 16 that He has "other sheep that are not of this sheep pen." The word "other" (*allos*), in contrast to *heteros*, refers to others without making any distinction in kind. They are sheep with similar hazards and needs. The "sheep pen" of the immediate context must be the Jewish people, of which Jesus was a part. Because anyone who is not Jewish is a Gentile, the "other sheep" must refer to Gentiles. This is consistent with the fact that Jesus is the Savior not only of the Jews and Samaritans, but of the whole world as well (4:42).

Jesus has sheep outside the fold of Judaism (cf. Matt. 8:11). Note that they are His "sheep," a term used throughout this passage to refer to those who are His own. These refer to elect individuals of Gentile background who are not yet part of God's spiritual family (cf. Acts 18:10). Jesus declares, "I must bring them also." The word "must" (*dei*) suggests a divine necessity. It is His sure duty and the Father's decree.

Like the sheep of the house of Israel, the Gentile sheep will also respond to the voice of the shepherd. Jesus anticipates a day when there will be "one flock and one shepherd." He is speaking here of the union of Jew and Gentile into one spiritual family on the basis of personal faith (cf. Eph. 2:12-18; 3:6; Col. 3:11). Morris observes, "The unity is not a natural unity but one brought about by the activity of the Shepherd in 'bringing' them."[7]

7. Morris, *The Gospel According to John*, p. 512.

10:17 The Son's sacrificial death ("I lay down my life"; cf. 10:11, 15) is the "reason" (*dia touto*) given for the Father's love. This does not suggest the Father had no love for the Son apart from His voluntary death. Rather, the Father's love is drawn out and intensified by Jesus' personal sacrifice.

Jesus links His death with His resurrection. He lays down His life "only to take it up again." The Greek uses the purpose clause with *hina* ("in order that") with the aorist subjunctive of *lambanō*, "to take." He died with a view to and for the purpose of His resurrection. Jesus therefore was able, at the time of this discourse, to look beyond His suffering and death to the "joy" (Heb. 12:2) and "glories" that would follow (1 Pet. 2:11). For Jesus, death was the beginning, not the end. The death and resurrection were looked upon as one event, not separate, isolated actions.

10:18 Jesus emphasizes that His death is entirely voluntary and that both His death and resurrection are according to the Father's will. No one took Jesus' life from Him. As John records, He "gave up his spirit" (John 19:30; cf. Luke 23:46). He gave up His life by His own accord and by His own authority (cf. John 5:27). Both His death and resurrection fell under the exercise of His authority (*exousia*), a concept stressed twice in this verse. Yet those events were not of His own initiative. Jesus explains, "This command I received from my Father."

John is presenting a delicate balance between Jesus' sovereign authority and His submission to the Father. He has divine authority, but He exercises it in accordance with God's will.

THE RESPONSE OF THE JEWS, 10:19-21

10:19 Once again, Jesus' teaching resulted in divided opinion (7:43) or *schisma* (from which "schism" is derived).

10:20 To some it was clear that Jesus was "demon possessed" (cf. 7:20; 8:48, 52). Being "mad" seems to be equated here with being demon possessed. Perhaps the thought is, "Because He has a demon, He must be crazy." There seemed to be no reason to listen to such a person.

10:21 Yet others were impressed by what Jesus was teaching and doing. His words did not seem to be those of a demented person. The rhetorical question, "Can a demon open the eyes of the blind?" expects a negative answer. The question relates to Christ's miraculous healing of the blind man (9:1-7).

THE UNITY OF THE FATHER AND SON, 10:22-30

The time note in v. 22 seems to suggest an occasion different from that which precedes (9:1–10:21). Yet, the mention of "my sheep" (10:26-27) links this section thematically with the Good Shepherd discourse. Although the shepherd motif continues, the focus here is on the Person of Christ and His relationship with God the Father.

10:22 The word "Then" (*tote*) does not mean that the events recorded here followed immediately the events of 10:1-21. The events of 8:53–10:21 seem to have followed the Feast of Tabernacles (7:2). The teaching of 10:22-39 is associated with the Feast of Dedication. There may have been a lapse of as much as three months following 10:21. Jesus may have spent that period in or near Jerusalem.

The Feast of Dedication took place in the winter. It was December 18, A.D. 32, just three and a half months before Christ's crucifixion. The Feast of Dedication (*Hanakkah*) was not of Mosaic origin but was instituted to commemorate the cleansing and rededication of the Temple by Judas Maccabaeus in 164 B.C. after it had been defiled by Antiochus IV Epiphanes (cf. 1 Macc. 1:10-67; 2 Macc. 6-7; Josephus *Antiquities* 12.248-56; Dan. 8:9-14; 11:12-31). The celebration is also called "Feast of Lights" (Josephus *Antiquities* 12.325). Jewish tradition recorded in a marginal note in the Talmud states that one small vessel of consecrated oil lasted for eight days until new oil could be prepared for the Temple lamps (*Megillath Ta'anith* 23).

Wescott suggests that the mention of the feast was designed to connect Jesus' teaching with the hopes associated with the Maccabean deliverance.[8] The thoughts of the Jewish people during this season were on the mighty deliverance accomplished by the Maccabees. Perhaps it had not yet occurred to them that Jesus, in His cleansing of the Jewish Temple (John 2:14-17), followed in the great Maccabean tradition. Their prayers for another deliverance could be realized in Him.

10:23 The mention of "winter" (10:22) serves to explain why Jesus was walking in Solomon's Colonnade (cf. Acts 3:11; 5:12). Winter is the rainy season in Israel and the covered, colonnaded porch would provide some protection against wet and windy weather. According to Josephus, colonnaded porches completely surrounded the Court of the Gentiles in the Temple area (*Jewish Wars* 5.192). He describes the Royal Portico, on the south, in great detail (*Antiquities* 15.410-16). Sol-

8. B. F. Westcott, *The Gospel According to St. John* (Grand Rapids: Eerdmans, 1973), p. 157.

omon's Colonnade was smaller and appears to have been stretched along the east side of the Temple court.[9] It was popularly believed to have been part of Solomon's Temple.

10:24 As Jesus was walking along, a number of Jews "gathered around him." The Greek word means "encircled" (*kukloō*). They were determined that He would not get away without answering their questions (cf. 8:59). They were struggling between doubting Jesus' messianic claims and fearing that He might possibly be the promised one. How long would Jesus keep them in suspense? They demanded a straight answer. "If you are the Christ, tell us plainly." The adverb translated "plainly" (*parrēsia*) literally means "all speech." The people wanted a clear statement as to the identity of Christ. This is *the* key issue and one that coincides with the purpose of the gospel (20:31). The first-class condition ("If") assumes that He is the Messiah, at least for the sake of argument.

10:25 Because of the political connotations associated with the term "Messiah," Jesus declined to use this term in identifying Himself. Jesus explained that He had already answered their question (cf. 1:51; 4:26; 8:58; 9:37). Although His "miracles" (*erga*, "works") had served to substantiate His claims, the Jews persisted in their unbelief.

In ancient times a person's name was believed to reflect something of his person. People were often named or renamed on the basis of a developing character trait (cf. Num. 13:16; Matt. 1:21; John 1:42). The "Father's name" refers to all that God stands for in terms of His reputation and attributes. The miracles done "in my Father's name" were consistent with God's character and in accord with all that He stands for. Jesus ministered in relationship with the Father. His miracles were consistent with God's will.

10:26-27 Jesus explains the ultimate basis for the Jews' unbelief. His messiahship can be recognized only by His sheep. Repeating some of the thoughts of 10:4, 14, Jesus points out that the sheep hear the shepherd's voice and respond to His teaching. There is a relationship of intimacy between sheep and shepherd ("I know them") and obedience ("they follow me"). The unbelief of the Jews resulted from their not having been Christ's sheep. In spite of their Jewish heritage, those who rejected the Messiah shepherd were not among the chosen people of God.

9. John Wilkinson, *The Jerusalem Jesus Knew* (Nashville: Thomas Nelson, 1978), p. 76.

10:28   Jesus explains that He gives eternal life to His sheep. This is a present provision (literally, "I am giving"), not merely a future prospect. The life that Jesus gives (cf. 5:24) is eternal. Jesus uses the double negative (*ou me*) to emphasize that His sheep "shall never perish." They may suffer physical death (cf. 16:2) but not spiritual or eternal death.

To emphasize further the security of the true sheep, those who listen to His voice and follow, Jesus declares, "No one can snatch them out of my hand." The word "snatch" (*arpazō*) is used in 10:12 of the wolf's "attack" and suggests an act of aggression or violence. Eternal security rests not on the believers' ability to cling but upon Christ's infinite power to keep His own in His hand. This doctrine has great practical application for believers. There is a freedom and joy that comes with knowing there is nothing that will ever separate a true Christian from Christ (cf. Rom. 8:31-39). Some fear teaching this truth because they believe it will encourage Christians to be less disciplined and more inclined toward sin. The solution is in teaching the whole counsel of God—both eternal security and Christian accountability.

10:29   The sheep may feel secure because they are secure. They are secure in the hand of the Father as well as the hand of the Son (10:28).

The major difficulty with this verse is determining whether the relative pronoun is masculine (*hos*, "who") or neuter (*ho*, "which"). The masculine pronoun would refer to God the Father "who has given" them as greater than all. The security of the sheep would be grounded in the greatness of the Father. The neuter pronoun would refer to the believers "which the Father has given" as something of highest value. Because Christ's sheep are of such great value, they are certain of God's protection. The manuscript evidence seems rather evenly divided. Although debated, it seems that theological concerns with the concept of the Father as "greater than all" may have motivated a scribal alteration of the text. Anti-Trinitarians have used the verse to show the superiority of the Father over the Son. They do so at the expense of the truth clearly taught in v. 30.

10:30   In careful theological balance with the statement of the Father's greatness (10:29), Jesus declares, "I and the Father are one." Here Jesus answers the question raised by the Jews in 10:24. He clearly claims to share an essential unity with God the Father. The word "one" (*hen*) is neuter and speaks of one essence, not one person. To speak of one person would constitute a denial of the Trinity and contradict what John said about the "face to face" (*pros ton theon*) relationship between God and the divine Logos (1:1). The Father and Son share a oneness of divine essence yet remain two distinct Persons within the godhead. This truth can be affirmed but not fully understood.

THE UNBELIEF OF THE JEWS, 10:31-39

The unbelief of the Jews, proved by their hostile reaction to Jesus' teaching, is quite consistent with the thematic development of this section (chaps. 5-11).

10:31   There was no doubt in the minds of the Jewish listeners that Jesus was claiming deity. According to Leviticus 24:16, the penalty for blasphemy was stoning. The Jews picked up stones, perhaps from a construction site within the Temple court (cf. 2:20), for the purpose (*hina*) of stoning Jesus. Although the Jews did not customarily have authority to carry out executions (cf. 19:31), Josephus mentions one exception having to do with the sanctity of the Temple (*Jewish Wars* 6.126). That incident, however, appears to have been more like a case of mob violence.

10:32   Jesus was calm in the face of violent hostility. He simply raised the issue of His undeniably great miracles. He linked His miracles with the Father. Once again (cf. 10:25), Jesus emphasized that He did not act as an independent agent. He functioned in relationship with the Father and did His will.

In the face of His attackers, Jesus raised the question, "For which of these [miracles] do you stone me?" What miracle ever called for the death penalty?

10:33   The Jews denied that they were stoning Jesus for a good work. Rather, it was because of His "blasphemy" (*blasphēmia*), or impious speech. Jesus, "a mere man," claimed to be God. There is no denying that Jesus claimed deity. Even His enemies acknowledged that He made such a claim. Had Jesus not intended to be so understood, this would have been a wonderful opportunity for Him to clear up the issue with a denial of any divine claims.

10:34   Jesus appeals to the Old Testament in a typically rabbinical argument to answer His accusers. Sensitive to the religious culture and environment, Jesus was able to adapt His presentation to communicate to the hearts and minds of His listeners. He is a good example to all who would seek to communicate cross-culturally. The term "law" (*nomos*) is used here in the general sense of God's revelation that embraces the whole of Scripture. The passage "I have said you are gods" is a direct quote from Psalm 82:6 as translated in the Septuagint. The psalm refers to the judges of Israel as "gods" (elohim) because they were to be God's representatives and administrators of His justice.[10] From this historical situation Jesus derives the principle that "divine commissioning permits individuals to bear the divine title" (cf. Ex. 4:16; 21:6; Deut. 19:17; 2 Chron. 19:6-7).[11] Jesus cites Psalm 82:6 not to demonstrate that mere men are "gods," but to answer the charge concerning His own identity.[12]

10:35   Using the argument from the lesser to the greater, Jesus proceeds to show the implications of the Old Testament's use of the term "gods" to refer to God's representatives. If the term can be applied to human judges (the lesser), certainly it can be applied to Jesus (the greater). The Scripture citation is used to drive home His own legitimate claim to deity.

The statement "And the Scripture cannot be broken" is a strong affirmation of Jesus' high regard for the written Word of God. The word "broken" (*luthēnai*) translates the Greek word *luō*, which is elsewhere rendered "untie" (John 1:27), "destroy" (2:19), and "break" (5:18). Jesus is saying that the Word of God cannot be set aside or deprived of its binding authority.

10:36   The greatness of Jesus over human judges is highlighted by two phrases. Jesus is the one whom the Father has "set apart" (*hagiazō*) or "consecrated" for His messianic work. He is also the one whom God has "sent into the world" on a divine mission. Taken together, these phrases emphasize the fact of Christ's messianic mission and demonstrate that the term "God" is appropriate for Him.

Jesus drives home His point with the rhetorical question at the end of v. 36: "Why then do you accuse me of blasphemy because I said, 'I am God's Son'?" Although Jesus did not use this term in the immediate context, He referred to Himself as "the Son of God" in His controversy with the Jews following the healing of the lame man

---

10. In his *Exposition of the Psalms* (Grand Rapids: Baker, 1969), pp. 593-94, H. C. Leupold demonstrates the appropriateness of the use of "Elohim" for those who represent God in courts of law.

11. W. Gary Phillips, "An Apologetic Study of John 10:34-36," *Bibliotheca Sacra* 146 (October-December 1989): 409.

12. Stephen L. Homcy, "'You Are Gods'? Spirituality and a Difficult Text," *JETS* 32 (December 1989): 491.

(5:25). If it is permitted, without risk of blasphemy, to call human judges "gods," what is the objection to Jesus' referring to Himself as "God's Son"?[13]

10:37   Having answered their objection to His use of the term "God's Son," Jesus commanded the Jews, "Do not believe me unless I do what my Father does." (The Greek uses *mē* with the present imperative, "Cease believing me.") Jesus was ready to let the truth of His Person stand or fall on His works. Because Jesus and the Father are one (10:30), They act as one. Jesus should not be believed unless He does the Father's works (cf. 9:4; 10:25).

10:38   Verse 38 presents the flip side of Jesus' statement in v. 37. If Jesus did the Father's works, then He should be believed. The first class condition indicates that the assumption ("if") should be regarded as true. But even if the Jews were not ready to believe in Jesus, they were challenged to "believe the miracles." The purpose clause with *hina* ("that you may know") explains why. A proper perception of Christ's miracles will result in a correct understanding of the relationship between the Father and Son.

The words "know and understand" are the same word (*ginōskō*) in the original. But the first is aorist tense and the second is present. The aorist tense emphasizes the single act of knowing, whereas the present tense calls attention to the continual process of knowing. Jesus wanted the Jews to come to know (the beginning of faith) and to continue to grow in their knowledge of His Person.

What Jesus wanted the Jews to know is capsulized in the words "That the Father is in me, and I in the Father." This claim is repeated in 14:10-11. The mutual indwelling of the Father and Son is similar in concept to the mutual knowledge of the Father and Son (10:15) and seems to suggest the basic truth of 10:30 that the Father and the Son share one divine essence.

10:39   Once again (cf. 7:30, 44; 8:20) the Jewish leaders tried to sieze Jesus. The imperfect tense of the verb "seize" (*paizō*) indicates they made the attempt repeatedly. But Jesus eluded their grasp and departed from their midst. Nothing miraculous seems to be suggested by this description of His departure from the encircled Jews (10:24).

13. For further study, see Jerome H. Neyrey, "'I Said: You are Gods': Psalm 82:6 and John 10," *JBL* 108 (1989): 647-63.

RETURN TO PEREA, 10:40-42

Chapter 10 concludes with a historical footnote describing Jesus' return to Perea, east of the Jordan, where His public ministry had been inaugurated by John's baptism (cf. 1:28-34).

10:40   Leaving the hostility of the religious authorities in Jerusalem, Jesus withdrew across the Jordan to the small ford community of Bethany. For a discussion of the location, see comments on John 1:28. It was at Bethany that John the Baptist first carried on his ministry of baptizing. Jesus stayed there for an indefinite time.

10:41   During the period of His stay at Bethany, many people were coming to Jesus. They were much more open and responsive than the religious leaders in Jerusalem. John reports what was repeated by many who met Jesus. The imperfect tense of the verb "said" indicates it was a common remark. Although John the Baptist never did any miracles to confirm his teaching, the people recognized beyond doubt that everything John said about Jesus was true. John, the forerunner (1:23), had prepared the way for many to accept the Messiah.

10:42   John concludes the brief account by reporting that "many believed in Jesus" in that place (10:40). The word translated "that place" (*ekei*) appears at the end of the sentence, in the place of emphasis. John is making a clear contrast with Jerusalem, the place where many did not believe (10:36-39).

HOMILETICAL SUGGESTIONS

John 10 would fit well into a series on the "I am's" of the gospel (6:35; 8:12; 10:7; 10:14; and 11:25). The chapter is well illustrated by virtue of the "door" and "shepherd" metaphors used by Jesus in His teaching. It would not take too much creativity to enhance and personalize these vivid pictures of the Person of Christ.

For example, in a message on the Good Shepherd (10:11-18), it would be essential to present a thorough background of the relationship between the sheep and their shepherd in the ancient Near East. One also ought to highlight the Old Testament's use of the shepherd metaphor to refer to the leaders of Israel (cf. Isa. 56:9-12; Jer. 23:1-4; 25:32-38; Ezek. 34; Zech. 11).

In John 10:11-18 Jesus fulfills all that the rulers of Israel failed to accomplish in terms of national leadership. The passage is an excellent place to emphasize the loving and personal relationship that believers have with the Lord Jesus.

The Feast of Dedication ("Hanakkah") provides the context for Jesus' teaching on His unity with the Father (10:22-30). An explanation of the nature of this feast would help people realize why the Jews were rejecting Jesus. He was not living up to their expectations as a great "Maccabean-style" deliverer. The people were guilty of imposing their own messianic expectations on Jesus. They were disappointed because He did not match their preconceived notions. What do we expect from God? Are our expectations accurate and biblically based?

JOHN
CHAPTER
ELEVEN

RESURRECTION AND LIFE

THE RAISING OF LAZARUS, CHAP. 11

The raising of Lazarus is the seventh miracle recorded by John in his gospel. This chapter vindicates Christ's authority to give life (5:21) and to resurrect the dead (5:28-29). The miraculous raising of Lazarus from the dead confirms Christ's claim to be "the resurrection and the life" (11:25).

Chapter 11 also illustrates the progress of belief. This is seen in the lives of Mary and Martha, whose faith was strengthened by the miracle they witnessed. Yet, consistent with the major thrust of this section (5-12), unbelief is strongly evident, as seen in the response by the Jewish leaders (11:53).

THE DEATH OF LAZARUS, 11:1-16

In telling this story, John first reports the preparation for the miracle, including the death of Lazarus and Jesus' return to Judea.

11:1 Lazarus, the brother of Mary and Martha, was sick in Bethany (cf. 12:1-3). Bethany was a small village located about two miles southeast of Jerusalem on the eastern slopes of the Mount of Olives. It was the village situated near Bethphage on the road to Jericho (cf. Mark 10:46; 11:1). The name is written *Beth 'Anya* in the Syriac version, which may be a shortened form of Beth Ananiah.[1] The Ananiah mentioned right after Anathoth and Nob in Nehemiah 11:32 could be the New Testament Bethany near Jerusalem. Bethany is identified today with the village of *el 'Azariyeh*, "the place of Lazarus." Since about A.D. 300, the tomb visited by pilgrims there has been regarded as the place of Lazarus's resurrection.

11:2   John provides a parenthetical explanation for the purpose of identifying the "Mary" named in v. 1. Lazarus's sister Mary was the one known to have poured an expensive ointment on Jesus and wiped His feet with her hair. The term "perfume" (*muron*) refers to a strongly aromatic ointment used in incense, cosmetics, medicine, and to anoint a body for burial. This incident, with which the readers must have been familiar, is detailed in John 12:1-8.

11:3   The close tie between Lazarus's family and Jesus is reflected by the comments in v. 3. When Lazarus became ill, the sisters sent word to Jesus, "Lord, the one you love is sick." The expression "the one you love" is a way of speaking of a close friend. The word "love" (*phileō*) means "to love as a friend."

Unlike the royal official whose son lay sick at Capernaum (cf. 4:47), Mary and Martha did not ask Jesus to come and heal Lazarus. They wanted Jesus to be aware of the situation but seemed careful not to impose on Him.

It is encouraging to know that Jesus loves those who are His. Verse 3 contains a petition that could be appropriated by believers interceding on behalf of someone who is ill. Jesus, the Great Physician, cares for His own.

11:4   After He received the message from Lazarus's sisters, Jesus explained to the disciples, "This sickness will not end in death." Jesus did not mean, of course, that Lazarus would not die (cf. 11:14, 21). Rather, He was saying that physical death would not be the final outcome of Lazarus's sickness.

The strong adversative (*alla*), translated "No" by the NIV, is used to contrast the positive outcome with death. Lazarus's sickness is "for God's glory so that God's Son may be glorified through it." The word *doxa* ("glory") is the Greek equivalent of the Hebrew word *kavod*, meaning "weight" or "social weight." Used of God, *kavod* speaks of God's weighty reputation or attributes. When used of God, *doxa* ("glory") speaks of the splendor of His fame, honor, or reputation.

---

1. Emil G. Kraeling, *Rand McNally Bible Atlas* (London: Rand McNally, 1956), pp. 393-94.

THE LOCATION OF BETHANY OF JUDEA
John 11:1

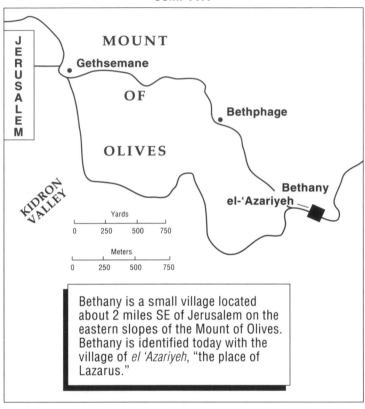

Bethany is a small village located about 2 miles SE of Jerusalem on the eastern slopes of the Mount of Olives. Bethany is identified today with the village of *el 'Azariyeh*, "the place of Lazarus."

Jesus was telling His disciples not only that death would not be the final outcome of Lazarus' sickness but that the splendor of God's reputation and that of His divine Son would be magnified through the events about to transpire. God can also use the physical sickness and affliction of believers today to bring glory to His name.

11:5 John comments that Jesus "loved" (*agapaō*) the sisters and their brother Lazarus. (The imperfect tense pictures an ongoing love.) This remark is probably intended to assure the readers that the delay in returning to Bethany was not because of a lack of love for the family. In this particular context, the two words for "love," *agapaō* here and *phileō* in v. 3, appear to be used without distinction.

11:6 Although He had heard that Lazarus was sick, Jesus stayed two more days in Perea (cf. 10:40) before traveling to Bethany. The delay indicates that Jesus was operating by a divine plan and according to a divine timetable. For Jesus, neither the need nor the opportunity constituted the call to minister. Although not stated here, He "already had in mind what He was going to do" (6:6).

11:7 After the two days had elapsed, Jesus spoke to the disciples, "Let us go back to Judea." It is probably significant that He spoke of "Judea" rather than "Bethany." It was in Judea where He had met with such strong opposition.

11:8 Jesus' proposal was not received with enthusiasm. The disciples respectfully expressed their astonishment that Jesus would suggest returning to Judea when He had but recently escaped a death threat by the Jewish leaders in Jerusalem (10:39). The imperfect tense of the verb "tried" (*zēteō*) suggests there were repeated attempts on Jesus' life. The term "rabbi," transliterated from the Hebrew word *rab* ("great"), was a title of respectful address for Jewish teachers.

11:9 In vv. 9-10 Jesus teaches the disciples an important lesson for ministry. A believer can rely upon God's protection while fulfilling His will. Jesus begins with a rhetorical question, "Are there not twelve hours of daylight?" The question expects the answer "Yes." Both the Jews and the Romans divided the period from sunrise to sunset into twelve hours.[2]

Jesus then sets forth a simple lesson based on the light-darkness contrast. The man who walks during the day will not stumble, because the sun sheds its light on obstacles to be avoided.

---

2. Jack Finegan, *Handbook of Biblical Chronology* (Princeton, N. J.: Princeton U., 1964), pp. 11-12.

11:10   Similarly, the one who walks during the night will stumble, because the darkness obscures obstacles in the path. The basic lesson is that "walking in the light prevents stumbling." Christ is the light of the world (8:12; 9:5). Those who walk in His light and according to His will have no need to fear. They can rely upon the "light" to keep them from stumbling. Those who walk at night, outside of Christ and contrary to His will, face uncertainty and stumbling. Jesus, "the Light," is saying that the disciples have no need to fear returning to Judea if they are walking with Him and doing His will.

11:11   After these remarks (11:9-10), Jesus announced, "Our friend Lazarus has fallen asleep." As in Mark 5:39, He used the metaphor of sleep to refer to death. This metaphor appears fourteen times in the New Testament. For believers, death is like sleep in that it is only a temporary repose. Believers will "awaken" from death in the resurrection. The term "cemetery," literally, "sleeping place," is derived from the same Greek root as the word translated "has fallen asleep" (*kekoimetai*). The imagery of death as "sleep" is an encouraging thought for believers. The sleep of death leads to an awakening at the resurrection. This imagery should not be mistaken for the doctrine of soul sleep, which teaches that the soul actually sleeps from death until resurrection day. The Bible teaches that to be absent from the body is to be present with Christ (2 Cor. 5:8; Phil. 1:23).

11:12   The disciples' reply, "Lord, if he sleeps, he will get better," reflects their misunderstanding of Jesus' allusion to Lazarus's death. The word translated "he will get better" literally means "he shall be saved," but it is used elsewhere of restoration to health (cf. Mark 5:23). A peaceful sleep would indicate that Lazarus would be delivered from sickness and restored to health.

11:13   John explains for the benefit of the readers that Jesus had been speaking of Lazarus's death, but the disciples misunderstood and thought He was speaking of natural sleep. The slowness of the disciples to understand shows that resurrection from death was still a relatively new concept for them.

11:14   Setting aside metaphorical language, Jesus cleared up the misunderstanding by telling His disciples straight out, "Lazarus is dead."

11:15   Jesus was glad (literally, "I am rejoicing"), not that Lazarus died but that—for the sake of the disciples—He was not there. The events to follow would greatly enhance their understanding of Jesus'

Person and work. He broke off suddenly (*alla*) with the invitation "Let us go to him."

The purpose clause with *hina* and the aorist subjunctive "so that you might believe" is the key to how this story fits within the purpose of John's gospel (20:31). The miracle Jesus would perform was designed to advance the faith of His disciples. John records it to advance the faith of his readers.

It has been noted that "this verse is written as if 2:11 had not been included in the Gospel."[3] Although the disciples "put their faith in him" (literally, "believed") as a result of Jesus' miracle at Cana (2:11), John is concerned to show that biblical faith is not static but progressive. The disciples had believed, and they must continue believing. Although the aorist tense (*pisteusēte*) may suggest the commencement of faith, here the sense is that of a confirmation and strengthening of faith. The disciples have taken a step of faith, and they need to take another.

11:16   The words of Thomas, "Let us also go, that we may die with him," reflect the disciples' concern over the danger involved in returning to Judea (cf. 11:7-8). Thomas apparently did not expect Jesus to survive another trip to hostile Jerusalem. Yet, to his credit, Thomas resolved to go with Jesus though it might cost him his life (cf. 12:23-26).

Three times in his gospel John reminds his readers that Thomas (his Hebrew name) is also known as Didymus, his Greek name (cf. 20:24; 21:2). Thomas appears to be derived from the Hebrew *to'as*, meaning "twin." Didymus is Greek for "twin." This must have been a nickname. In the Syrian-speaking churches he was known as Judas Thomas ("Judas the twin"), as seen in the apocryphal Acts of Thomas. His twin is never identified in Scripture. His character is revealed only in John's gospel (20:24-29). Elsewhere in Scripture he is merely named among the apostles.

THE CONVERSATION WITH MARTHA, 11:17-27

As Jesus approached Bethany, He was met by Lazarus's sister Martha. Jesus offered her words of comfort and sought to strengthen her faith.

11:17   John reports that by the time Jesus came to the vicinity of Bethany, Lazarus had been in the tomb four days. It was the custom of

3. Barclay M. Newman and Eugene A. Nida, *A Translator's Handbook on the Gospel of John* (London: United Bible Societies, 1980), p. 361.

the Jews, as well as other people of the Near East generally, to bury their dead on the day of death (cf. Acts 5:1-10). A speedy burial was necessary because embalming was not a custom practiced by the Jews.[4] The body would be washed, anointed with perfumes, and wrapped in white cloth.

11:18   John notes briefly that Bethany was "less than two miles," literally, "fifteen stadia," from Jerusalem. The *stadion* was a Roman measurement of a little more than 606 feet. Bethany was about 9,090 feet, or 1.72 miles, from Jerusalem.

11:19   Among the Jews, the dead were mourned for a period of thirty days. No work was done during the first three days. Deep mourning or lamenting lasted the rest of the week. The very religious would not wash, shave, or wear clean clothes during mourning.[5] While Martha and Mary were mourning the death of Lazarus, they received a number of visitors who came for the purpose of (*hina* with the aorist subjunctive) comforting them in the loss of their brother.

11:20   Verse 20 reflects something of the personality differences between the two sisters (cf. Luke 10:38-42). Although children grow up in the same home, parents should not expect them to all be the same. God seems to prefer variety. Martha seems to have been a busy woman, always caring for the needs of visitors. Mary was more content to sit quietly and reflect.

Hearing that Jesus was approaching, Martha, concerned to extend hospitality, went out to meet Him. Mary, on the other hand, remained seated at home.

11:21   Upon meeting Jesus, Martha expressed what must have been in her mind for the last four days, "Lord, if you had been here, my brother would not have died." Her words are not a rebuke but an expression of deep regret. At the same time, they are an expression of her faith. Jesus, had He been there, could have done something to prevent Lazarus's death.

11:22   Martha's comment in v. 22 is somewhat difficult in that she seems to express hope that is not apparent in the verses that follow (11:39). Perhaps she was expressing to Jesus her confidence that God would answer Jesus' prayer ("whatever you ask"). It had not yet occurred to her that Jesus was God and could raise Lazarus Himself.

---

4. Roland de Vaux, *Ancient Israel*, vol. 1 of *Social Institutions* (New York: McGraw-Hill, 1965), p. 56.

5. Peter Connolly, *Living in the Time of Jesus* (Tel Aviv: Steimatzky, 1988), p. 61.

Martha's remark hinted at the possibility of a miracle, but she did not presume upon God. Her term "whatever" expressed an attitude of submission to God's will. The repetition of the term "God" serves to emphasize her faith in His name and power.

11:23 Jesus' statement to Martha "Your brother will rise again" may have been designed to strengthen her faith. The word translated "will rise again" is the Greek *anistēmi*, meaning "to rise," "stand up," "get up." It is often used of the resurrection of the dead, particularly of Jesus' resurrection.

11:24 Although Jesus may have referred to the resurrection that was about to take place, Martha apparently did not understand His comment as referring to an immediate event. She did express faith in God's power to resurrect the dead. The expression "last day" (*eschatē hēmera*) is peculiar to John (6:39, 40, 44, 54; 12:48). It is always used with reference to the end-time events of resurrection and judgment.

Even though the doctrine of the resurrection was clearly taught in the Hebrew Scriptures (cf. Ps. 16:8-11; 73:23-26; Isa. 26:14; Dan. 12:1-4),[6] there was not total agreement on this among the Jews of the first century. The Pharisees affirmed the resurrection of the just (Acts 23:8; Josephus *Jewish Wars* 2.163-64). So did the Essenes (Josephus *Jewish Wars* 2.154). The Sadducees, on the other hand, denied this doctrine as not "Mosaic" (Matt. 22:23; Mark 12:18; Josephus *Jewish Wars* 2.165).

11:25 Jesus advanced Martha's understanding of His Person as He presented His fifth "I am" (*ego eimi*). As noted in previous comments on this phrase (cf. 10:58), this constitutes a strong affirmation of deity. Martha was thinking in terms of a future resurrection, but Jesus' statement related to the present situation. He declared, "I am the resurrection and the life." He is the one in whom "resurrection and life" have their most magnificent presentation. The power and authority to resurrect and give life reside within His divine Person (cf. 5:21, 28-29).

Jesus makes two statements after His claim to be the resurrection and the life. The statements say much the same thing, but they are not synonymous. C. H. Dodd has suggested that the first statement elucidates the claim "I am the resurrection" and the second statement elucidates the claim "I am the life." Thus his paraphrase: "I am the resur-

6. James Orr, "Immortality in the Old Testament," in *Classical Evangelical Essays*, ed. Walter C. Kaiser, Jr. (Grand Rapids: Baker, 1972), pp. 253-65.

rection: he who has faith in me, even if he dies, will live again. I am the life: he who is alive and has faith in me will never die."[7]

Belief in Jesus may not prevent physical death, but most assuredly it prevents perishing (cf. 10:28). Spiritual life means eternal life. A resurrection hope, for all who believe, is a fundamental and essential Christian doctrine (cf. 1 Cor. 15).

11:26 Elucidating his claim "I am the life," Jesus adds, "And whoever lives and believes in me will never die." The term "lives" (present participle of *zaō*) may refer to physical or spiritual life. Following Dodd's view, it must refer to physical life. Others take the term "lives" to refer here to spiritual (or eternal) life. For those who believe, physical death has no effect on life. The word "never" translates the strong double negative *ou mē*, which appears in the Greek.

Jesus' question to Martha, "Do you believe this?" includes the full content of His teaching in vv. 25 and 26. The question emphasizes that faith requires a personal response.

11:27 Martha's answer reflects a settled conviction (perfect tense of *pisteuō*, "to believe") that Jesus is the Messiah ("the Christ") and the divine Son of God. The words "who was to come into the world" reflect her understanding that Jesus is the promised one spoken of by the prophets. Her answer is not only a great declaration of personal faith, but it also serves to advance the purpose of John's gospel. It is presented here to encourage like faith in others.

THE CONVERSATION WITH MARY, 11:28-37

In His conversation with Mary, Jesus shows sensitivity to her particular need. Whereas Martha needed instruction to cope with her loss, Mary needed an understanding friend who would weep with her.

11:28 After her conversation with Jesus, Martha returned to her home and told her sister, "The Teacher is here and is asking for you." The term "teacher" (*didaskalos*) is the same word used of the prominent Jewish leader Nicodemus (3:10). It is significant that Martha called Jesus "the Teacher." Many of the rabbis refused to instruct women. The Jerusalem Talmud records the opinion of Rabbi Eliezer, who said, "It is better that the words of the Law would be burned than that they should be given to a woman" (*Sotah* 3.4). Although Jewish

---

7. C. H. Dodd, *The Interpretation of the Fourth Gospel* (Cambridge: At the University Press, 1953), p. 365.

women in the first century could attend worship and pray individually, it was generally believed that instruction in the law was for men
only.[8] It is evident by Martha's term "the Teacher" that Jesus did not
share this opinion.

11:29   When Mary heard that Jesus was asking for her, she arose
quickly and went out to meet Him. Would that all believers would
respond so promptly to His call!

11:30   John explains in v. 30 that Jesus had not yet entered the village of Bethany. He was waiting for Mary at the place He had spoken
to Martha. He apparently wanted to speak with her privately, apart
from the other sympathizers.

11:31   Although a private conversation may have been desired, it
apparently was not to be. The other comforters followed Mary out of
the house, thinking that she intended (purpose clause with *hina*) to
mourn (literally, "weep") at Lazarus's tomb. The word "weep" (*klaiō*)
refers to any loud expression of pain or sorrow. Mourning in the Middle East, even today, is quite loud and expressive.

11:32   When Mary reached Jesus, she fell at His feet and said, "Lord,
if you had been here, my brother would not have died." These are the
exact words spoken by Martha in v. 21 (although the word order in
the Greek is slightly altered). Mary seems to be the more expressive
of the two sisters. There is no mention of Martha falling at Jesus' feet.
(Note again the personality differences between these siblings.)

11:33   The presence of the Jewish friends who had come along
with Mary may have prevented further conversation. Seeing Mary and
her comforters weeping (cf. comments on "weep" in 11:31), Jesus was
"deeply moved in spirit and troubled." The word translated "deeply
moved" (*embrimaomai*) is used elsewhere in the New Testament of a
stern warning (Matt. 9:30; Mark 1:43) or scolding (Mark 14:5). In classical Greek literature it is used in the sense of a horse's "snort." In
these contexts, the word seems to express some sense of anger or
displeasure. The word "troubled" (*tarassō*) is used of stirring up water (5:4). Used figuratively, it means to disturb, unsettle, or throw into
confusion. This word is used of Jesus in 12:27 and 13:21.

    The two words taken together indicate that Jesus was perturbed
or agitated. One might say, "He was upset." What was it that raised

8. James B. Hurley, *Man and Woman in Biblical Perspective* (Grand Rapids: Zondervan, 1981),
pp. 71-73.

such a response? The opinions are as varied as the commentators. The most prominent views are listed:

1. Jesus was agitated by the unbelief of the Jews, and perhaps the sisters (Bultmann).
2. Jesus was agitated at the ravages of death, which had entered the world because of sin (Tenney).
3. Jesus was agitated by the presence of sickness and death, and the havoc they wrought in human life (Bruce).
4. Jesus was agitated by the hypocritical and sentimental lamentations of the Jews mingled with the heartfelt lamentations of Mary (Plummer).
5. Jesus was agitated by the attitude of the mourners who so completely misunderstood the nature of death and the Person of the Son (Morris).
6. Jesus was agitated by the sisters and the Jews, who appear to be almost forcing a miracle upon Him (Barrett).
7. Jesus was angry because He was face to face with the realm of Satan, represented by death (Brown).
8. Jesus was agitated by several factors. Westcott, for example, suggests a combination of views 1 and 2.

The many views of capable scholars suggest that there can be no degree of certainty over the cause of agitation. It may have been a combination of factors. Had John thought it important, he could have presented a parenthetical explanation. In the midst of these mourners, Jesus struggled with His own emotions. Perhaps it was the kind of response felt by those attending a funeral and seeing the grieving family seated before a casket. The swelling up of emotion is difficult to analyze.

11:34   The conversation with Mary having been interrupted, Jesus asked a simple question, "Where have you laid him?" He wanted directions to the tomb. The people offered to show Him the way, "Come and see, Lord."

11:35   This brief remark by John shows that Jesus was fully human and experienced a broad spectrum of human emotions (Heb. 4:15). The word "wept" (*dakruō*) is used only here in the New Testament and means "to shed tears." The reasons for this weeping are much the same as those offered for Jesus' agitation in v. 33. Suffice it to note that

Jesus exemplified the admonition later given by Paul, "Mourn with those who mourn" (Rom. 12:15).

John 11:35 is often regarded as the shortest verse in the Bible. But it contains three words in the Greek, whereas 1 Thessalonians 5:17, "Pray continually," contains only two.

11:36 Jesus' weeping was interpreted by the Jews as a reflection of the great love He had for Lazarus (cf. John 11:3). The words "said" and "loved" are in the imperfect tense. They "kept saying" how Jesus "used to love" Lazarus. Evidence of genuine love for others can have a powerful impact on those who witness it. No wonder Jesus identified love as the mark of the Christian (cf. 13:34-35).

11:37 The comment about Jesus' love for Lazarus elicited what appears to be an objection. The healing of the blind man (9:1-7) had made a lasting impression on the Jews. Their thinking may have been something like this: "If Jesus could give sight to the blind, couldn't He have prevented the death of Lazarus? If He had the power to do so, why didn't He? What kind of 'love' is this that lets a friend die?"

THE RESURRECTION OF LAZARUS, 11:38-44

The resurrection of Lazarus anticipates Jesus' own victory over the ultimate consequence of sin—death.

11:38 It may have been the sight of the tomb or a combination of other factors (cf. 11:33) that caused Jesus once again to be "deeply moved." John briefly describes that burial place. As was often the custom in Israel, a cave (*spēlaion*) had been made into a tomb. The use of a private burial place indicates that the family was well off financially.

In Hellenistic and Roman times, the poor were buried in communal graves or unused cisterns, whereas the wealthier families had tombs cut out of rock. A simple tomb consisted of a rectangular room with ledges or horizontal shafts where the bodies would be placed. Each shaft grave had its own little door. The small opening into the tomb complex was sealed with a rolling stone (cf. Matt. 27:60).[9]

11:39 Jesus must have startled Martha and the rest of the mourners when He ordered, "Take away the stone." As Lazarus's sister, Martha politely objected to the action. She pointed out to Jesus that the body had begun to decompose. Translated literally, her remark reads "Al-

9. Connolly, *Living in the Time of Jesus,* pp. 60-61.

ready he stinks." Martha explained that Lazarus had been in the tomb "four days."

The "four days" is significant from the rabbinical viewpoint. According to the rabbinical commentary, *Leviticus Rabba* 18:1 (on Lev. 15:1), the soul is said to hover over the body for three days after death. But it departs on the fourth day when decomposition becomes evident. It is uncertain whether this opinion was prominent among the Jews of the first century.

11:40 Jesus reminded Martha of what He had spoken earlier (cf. 11:23-26). In 11:26 she had been challenged regarding her belief. The promise "would see the glory of God" must refer to the resurrection of Lazarus. Jesus had told the disciples that Lazarus's sickness was "for God's glory" (11:4). The prospect of gaining insight into the reputation and attributes of God ("the glory of God") was not mentioned in 11:23-26, but more may have been said than is recorded.

11:41 Following the instruction of Jesus, the stone was removed from the opening of the tomb. Then Jesus prayed. He addressed God as "Father," thanking Him for having heard His prayer. It is not completely clear to which prayer Jesus refers. The aorist tense of the verb "heard" (*akouō*) may suggest a previous prayer that is not recorded. The context, however, would indicate that the present prayer is in view.

Many critical scholars view this prayer (vv. 41*b*-42) as suspect—one that was created by John and put into the mouth of Jesus. Some interpreters believe the prayer offends religious sensitivities because Jesus prays to the Father "for the benefit of the people" who would overhear His words (v. 42). Hunter has answered these objections by showing that the prayer is an essential element in the miracle narrative and is part of a tradition of piety exemplified by the Jewish personal thanksgiving psalm—prayers that both God and spectators are meant to hear.[10]

11:42 Jesus acknowledged to the Father that this prayer of thanksgiving was for the benefit of the people, "that they may believe that you sent me." The prayer was intended (purpose clause with *hina* and the subjunctive of *pisteuō*) to lead the observers to faith in Jesus' divine mission as sent by the Father. Once again it is demonstrated by

10. W. Bingham Hunter, "Contextual and Genre Implications for the Historicity of John 11:41*b*-42," *JETS* 28 (1985): 53-70.

John that Jesus, the Sent One, acts not on His own initiative but in submission to and dependence upon the Father (cf. 3:17; 7:16; 8:28; 10:18).

11:43   After praying, Jesus called out in a loud voice, "Lazarus, come out!" (Someone has said it is a good thing He named Lazarus, otherwise He might have emptied the whole cemetery.) The word translated "called out" (*kraugazō*) is used later of the crowds who wanted to crucify Jesus. The "loud voice" was probably not for the sake of Lazarus but that the crowds could hear and link the resurrection with Christ's command.

11:44   In response to the command of Jesus, Lazarus came out of the tomb. As was the custom in first-century Palestine, Lazarus was wrapped in graveclothes (*keiria*), or linen strips. Those wrappings and a face cloth (*soudarion*, cf. 20:7), something like a handkerchief, were still on his body when he came out of the tomb. Jesus instructed the shocked onlookers, "Take off the graveclothes and let him go."

By this miracle, Jesus vindicated His claim to give life and resurrect the dead (cf. 5:21, 28-29). In restoring life to the dead, Jesus demonstrated His authority to turn back the effects of sin (cf. Gen. 2:17; Rom. 5:12). The resurrection of Lazarus exhibited in a small but significant way that death will not be characteristic of the messianic kingdom (Isa. 25:8).

THE RESPONSE TO THE MIRACLE, 11:45-53
The miracles of Jesus often brought different results among people. In response to the raising of Lazarus, some believed. Others, however, reported the miracle to the religious leaders, who took counsel to put Jesus to death.

11:45   John reports the immediate result of the miracle. Many Jews believed (*episteusan*) in Jesus. By personal faith, they came to trust Him. But not all responded in this manner. The Jews to whom John refers are described as those who "had come to visit Mary, and had seen what Jesus did." They had witnessed the miracle and understood its significance (cf. 3:2).

11:46   Although many of the Jews who had seen the miracle believed, there were others who exhibited a more hostile response. John refers here to the Jews generally, as distinguished from those who saw and believed (v. 45).[11] These other Jews apparently heard

11. A. Plummer, *The Gospel According to St. John* (Cambridge: At the University Press, 1899), p. 241.

about the miracle second-hand. They reported the events to the "Pharisees" (see comments on 1:24), whom they regarded as religious authorities. Their motives in presenting this report, whether good-intentioned or otherwise, are not revealed.

11:47   The Pharisees and the "chief priests" (see comments on 7:32) convened a meeting of the "Sanhedrin" (*sunedrion*). Although mentioned in the synoptics and Acts, this is the only time John mentions the Sanhedrin. The term is a Greek word meaning "assembly" or "council," derived from *sun* ("with") and *hedra* ("seat"). It is used to refer to the supreme religious, political, and judicial Jewish authority in postexilic Palestine. The Sanhedrin was composed of seventy-one members, including the presiding high priest. The three main sources of information concerning the Sanhedrin are the New Testament, Josephus, and rabbinic literature (M. *Sanhedrin*).

When Judea became a Roman province in A.D. 6 after the banishment of Herod's son Archelaus, the Sanhedrin was given almost exclusive control of the internal government and affairs of the people. Although answerable to the Roman governor, it was during this period (A.D. 6-66) that the Sanhedrin came to possess its greatest power and jurisdiction.

As the Sanhedrin convened, the religious leaders discussed the problem of Jesus' ministry and miracles. Frustrated by the ineffectiveness of their efforts to dissuade people from believing in Jesus, they questioned, "What are we accomplishing?" They could not deny the miracles, but they refused to accept the implications of the evidence before them.

11:48   The primary concern of the religious authorities is expressed here. Fear of political upheaval due to popular messianic expectations could have resulted in future subjugation to Rome. The leaders presumed that if the present course of events went unchecked, "the Romans will come and take away both our place and our nation." The "place" (*tupon*) may refer to the Temple itself (2 Macc. 5:19) or Jerusalem as the seat of the Sanhedrin.

11:49   John reports the words of Caiaphas, son-in-law of Annas (18:13) and high priest from A.D. 18 to A.D. 36. Caiaphas, a Sadducee, was also known as Joseph (Josephus *Antiquities* 18.35). Although the rabbinic sources speak of a "president" (*nasi*) of the Sanhedrin, the New Testament and Josephus portray the Sanhedrin as headed by the high priest (Josephus *Antiquities* 20.10; *Apion* 2.23; Acts 5:17ff.; 7:1;

9:1, 2; 22:5). The words "that year" (cf. 11:51; 18:13) refer to that memorable year of Messiah's death and resurrection.

Caiaphas brushed aside the hesitant and uncertain questions of the other religious leaders (11:47) with his contemptuous comment "You know nothing at all." His remark is consistent with Josephus's report that the Sadducees "in their intercourse with their peers are as rude as to aliens" (*Jewish Wars* 2.166).

11:50   Caiaphas continued his rebuke: "You do not realize that it is better for you that one man die for the people than that the whole nation perish." According to his reasoning, it would be better to murder the controversial Galilean rabbi than to give Rome cause to subject Judea to a heavier yoke. The word "for" represents the Greek *huper*, "instead of." *Huper* is used of one who takes the place of another and in this context has implications concerning substitutionary atonement.

11:51   Reflecting on the words of Caiaphas, John explains that he did not speak on his own initiative. Unknowingly, Caiaphas uttered a prophecy. As God spoke through unbelieving Balaam (Num. 22-25), so God spoke through Caiaphas to predict Christ's death for the Jewish nation. John comments that he spoke this prophecy "as high priest that year." The high priestly office was associated with the giving of divine revelation by means of the Urim and Thummim (cf. Num. 27:21).

11:52   In keeping with the purpose of his gospel (20:30-31), John explains that the death of Jesus prophesied by Caiaphas was not for the Jewish nation only. Consistent with the promise of the Abrahamic Covenant (Gen. 12:3), Messiah's death would have worldwide impact. It was also designed to gather into one body the "scattered children of God."

The concept of a "scattered children of God" is similar if not identical to Jesus' reference to "sheep that are not of this sheep pen" (10:16). One of God's purposes in Christ's death is to gather the elect who have expressed personal faith into one spiritual Body (Eph. 2:14-16; 3:6).

11:53   The meeting of the Sanhedrin and the comments by Caiaphas marked a significant turning point. Although not apparent in the NIV translation of v. 53, the word "therefore" (*oun*) is prominent in the Greek text. The actions that followed were as a consequence of Caiaphas's analysis. From that day on, the religious leaders plotted the death of Jesus.

THE WILDERNESS RETREAT, 11:54

11:54   The plot of the Sanhedrin and the increasingly hostile climate in Judea soon limited Jesus' public ministry. To avoid premature seizure by the Jews, He withdrew to a remote region near the wilderness. Jesus and His disciples stayed in the village called "Ephraim" (2 Sam. 13:23). Josephus mentions a village called Ephraim near Bethel (*Jewish Wars* 4.551). Most geographers identify Ephraim with modern et-Taiyibeh, located about 12 miles northeast of Jerusalem.[12]

THE PASSOVER PILGRIMAGE, 11:55-57

It was the spring of A.D. 33, and the Passover was approaching. According to the synoptics, Jesus journeyed north from Ephraim to the border between Galilee and Samaria (Luke 17:11) where He joined the pilgrims traveling through Perea en route to the Passover (Matt. 19:1; Mark 10:1). Jesus had many wonderful opportunities to teach and minister to the travelers along the way.

11:55   Passover was one of the three great pilgrim festivals to be observed by the Jews in Jerusalem (Deut. 16:16). The feast, observed annually on the fourteenth of Nisan, commemorated God's deliverance of the Jews from bondage in Egypt (cf. John 2:23; 6:4). John refers to the Jewish custom of going up to Jerusalem for ceremonial cleansing before Passover.

Ceremonial defilement disqualified a man from observing the Passover (cf. Lev. 7:21; Num. 9:6). Hence it was important to arrive in sufficient time to participate in the appropriate cleansing. According to the Mishnah, this was done by immersion in a ritual bath called a *miqveh* (*Mikva'ot* 4.1). Excavations south of the Temple area have uncovered 48 *miqva'ot* (the plural of *miqveh*) that served the pilgrims who sought purification before climbing the steps to the Temple area.[13]

The phrase "went up" indicates that Jerusalem is in the mountains, and nearly any approach to the city requires an ascent in elevation.

11:56   The pilgrims who arrived early in Jerusalem kept looking around for Jesus and wondering among themselves about Him. Would He come to the feast or not? The use of the negative particle

12. Kraeling, *Rand McNally Bible Atlas*, p. 394.
13. William Sanford La Sor, "Discovering What Jewish *Miqva'ot* Can Tell Us About Christian Baptism," *Biblical Archaeology Review* (January/February 1987): 52-59.

ou mē in the second question ("Isn't he coming to the Feast at all?") assumes strongly that the expected answer is "No." They doubted that Jesus would be so foolish as to endanger Himself by returning to the center of Jewish hostility.

11:57   Verse 57 explains why the people doubted that Jesus would return to Jerusalem. The chief priests and Pharisees (cf. 7:32; 11:47) had given orders that anyone knowing of Jesus' whereabouts should report it so that they might arrest Him.

HOMILETICAL SUGGESTIONS

The raising of Lazarus is the seventh miracle of John's gospel and could serve as the final message in a series on the seven signs. The chapter is probably too long for one sermon and should be divided into reasonable homiletical units.

The account of the death of Lazarus (11:1-16) provides an opportunity to present Christians with a more positive view of death. Here we see that sickness and death may be used to bring glory to God. The imagery of sleep can be elaborated to show that death is only a brief step to resurrection life. Although death remains an enemy, its sting has been removed through Christ's resurrection (1 Cor. 15:54-57).

Jesus' conversations with Mary (John 11:17-27) and Martha (11:28-37) provide material to expound upon Jesus' way of ministering to the grieving. It is significant that He taught Martha and wept with Mary. He knew their needs and ministered accordingly. Verse 25 records the fifth "I am" in John's gospel and serves to conclude this series.

With the raising of Lazarus (11:38-44), the preacher is provided with a text that demonstrates the authority of Christ as giver of life. In this miracle, the effects of the Fall are reversed, showing Christ's ability to deal with the ultimate issue—man's sin. Lazarus's resurrection gives hope for all believers whose loved ones have died in Christ. These believers and their loved ones will all one day be raised and reunited.

JOHN
CHAPTER
TWELVE

HOSANNA! KING OF ISRAEL

THE CLOSE OF CHRIST'S PUBLIC MINISTRY, CHAP. 12

Chapter 12 is a key turning point in John's development of the life of Christ. It describes a point of crisis in Jerusalem (12:23) and the transition in Jesus' career from public to private ministry (12:26).

On His last journey to Jerusalem, Jesus traveled north from Ephraim to the border between Galilee and Samaria (Luke 17:11) where He joined the pilgrims traveling through Perea en route to Jerusalem to celebrate Passover (Matt. 19:1; Mark 10:1). Jesus probably crossed the Jordan at Bethany, east of Jericho (Matt. 20:29; Luke 18:35). He would have then proceeded from Jericho to Jerusalem, ascending the hill country by the Roman road that leads through the Wadi Qilt.[1]

THE ANOINTING AT BETHANY, 12:1-8

12:1 It was six days before the Passover in the spring of A.D. 33 when Jesus arrived in Jerusalem. Because Passover (the 14th of Nisan) took place on Friday that year, "six days" earlier would be Saturday, the eighth of Nisan. Bethany, the home of Mary, Martha, and Lazarus, was located on the eastern slopes of the Mount of Olives about two miles southeast of Jerusalem (see 11:1). John identifies the village in

---

1. J. Carl Laney, *Baker's Concise Bible Atlas* (Grand Rapids: Baker, 1988), p. 205.

relationship to the great miracle that occurred there—the resurrection of Lazarus.

Although not translated by the NIV, the word "therefore" (*oun*) appears at the beginning of the verse in the Greek text. It may be translated "then" and serves to resume the narrative from where it left off in 11:55.

12:2   After Jesus' arrival in Bethany, a dinner was held in His honor. According to the account in Matthew and Mark, the dinner was given in the home of Simon the leper (Matt. 26:6; Mark 14:3), who may have been healed by Jesus. The fact that "Martha served" and Lazarus was among the dinner guests suggests that Simon was a personal friend of Lazarus and his sisters. The imperfect tense of the verb "served" (*diakoneō*) indicates that Martha continued in this manner through the dinner. As in Luke 10:38-42, the two sisters are contrasted—Martha serving and Mary worshiping. It was customary in ancient times for dinner guests to recline on cushions around a low table.

12:3   Mary's love for Jesus was expressed by her giving an expensive gift. John reports that she took a large quantity of extremely expensive perfume and poured it on the feet of Jesus, wiping the excess with her hair. John describes the amount, the ointment, and the cost in such a way as to give the reader the full force of this expression of worship. The amount, a *litra* (NIV, "pint"), was a measure of both weight and capacity and is the equivalent of a Roman pound (12 ounces). The ointment was a perfumed oil made from an East Indian plant, *Nardostachys jatamansi.* John reports that the ointment was "pure," in contrast with that which had been diluted. It's value is noted by John and highlighted by Judas, who regarded it as the equivalent of a years' wages (12:5). Nard ointment was imported from India in carefully sealed alabaster jars. Only on a special occasion would the seal of the jar be broken so as to do the anointing.[2]

The synoptic accounts record Mary's anointing of Jesus' head. John alone records the anointing of His feet. To attend to the feet was the task of the most lowly slave. Mary's action reflects her great humility and devotion. This account is similar to, but not identical with, Luke's account of the sinful woman who anointed Christ's feet with her tears and perfume (Luke 7:36-50).

2. W. E. Shewell-Cooper, "Spikenard," in *The Zondervan Pictorial Encyclopedia of the Bible*, ed. Merrill C. Tenney (Grand Rapids: Zondervan, 1975), 5:502.

12:4   The loving act of Mary is set in contrast with the selfish objection raised by the betrayer, Judas Iscariot. As in John 6:71, Judas is described as the one "who was later to betray ["deliver over"; Greek, *paradidōmi*] him" (which was in keeping with the sovereign purposes of God). However, the sovereignty of God never annuls human responsibility (cf. Matt. 26:24).

12:5   Judas objected to the high cost of Mary's expression of worship. He pointed out that the perfume was the equivalent of a "year's wages," literally, three hundred denarii. The denarius, a Roman coin, had the purchasing power of approximately one day's wages (cf. Matt. 20:1-16). Judas demanded to know why the perfume was not sold and the money given to the poor. Judas was thinking with his pocketbook instead of with his heart. It is important to remember that although good stewardship over finances and budgets is important, one cannot place a monetary price on Jesus. His worth is infinite, and He fully deserves *all* our affection and support.

12:6   John explains in v. 6 the selfish motivation behind Judas's comment. Judas was not so much concerned about the poor as he was about his own enrichment. Judas was the treasurer for the twelve and the custodian of the money bag. Although the disciples did not then know that Judas was a thief, it became evident after his betrayal of Jesus. John reports that he used to pilfer from the purse. The imperfect tense of *bastazō* ("to pick up") indicates that it was a regular occurrence. Judas's weak character, greed, and lack of accountability were no doubt factors in his sin.

12:7   Jesus spoke in defense of Mary's actions and explained that the anointing was for His burial. Mary's worship was not to be disrupted. The words "It was intended that she should save this perfume for the day of my burial" may be understood in at least two different ways. Jesus could be referring to keeping the custom of anointing the dead, or to saving the remainder for His burial. The former is more in keeping with the context and Jesus' defense of her actions. Mary must have sensed the darkness of the hour (10:11, 17-18) and sought to honor Jesus before His impending death (Mark 14:8). She provides a model for sacrificial giving, doing it joyfully as an expression of her love for Jesus. Based on human experience, we can reasonably assume that Mary enjoyed giving the gift.

12:8   Jesus' comment regarding the poor is quite in keeping with the thought of Deuteronomy 15:11, "There will always be poor people in the land." Jesus is certainly not suggesting that the poor be neglected. What is emphasized in the original is the contrast. The "poor" and the "me" are in the emphatic positions in the original. There would always be time and opportunity to care for the poor—a good and necessary work. But there was only limited opportunity to express one's personal love for Jesus.

THE HOSTILITY OF THE PRIESTS, 12:9-11

Verses 9-11 are transitional and record the plans of the priests to kill Lazarus as well as Jesus. According to Hoehner's chronology, the events recorded here took place on Sunday, the ninth of Nisan.[3]

12:9 Word spread fast among the Passover pilgrims that Jesus was staying in Bethany. Soon a large crowd gathered there. The people came because of Jesus, but they also wanted to see Lazarus, whom Jesus had raised from the dead.

12:10 Lazarus served as "exhibit A" that the claims of Jesus were true and that He did have divine authority to give life and resurrect the dead. One way to limit Jesus' popularity was to eliminate the evidence that His claims were true. The "chief priests" (cf. 7:32) had already made plans to kill Jesus (cf. 11:53). Now they decided to kill Lazarus too.

12:11 John explains the reason (causal use of *hoti*) for the Jewish leaders' hostility against Lazarus. It was because of Lazarus that many were leaving the ranks of Jewish orthodoxy by expressing personal faith in Jesus. The imperfect of *pisteuō* ("putting their faith in") indicates that the action was ongoing. The religious leaders were in danger of facing a massive people's movement away from Judaism.

THE ROYAL ENTRY, 12:12-19

The royal entry of Jesus into Jerusalem served as His official presentation to the nation as Messiah and King. He came on the prophesied day, in fulfillment of the sixty-nine weeks (Dan. 9:24-27), and in the prophesied way, riding on the colt of a donkey (Zech. 9:9). The entry of Jesus into Jerusalem is recorded in all four gospels (Matt. 21:1-11; Mark 11:1-11; Luke 19:28-40; John 12:12-19). Although the event is commonly referred to as His "Triumphal Entry," the "royal entry" designation is probably better because He entered the city as

---

3. Harold W. Hoehner, *Chronological Aspects of the Life of Christ* (Grand Rapids: Zondervan, 1970), p. 91.

NEW TESTAMENT JERUSALEM
John 12:1

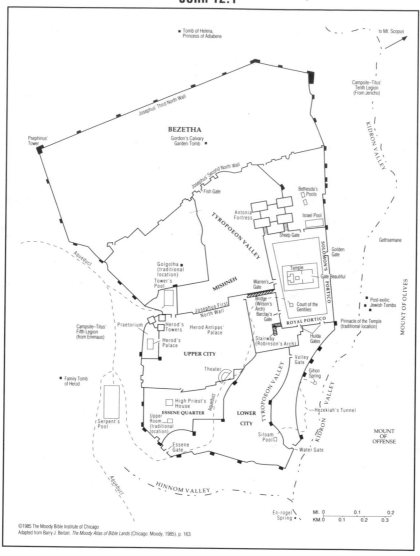

■ Tomb of Helena,
Princess of Adiabene

to Mt. Scopus

Campsite–Titus'
Tenth Legion
(From Jericho)

KIDRON VALLEY

Josephus' Third North Wall

BEZETHA

Psephinus'
Tower

Gordon's Calvary
Garden Tomb ■

Josephus' Second North Wall

Fish Gate

Bethesda's
Pools

Israel Pool

Antonia
Fortress

Sheep Gate

TYROPOEON VALLEY

Golden
Gate

Gethsemane

SOLOMON'S PORTICO

Temple

Gate Beautiful

Aqueduct

Golgotha
(traditional
location)

Tower's
Pool

MISHNEH

Warren's
Gate

Post-exilic
Jewish Tombs ■

MOUNT OF OLIVES

Josephus' First
North Wall

Bridge
(Wilson's
Arch)

Barclay's
Gate

Court of the
Gentiles

ROYAL PORTICO

Pinnacle of the Temple
(traditional location)

Campsite–Titus'
Fifth Legion
(from Emmaus)

Praetorium

Herod's
Towers

Herod Antipas'
Palace

Stairway
(Robinson's Arch)

Hulda
Gates

Herod's
Palace

UPPER CITY

Theater

Valley
Gate

Gihon
Spring

■ Family Tomb
of Herod

High Priest's
House

Aqueduct

ESSENE QUARTER

Upper
Room
(traditional
location)

**LOWER
CITY**

TYROPOEON VALLEY

Hezekiah's Tunnel

KIDRON VALLEY

MOUNT
OF
OFFENSE

Serpent's
Pool

Essene
Gate

Siloam
Pool

Water Gate

Aqueduct

HINNOM VALLEY

En-rogel
Spring ●

MI. 0   0.1   0.2

KM. 0   0.1   0.2   0.3

©1985 The Moody Bible Institute of Chicago
Adapted from Barry J. Beitzel, *The Moody Atlas of Bible Lands* (Chicago: Moody, 1985), p. 163.

Messiah and King (12:15). (Perhaps the usage of Triumphal Entry is better reserved for His second advent.)

12:12 The "next day" appears to refer to the day after the great crowds of Jews came to Bethany (12:9). It was probably Monday, rather than Sunday, that Jesus' official entrance into Jerusalem took place.[4] Monday was the tenth of Nisan, the very day the Passover lamb was to be selected and set aside for sacrifice (Ex. 12:3). It was on that day that Jesus presented himself as Israel's Paschal lamb (1 Cor. 5:7).

John refers to the "great crowd" that came to Jerusalem for the Passover feast. Josephus reports crowds exceeding 2.7 million (*Jewish Wars* 6.425). Jeremias estimates that the population of Jerusalem swelled from 55,000 to 180,000 during Passover.[5] The crowd that had come to Jerusalem for the Passover observance learned that Jesus was approaching the city. Many undoubtedly believed in Him and hoped that He would make good His claims concerning His kingdom and authority.

12:13 Taking palm branches, the people went out to meet Jesus. Palm branches were used in celebrating the Feast of Tabernacles (Lev. 23:40; Neh. 8:15). A palm design ornamented the walls of Solomon's Temple (1 Kings 6:29). Palm branches were carried by the Jews who celebrated Simon's entry into Jerusalem at the climax of the Maccabaean Revolt (1 Macc. 13:51). In time, the palm became a symbol of Jewish nationalism and victory.[6]

As the people met Jesus coming along the road from Bethany, they began shouting quotations from Psalm 118:25-26. The words "Hosanna" are a transliteration of the Hebrew hiphil imperative *yasha'*, meaning "to help," "save," or "rescue," with the additional *na*, a particle of entreaty meaning "We pray!" or "Please!" The words "Blessed is he who comes in the name of the Lord" are a direct quote from the Septuagint. The one who came in the Lord's name was none other than Jesus. The Greek word structure equates "him who comes in the name of the Lord" with "the king of Israel." The people recognized what John wants to emphasize, that Jesus was Israel's king (cf. 1:49; Ps. 2:6-7).

---

4. Ibid., p. 91.

5. J. Jeremias, *Jerusalem in the Time of Jesus* (Philadelphia: Fortress, 1969), pp. 82-84.

6. Palm trees ornamented Roman coins celebrating the demise of Jewish independence with Titus's capture of Jerusalem in A.D. 70. Jewish coins minted during the Second Jewish Revolt (A.D. 132-35) also featured palm trees.

12:14   John summarizes briefly an incident reported in greater detail in the synoptics. He records that Jesus found a young donkey. Matthew 21:2-3; Mark 11:2-6; and Luke 19:30-35 tell how the donkey was acquired. The Greek word translated "young donkey" appears only here in the New Testament. It is a diminutive form meaning "a small donkey." Matthew 21:2,7 indicates that there were two animals brought to Jesus, a donkey and a colt. The donkey accompanied the colt, the younger animal that Jesus rode.

12:15   John is interested to show that the entrance of Jesus into Jerusalem was in keeping with what had been foretold by the Hebrew Scriptures. He quotes rather freely Zechariah 9:9, abbreviating the text and substituting the words "Do not be afraid" for "Rejoice greatly." Many have called attention to the fact that the Messiah King is depicted riding on a humble donkey instead of a splendid horse. But it should be recognized that a donkey was not considered a lowly creature in the ancient Near East. It was the mount of princes (Judg. 5:10; 10:4; 12:14) and kings (2 Sam. 16:1-2). Both Asherah and Baal are depicted in ancient literature as riding on donkeys. Jesus came riding into Jerusalem on a mount appropriate to His royal position.

12:16   John shares another candid comment (cf. 2:22; 7:39) regarding the disciples' failure to understand fully the significance of the events they were witnessing. Much of what was obscure during the life and ministry of Jesus was brought to the disciples' remembrance and made clear through the ministry of the Holy Spirit (14:26; 16:13-15). This new insight and understanding came to them "after Jesus was glorified" through His death and resurrection (cf. 7:39). Even the apostles who lived and traveled with Jesus were limited in their spiritual understanding prior to the sending of the Holy Spirit.

12:17   John refers in v. 17 to those who were present in Bethany when Jesus raised Lazarus from the dead. Caught up by the enthusiasm of the crowds welcoming Jesus, they were encouraged to tell others what they had seen at Lazarus's tomb. The imperfect tense is reflected in the NIV translation, "continued to spread the word" (literally, "continued bearing witness," *martureō*). When persons' lives have been touched by Christ's resurrection power, it is hard for them to keep silent about it.

12:18   It appears that two groups of people welcomed Jesus at His royal entry. There were those who followed Him from Bethany and those who came out from Jerusalem to meet Him (Matt. 21:9; Mark

11:9). Verse 18 refers to the latter group, the same crowd referred to in 12:13. This group is distinct from those who were present at the raising of Lazarus (12:17).

Hearing about the great miracle (*sēmeion*) of Lazarus's resurrection, a crowd of people went out to meet Jesus. Like Nicodemus (3:2), they responded to the reported miracles by seeking personal confirmation of those things. Many undoubtedly wondered, *Could this be the Messiah?*

12:19 The Pharisees (cf. 1:24) were not at all pleased when they observed the crowd's enthusiasm for Jesus. It seemed their efforts to diminish His influence (cf. 11:47, 57) were completely unsuccessful. In contrast with their failure was the seeming success of Jesus' ministry. Using strong hyperbole (exaggeration for emphasis), they noted, "Look how the whole world has gone after him!" The word "Look" (*ide*) is used to introduce something unexpected.

THE PREDICTION OF JESUS' DEATH, 12:20-36

Although the royal entry seemed to reflect a positive response to Jesus, He knew that the enthusiasm of the crowd would soon wane in response to the persuasions of the religious leaders. With this in mind, Jesus announced His impending death and expressed His resolve to do the Father's will.

This section serves as a conclusion to Christ's public ministry and is climactic in that it tells of Gentiles seeking Jesus (12:20-21). This development is quite significant in light of John's emphasis on the universal provision of Messiah's saving work (1:11-12; 3:16; 4:42; 5:24; 20:30-31).

12:20 John reports that there were some "Greeks" who had traveled up to Jerusalem to participate in the Passover observance. The term "Greeks" (*hellēnes*) is used to refer to non-Jews, or Gentiles. These Greeks are to be distinguished from the "Grecian Jews" (*hellēnistēs*) mentioned in Acts 6:1 and 9:29. The latter were Jews who spoke Greek rather than Aramaic. The Greeks referred to here were probably God-fearers like Cornelius (Acts 10:1-2). They believed in the God of Israel and desired to worship Him but had not taken the steps necessary to become Jewish proselytes.

12:21 Having heard that Jesus was in Jerusalem, the Greeks approached Philip (1:43) of Bethsaida (1:44), asking to be introduced to Jesus. Why they came to Philip is not revealed in the text. There may have been some previous acquaintance, or perhaps his Greek name attracted their attention. It was a simple and polite request, "Sir, we would like to see Jesus." Perhaps they had heard about Jesus' miracles and teachings and wanted to become acquainted with this messianic figure. Within the framework of John's gospel, the inquiry has a significant theological point. In the words of Morris, "Jesus was the Saviour of the world and this group of Gentiles symbolically represents the world seeking its salvation from Jesus."[7]

The words "Sir, we would like to see Jesus" have often been engraved into pulpits where preachers can be reminded of the ultimate objective—to present Jesus. Every sermon should be evaluated in light of this goal.

12:22 Philip reported the request to Andrew (1:40-41, 44; 6:8-9), another apostle with a Greek name. John does not record why Philip went first to Andrew. Perhaps he was uncertain as to what to do. Jesus had spoken about "other sheep" (10:16) but had not elaborated. Andrew apparently had no solution, and the matter was brought to Jesus.

12:23 Jesus came unto His own Jewish people, and they rejected Him. Now the Gentiles were seeking Him. Jesus highlighted the significance of this turning point with the climactic words "The hour has come for the Son of Man to be glorified." The perfect tense of "has come" (*elēluthen*) suggests the ongoing result of this moment. The word "hour" (*hora*) refers not to the hour of the day but a *time* of crisis. This long awaited hour is mentioned repeatedly by Jesus (2:4; 7:6, 30; 13:1; 17:1). For the messianic designation "Son of Man," see 1:51. The word "glorified" (*doxazō*) speaks of magnifying Jesus through the display of His divine attributes. Within a few days, Jesus' reputation would be enlarged though His sacrificial death and miraculous resurrection.

12:24 Jesus moves to a prediction and analysis of His impending death (12:24-33). He begins with the solemn formula "I tell you the truth" (cf. 1:51). Jesus speaks of death in v. 24 using an agricultural analogy. A kernel of wheat remains singular and solitary unless it "falls to the ground and dies." Jesus' use of the word "dies" may raise some objections. A seed producing life germinates; it does not die. But there is the appearance of death in that the seed is buried. The kernel that "dies" and is buried produces many seeds. In the analogy of the seed, death is the means of producing life. Paul uses a similar illustration in 1 Corinthians 15:36.

---

7. Leon Morris, *The Gospel According to John*, NICNT (Grand Rapids: Eerdmans, 1971), p. 592.

12:25   Jesus goes on in v. 25 to make an application. As with the seed, so with man. There is no fruit-bearing without dying. The man who "loves his life" will lose (literally, "destroy") it. The man who "hates his life will keep it for eternal life." Jesus uses two different words for "life" here. The first two appearances of the word translate the Greek *psuchē*, meaning one's natural life. The second word, *zoē*, is used in connection with the word "eternal" and is used in John of spiritual life—both present and eternal—kingdom life with God (3:16; 5:24; 10:10).

Paradoxically, losing natural life results in gaining spiritual life. Clinging to life in this world means losing life for eternity. Note the vivid contrast reflected in the words "loves" and "hates." The one who loves Christ will recognize spiritual priorities. Things of the world will be hated by comparison. Do we hate the world in comparison to Christ? I am afraid that believers today are much too invested with the world to "hate" it as this comparison urges. Similar teaching was given earlier in Christ's ministry (Matt. 10:39; 16:25; Mark 8:35; Luke 9:24; 17:33).

12:26   Not only is self-sacrifice the way to life (John 12:25), service is the way to honor (12:26). The one who serves Christ must be willing to follow Christ. The present subjunctive of *diakoneō* ("keep on serving") and the present imperative of *akoloutheō* ("keep on following") emphasize the ongoing duty of disciples. The disciple who follows Christ is promised His companionship; the disciple who serves Christ is promised the Father's honor. This verse advances the thought of 12:25, revealing the ultimate results of the two different perspectives on life.

12:27   Having contemplated His approaching death, Jesus realized there were only two alternatives—deliverance from the hour of crisis or glorification of the Father through death. It was a troubling thought, and this is reflected in His own admission "Now my heart is troubled, and what shall I say?" Needless to say, John does not hide the humanity of Christ from his readers. Jesus was "troubled" (*tarassō*), or "disturbed," as He was at the tomb of Lazarus (11:33). The perfect tense means that He had been and still was "troubled." It was a decisive moment. What should He say? How should He respond?

Believers facing an hour of crisis can be encouraged that Jesus faced one too. And by God's enablement He went forward with His life's mission and work.

One possibility was to ask the Father to deliver Him from "the hour," the time of crisis He would face on the cross. But setting that alternative aside, Jesus acknowledged that it was for this very purpose that He came to earth—to suffer and die for sinners. As in the Garden of Gethsemane (Matt. 26:39-42), Jesus wrestled with the will of God and brought Himself into subjection to it.

12:28   The other possibility before Jesus was to pray that His death on the cross would magnify the Father's name. Jesus' decision is reflected in His prayer "Father, glorify your name!" The word *doxazō* suggests that Jesus was asking that the Father's name, or reputation, would be magnified through His sacrificial death on the cross.

After Jesus voiced His commitment to glorify the Father, a voice resounded from heaven, "I have glorified it, and will glorify it again." There were two other occasions in the life of Christ where God spoke from heaven: His baptism (Matt. 3:17; Mark 1:11; Luke 3:22) and His transfiguration (Matt. 17:5; Mark 9:7; Luke 9:35). God had glorified His name in the past through many mighty works; He would glorify it again in the immediate future through the death and resurrection of Jesus.

12:29   The voice from heaven was variously interpreted by the crowd that was with Jesus. Some thought that it was thunder. In the Old Testament thunder is often spoken of as the voice of God (cf. 2 Sam. 22:14; Job 37:4; Ps. 29:3). Others thought an angel had spoken to him. To Jesus the words were clear, but others could not distinguish them. Perhaps a rumble of thunder accompanied the voice and caused people to question what they heard.

12:30   Hearing the people's discussion over the nature of the sound, Jesus settled the issue by calling it a "voice." He then explained that the voice was not for His benefit but for their sakes. This raises the obvious question, If the voice was for their sakes, why didn't they understand what God had said? Their confusion may have been due to their lack of spiritual perception (12:39-40).

12:31   Verses 21-32 present three results of Jesus' death: judgment on the world (v. 31*a*), defeat of Satan (31*b*), and the drawing of men to Christ (v. 32). In spite of the misunderstanding and outright unbelief, Jesus anticipated the victory that would be achieved at the cross. The "judgment on this world" refers to the judgment (*krisis*) on sin and unbelief that would be poured out on Christ (3:17; Rom. 3:25; 2 Cor. 5:21). The "prince" (or "ruler," *archōn*) of this world alludes to

Satan, who rules over the unbelieving world system. For Satan, the cross is a defeat. By Christ's death he was "driven out" (*ekballō*, "to cast out") from his position of power and earthly influence. Paul speaks in Col. 2:15 of Satan and his associates having been "disarmed" by the cross. This is the beginning of a series of judgments that will conclude with Satan's being cast into the lake of fire (Rev. 20:7-10).

12:32   Jesus once again anticipated being "lifted up" (3:14; 8:28). The words speak of His crucifixion, as John explains (12:33), but probably more. His crucifixion would be followed by His resurrection and ascension. On the basis of His triumph over death and exaltation to heaven Jesus will "draw all men" to Himself.

The "all men" (*pantas*) does not mean that all will be saved (3:16-18). Certainly, those who resist His call to salvation will face Him one day in judgment (5:28-29). Perhaps the "all men" refers not to a universal encounter (either salvation or judgment) but to a universal opportunity. Bruce suggests, "This, then, is his answer to the request of the Greeks: in a short time, they may come to him as freely as (at present) his Jewish disciples do. His death would obliterate all racial and religious barriers."[8] It is exciting to think about heaven as a place where ethnic and cultural differences that tend to separate Christians on earth will dissipate as believers enjoy the fulness of their unity in Christ.

12:33   As is often his custom, John adds a brief explanatory note to the remarks of Jesus (6:6, 71; 11:31, 51; 13:11, 28). Jesus knew of both His coming death and the manner in which He was about to die.

12:34   Jesus' remark about His being lifted up raised a question in the minds of the people. It was their understanding from the "Law" that the Messiah would live and rule forever. The people could not reconcile Jesus' claims as Messiah and this death announcement. Perhaps He was not the Messiah after all.

The term "Law" is used in its widest sense as "Scripture." Commentators suggest that the crowd had in mind such texts as Psalm 89:36; 110:4; Isaiah 9:7; Ezekiel 37:25; and Daniel 7:14. Bampfylde argues convincingly that Psalm 61:6-7 contains all three elements mentioned in the quote: the Christ, remains, and forever, and that this is the Scripture the people had in mind.[9]

---

8. F. F. Bruce, *The Gospel of John: Introduction, Exposition and Notes* (Grand Rapids: Eerdmans, 1983), p. 268.

9. Gillian Bampfylde, "More Light on John 12:34," *Journal for the Study of the New Testament* 17 (1983): 87-89.

There seems to be a note of contempt in their question, "Who is this 'Son of Man'?" "Would the true Messiah come and not stay? What kind of a 'Son of Man' is this anyway?" This difficulty may be the clue as to why the same crowd that hailed Him as king was later that week to cry out for His crucifixion. Jesus simply did not conform to the crowd's messianic expectations. This attitude is often present today as God's self-revelation does not fit secular society's mold.

12:35 Having predicted His coming death, Jesus concluded His interaction with members of the crowd by offering them an invitation to believe in the light. Jesus had made quite clear that He was "the light" (8:12; 9:5). He now warned them that the light of His Person would be available for just a little longer. With His death and ascension, Jesus' physical presence would be removed from the earth. There was only a short time in which to respond to the light available. With that in mind, Jesus exhorted the crowd, "Walk while you have the light, before darkness overtakes you." In understanding this metaphor, it is helpful to note that in ancient cities the streets were dark and shadowy. It would be dangerous in such streets without any light. The expression "walk" is a metaphor of living (cf. Eph. 4:1; 5:2). They needed to respond to the light while it was available. Failure to do so results in "darkness," a metaphor descriptive of the uncertainties and dangers of unbelief.

12:36 With a strong imperative, Jesus exhorted His listeners, "Put your trust in the light while you have it." He was calling for a decision, a step of faith. The invitation is followed in the Greek by a purpose clause, "so that" (*hina*). The expression "sons of light" speaks of those who are characterized by the quality of light (Eph. 5:8; 1 Thess. 5:5). Those who believe will be like Christ. They will be enlightened spiritually and serve as instruments for enlightening others. This was Israel's intended destiny (Isa. 42:6). The people of Israel were to be enlightened and then to share that light with others.

When He finished speaking, Jesus left the crowd and "was hidden from them" (second aorist passive indicative of *kruptō*, "to hide"). This marks a significant transition from Jesus' public to private ministry in the gospel of John. Jesus came as the light, inviting people to believe in Him. But now the light was gone. Unbelievers were left in darkness. Jesus left the crowds to spend the last few days before His death with His disciples.

THE EXPLANATION FOR UNBELIEF, 12:37-43

John the apostle sums up the public ministry of Jesus that had just come to a close and explains the tragedy of the Jews' unbelief.

12:37   In the face of all the miraculous signs (*sēmeia*) Jesus had done to validate His messiahship and deity, most people were not believing in Him. The negative with the imperfect may be rendered "They kept on not believing on him." His miracles could not be denied (7:31; 11:47), but most of the people failed to appreciate their full messianic significance. Unbelief is stubborn and persistent. Only by the grace of God can light break through and penetrate the darkness of the human heart.

12:38   Reflecting on the unbelief of the Jewish people, John still sees God's purposes being fulfilled and accomplished rather than thwarted. The Scripture foretold that many would not believe on the Messiah. The unbelief of the Jews is seen as a direct fulfillment of Isaiah 53:1 and 6:10, quoted by John in vv. 38 and 40, respectively.

The words "This was to fulfill" (*hina*) indicate that divine purpose was involved. In the case of those who chose to disbelieve, God's purposes were accomplished as their unbelief fulfilled Scripture. God's purposes are accomplished, not frustrated, through the opposition and unbelief of evil men.

The Scripture quoted (nearly verbatim from the Septuagint) is Isaiah 53:1. There enlightened Israel, believing Jews of a future day (Zech. 12:10–13:1; Rom. 11:26), laments that so few believed the message concerning Messiah. The rhetorical question is really more of an exclamation designed to call attention to the paucity of true believers among the Jews.[10] The "arm of the Lord," a figure for the Lord's strength, is another way of referring to the "message," the report of a mighty salvation.

12:39   The words "For this reason" (*dia touto*) look back to what precedes in v. 38, whereas "because" (*hoti*) looks ahead to what follows in v. 40. Both emphasize causality and serve to explain the unbelief of the Jewish people. The words "They could not believe" express in the strongest possible terms the sovereignty of God over the Jews' rejection of Christ. Yet the truth of God's absolute sovereignty must always be balanced with the truth of man's responsibility (cf. Acts 2:23). God's sovereignty never does away with the principle of personal accountability.

10. Edward J. Young, *The Book of Isaiah*, 2d ed., NICOT (Grand Rapids: Eerdmans, 1972), 3:340.

12:40   John quotes rather freely from Isaiah to explain further the unbelief of the Jews in his day. The quote appears to be a rather free rendering of Isaiah 6:10—a rendering that does not follow precisely the Septuagint or the Hebrew text. Jesus quotes this same text to explain why He teaches in parables (Matt. 13:14-15), and Paul quotes it to explain the rejection of His preaching by the Jews in Rome (Acts 28:26). Evans suggests that John composed the quotation from several related Isaianic texts (Isa. 6:10; 29:10; 42:18-19; 56:10) to show that God sovereignly intended to blind the Jewish people to the truth of Jesus' message.[11]

The prophet Isaiah was commissioned to speak in such a way as to harden hearts and render the people unresponsive to God's word in anticipation of their coming judgment (Isa. 6:9-10). Building on this key text, and supplementing it with others, John describes what God had done in Jesus' day. The quotation not only provides scriptural rationale for the Lord's rejection but also shows that this rejection was actually part of God's plan. God had hardened the hearts of the people so that they could not believe in His Son.

This raises all sorts of theological objections such as, "How can God hold people responsible for their unbelief when it has been sovereignly determined by divine election?" There are mysterious matters for which God has not provided complete answers. Believers can be assured, however, that God is good, loving, and just. None of His sovereign actions will contradict those attributes. Nor will God's sovereignty contradict human responsibility. A comment from Morris may be helpful at this point:

> But when John quotes "he hath blinded their eyes . . ." he does not mean that the blinding takes place without the will or against the will of these people. So with the hardening of their heart. These men chose evil. It was their own deliberate choice, their own fault. Make no mistake about that. Throughout his Gospel John has insisted upon the seriousness of the decision forced on the Jews by the presence of Jesus, on their responsibility, and on their guilt. He is not now removing all that.[12]

---

11. Craig A. Evans, "The Function of Isaiah 6:9-10 in Mark and John," *Novum Testamentum* 24 (1982): 124-38.

12. Morris, *The Gospel According to John*, p. 604.

If Christians have a problem with God's sovereignty in accomplishing His purposes even through man's unbelief, perhaps it is because they conceive of Him as a little less than God. In a world of precision and accuracy believers must beware of theologizing away the mystery of the Godhead.

12:41   Referring once again to the prophecies of Isaiah, John comments, "Isaiah said this because he saw Jesus' glory and spoke about him." The account is recorded in Isaiah 6:1-4. There Isaiah tells of his vision of the glorious Lord sitting on His throne in the Temple. What Isaiah saw, declares John, was none other than the preincarnate Messiah. Isaiah, like Abraham (John 8:56), saw the coming of Christ.

12:42   In spite of the general rejection of Jesus by the Jewish people of His day, John reports that many, even among the religious leaders, believed in Him. Unbelief prevailed, but not without exception. Nicodemus and Joseph of Arimathea apparently believed (John 7:50; 19:38). John indicates there may have been others. But because of the outspoken views of the Pharisees (7:47-49), they were fearful of making an open profession of their faith. For the threat of being "put out of the synagogue," see comments on 9:22.

12:43   John comments rather frankly regarding the unwillingness of those secret believers to make their faith known. They "loved praise from men more than praise from God." Putting it another way, they valued their reputation among men more than the approval that comes from God. Many opportunities of witness are lost in attempting to maintain man's approval and praise.

THE CONSEQUENCES OF UNBELIEF, 12:44-50

Verses 44-50 summarize the key elements of the message Jesus had been proclaiming for the previous three and one-half years. Some scholars suggest that these verses are not in the proper place because v. 36 indicates the conclusion of Jesus' public ministry. However, there is no textual evidence for placing them anywhere else. It is more likely that the words were spoken earlier but inserted here as an appropriate summary of Jesus' message.

12:44   The word "then" (*de*) may be misleading if it is taken to refer to the immediate occasion of 12:20-43. The particle *de* may be translated "but" when a contrast is clearly implied, or as a simple connective "and." Frequently it cannot be translated at all, which may be the case here. The words "cried out" speak of public teaching. The expression is used when Jesus taught in the Temple (7:37).

The message is one that had been emphasized earlier (5:36; 8:19). Belief in Jesus implies, even demands, belief in the Father who sent Him. Jesus came as the Father's representative. To believe in the Son in a genuine and regenerating way is to believe in the Father also.

12:45   Verse 45 is parallel in thought with verse 44. As believing in the Son means believing in the Father, so to see the Son is to see the Father who sent him (cf. 14:9).

12:46   The grand theme of Christ the light appears once again (1:4, 9; 3:19; 8:12; 9:5; 12:35). Jesus came as the light (*phos*). Belief in His Person removes one from the sphere of spiritual darkness to the realm of spiritual light. All were once in darkness. But because the light has come, darkness is a choice, not a necessity.

12:47   Rejection of Christ the light results in judgment (5:45). Jesus distinguishes here between obeying His words and merely hearing them (cf. Matt. 7:24-27; Luke 6:47-49; James 1:22-25). The one who hears and refuses to obey stands under God's judgment, apart from any sentence of condemnation by Jesus (John 3:18).

It may be troubling to see in John some passages that indicate Jesus acts as judge (5:22, 27; 8:16, 26) and other texts that indicate He does not (3:17; 8:15; 12:47). The apparent contradiction may be resolved by distinguishing between purpose and result. The purpose of the sun is to provide light. When that purpose is thwarted, a shadow results. Jesus' purpose was to bring salvation to the world. Therefore, judgment is the inevitable result or outcome of rejecting this gracious provision.

12:48   Although Jesus did not come for the specific purpose of functioning as judge of the world, those who reject His saving provision will face judgment. That very word that Christ spoke will be used to condemn (*krinō*) unbelievers in "the last day," the day of resurrection and final judgment.

12:49   Verse 49 provides a reason ("For") that those who reject Christ face judgment (12:48). Here Jesus summarizes a theme elaborated in an earlier discourse (5:19-30). Jesus did not speak His own message at His own will. Rather, He spoke what the sending Father commanded. The word of the Son is, therefore, the word of the Father. To reject the word of the Son is to reject the word of the Father who commissioned Him.

12:50   Jesus affirms that the "command" (*entolē*), or message, of the Father leads to eternal life. The phrase "eternal life" (*zōē aiōnios*) occurs seventeen times in the gospel of John in comparison with only eight occurrences in the synoptics. Eternal life is life with God, life with blessing, life that precludes perishing. It was the great mission of Jesus to provide eternal life to those who would receive the gift. John's purpose in writing the gospel was to bring the readers to eternal life through faith in Jesus (20:30-31).

In the last sentence of v. 50 Jesus once again expresses His submission to the Father (5:19, 30; 6:38). Plummer comments, "The revelation comes from the Father, the external expression of it from the Son."[13]

Thus concludes a major division of John's gospel (chaps. 5-12). His public ministry is over. John devotes the next major section of the gospel to a private ministry Jesus had with a select group of disciples in the Upper Room on the night before His death.

HOMILETICAL SUGGESTIONS

Although it contains no signs or "I am's," chapter 12 is crucial to the development of John's gospel. The chapter highlights the crisis (12:33) that led to a key turning point in Jesus' career.

The royal entry of Jesus (12:12-19) serves as an excellent Palm Sunday text. The passage recounts how Jesus came into Jerusalem in fulfillment of messianic prophecy. Here we see great rejoicing and expressions of worship. The text could be used to emphasize the enthusiasm and excitement of creative and spontaneous worship. Is our worship motivated by encouraging circumstances, or is it based on God's character alone? Is our worship superficial and temporary, or genuine and lasting?

John 12:37-43 highlights God's sovereignty over belief and unbelief. Are God's purposes thwarted by the world's unbelief? No! God is so absolutely sovereign over His creation that His purposes are accomplished even through the spiritual hardness and unbelief of ungodly people. This teaching can be a source of comfort when it seems the world has spun out of control.

Verses 44-50 summarize the message Jesus preached for three and one-half years. This text sets forth the requirement of faith and the consequences of unbelief. It would serve well as an evangelistic text or as a summary of the gospel.

13. A. Plummer, *The Gospel According to St. John* (Cambridge: At the University Press, 1899), p. 260.

JOHN

CHAPTER

THIRTEEN

DINNER DIALOGUE

THE STRENGTHENING OF BELIEF, CHAPS. 13-17

The last conversation with a loved one is remembered and cherished long after that person's death. So it is with the Upper Room discourse, the last instructions of Jesus to His disciples before His crucifixion. In this discourse Jesus seeks to strengthen the disciples' faith in preparation for the challenges soon to follow.

In His farewell discourse Jesus taught the disciples many great principles of the Christian faith, including servanthood, love, heaven, the Holy Spirit, peace, fruit-bearing, persecution, witness, joy, victory, and prayer. These truths made a difference in the lives of the apostles. Faithfully applied, they will make a difference in the lives of Christians today.

THE EXAMPLE OF HUMBLE SERVICE, 13:1-17

Although there is common ground between the synoptics and John's account of the events in the Upper Room, the fourth gospel makes some unique contributions, the first of which is the lesson of the foot washing.

THE CIRCUMSTANCES AT THE SUPPER, 13:1-3

13:1 John links this discourse with the Jewish Passover (*pesach*), one of the three great pilgrim feasts celebrated annually in Jerusalem

237

(cf. Deut. 16:16). It was Thursday evening, April 2, A.D. 33. Earlier in the day Peter and John had made preparations for the Passover Supper (Luke 22:7-8). Such preparations would have included the sacrifice of an unblemished lamb, which was then roasted on a spit so that no bones would be broken (Ex. 12:46). The Passover meal was to be eaten at night within the city of Jerusalem. It was generally a family supper over which the father presided, explaining the meaning of the feast (cf. Ex. 12:26-27; 13:8). Because none of the disciples resided in Jerusalem, they observed the Passover meal in a large, furnished upper room that was made available to them (Luke 22:9-12).

On the night before His death Jesus knew that the hour for His impending death and departure from the world had come (John 12:23). This knowledge prompted Christ's crowning display of His love for His own disciples there in the upper room. John records, "he now showed them the full extent of his love." The NIV renders nicely John's phrase, *eis telos.* Jesus did not simply love them unto the end of His life. He loved "unto the uttermost degree." And He was about to demonstrate something of this love by washing the disciples' feet.

13:2   Verse 2 contains a textual difficulty that involves a single Greek letter but makes a significant difference in translation. The King James reads *deipnou genomenou* (second aorist participle), "supper being ended," whereas the superior manuscript evidence (Codex Sinaiticus and Codex Vaticanus) reads *deipnou ginomenou* (present participle), "when supper was beginning." The context indicates the supper was in progress (13:4, 26) and supports the latter view.[1]

The love of Jesus for His own is set in stark contrast with the selfishness of Judas who had already arranged for Christ's betrayal. John indicates that the devil had prompted (literally, "put into the heart") the betrayal. Although Judas was motivated by money (Matt. 26:15), he was also strongly influenced by Satan (cf. 13:27).

13:3   John reports that as the hour of crisis approached, Jesus was conscious of His authority and His commission. The perfect active participle *eidōs* ("knowing") emphasizes His complete awareness of the situation at hand. In terms of authority, He knew the Father had "put all things under his power" (literally, "into His hands"). God had given Him the authority to give life and execute judgment (John 5:25-27). He knew He had the authority to call upon the angels for deliver-

---

1. Bruce M. Metzger, *A Textual Commentary on the Greek New Testament* (London: United Bible Societies, 1971), p. 239.

ance (Matt. 26:53), but Jesus yielded that prerogative. In terms of His commission, Jesus knew it was from God and that He would return to God with His mission accomplished.

Why does John focus the reader's attention on the fact that Jesus was conscious of His authority and commission? John is about to describe a situation in which Jesus took on a very lowly position. But the apostle does not want the reader to forget that the highest possible place is His by divine right.[2]

Jesus was able to serve in a humble manner because He had a complete grasp of His own spiritual status and the needs of His disciples. A knowledge of who we are in Christ is foundational to any ministry.

THE EXAMPLE OF HUMBLE SERVICE, 13:4-11

To understand the lesson of the foot washing one must appreciate what was going on among the disciples that night. Luke 22:24-27 reports that the disciples were quarrelling among themselves over who was going to be the greatest in Christ's kingdom. Jesus had taught them that greatness in His kingdom comes through serving others (Matt. 20:26-27), but they had apparently not learned the lesson. Now in the upper room Jesus proceeded to give them an unforgettable illustration of this truth.

13:4   In Palestine the roads are dusty, and though guests would normally bathe before a social gathering like Passover, after a walk across the city their feet would be dirty. A basin of water and towels were customarily placed at the door of a home for washing. The task of washing guests' feet was generally assigned to a household servant. A basin of water and towel had been left in the upper room for the disciples use, but not one of them had taken on the responsibility for washing the others' feet. They were too busy thinking of themselves to think of others.

Rising from the Passover supper, Jesus took off His outer robe and wrapped Himself with a large towel. In describing this scene, John uses present tense in a dramatic sense, that is, "He rises; He takes off." Jesus was about to assume a servant's task and dressed appropriate to the position.

13:5   Jesus poured (literally, "pours") the water into a basin. Once again, the dramatic present is in use. After pouring water into the ba-

2. Leon Morris, *The Gospel According to John*, NICNT (Grand Rapids: Eerdmans, 1971), p. 615.

sin, Jesus began to wash the disciples' feet. Jesus was illustrating the truth He had taught the Passover pilgrims en route to Jerusalem, "the Son of Man did not come to be served, but to serve," (Matt. 20:28; cf. Luke 22:27). John's description of Jesus' example of supreme condescension illustrates the statement of Philippians 2:7 that Jesus took "the very nature of a servant." *Niptō* ("wash") is a common term for washing parts of the body like hands and feet.

13:6   The disciples must have been quiet as they watched the Master doing servants' work. Then He approached Simon Peter, who challenged the procedure. The Greek reflects a strong contrast between "you" (Jesus) and "my" (Peter). It was not the time or place for foot washing (the supper had already begun), nor was Jesus the one to do it.

13:7   Jesus explained to Peter that although His intended purpose was not immediately clear, he would understand (*ginōskō*) later (literally, "after these things"). Although the indefinite time note "later" could refer to the Spirit's illumination of Jesus' teaching after Pentecost (cf. 14:26; 16:13), the context would suggest that Jesus had something more immediate in mind. He would explain to Peter after He finished the foot washing (13:12).

13:8   Peter continued to protest what he regarded as an inappropriate procedure. Using the strongest possible form of the negative (*ou mē*), Peter declared, "No, you shall never wash my feet." Commentators have debated the meaning of Jesus' response, "Unless I wash you, you have no part with me." The context suggests that "wash" (*niptō*) must refer to the washing of feet, but some believe that a double meaning is present. Morris believes the words point to a "washing free from sin."[3] Tenney interprets Jesus to refer to the need for "cleansing" Peter's personality to make him fit for the kingdom.[4] Westcott argues that Jesus is referring to "self-surrender" as the first condition of discipleship.[5]

Students of Scripture must avoid such speculation and interpret the passage quite literally. In washing the disciples feet, Jesus was serving. He had come for this very purpose (Mark 10:45). Peter's refusal of His service was in essence a rejection of Christ's Person. Jesus was saying, "Peter, if you do not receive My ministry, of which this

3. Ibid, p. 617.
4. Merrill C. Tenney, "The Gospel of John," in *The Expositor's Bible Commentary*, ed. Frank Gaebelein (Grand Rapids: Zondervan, 1981), 9:136.
5. B. F. Westcott, *The Gospel According to St. John* (Grand Rapids: Eerdmans, 1973), p. 191.

foot washing is a mere token, then you are guilty of rejecting my Person and cannot be My disciple."

Sometimes it is easier for us to serve rather than be served. It is easier to take a meal to a sick church member than to receive one graciously when we are not well. Pride may be the key factor that keeps believers from accepting God's gifts in such situations.

13:9   Peter, a man of deep sincerity but inclined toward extremes, replied, "Then, Lord, not just my feet but my hands and my head as well!" Under no circumstances did Peter want to be guilty of rejecting the Person of Christ. If a foot washing was necessary, he would gladly take it a step or two further and include his "hands" and "head."

13:10   Jesus patiently reminded Peter that one who has already bathed (perfect passive participle of *louō*, "to bathe the body") needs only to wash (first aorist middle infinitive of *piptō*, "to wash parts of the body") his feet in order to be completely clean. There is some debate among textual scholars whether the phrase *ei mē tous podas* (NIV, "only his feet") should be included or omitted. John Christopher Thomas argues that the support in favor of inclusion is strong, early, and well-distributed.[6] The omission of the phrase may have been due to the difficulty in reconciling the words "needs only to wash his feet" with "his whole body is clean."

In the last part of the verse Jesus elevates the conversation from the discussion of physical footwashing to the spiritual realm. "And you are clean, though not every one of you." The disciples were "clean" (*katharos*), a metaphor of spiritual purity reflective of a life of faith (cf. 15:3). Judas was the one exception to this "clean" condition. John elaborates on this in the next verse.

Many expositors interpret 13:10 to teach the need for confession and cleansing from sin. The word "bathed" (*louō*) is interpreted to refer to the washing of regeneration (Titus 3:5), and the word "washed" (*niptō*) would point to the cleansing of 1 John 1:9. Accordingly, Jesus would be teaching, "If you have 'bathed' (i.e.,'been regenerated'), then you need only to be 'washed' (cleansed from sin through confession)."

Granted, there is a difference between the Greek words translated "washed" and "bathed." "Washed" (*louo*) speaks of washing the

---

6. John Christopher Thomas, "A Note on the Text of John 13:10," *Novum Testamentum* 24 (1987): 46-52.

entire body, whereas "bathed" (*niptō*) usually refers to washing a part of the body. But what logic compels the interpreter to see spiritual cleansing as the point of the passage? Although the bathing and washing imagery could well illustrate the teaching of Titus 3:5 and 1 John 1:9, spiritual cleansing from sin is not the point of this passage (cf. 13:12-17). First, Jesus was dealing with the problem of humility, not sin. Second, in His explanation Jesus makes no reference to the washing of regeneration or the cleansing from sin. Third, Jesus commanded His disciples to follow His example (12:14-15, 17), and they have no authority to cleanse others from sin. Fourth, Judas' feet were washed, yet he was unsaved. There was no cleansing from the defilement of sin in his case.

13:11   John explains the comment made by Jesus, "And you are clean, though not every one of you." The single exception was Judas. The present participle of *paradidōmi* is used to describe Judas as "the one betraying him," indicating that Judas was already engaged in the betrayal. He had made plans to hand Jesus over to the religious authorities (cf. Matt. 26:14-16).

THE EXPLANATION OF THE FOOT WASHING, 13:12-17

A foundational principle of hermeneutics is, "Do not add to the interpretation when an explanation is given in the text." Another helpful guide is, "Always prefer the clear meaning over an obscure interpretation." Applying these principles to John 13:4-11 one discovers in Jesus' own explanation (13:12-20) that the foot washing teaches a simple but profound lesson concerning the humble service each believer ought to pursue. What is emphasized here is the attitude of service that is to be manifested in daily Christian living.

13:12   When He had finished washing the disciples feet, Jesus returned to the table and began to probe the disciples, "Do you understand what I have done for you?" Obviously, they did not (cf. 13:7). Jesus asked this leading question to prepare them to receive the explanation He was about to provide.

13:13   Jesus reminded the disciples how they had addressed Him with such honorable terms as "Teacher" (*ho didaskalos*) and "Lord" (*ho kurios*). These were the ordinary titles of respect used to address a rabbi. Such designations were appropriate and in keeping with His dignity and position. The term "Lord" (*kurios*) may be a reference to Jesus' deity (cf. 20:28).

13:14   Jesus proceeded to make a personal application. If one with such dignity and position was willing to take the role of a servant and wash their feet, then the disciples should certainly be willing to "wash one another's feet." The argument here is from the greater to the lesser. If the greater (Jesus) serves (the condition of first class, indicated by *ei*, assumes the truth of the premise), certainly the disciples (the lesser) should be willing to serve.

13:15   Explaining the act of foot washing, Jesus declared, "I have set you an example that you should do as I have done for you." The word "example" (*hupodeigma*) is the key to the lesson Jesus was teaching. The Greek word *hupodeigma* means a "token" or "pattern" and is often used of something that should spur others to imitate the example. The term is used of Eleazar, a noble teacher of the law, who chose martyrdom rather than swallow pig's flesh (2 Macc. 6:31). In the foot washing, Jesus gave the disciples something to pattern their lives after. (In the Greek, "do" is present tense, "keep on doing.") It is significant that Jesus did not use the word *tupos*, which would refer to an exact replica. Jesus was not asking the disciples to replicate His specific actions, i.e., "wash feet." Rather, He was calling them to follow His humble pattern of serving others exemplified in the foot washing.

There is no evidence in the book of Acts that foot washing was practiced by the disciples or the early church. The reference in 1 Timothy 5:10 refers not to a rite of foot washing and should be interpreted as a metaphor of humble service. However, an actual foot washing can be used as a memorable illustration of servant leadership in the context of a church service or deacons' retreat. My children have never forgotten when a missionary couple washed their feet to illustrate the kind of work the missionaries' anticipated in their overseas ministry. Nor have I forgotten when my feet were washed by a beloved student after three weeks of ministry in Asia.

13:16   Jesus reminds His followers of their status as servants and messengers. The slave is not greater than his master, nor is a messenger greater than the one who sends him. The word "messenger" is the word *apostolos*, from which the English word *apostle* ("sent one") is derived. The point is that if Christ the Master serves, how much more ought the disciples to serve. Rather than seeking the honors due Christ, disciples should serve others with an attitude of humility (cf. John 3:26-30).

Humility involves the simple recognition that we are what we are and are able to do what we do only by the grace of God. My teaching, preaching, and writing does not reflect my own intelligence or ability, but God's gifting of a lowly clay pot He has chosen to use for His glory.

The saying "no servant is greater than his master" occurs four times in the gospels, but each in a different context (cf. Matt. 10:24; 15:20; Luke 6:40). This appears to have been one of Christ's frequent sayings. The words "I tell you the truth" reflect its importance (cf. John 1:51).

13:17   Jesus remarks in v. 17 regarding the blessing enjoyed by those who practice His teachings. The word "blessed" (*makarios*) literally means "happy." It is great to know the teachings of Jesus about humble service to others, but there is no blessing or happiness where these truths are not applied. Truth is not revealed by God as an end in itself. As D. L. Moody once said, "The Scriptures were not given for our information, but for our transformation." The present subjunctive of *poieō* ("to do") may be better translated, "keep on doing." Jesus is referring to the works that accompany regenerating faith (James 1:22-25).

THE PREDICTION OF JESUS' BETRAYAL, 13:18-30

John returns in this section to the matter of Judas, the betrayer (13:11). Jesus predicted the betrayal by Judas and dismissed him from the upper room before continuing His teaching.

THE ANNOUNCEMENT TO THE DISCIPLES, 13:18-22

13:18   The betrayal by Judas came as no surprise to Jesus. He knew Judas' heart from the beginning (cf. 6:64, 70). The words, "I am not referring to all of you," introduce Jesus' next words, although the topic is not completely new to the conversation. Jesus made it clear that He was not deceived by Judas. He knew the hearts of the men "chosen" to be with Him. He made a sovereign decision to include Judas among the twelve. This served to fulfill Scripture (*graphē*). Jesus quoted from the Hebrew text of Psalm 41:9 as finding its ultimate fulfillment in His betrayal by Judas.

Eating bread with someone is a picture of fellowship. To eat someone's bread is to receive hospitality. The background of the metaphor "lifted up his heel" is uncertain. Some commentators suggest it refers to a horse's hoof lifted in preparation to kick. Others believe it refers to tripping with the heel. The Psalms quotation paints a graphic picture of treachery against one who has provided close fellowship and hospitality.

13:19   Jesus explains to His disciples that He told them of the impending treachery of Judas so that their faith would be strengthened rather than shaken when the events transpired. The content of their faith is reflected in the words, "that I am He." The words "I am He" (*egō eimi*) are used by Jesus in John's gospel to refer to His deity (4:26; 8:24, 28, 58). By revealing His betrayal beforehand, Jesus wanted the disciples to know that He was God. The words "you will believe" are in the present tense and could be rendered "you will keep on believing."

13:20   Some might conclude that the treachery announced in v. 18 might mean an end to the disciples' work. But Jesus implied that their commission was still in force. Once again Jesus emphasized the oneness of the disciples with Christ and the oneness of the Father and Son (Matt. 10:40). Those who accept the disciples as Christ's spokesmen and representatives are in fact accepting Christ. And those who accept Christ are accepting the Father who sent him. The word "accepts" (*lambanō*), used four times here, may be understood in this context in the sense of "to welcome." For the solemn introductory phrase, see John 1:51.

13:21   For the third time in the upper room Jesus referred to the betrayer (13:10, 18). Now He became much more specific. John's comment, "Jesus was troubled in spirit," reflects the human emotions Jesus was feeling at this time (cf. 11:33). The words "I tell you the truth" reflect the solemnity of what He was about to disclose.

This verse may serve as an encouragement to those who have been betrayed by a friend, a business partner, or a spouse. It is a sad thing to have one's trust violated and exploited. But we are not alone when such things happen. Jesus has been there. He has experienced betrayal too.

13:22   The disciples were undoubtedly shocked to hear Jesus say, "One of you is going to betray me" (13:21). As the disciples looked about the room at each other, none could comprehend who would do such a thing. The synoptics report that each disciple responded, one after another, "Surely not I, Lord?" (Matt. 26:22; Mark 14:19).

THE IDENTITY OF THE BETRAYER, 13:23-27

An understanding of the cultural situation is of great help in interpreting v. 23 and understanding the dynamics of the narrative that follows. In first-century Palestine the triclinium was coming into use. A triclinium was a low, rectangular dining table around which couches were arranged on three of the four sides. The fourth side, the "foot" of the table, was left open so that food could be served. Guests would eat in a reclining position around the table. A cushion would be provided for the left arm. The right arm would then be free to reach for food on the low table. Of the three positions around the table, the middle position (opposite the "foot" of the table) was regarded as the most honorable. It was here at the "head" of the table that the principal guests would recline.[7] The reference to the reclining position of the disciples around the table suggests that the Passover meal with Jesus was observed in triclinium fashion.

It is safe to assume that Jesus would be situated at the head of the table as the principal guest. To His right and left were the principal places of honor (cf. Mark 10:35-37). To His right, in the place of special honor reclined the apostle John (John 13:23). On His left, in the next highest place, was Judas, the betrayer (13:26). With this cultural situation in mind, one is better able to follow the narrative.

13:23   The "disciple whom Jesus loved" is described as reclining next to Him (literally, "in the sphere of [*en*] his breast"). The disciple "whom Jesus loved" is identified in 21:20, 24 as the author of the gospel, the apostle John. John must have sensed a close relationship with Jesus and repeatedly uses this designation to refer to Himself (19:26; 20:2; 21:7). He loved Jesus and sensed that his love was reciprocated. John was just to the right of Jesus, who was propped up on His left elbow. John's back was in close proximity to (*en*, "in the sphere of") Jesus' breast or chest (*kolpos*).

13:24   Simon Peter was apparently reclining on one of the side tables near John but was not in a suitable position to carry on a conversation with Jesus. He was troubled by the announcement of the betrayal and wanted the culprit identified. Getting John's attention, he said, "Ask him which one he means."

13:25   In order to speak privately with someone to your left at a triclinium you would lean back and speak over your right shoulder. Leaning back in this manner, a guest would be nearly "reclining upon [*epi*] the breast" of his neighbor to the left, which is exactly how the

7. Ralph Gower, *The New Manners and Customs of Bible Times* (Chicago: Moody, 1987), p. 247; J. Robert Teringo, *The Land and People Jesus Knew* (Minneapolis: Bethany House, 1985), p. 53.

Greek text renders v. 25. Leaning back toward Jesus in this manner, John asked the question, "Lord, who is it?" The source of this question was not idle curiosity or meddling. Both Peter and John were concerned for the personal well-being of Jesus.

13:26   Jesus responded by telling John that He would identify the betrayer by giving him a piece of bread (*psōmion*) after dipping it in the dish. The giving of a morsel of bread at a feast was a traditional expression of love and friendship in biblical times. It was given as a mark of special respect and a manifestation of good will. In giving the morsel of bread to Judas, Jesus may have been making one final appeal for him to repent.

The morsel given to Judas may be identified with the "sandwich" made from two pieces of unleavened bread (*matzah*) and bitter herbs (*maror*). The "sandwich" was then dipped in the *charoseth*, a mixture of chopped apples, nuts, and spices representing the clay from which the Israelites made bricks for pharaoh. This was eaten in memory of the first-century rabbi Hillel, who ate the paschal lamb literally "upon" unleavened bread and bitter herbs (based on the Hebrew preposition *'al* ["upon"] in the command of Ex. 12:8).[8]

Judas is distinguished from the other disciples by name (cf. Luke 6:16) by the epithet "Iscariot." This may be a Hellenized form of the Hebrew *ish Kerioth*, "man of Kerioth." If Judas came from the Judean city of Kerioth (about 14 miles south of Hebron), he was the only one of the disciples who was not a Galilean (cf. Acts 1:11). Another possibility is that "Iscariot" is related to the Latin term *sicarius*, used as the designation of a radical Zealot, a member of that party of Jewish patriots who so zealously and violently opposed Roman rule in Palestine (cf. Josephus *Jewish Wars* 4.160-61; 7.268-74). Members of the *sicarii* armed themselves with a *sica*, or "dagger," which they concealed in their robes and used in crowded market places on community leaders and public officials not sympathetic to their cause (*Jewish Wars* 2.254-57).[9] At least one of the twelve, Simon, is designated a "Zealot" (cf. Matt. 10:4; Mark 3:18).

13:27   After Judas received the morsel of bread from Jesus, John reports that "Satan entered into him." John records in 13:2 that the devil put it into the heart of Judas to betray Jesus. At this point, Satan

---

8. *The Jewish Encyclopedia*, 1905 ed., s.v. "Seder," 11:146.

9. For a discussion of the relationship between the terms *Zealot* and *sicarri*, see F. F. Bruce, *New Testament History* (Garden City, N.Y.: Doubleday, Anchor Books, 1972), pp. 98-100.

(*satanas*) apparently took possession of Judas to accomplish the evil deed.

Knowing full well Judas's plans to betray Him, Jesus commanded, "What you do, do quickly." These words set into motion a chain of events that would ultimately result in Jesus' crucifixion.

THE DEPARTURE OF JUDAS, 13:28-30

The departure of Judas from the upper room enabled Jesus to devote His attention to instructing His faithful disciples on truths that would sustain them after His death.

13:28 Those reclining at the Passover table did not understand the meaning or significance of Jesus' words. It seems as though John himself failed to comprehend what was going on. If he had, perhaps some action would have been taken to thwart the plans of Judas. It is not that the disciples were dull. They simply did not have the understanding of the events, which comes with time and perspective.

13:29 Some of the disciples thought that because Judas had charge of the disciples' money bag (cf. 12:6), Jesus had directed him to go and buy something necessary for the feast or to give alms to the poor. Alms giving was regarded, along with prayer and fasting, as one of the three great pillars of Jewish piety (cf. Tobit 12:8).

13:30 John reports that Judas left the upper room as soon as he had taken the morsel from Jesus. The apostle adds a brief note, "and it was night." Was it necessary to tell the readers of the gospel that it was dark outside on Passover evening? In view of the light vs. darkness contrast reflected in John's writings (cf. 1:4-5; 3:19-21; 8:12; 12:35-36; 1 John 1:5-7; 2:8-11), it is likely that he intended this as a theological commentary on the state of Judas's soul. Judas had cut himself off from Jesus, the light of the world, and had entered the realm of impenetrable spiritual darkness.

Every person must make the choice of whether to accept the redemption of God's promised one or to remain in the darkness of unbelief. Judas made the choice and must face the consequences. For others, there is yet opportunity to repent.

THE PREPARATION FOR DEPARTURE, 13:31–14:31

This section of the discourse is occupied with answering the disciples' questions regarding the announcement of His departure to heaven (13:33). Here Jesus teaches his disciples through dialogue. He makes statements that raise questions and provide Him the opportunity to give instruction.

THE NEW COMMANDMENT, 13:31-35

The betrayal by Judas was a sin against love. Instead of showing love for the one who had extended grace and friendship, Judas responded with deception and hostility. It is in the context of Judas's sin against love that Jesus reveals to His disciples the mark of the Christian.

13:31   The departure of Judas from the upper room initiated a sequence of events that would result in Jesus' death and glorification. Thus Jesus declares, "Now is the Son of Man glorified and God is glorified in him." The word "now" (*nun*) indicates that the process of glorification had commenced. The word "glorify" (*doxazō*) means to magnify or increase the estimation in which one is held. Jesus acknowledges that His sacrificial death will magnify His reputation and God the Father's as well. For the term "Son of Man," see comments on 1:51.

13:32   The first phrase in v. 32, "If God is glorified in him," is uncertain because the words are omitted in the best Greek manuscripts. The words may have been accidentally left out in transcription due to repetition (cf. 13:31). On the other hand, the words may have been deliberately deleted because of supposed redundancy of thought. Yet, there is a logical connection expressed between the glorification in v. 31 and the glorification in v. 32, and such step-parallelism is characteristic of John's writings.[10] The "if" clause is assumed as true (a first class condition), and so the text could be translated, "Since God will be glorified in Him, God will glorify the Son in Himself." As the Father is glorified in the Son through His passion, so the Father will glorify the Son. The glorification of the Son will take place "at once," an apparent allusion to the resurrection that followed three days after Christ's death. The Son will be glorified by the Father without delay.

13:33   Here Jesus again announces His imminent departure from the earth and speaks of His separation from His beloved disciples, which would follow His return to heaven. He had spoken of this departure to the Jews at the Feast of Tabernacles (cf. 7:33-34; 8:21-22),

---

10. Bruce Metzger, *A Textual Commentary on the Greek New Testament* (London: United Bible Societies, 1971), p. 242.

but now He repeated the announcement for the benefit of the disciples. The expression of endearment "My children" (*teknia*) reflects Jesus' fatherly affection for His disciples, who will be somewhat orphaned by His departure. Although the expression appears nowhere else in the gospels, it occurs frequently in 1 John (2:1, 12, 28; 3:7, 18; 4:4; 5:21). Jesus instructed His disciples that there would be a time of separation due to His death and departure to the Father. His statement "Where I am going, you cannot come" raised some key questions in the minds of the disciples—questions Jesus would respond to in the dialogue that followed (13:36–14:24).

13:34   Jesus introduces the disciples to the command to "love one another" (cf. 15:12). The word Jesus uses for "love" is *agapaō* and refers in this context to a volitional love that can be commanded. Jesus is not speaking of a merely emotional attachment or personal affection, but rather a commitment that seeks the ultimate good of the other person—even to the point of personal sacrifice. The present tense of *agapaō* calls attention to the continuous nature of the action, that is, "keep on loving."

Jesus calls this "a new command." But the command itself is not new. God had instructed His people through Moses, "love your neighbor as yourself" (Lev. 19:18). So what is "new" about the "new command"? It is the measure of the love "as I have loved you" that made Jesus' command "new" or "fresh" (*kainos*). John records that Jesus loved His own to the point of sacrificing His life (John 10:11; 15:12-13). Paul describes the same kind of sacrificial love in Ephesians 5:1-2. The measure of the disciples' love for others is determined by Christ's love for them.

13:35   Jesus points out that *agapē*, "sacrificial commitment" for one another, is to be the distinguishing mark of His followers. Their love for one another will identify Christ's disciples to all the world. Note that an "if" (*ean*) is involved. The new commandment can be violated. Believers can sin against love even as unbelieving Judas did. On the other hand, if the command is followed, those who "love" will identify themselves to the world as Christ's disciples. Francis Schaeffer writes, "The point is that it is possible to be a Christian without showing the mark, but if we expect non-Christians to know that we are Christians, we must show the mark."[11] (I was saddened to hear a Christian say one time that non-Christian friends had treated him in a

---

11. Francis A. Schaeffer, *The Mark of the Christian* (Downers Grove, Ill.: InterVarsity, 1970), p. 8.

more loving manner than many of those in his church. This is the exact opposite of how things ought to be.)

THE QUESTION OF PETER, 13:36–14:4

Jesus had just spoken of His departure from the disciples (13:33). He was going away, and the disciples would not be able to follow. That remark raised a question in the mind of Peter. His question provided Jesus an opportunity to teach something about heaven.

13:36 Picking up on Jesus' word "where" in 13:33, Peter asked the Master, "Lord, where are you going?" Jesus responded but did not immediately answer Peter's question. Instead He explained, "Where I am going, you cannot follow now, but you will follow later." Jesus appears to be telling Peter that they will one day be reunited in heaven. He may also be alluding to Peter's death (cf. 21:18-19).

13:37 Peter, who was determined to remain with Jesus whatever the cost (cf. Matt. 26:31-33), pressed Jesus for an explanation. "Lord, why can't I follow you now?" As if to emphasize his own love and commitment, Peter adds, "I will lay down my life for you." He used words nearly identical to those of the Good Shepherd (John 10:11). Peter undoubtedly meant what he said (cf. 18:10-11), but he overestimated the strength of his own commitment (cf. Matt. 26:56, 69-75).

13:38 Jesus picked up on Peter's words and challenged his boast of loyalty. Introducing the solemn announcement with the words "I tell you the truth" (cf. John 1:51), Jesus declared, "before the rooster crows, you will disown me three times!"

Both Luke and John record the prediction of Peter's triple denial in the upper room, but Matthew and Mark indicate that it occurred on the way to Gethsemane (Matt. 26:30-35; Mark 14:26-30). It is possible that the prediction was repeated.

HOMILETICAL SUGGESTIONS

John 13 is a rich text for preachers. Verses 4-11 present a vivid illustration of what the word *ministry* is all about. The ministry is not just preaching, teaching, or going on a mission. By Jesus' own explanation (vv. 12-17), the ministry is service. It is humble service. It is service to others. And it is service that issues in blessing.

The prediction of the betrayal of Judas (13:18-30) provides an opportunity to speak on what it means to be a genuine friend, not just a casual associate. Friendship involves faithfulness and loyalty. These qualities were lacking in Judas. There was no genuine love for Jesus in his heart. The words "and it was night" present a powerful image of Judas's choice for the world's darkness over against the light offered by Jesus.

The new commandment (13:31-35) is a wonderful text for any season, but it fits well in the middle of February when people are thinking about Valentines and romantic love. Here we see that the biblical concept of love is far different from the silly sentimentalism associated with February 14. The love Christ calls for is expressed in lasting committment and personal sacrifice.

John 13:36–14:4 is a literary unit dealing with Peter's question, "Lord, where are you going." This text provides an excellent opportunity to speak on our heavenly home. This is further discussed in the homiletical suggestions for chapter 14.

JOHN
CHAPTER
FOURTEEN

QUESTIONS FOR THE MASTER

In John 14 Jesus continues his response to Peter's question, "Lord, where are you going?" (13:36). He goes on in the chapter to raise other questions and provide instruction concerning obedience, prayer, the Holy Spirit, and peace.

THE QUESTION OF PETER (CONT.), 13:36–14:4

14:1 Jesus' announcement of His departure (13:33) and prediction of Peter's denial (13:38) brought an atmosphere of gloom to the upper room. Some sense of anxiety must have been evident on the faces of the disciples. Jesus immediately sought to deal with this concern and went on to answer Peter's question (13:36).

He commanded His disciples, "Do not let your hearts be troubled." The word "trouble" (*tarassō*) is used by Jesus in 11:33 and 13:31. He knew what it was like to have a troubled heart and sought to correct this among His disciples. The negative particle *mē* with the imperative means "stop (what you are doing)." Their concern and anxiety was to cease.

Because the indicative and the imperative take the same form in the second person plural, the second half of the verse can be translated four different ways: (1) Trust in God; trust also in Me, (2) You are trusting in God; you are also trusting in Me, (3) Trust in God; you are also trusting in Me, and (4) You are trusting in God, trust also in Me. The imperative is probably intended in both occurrences of *pisteuō*.

253

The thrust of the commands would be, "Keep on trusting in God and in Me, His Son." Jesus was simply exhorting the disciples to "keep the faith." Continued trust in the Father and Son is a divine antidote to discouragement and despair.

14:2 Verse 2 contains the long-awaited answer to Peter's question, "Lord, where are you going?" (13:36). On the day of His royal entry into Jerusalem, Jesus had said, "Where I am, my servant also will be" (12:26). He now elaborates further on that statement. Jesus explains that He is returning to His "Father's house" to prepare a place for the disciples. In 2:16 Jesus refers to the Jerusalem Temple as "my Father's house." But here He refers to a place clearly not earthly. Jesus had instructed His disciples to pray, "Our Father in heaven" (Matt. 6:9). The "Father's house" is obviously in heaven. The "house" (*oikia*) is made up of many "rooms" (NIV), or "dwelling places" (NASB). The Greek word *monē* appears only here and in v. 23. It is derived from *menō*, "to remain," and can refer to either temporary or permanent dwellings. The latter is suggested in this context. Cook observes, "The picture is of each child having a suite of rooms in the Father's house. All will be with the Father, enjoying His hospitality and sharing His love."[1]

Jesus' words in 14:2 are strikingly similar to words found in a Jewish apocalypse probably written during the century in which Jesus lived, "in the great age many shelters have been prepared for people" (2 Enoch 61:2).[2]

14:3 Jesus goes on to assure His disciples that His departure will not be permanent. Someday Christ will return to take all believers to be with Him in heaven. Note the sequence, "And if I go . . . , I will come back . . . ." His return is as certain as His departure.

Jesus does not elaborate on the details of His *parousia* ("coming") as does Paul in 1 Thessalonians 4:13-18, 2 Thessalonians 2:3-8, and 1 Corinthians 15:51-53. Yet it is helpful to distinguish between the imminent coming of Christ for His church (the rapture) and His second coming to judge the earth and establish His kingdom. Christ will first come for His saints and then, after the seven-year Tribulation, will come with His angels to establish the millennial kingdom (Rev. 19:11–20:4). Whereas the second coming is heralded by many signs (Matt. 24:3-30), the rapture is unannounced and could occur at any time.

1. W. Robert Cook, *The Theology of John* (Chicago: Moody, 1979), pp. 229-30.
2. J. H. Charlesworth, *Jesus Within Judaism* (New York: Doubleday, 1988), pp. ix-x.

The purpose for His departure and His return is reflected in the last clause of the verse (*hina* with the present active subjunctive of *eimi*). Jesus is going away to prepare a heavenly home, and He will come again for His saints so that believers will be with Him forever. This is the ultimate plan of God for His people.

14:4   Having answered Peter's question, "Lord, where are you going?" Jesus advances the discussion a step further. "You know the way to the place where I am going." Although Peter's understanding of heaven was minimal, at least the disciples knew "the way" to get there. Jesus, the master teacher, was "baiting the hook" for further interaction. This statement leads to Thomas's question.

THE QUESTION OF THOMAS, 14:5-7

14:5   Thomas (11:16; 20:26-28) was perplexed by the answer regarding "the place" (14:4) where Jesus was going. Because he did not understand the place, he certainly could not know the way (*tēn hodon*). He took the bait offered by Jesus in v. 4. His question, "How can we know the way?" gives Jesus the opportunity to provide the disciples further instruction.

14:6   Jesus explains to the disciples that He is "the way" (*hē hodos*) to the Father and His heavenly abode. He adds, "No man comes to the Father except through me." Jesus is quite narrow and exclusive on this point. Many say it does not matter what religion you choose—just that you are sincere. This is one of Satan's most propagated lies. There is only one way into the sheepfold, and Jesus claimed to be "the gate for the sheep" (10:7). He said, "Whoever enters through me will be saved" (10:9). There is just one way to the Father, and Christ is that way.

Jesus also claimed to be "the truth" (*hē alētheia*). Hawkins presents a thorough discussion of the range of meanings of this key concept in Johannine theology.[3] In Greek thought *alētheia* can refer to an abstract quality of truthfulness or "reality" as opposed to "appearance." The Hebrew concept of truth, derived from the Hebrew *'emet*, is moral rather than intellectual. The key idea in Hebraic thought would be that of "fidelity." Hawkins suggests that in John's writings the Hebraic and Greek viewpoints are combined to form a concept of

3. David J. Hawkins, "The Johannine Concept of Truth and Its Implications for a Technological Society," *The Evangelical Quarterly* 59 (1987): 3-13.

truth that is moral (fidelity) but nuanced to include the concept of "revealed truth."

As "the truth," Jesus is "the word of the Father addressed to men."[4] Or in the words of Ladd, Jesus is "the full revelation and embodiment of the redemptive purpose of God."[5] God's redemptive truth has its ultimate realization in and through the Person of Christ (1:17). Truth is found in Jesus. To know Jesus is to know the truth. This truth is not something to be contemplated, but a divine reality to be embraced and lived.

In addition to being the "way" and the "truth," Jesus also claims to be "the life" (*he zōē*). He has "life" in Himself (5:26) and authority to give life to whom He wishes (5:21). The resurrection of Lazarus authenticates His claim to be "the life" (11:25).

Thomas à Kempis sums up the importance of this verse, "Without the way there is no going; without the truth there is no knowing; without the life there is no living."[6] Jesus is the way to follow; the truth to believe; the life for which we hope.

14:7   Addressing all His disciples in the upper room, Jesus said, "If you really knew me, you would know my Father as well." The conditional construction ("if") implies that the disciples had not really known (*ginōskō*) Christ, and thus had not known the Father.[7] (The Greek word *ginōskō* refers to knowing by personal experience.) They knew Jesus, but not in the fullest sense of His messianic Person and work. But "from now on" things would be different. These words refer not to that precise moment but to the time of Jesus' passion. As a result of their fuller understanding of Jesus (through His death and resurrection), the disciples would know and experience the Father. In light of Exodus 33:20, this is a bold claim. To *know* (*ginōskō*) Jesus is to *see* (*horaō*) the Father (cf. John 1:18). This is a strong affirmation of Jesus' deity.

THE QUESTION OF PHILIP, 14:8-21

14:8   Jesus' words about seeing the Father elicited a request from Philip (1:43-46; 6:5-7; 12:21-22). He said, "Lord, show us the Father and that will be enough for us." Philip, like Moses (cf. Ex. 33:18),

---

4. Ibid., p. 11.

5. G. E. Ladd, *A Theology of the New Testament* (Grand Rapids: Eerdmans, 1974), p. 266.

6. Thomas à Kempis *The Imitation of Christ* 56.1.

7. Leon Morris, *The Gospel According to John*, NICNT (Grand Rapids: Eerdmans, 1971), p. 641.

longed to see a glorious glimpse of God. He quite obviously missed the point Jesus was making in v. 7. Yet his request prepared the way for Jesus' teaching concerning the intimate relationship existing between God the Father and Jesus the Son.

14:9   Jesus responded to Philip's request with a gentle rebuke, "Don't you know me, Philip, even after I have been among you such a long time?" (Once again Jesus uses the word *ginōskō* to describe an intimate and personal knowledge [cf. v. 7].) Although Philip had been with Jesus since the beginning of His public ministry (1:44), He had not yet grasped the full significance of His Person. Then Jesus made a simple but profound statement regarding His relationship with the Father: "Anyone who has seen me has seen the Father." Earlier in His ministry Jesus had declared, "I and the Father are one" (10:30). Even though there are three Persons in the Godhead, there is only one God. Verse 9 advances the thought a bit further. Philip was having his glimpse of God in the Person of Jesus.

Although believers today do not see Jesus in physical form, they do see Him in God's Word, and through this revelation they both see and know the Father.

14:10   Jesus returns to a concept first introduced in 10:38 during His interaction with the Jews at the Feast of Dedication. Once again He teaches the mutual indwelling of the Father and the Son. Jesus questions Philip, "Don't you believe that I am in the Father, and that the Father is in me?" Jesus is saying, "I am one with the Father, and the Father is one with me. You may meet the Father in me."[8] Jesus' question suggests that Philip did not believe this truth, but that he should.

Jesus appeals to His words and works as evidence of His union with the Father. The words He speaks are the Father's, not His own (cf. 7:16-17). The word *rēma* speaks of His *spoken* statements or instructions. And it is the Father living in Him who is "doing his work" (cf. 5:19, 36; 10:25, 38; 15:24). The word "work" (*ergon*) is the term most often used by Jesus to refer to His miracles. Morris observes, "What to men are miracles, to God and to Christ are no more than 'works.'"[9]

---

8. Barclay M. Newman and Eugene A. Nida, *A Translator's Handbook on the Gospel of John* (London: United Bible Societies, 1980), p. 460.

9. Morris, *The Gospel According to John*, p. 690.

14:11   Jesus here reinforces His instruction to Philip in v. 10 with a command to all His disciples. He calls on them to "keep on believing" (present active imperative of *pisteuō*) the truth of His mutual indwelling with the Father. Then He adds, "Or at least believe on the evidence of the miracles themselves." Nicodemus was properly responding to Jesus' "works" when he said, "Rabbi, we know that you are a teacher who has come from God. For no one could perform the miraculous signs you are doing if God were not with him" (3:2). The miracles of Jesus were designed to lead to the truth concerning His Person (cf. 10:38; 20:30-31). They still accomplish that purpose as God through the Holy Spirit touches hearts and draws people to Christ.

14:12   Jesus presents a great promise for believers ("anyone who has faith in me"). The introductory formula, "I tell you the truth," underlines the importance of what He is about to say. Jesus promises that those who believe "will do what I have been doing." Then He adds, "He will do even greater things than these, because I am going to the Father."

What is Jesus promising believers? What are the "greater things" they will accomplish? Many suggest that Jesus is speaking about His miracles. This view does have a basis in the immediate context (cf. 14:11). But did the disciples do more miracles than Jesus? There is no evidence in Scripture that they did. There are thirty-six specifically recorded miracles found in the gospels, and only twenty specifically recorded miracles in Acts. Did Jesus mean that the disciples would do greater miracles than He? Apparently not. The miracles of the apostles were primarily healing miracles. No apostle in Acts ever walked on water, stilled a storm, or fed five thousand. Could the "greater things" refer to more conversions?[10] This is possible. The ministry of the disciples resulted in innumerable conversions and tremendous church growth throughout the Mediterranean world. Perhaps the "greater things" are spiritual works accomplished by the power of the Holy Spirit (cf. 16:7) in the lives of the disciples. This view has possibilities, but it leaves the nature of the "greater things" rather general and elusive.

There is yet another view to consider. The last words of the verse, "because I am going to the Father," indicate that Christ's position with the Father provides the basis for these works. The discussion

10. Ibid., p. 646; F. F. Bruce, *The Gospel of John: Introduction, Exposition and Notes* (Grand Rapids: Eerdmans, 1983), p. 300.

leads in vv. 13-14 to the subject of prayer. The context of v. 12 would indicate that the "greater things" mentioned by Jesus are those things that will be accomplished by prayer in His name (cf. Heb. 4:14-16; 7:24-25). This view fits better with the phrase "anyone who has faith" (lit., "everyone who believes"). Most would agree that not everyone who believes has authority to do miracles (cf. 1 Cor. 12:29). On the other hand, all believers do have the privilege of intercessory prayer. In emphasizing the importance of prayer, it is well to remember that the capacity for greater works is not in the mechanics of prayer but in the power of almighty God.

14:13 Verse 13 may be either a continuation of the last line of v. 12 or may be an independent clause carrying the thought of v. 12 one stage further.[11] Either way, the two verses are closely related contextually. Verse 13 contains a great promise and reveals a completely new truth to the disciples. In Matthew 6:9 Jesus taught the disciples to pray to the "Father" in heaven. Now He reveals that their prayers will be answered when asked in His name (*onoma*). John 14:13 is the first of a series of references to prayer "in Jesus' name" (cf. 15:21; 16:23, 24, 26).

Jesus promises that He will do "whatever you ask in my name." Bruce points out that this is the Johannine counterpart to the synoptic promise of Matt. 18:19.[12] What does it mean to pray "in Jesus' name"? Often this becomes something of a ritual formula attached to Christian prayers with little thought or reflection on the significance. In ancient times a man's name was almost synonymous with his reputation. Children were often named or renamed to commemorate a significant event or call attention to a character trait. The name of the prophet Samuel ("name of God") commemorated that his birth was God's answer to Hannah's prayer. Moses changed the name of his successor, Hosea ("salvation"), to Joshua in order to remind him and the Israelites that "Yahweh is salvation" (Num. 3:8, 16).

Praying in Jesus' name means that a believer's requests are presented to the Father on the basis of Christ's Person and work—all that He is and has done. Specifically, this means (1) to pray in accordance with all that Jesus' name stands for as divine Son of God who died for our sins; (2) to appeal to the Father on the basis of Jesus' merits and influence as the believers' High Priest, Heb. 4:14-16; 7:25; (3) to pray a

---

11. B. F. Wescott, *The Gospel According to St. John* (Grand Rapids: Eerdmans, 1973), p. 204.
12. Bruce, *The Gospel of John*, p. 301.

prayer consistent with Jesus' holy and righteous character; (4) to request of the Father what Jesus would want; (5) to seek that which would glorify the Father, John 14:13; 17:4; (6) to pray believing that God will grant the request for Jesus' sake, Matthew 21:22. To pray in Jesus' name is like signing His name to our prayer. Jesus was not asking His disciples merely to adopt a new formula but rather to appropriate a totally new concept of prayer. There is no limit to the power and potential available to the believer through prayer in Jesus' name.

The purpose of the promise must be noted "so that the Son may bring glory to the Father." God is glorified (*doxazō*) when His reputation is enhanced and magnified. This provides a key to knowing whether or not a particular request is according to God's will (cf. 1 John 5:14). If the prayer is answered, will the Father be glorified?

14:14 Verse 14 repeats the promise of v. 13 concerning the effectiveness of prayer in Jesus' name. A number of Greek manuscripts omit this verse entirely, including several important ancient versions.[13] The omission may be due to an accident in transmission, the eye of the scribe having passed from *ean* at the beginning of v. 14 to *ean* at the beginning of v. 15. Because the verse seemed redundant after v. 13, the error was never corrected and the omission was passed on by transcription. A variety of manuscript witnesses omit "me." Several others replace "me" with "the Father," possibly in an attempt to avoid contradiction with 16:23. Codices Vaticanus and Sinaiticus and other important manuscripts support the inclusion of "me."

This verse does not merely repeat v. 13 for emphasis. It adds the thought that prayer may be addressed to the Son as well as the Father (cf. Acts 7:59; Rev. 22:20). If the reading "me" is genuine in v. 14, this is a clear indication that prayer may be addressed to Jesus. Comparing vv. 13 and 14, Morris notes the characteristic Johannine habit of introducing slight variations when a statement is repeated.[14]

14:15 Verse 15 introduces a thought that Jesus will develop further in 14:21-24. Jesus points out that the disciples' relationship with Christ involves ethical responsibilities. Jesus declares, "If you love me, you will obey what I command." The one who truly loves (*agapaō*) Christ will demonstrate it by obedience. The present tense is used in both verbs and could be rendered, "If you keep on loving . . . , you will

---

13. Bruce M. Metzger, *A Textual Commentary on the Greek New Testament* (London: United Bible Societies, 1971), p. 14.

14. Morris, *The Gospel According to John*, p. 647.

keep on obeying." One's love for Christ is measured by obedience. Continued love for Christ serves as a preventative against disobedience.

Many people claim to love God. Some would even tell Him so. Yet the genuineness of our love is most effectively communicated through actions. The authenticity of our love for Christ is measured by our obedience to His will.

14:16 Verses 14-16 introduce the first of an important series of references about the Holy Spirit (cf. 14:26; 15:26; 16:7-15). Here the Holy Spirit is promised by Jesus and will be given by the Father at the request of the Son. It is noteworthy that in vv. 13-14 Jesus commands His disciples to "ask" (*aiteō*), the word used of an inferior asking a superior. But here Jesus uses the word *erotaō* ("ask"), a word used of a request made to an equal. This has significant implications in terms of Jesus' deity. Although submissive to the Father, Jesus regarded Himself as an equal (cf. 10:30; 14:9).

The Holy Spirit is designated as "another" Counselor. The word "another" (*allos*) means "another of the same kind." This means that the Holy Spirit shares the same character and quality as the divine Christ (cf. Matt. 28:19; Acts 5:3-4; 2 Cor. 13:14). The word "Counselor" (*paraklētos*) is a word that can be used in a legal sense of a friend of the accused—an advocate or counsel for the defense (cf. 1 John 2:1). But the more common usage is the general sense of "helper." The translation "Counselor" is probably too narrow. The *paraklētos* is literally "one called alongside" to help, counsel, or encourage. This concept is illustrated in the ancient Greek world where the word *paraklētos* is used of one who would come alongside and help shoulder a heavy burden.

The Holy Spirit is promised in light of Christ's departure. Christ's stay on earth was temporary, a mere three-and-one-half years, but the Holy Spirit is sent "to be with you forever." What an encouragement to know that when we face burdens that are beyond our ability to cope, the Holy Spirit is ever present to provide necessary assistance.

14:17 Jesus designates the Holy Spirit as "the Spirit of truth" (cf. 15:26; 16:13). The genitive "of truth" (*tēs alētheias*) should not be understood too narrowly. It may be both descriptive, indicating that the Spirit is marked or characterized by truth, and subjective, indicating that the Spirit communicates truth (cf. 16:13).

Jesus explained to His disciples that the unbelieving "world" would not receive the Spirit because unbelievers did not know Him

261

nor did they understand His working. But the disciples did "know him" because they had believed in Jesus who had revealed God (cf. 14:9).

In the last phrase of v. 17 Jesus alludes to a change in the Holy Spirit's manner of working from the Old Covenant to the New Covenant economy. Under the Old Covenant the Holy Spirit had been readily available and present with some believing individuals (Judg. 3:10; 6:34; 11:29; 13:25). Yet the ministry of the Spirit was selective and temporary (1 Sam. 16:14; Ps. 51:11). Jesus anticipated a change when He told the disciples, "For he lives with you and will be in you." The Holy Spirit was presently "with" (*para*) the disciples but would soon be "in" (*en*) them. Under the provisions of the New Covenant the Holy Spirit permanently indwells all believers (cf. Ezek. 36:27; 1 Cor. 6:19; 12:13; Rom. 8:9). It is the indwelling ministry of the Holy Spirit that empowers believers for obedience and sanctification (cf. Rom. 8:4).

14:18 Although Jesus had made it clear that He was going away (13:33; 14:2), He promised the disciples, "I will not leave you as orphans." The term "orphan" (*orphanos*) is used commonly of orphaned children. But here it is used in a more general sense of "one left without anyone to care for him."[15] The disciples of Socrates were said to have been left "orphans" at his death.[16] Jesus promised His disciples that He would not leave them like helpless orphans. There are no orphans in the family of God. We are in the care of one who will never leave us nor forsake us (cf. Heb. 13:5). Jesus' words "I will come to you" refer in this context (cf. John 14:19-20) to His postresurrection appearances.

14:19 Jesus instructed His disciples that in a short time, "before long," the unbelieving world would no longer see Him. The last the world would see of Him would be at His crucifixion. But to the disciples He said, "You will see me." They would see (*theōreō*) Him again at His resurrection (20:19-29).

The words "Because I live, you also will live" indicate clearly that Jesus is referring in this context to His resurrection and postresurrection appearances. Jesus links the disciples' resurrection life to His own. Jesus is the "first fruits" of a resurrection (1 Cor. 15:20, 23) of which all believers have a part. He has "life in himself" (5:26) and the authority to give life to others (5:21).

15. Nida and Newman, *A Translator's Handbook on the Gospel of John*, p. 469.
16. Plato *Phaedo* 116 A.

14:20   Jesus anticipates here that something culminative will happen "on that day," the day of His resurrection when the disciples will see Him again. The impact of the resurrection will convince the disciples experientially (*ginōskō*) of the essential unity of the Father and Son ("I am in my Father") and the intimate relationship Jesus shares with believers ("you are in me, and I am in you"). Verse 20 indicates that the disciples' faith was progressive. They had believed Jesus enough to follow Him and give Him their allegiance. But the resurrection of Jesus would be a culminating factor in the strengthening and confirmation of their faith (20:8, 27-28).

14:21   Jesus returns in v. 21 to the thought of love and obedience introduced in v. 15. It is not enough to know the Word of God or even believe it. It is obedience to His teachings that marks one as truly loving Christ. The word Jesus uses for "love" is *agapaō*, a sacrificial commitment (cf. 13:34-35).

Jesus goes on to reveal that He who loves the Son will be loved by the Father. This is not to suggest that the Father's love is earned by loving Jesus. Rather, the Father is not indifferent to the manner in which people respond to His Son. Bruce comments, "The Father who loves the Son (John 3:35; 5:20) loves those who are united to the Son, and they, thus loved by the Father, have the assurance that the Son loves them." [17] Added to these comments on reciprocal love, Jesus introduces the subject of His self-disclosure. He promises to "show" (*emphanizō*) Himself to His disciples ("he who loves me"). Jesus is apparently referring to the self-disclosure that would take place through the Holy Spirit (16:13-15).

THE QUESTION OF JUDAS (NOT ISCARIOT), 14:22-24

The mention of Jesus' self-disclosure to His disciples raised a serious question in the mind of Judas. This provided the opportunity for Jesus to explain that obedience is the prerequisite for enlightenment.

14:22   The "Judas" spoken of here is not to be identified with Judas Iscariot. This Judas was the son of James (cf. Luke 6:16; Acts 1:13). He questioned Jesus, "But, Lord, why do you intend to show yourself to us and not to the world?" He was concerned over the prospect of Christ's disclosure being private rather than public. Like his Jewish countrymen, Judas expected the Messiah to appear in glory before the

17. Bruce, *The Gospel of John*, p. 304.

whole world, judge the Gentiles, and restore the kingdom to the Jews (John 7:4; cf. Dan. 7:13-14; Zech. 14:1-5). Jesus had announced in His Olivet discourse that "all the nations" would see "the Son of Man coming" (Matt. 24:30). Now Judas wondered why this previously announced plan had changed.

14:23   Jesus answered Judas's question by repeating and developing the concepts introduced in vv. 15 and 21. Here once again Jesus links love with obedience. Essentially Jesus is saying that love issuing in obedience is the necessary prerequisite for His self-disclosure to His disciples. Those who are characterized by loving obedience will be loved by the Father and will enjoy a special fellowship with the Father and Son. Jesus promises, "And we will come to him and make our home with him."

The word translated "home" (*monē*) is used in 14:2 with reference to heaven. Jesus is promising that the Father and Son will make Their united home in the lives of His obedient disciples. The idea of God's dwelling among His people was not unfamiliar to the Jews (Ex. 25:8; 29:45; Zech. 2:10). But the united dwelling of the Father and Son was a new concept. How encouraging to know that believers need never be alone. The Father and Son dwell with those who love and obey Jesus.

14:24   Verse 24 contrasts with v. 23, showing the actions of those who do not love Christ. Jesus uses the present participle with the negative *mē*, which could be rendered "the one who keeps on not loving me." Jesus points out once again that His teaching is not His own, but comes from the Father (7:16; 8:28; 12:49; 14:10).

THE CONCLUDING WORDS OF ENCOURAGEMENT, 14:25-31

This section of the discourse concludes with a renewed emphasis on Jesus' departure and its consequences for the disciples.

14:25   Jesus had taught the disciples many things during His earthly ministry. The words "while still with you" contain a veiled reference to His departure. Jesus was physically present with His disciples, but that was soon to change.

14:26   It was in light of His anticipated departure that Jesus provided further instruction on the ministry of the Holy Spirit (14:16-17). Jesus revealed that the Holy Spirit, the "Counselor" (*paraklētos*), would be sent by the Father in the name of the Son (cf. 15:26). To send the Spirit "in my name" means to send Him "at my request." His ministry would include teaching the disciples "all things" (cf. 1 John

2:27) and reminding them of "everything" Jesus had taught them. The Spirit's ministry is not limited to the apostles but was especially for their benefit as writers of Scripture. After receiving the Spirit they would better recall and understand the teachings of Jesus.

14:27 Because the disciples were troubled over the prospect of Jesus' impending departure (John 13:36; 14:1, 5), Jesus promised them His own "peace" to encourage them in their struggles ahead. The Greek word for "peace" (*eirēnē*) has much the same meaning and usage as the Hebrew word *shalom*. The word was used in New Testament times both as a greeting (20:19, 21; Gal. 1:3) and for a farewell (Eph. 6:23). The word "peace" is also used to describe harmonious relationships between men (Mark 9:50; Rom. 14:19) and between nations (Rev. 6:4). The prophets anticipated a messianic age of peace. Both national (Isa. 2:2-4; 11:6-9; Zech. 9:9-10) and individual (Isa. 32:17-18; 53:5; 54:13; 55:12) peace was anticipated during Messiah's reign. The word "peace" is also used in the New Testament to describe the spiritual well-being of true believers (Rom. 5:1; Eph. 2:14; Col. 1:20). The message of salvation in Christ is essentially a message of peace between God and mankind.

Peace, then, is the spiritual well-being that results from being rightly related to God through Jesus Christ. This is what Jesus has in mind when He promises, "Peace I leave with you; my peace I give you." A major feature of such peace is inward contentment. This is not the kind of peace that the world offers. The world offers a "peace" based on favorable conditions and circumstances. The legacy of peace Jesus provides is independent of external circumstances. He promises trouble in this world (John 15:18-25; 16:1-4) but peace in Him (16:33).

It is in view of this legacy of peace that Jesus is able to say, "Do not let your hearts be troubled and do not be afraid." This is nearly identical to the words in 14:1, with the addition of "and do not be afraid" (*mēde deiliatō*).

14:28 Jesus returns in v. 28 to the subject of His impending departure (13:33; 14:2-4). His promise "I am coming back to you" may refer either to His second coming (14:3) or His resurrection appearances (14:18-19). Jesus then calls attention to the way the disciples responded to the announcement of His departure: "If you loved me, you would be glad that I am going to the Father." The disciples should have viewed Jesus' return to the Father as an occasion for rejoicing. As it was, their thoughts were on themselves and what that loss would mean to them. They were apparently not loving Christ as they should, nor were they seeking His best interests rather than their own. Jesus' return to the Father was for His good and glory. The disciples, focusing on themselves, found no joy in the announcement.

Jesus' explanation "For the Father is greater than I" (cf. 10:29) has given impetus to the theological error that Christ is a created being and thus inferior to God the Father. The words in 14:28 must be understood in light of 10:30, "I and the Father are one." Jesus is clearly presented in John as the divine Son of God (20:30-31). Yet in relationship to His incarnation and messianic office, the Father is in a position of authority over Christ. Although coequal with the Father in the Godhead, in His incarnation Jesus became the submissive, obedient, subordinate Son (cf. 13:16; 1 Cor. 11:3; Phil. 2:6-8). Equality and hierarchy are not mutually exclusive concepts.

Bruce notes that the conjunction "for" before "the Father is greater than I" attaches to the preceding clause, "I am going to the Father." Jesus is on His way back to the Father who sent Him. Because "a messenger is not greater than the one who sent him" (John 13:16), Jesus must render to the Father an account of His mission.[18]

14:29   Jesus here informs the disciples that He has announced these things (cf. 14:28) beforehand in order to elicit faith ("so that when it does happen you will believe"). Realizing the fulfillment of His prophetic words would encourage belief in His Person and claims. This concept is quite in keeping with the purpose of the gospel (20:30-31).

14:30   Jesus explains to His disciples that His words will soon cease, "for the prince of this world is coming." The "prince of this world" (*ho tou kosmou archōn*) is a clear reference to Satan (cf. 12:31). The word *archōn* speaks of one who is a ruler or chief over others, referring to Satan's power over unbelievers and unseen spiritual forces. Satan was active and present in the person of Judas (13:2, 27), who was already in the process of betraying Jesus. Although Satan had laid claim to Judas (13:2, 27), Jesus points out that Satan, the ruler of this sin-darkened world, "has no hold on me." Nor does Satan have any hold on those who trust in the name of Jesus. Believers have nothing to fear from Satan when they rely on Christ. As the apostle notes elsewhere, "The one who is in you is greater than the one who is in the world" (1 John 4:4).

14:31   In previous verses Jesus has taught that love for Him must be demonstrated by obedience to His commands (John 14:15, 21, 23).

18. Ibid., p. 307, n. 15.

In v. 31 He points out that this principle applies to His own relation-ship with God the Father. His love for the Father is shown by His doing exactly what God commands. Soon He will die in obedience to His Father's command. The purpose clause in the Greek text ("But in order that the world may know that I love the Father") indicates that Christ's obedience is intended to show the world His love for God.

Chapter 14 concludes with the words "Come now; let us leave." Although this sounds like the end of the Upper Room discourse, Jesus continues teaching with no apparent departure from the room. Not until 18:1 is Jesus said to have crossed the Kidron Valley on His way to the Garden of Gethsemane. Some scholars believe that 14:31 is mis-placed (by scribal error) and originally marked the conclusion of the discourse after chapters 15 and 16. There is, however, no textual evi-dence to support this theory. Newman and Nida suggest that chapter 14 and chapters 15-17 contain alternative versions of Jesus' last dis-course, and that the author or final editor included both endings. The remark in 14:31 was allowed to remain, the editor not wanting to tamper with the text.[19] Others spiritualize the words, interpreting them as an appeal to go to the Father or forward to death and resur-rection. Westcott insists that Jesus and the disciples left the upper room at once and the rest of the discourse was given as they walked to Gethsemane.[20] Following R. H. Lightfoot, Morris believes that the words about departing mark the closing of a stage in Jesus' teaching.[21] Whether or not Jesus' words about departing indicate a change of scene, they at least reflect a break in the discourse at the end of chap-ter 14.

HOMILETICAL SUGGESTIONS

Peter's question (13:36–4:4) provides an excellent text for an ex-position on heaven. After an explanation of Jesus' preparations for heaven (4:2-3), one might turn to Revelation 21 for a glimpse of the New Jerusalem. Here it is discovered that heaven is a literal, large, and lovely place. Peter's question and Thomas's question (14:4-7) might be linked under the topic "Heaven: what it is like and how to get there."

19. Newman and Nida, *A Translator's Handbook on the Gospel of John*, p. 453.
20. Westcott, *The Gospel According to St. John*, p. 211.
21. Morris, *The Gospel According to John*, p. 661.

Thomas's question in 14:4-7 focuses on the claim of Jesus to be "the way, the truth, and the life." This provides an excellent text for an evangelistic message on the Person of Christ.

Philip's question (14:8-15) expresses the longing of most people to know something more about God. The answer to this longing is Jesus Christ. We know something more about God as we learn of Him.

John 14:12-14 is an excellent text on prayer. On the night before His death, Jesus taught the disciples a new concept of prayer. He told them to petition the Father in Jesus' name. We use the phrase "in Jesus' name" with little understanding of its significance. This text provides an opportunity to make this revolutionary concept clear.

Verses 14-16 introduce an important series of references to the Holy Spirit (cf. 14:26; 15:26; 16:7-15). These texts could be united into several messages on the Person and work of the Holy Spirit.

Judas's question (14:22-24) provides an opportunity to emphasize the importance of obedience in the believer's life. Obedience is not optional. It is the necessary prerequisite for further understanding and enlightenment.

The concluding section of the chapter (14:25-31) highlights the peace or spiritual well-being that comes from being rightly related to God (14:27). In a world that is insecure and upside down, people search for something or someone who can get them through anxious moments. Christ is the answer. He offers His very own peace that is independent of conditions or circumstances.

JOHN
CHAPTER
FIFTEEN

VINE AND BRANCHES

THE BELIEVER'S RELATIONSHIPS, CHAP. 15

John 15 is central to the Upper Room discourse both from the viewpoint of text and theology. Here Jesus brings the subject of "relationships" into primary focus. He teaches His disciples about His relationship with them—a relationship of "abiding." Then He discusses the disciples' relationship with each other ("love each other"), with the world ("the world hates you"), and with the Holy Spirit ("he will testify . . . and you must testify").

THE RELATIONSHIP WITH CHRIST, 15:1-11

The believer's relationship with Christ is presented by Jesus through the figure of the vine and branches. Jesus first presents the analogy (15:1-2), and then applies it (15:3-6). He follows this up with further instruction about remaining in Christ (15:7-11).

The Allegory, 15:1-2

Jesus presents the analogy and identifies the parts. Many commentators have suggested that Jesus appropriated the figure of the vine from vineyards located along the way from the upper room to the Garden of Gethsemane. It is more likely that the figure used by Jesus was drawn from the rich resource of imagery found in the Hebrew scriptures.

The vine is a familiar symbol for Israel in the prophets and Psalms (Ps. 80:8-16; Isa. 5:1-7; Jer. 2:21; 5:10; 12:10; Ezek. 15:1-8; 17:1-4; Hos. 10:1). This symbol was so well recognized that during the Maccabean period the image of a vine was stamped on the coins minted by the Jewish nation.[1] The use of this symbol continued in Judaism as evidenced by an elaborate allegorial portrayal of Israel in the Jewish Midrash, *Leviticus Rabbah* 36 (133*a*). Josephus reports that above the entrance doors of Herod's Temple "spread a golden vine with grape-clusters hanging from it" (*Antiqities* 15.395). Regarding the use of this imagery, Beasley-Murray observes, "It is striking that in every instance when Israel in its historical life is depicted in the OT as a vine or vineyard, the nation is set under the judgment of God for its corruption, sometimes explicitly for its failure to produce good fruit (e.g., Isa. 5:1-7; Jer. 2:21)."[2] Themes common to the vine imagery include fruitlessness, degeneracy, removal of branches, burning, and destruction. These are the very themes Jesus appropriates in the analogy of John 15.

15:1 Introducing the analogy, Jesus identifies Himself as the vine. The definite article with the adjective *alēthinos* indicates Jesus is "the true," or genuine, vine. In contrast to the degenerate and unfruitful vine (unbelieving Israel), Jesus fulfills God's expectation for His people. A vineyard needs care, and in this analogy God the Father is identified as the farmer or "gardener." He does the plowing, planting, watering, and pruning. The vineyard is under His sovereign care and authority.

15:2 Jesus goes on to describe the work of the gardener (God the Father) in relationship to the branches (*klēma*). Jesus does not specifically identify the "branches" with any particular group of followers, but He does identify two kinds: fruit-bearing and fruitless. It is obvious that Jesus is talking here about people, not plants. The context would suggest that He is referring to disciples, broadly defined as interested listeners. Some disciples bear fruit, and others, like the "disciples" who turned away from Jesus' hard teaching (6:60, 66), bear none.

Two sovereign actions are taken with regard to the branches. The fruit-bearing branches "he prunes," and the fruitless branches "he cuts off." The word translated "prunes" (*kathairō*) literally means

---

1. William Barclay, *The Gospel of John* (Philadelphia: Westminster, 1956), 2:201.
2. George R. Beasley-Murray, *John*, Word Biblical Commentary (Waco, Tex.: Word, 1987), p. 272.

"to cleanse," "to purge," "to purify." The verb was commonly used of ceremonial cleansing.[3] It is not the normal word for pruning but is used here because Jesus was talking about people rather than vines. Regular pruning is necessary to maximize the fruit production of a vine (*M. Peah* 7.4-5). This includes pinching off the tip of a vigorous shoot to prevent its being broken off by the wind, thinning clusters of flowers or fruit to enable the rest of the branch to bear a better quality of fruit, cutting away suckers that arise from the ground or from the trunk of the vine, and a fall or winter pruning back of the vines to the main stalk, except for several main shoots.[4]

As the vinedresser cuts away that which would hinder the productivity of the vine, so God the Father, through loving discipline (cleansing, purging, purifying), removes things from the lives of believers that do not contribute to their spiritual fruitfulness (cf. 2 Cor. 12:7; Heb. 12:6-11).

Whereas the fruitful branches are pruned, the fruitless branches "He [God] takes away" (*airō*). The word *airō* is used twenty-three times in John's gospel. In eight places it could be translated "take or lift up" (5:8, 9, 10, 12; 8:59; 10:18, 24). In thirteen places it must be translated "take away" or "remove" (11:39, 41, 48; 16:22; 17:15; 19:15, 31, 38; 10:1, 2, 13, 15). How is Jesus using the word in this context?

Some commentators have argued that the fruitless branches are "lifted up" so that they can receive exposure to the sun and thus produce abundant fruit.[5] It has been suggested that the grapevine stalks that usually lie on the ground were raised during the growing season. It has yet to be proved that this was the practice in ancient Israel. The Mishnah speaks of two kinds of vines in Israel, the trellised and the ground-trained vine (*M. Peah* 7.8). Schultz points out that "most of the vines in Pal[atine] trail on the ground, because it is believed that the grapes ripen more slowly under the shadow of the leaves."[6] The context of v. 6, which describes the destruction of the fruitless vines, appears to contradict the view that the branches are "lifted" with a view to greater fruitfulness.

3. J. H. Moulton and G. Milligan, *The Vocabulary of the Greek Testament* (Grand Rapids: Eerdmans, 1930), p. 310.

4. H. E. Jacob, "Grape Growing in California," Circular No. 116 (California Agricultural Extension Service, The College of Agriculture, University of California at Berkeley, April 1940).

5. A. W. Pink, *Exposition of the Gospel of John* (Cleveland: Bible Truth Depot, 1929), 3:337; James Montgomery Boice, *The Gospel of John* (Grand Rapids: Zondervan, 1978), 4:228.

6. A. C. Schultz, "Vine, Vineyard," in *Zondervan Pictorial Encyclopedia of the Bible*, ed. Merrill C. Tenney (Grand Rapids: Zondervan, 1975), 5:882.

Most commentators, save those mentioned above, interpret *airō* to refer to the removal of the unproductive branches.[7] This view fits best within the context of v. 6. The question remains, however, What is the ultimate fate of the fruitless branches?

Arminians have consistently interpreted the fruitless branches as Christians who lose their salvation. This viewpoint, however, is quite inconsistent with the words of Jesus in 10:28-29. Others have argued that the fruitless branches represent true Christians who are removed to heaven by physical death as God's final step in divine discipline. The major difficulty with this view is that v. 6 indicates that the removal of the fruitless branch is a prelude to judgment, not blessed fellowship with Christ in heaven. Such a judgment awaits only unbelievers (Matt. 3:12; 5:22; 18:8-9; 25:41; 2 Thess. 1:7-8; Rev. 20:15).

The view that best answers to the immediate context and theological themes of John's gospel is this: the fruitless branches represent disciples who have had an external association with Christ that is not matched by an internal, spiritual union entered into by personal faith and regeneration. As MacLaren comments: "If there be any real union there will be some life, and if there be any life, there will be some fruit, and, therefore, the branch that has no fruit has no life, because it has no real union."[8] The fruitless branches are lifeless branches— branches without Christ. This view has the advantage of consistency with the immediate context and with John's theology of progressive belief (1:50; 2:11, 22; 6:69; 11:15; 16:30; 17:8; 20:8). This view is also consistent with first-century agriculture. The Mishnah speaks of a "defective grape-cluster" that is "cut off" (*M. Peah* 7.4) and "dead branches" (of trees) that are pruned or lopped off (*M. Shebiith* 2.3).

The gospel of John also presents the reader with an enigma of "belief" that is not belief. In the progress of belief there is a stage that falls short of genuine or consummated faith resulting in salvation (2:23-25; 7:31; 8:31, 40, 45-46; 12:11, 37). Tenney refers to the "belief" that falls short of genuine faith as "superficial."[9] Morris calls it "transitory belief" that is not saving faith.[10] Many were inclined to believe

---

7. For further study, see my article "Abiding Is Believing: The Analogy of the Vine in John 15:1-6," *Bibliotheca Sacra* 146 (January-March 1989): 55-66. For an opposing viewpoint, see Joseph C. Dillow, "Abiding Is Remaining in Fellowship: Another Look at John 15:1-6," *Bibliotheca Sacra* 147 (January-March 1990): 44-53.

8. Alexander MacLaren, *Expositions of Holy Scripture* (Grand Rapids: Eerdmans, 1952), 7:5.

9. Merrill C. Tenney, "Topics from the Gospel of John: The Growth of Belief," *Bibliotheca SacSacra* 132 (October-December 1975): 351.

10. Leon Morris, *The Gospel According to John*, NICNT (Grand Rapids: Eerdmans, 1971), p. 603.

something about Jesus but were not willing to yield their allegiance to Him or trust Him as their personal sin-bearer.

The major objection against interpreting the fruitless branches as unbelievers is the presence of the phrase "in me" (*en emoi*). How could a fruitless, unbelieving branch be "in Christ"? Godet has suggested that the words "in me" may modify either the "branch" (adjectival) or the participle "bearing" (adverbial).[11] If interpreted adverbially, the verse would read, "He cuts of every branch that bears no fruit in me." The bearing of fruit takes place "in the sphere of" (*en*) Christ—by His influence and enablement. The emphasis of "in me" is apparently not the place of the branch but the process of fruit-bearing.

The Application, 15:3-6

Having presented the analogy of the vine, Jesus proceeds to teach the disciples the practical significance of what it means to be a branch in vital union with Christ the vine.

15:3 Jesus had spoken in 15:2 about the removal of fruitless branches. He explains to the disciples in v. 3 that they were not the branches in view. They were already "clean" (*katharos*) by virtue of their response to Christ's Person and message (cf. the use of *katharos* in 13:10-11). The remarks about the fruitless branch did not reflect the spiritual situation of the disciples with Jesus in the upper room. Rather, this teaching had primary application for those to whom they would minister—people who claimed to be Christ's followers but were not bearing fruit.

15:4 Jesus proceeds to explain that there is no fruit-bearing apart from remaining in Christ. He exhorts the disciples, "Remain in me, and I will remain in you." The Greek word "to remain" (*menō*) is used of someone who remains where he is (Acts 27:31). The word is used figuratively of someone who does not leave a particular realm or sphere (John 8:31).

There is a clear relationship in John's gospel between believing and remaining (abiding). The one who believes in Christ (6:40, 54) remains in Christ (6:56). Everyone who believes in Christ does not remain in "darkness" (12:46), a Johannine symbol of unbelief (12:35-36). The apostle equates confessing Jesus to be the Son of God with remaining in God (1 John 4:15; cf. 2:24; 3:23-24). These passages show

11. F. Godet, *Commentary on the Gospel of John*, 3d ed. (Edinburgh: T. and T. Clark, 1893), 3:162.

that believing in Jesus establishes a relationship of remaining or abiding. Kent comments, "Thus to abide [remain, *menō*] in Christ is equivalent to believing in Christ."[12] Yet the term *menō* suggests more than believing. It connotes "continuing to live in association or in union with" Christ.[13] Belief is the connection that initiates the ongoing faith that unites the vine and the branches. The aorist imperative "remain in me" may reflect the disciples' need to bring their faith union with Jesus to consummation, particularly in view of His imminent death and resurrection. The words "and I will remain in you" may be taken as the outcome of remaining in Christ. More likely, this is a word of encouragement, "and be assured I am remaining in union with you."

The main point is summed up at the end of v. 4. Just as a branch cannot bear fruit alone, neither can the disciples bear fruit apart from the life-giving connection with Christ, the vine. The present active indicative of *menō* ("remain") in the last line of the verse indicates that the abiding must be continual, that is, "keep on abiding."

15:5 Here Jesus elaborates further on the faith union He shares with the disciples. It involves a mutual indwelling ("in me, and I in him") and results in fruitbearing. Just as it is impossible to bear fruit without remaining in the vine (v. 4), so it is impossible not to bear fruit in quantity ("much fruit") where a life-giving union with the vine exists. Jesus' words "apart from me you can do nothing" capsulize the fundamental principle of spiritual life (cf. Phil. 4:13).

The concept of fruit (*karpos*) is quite varied as evidenced by many New Testament references. Fruit may include character that is Christlike (Gal. 5:22-23; Eph. 5:8-13), confession of Christ's name in praise (Heb. 13:15), contributing to those in need (Phil. 4:17), converts through witness (John 4:31-36), communication that blesses others (1 Cor. 14:14), and Christian conduct in general (1 Tim. 5:9-10; Titus 2:7-10).[14]

15:6 The natural flow of the context indicates that those being referred to in vv. 2 and 6 are the same people. Verse 6 simply extends and applies the truth presented in v. 2. Those who do not "remain in" (*menē en*) Christ cannot be expected to produce fruit. Like a branch that is "thrown away [*ballō exō*] and withers," they are "picked up, thrown into the fire and burned." Many texts speak of a fiery destiny for unbelievers (Matt. 3:12; 5:22; 18:8-9; 25:41; 2 Thess. 1:7-8; Rev.

12. Homer A. Kent, Jr., *Light in the Darkness* (Grand Rapids: Baker, 1974), p. 183.

13. Beasley-Murray, *John*, p. 272.

14. James E. Rosscup, "Fruit in the New Testament," *Bibliotheca Sacra* 125 (1968): 62-66.

20:15), but there is no parallel in the New Testament where believers are said to undergo judgment by fire in which they themselves are burned.

The description of judgment on the fruitless branch is strikingly similar to the judgment on the worthless vine in Ezekiel 15:6-7: "As I have given the wood of the vine among the trees of the forest as fuel for the fire, so will I treat the people living in Jerusalem. I will set my face against them. Although they have come out of the fire, the fire will yet consume them." Viticultural practices verify the image of destruction used both by Jesus and Ezekiel. Nogah Hareuveni, director of Noet Kedumim (the Biblical Landscape Reserve) in Israel, said in a telephone interview that the clippings from the vineyards in Israel have but one use. After they have dried, they are used for kindling.

More About Remaining in Christ, 15:7-11

In vv. 7-11 Jesus furthers the teaching on what it means to "remain" in Christ and the results of continuing in this life-giving relationship.

15:7   One result of an abiding relationship with Christ is answered prayer. Deviating slightly from the concept of mutual abiding in 15:5, Jesus had said, "If you remain in me and my words remain in you, ask whatever you wish, and it will be given to you" (14:13-14). The "words" of Jesus refer to His teachings (cf. 8:31). Because of the Person and work of His Son (14:13-14), the Father will answer the prayers of those who have a life-giving union with Christ, the vine. What an encouraging prospect for believers.

15:8   Jesus reveals in v. 8 that the Father is glorified when the disciples bear much fruit, and that fruit-bearing proves that one is a disciple of Christ. To "glorify" (*doxazō*) God means to magnify or elevate His estimation in the sight of others. God is glorified through believers who cause others to have a higher view of His Person and work. The Westminster Confession asks the famous question, "What is the chief end of man?" The answer is found here in 15:8. We are to glorify Christ by bearing much fruit.

There is a difficult textual problem with the word translated "showing yourselves to be." There are two possible readings: the subjunctive (*genēsthe*) or the future (*genēsesthe*) of *ginomai*, "to become." The United Bible Societies committee rates the reading "D,"

275

indicating a very high degree of doubt as to the original text.[15] The future tense suggests that the disciples will become more of what they already are, thus glorifying the Father. The subjunctive mood makes fruitbearing and becoming disciples grammatical coordinates that together glorify the Father. However the issue is decided, being a disciple means to bear fruit and thus glorify the Father.

15:9 Another aspect of remaining in Christ is the enjoyment of a loving relationship with Him. Jesus declares, "As the Father has loved me, so have I loved you." Jesus' love for the disciples is patterned after the Father's love for Him. Then He adds the command "Now, remain in my love." Here the constative aorist active imperative of *menō* ("remain") looks at the action of abiding in its entirety, from beginning to end.

It has been suggested that "my love" (*tē agapē tē emē*) is best taken in the sense of "my love for you," rather than "your love for me."[16] Although this seems preferable theologically, it is the less likely option grammatically. Wescott suggests that the phrase emphasizes the character of the love as that which answers to Christ's nature and work. "Thus the meaning of the words cannot be limited to the idea of Christ's love for men, or to that of man's love for Christ: they describe the absolute love which is manifested in these two ways, the love which perfectly corresponds with Christ's Being."[17] The imperative enjoins the disciples to remain mindful of and responsive to Christ's love.

15:10 Verse 10 elaborates on what it means to "remain in" Jesus' love (15:9). Jesus explains, "If you obey my commands, you will remain [future tense] in my love." As Jesus' love for the Father was demonstrated by His complete obedience to Him (8:29), so the disciples' love for Christ should be shown by their constant obedience (14:15).

Love and obedience are never viewed as isolated, unrelated concepts in Scripture (Deut. 7:7; 10:12-13). Love elicits obedience and obedience demonstrates love. Obedience, however, should not be viewed as a means of earning God's love, for divine love is a sovereign act that is totally unmerited (Deut. 7:7-9; Rom. 5:8).

5:11 Jesus now reveals the purpose (*hina*) of teaching these important lessons (15:1-10) to the disciples. "I have told you this so that

15. Bruce M. Metzger, *A Textual Commentary on the New Testament* (London: United Bible Societies, 1971), p. 246.

16. Barclay M. Newman and Eugene A. Nida, *A Translator's Handbook on the Gospel of John* (London: United Bible Societies, 1980), p. 484.

17. B. F. Westcott, *The Gospel According to St. John* (Grand Rapids: Eerdmans, 1973), p. 219.

my joy may be in you and that your joy may be complete" (cf. 1 John 1:4). Jesus' teaching, issuing in love and obedience, is intended to bring fullness of joy. The joy that the disciples may realize is not based on circumstances, which may be positive or adverse, but on an abiding relationship with Christ in which His joy becomes their own. This theme of "joy" becomes prominent in the last two chapters of the discourse (16:20-22, 24; 17:3).

THE RELATIONSHIP WITH DISCIPLES, 15:12-17

In this section of John 15, Jesus focuses on the disciples' relationship with one another. Here Jesus repeats the thrust of the new commandment (13:34-35), emphasizing the believers' responsibility to love one another.

15:12   In v. 10, Jesus said that obeying His commands was the way to abide in His love. Now He reminds them of one of those commands. The command "Love each other" was introduced in 13:34-35 as the "new command." This "love" (*agapē*) for one another is a commandment, not merely a suggestion. The kind of love commanded by Jesus is not just an emotion or feeling but a sacrificial commitment to the ultimate good of another person. This is suggested by the pattern of Jesus, "as I have loved you," which is presented in the present active subjunctive of *agapaō* and could be rendered "keep on loving."

15:13   The sacrificial love being called for by Jesus is highlighted in v. 13. The greatest love possible is a love that says no to self and yes to others. This is the kind of love exemplified by Jesus as He went to the cross. In Romans 5:6-8, Paul observes that cases of self-sacrifice for good men do occur, but they are rare. Jesus went beyond this by dying for sinners. Jesus uses the term "friends" because He was addressing the apostles. The words "lay down his life" (*tēn psuchēn autou thē*) are used in 10:11 to describe the work of the Good Shepherd.

15:14   Picking up on the mention of "friends" (v. 13), Jesus identifies the disciples as His "friends" (*philos*) and then elaborates what this friendship involves and implies. The phrase "You are my friends" has "you" (*humeis*) in the place of emphasis. Plummer renders the phrase "And when I say 'friends,' I mean you."[18] But the friendship spoken of by Jesus is no mere casual relationship. It involves commitment and obedience. And so He adds the condition "if you do what I

18. A. Plummer, *The Gospel According to St. John* (Cambridge: At the University Press, 1899), p. 290.

command." The test of true friendship with Christ is the disciple's obedience to His commands. After the pattern of Abraham, God's friend (2 Chron. 20:7; Isa. 41:8; James 2:23), the friends of Jesus are those who obey Him willingly.

15:15   Here Jesus reveals a second distinguishing characteristic of those who are His friends. He draws a contrast from the relationship of a slave with his master. Such a relationship is characterized by duty and obligation but could not be regarded as a friendship. A slave is expected to obey his master whether or not he understands or agrees with the master's command. No longer does Jesus regard the disciples as servants (cf. 12:26; 13:16) but as friends.

Jesus explains this change in their relationship: "Instead, I have called you friends, for everything that I learned from my Father I have made known to you." In contrast to dealing with servants, Jesus has shared intimately with His friends. He has kept nothing from them that they could presently bear (cf. 16:12). He has revealed to the disciples all that the Father made known to Him. A friend of Jesus is one who knows Him intimately (v. 15) and obeys Him willingly (v. 14).

There are many reasons for failure in the Christian life, but one of the most noteworthy is absence of a deep, personal friendship with the Savior. Many Christians serve Christ, they communicate the gospel, and they study the Bible. But they have never cultivated a meaningful and edifying relationship with Christ. Such a relationship can be developed only through time spent alone with the Lord, delighting in His blessings and friendship.

15:16   Jesus points out in the first part of v. 16 that His friendship with the disciples is the result of His choice, not theirs. The words "You did not choose me, but I chose you" reveal that it was His initiative, divine calling, and sovereign appointment that brought them to faith and gave them a mission. (The word "chose" [*eklegō*] is a strong argument for the doctrine of election.)

The purpose of God's choosing and appointment is expressed by the two present active subjunctives in the purpose clause introduced by *hina*, "to go and bear fruit—fruit that will last." The present tense emphasizes continued action, "keep on going" (their mission) and "keep on bearing fruit" (their ministry). The "fruit" (*karpos*) spoken of here draws from the analogy of the vine (15:2) and may refer to the conversion of souls (cf. 15:5). This is suggested in the mission word "go."

In connection with this ministry of going and fruit bearing, the disciples are here again promised that their prayers in Jesus' name will be effectual (cf. 14:13-14). The Father answers instead of Christ (cf. 14:14). The word "then" (*hina*) indicates that answered prayer grows out of obedience and fruit bearing.

15:17   Jesus concludes this section as He began it, with a restatement of the New Commandment (15:12). A believer's relationship with Christian brothers and sisters should be characterized by sacrificial (*agapaō*) love.

THE RELATIONSHIP WITH THE WORLD, 15:18-25

Having repeated once again the New Commandment to love one another, Jesus reveals by way of contrast that the world's attitude toward His disciples will be one of hatred and hostility. Here Jesus reveals the reason for the world's hatred, the extent of this hostility, and how believers can cope with it.

The Reasons for the Hostility, 15:18-21

15:18   Jesus tells His disciples in this verse, "If the world hates you, keep in mind that it hated me first." The first-class condition (*ei* with the indicative) indicates that the world's hatred is actual, not hypothetical as the English translation would suggest. The verse could be rendered, "Because the world hates you ..." The "world" (*kosmos*) refers here to the unbelieving world of mankind, particularly those who are part of Satan's world system that is so hostile toward God (cf. 12:31; 15:19; 17:14).

The world will have an attitude of hostility toward believers, but Jesus informs the disciples that this is nothing new. "Keep in mind," says Jesus, "that it hated me first." The words "keep in mind" (*ginōskete*) may be either indicative or imperative. The NIV is no doubt correct in taking *ginōskō* to be imperative.

15:19   Jesus goes on in vv. 19-21 to explain the reasons for the world's hatred toward His followers. The first reason (v. 19) is the essential difference in nature between the world and Christ's disciples. The words "if you belonged to the world" are in the second-class condition, expressing improbability. The phrase could be rendered "If you belonged to the world, and it is doubtful that you do..." The basic premise here is that the world has a friendly affection (*phileō*) for its own kind, but it hates (*miseō*) those who have turned their back on spiritual darkness to walk in the light. The old adage "Birds of a feather flock together" well illustrates the truth of v. 19. The world loves its own—those who belong to its system, commend its values, and follow its ways. Christ's disciples are hated by the world because they do not "belong to the world" but have been chosen "out of the world." The world hates believers because of the essential difference in nature between the unbelieving world and the followers of Jesus.

Few of those who live in countries with well-established religious freedoms personally experience the full extent of the world's hatred of Christ. But there are occasions, and they will increase by intensity and frequency as the world tumbles into the anti-God mentality of the last days.

15:20 The second reason given by Jesus for the world's hostility against believers is their identification with the rejected Christ. Jesus prefaces these next remarks with the admonition "Keep on remembering" (present imperative of *mnēmoneuō*). Jesus had already taught His disciples an important principle: "No servant is greater than his master" (cf. 13:16; Matt. 10:24). Reminding His disciples of this teaching He adds, "If they persecuted me, they will persecute you also. If they obeyed my teaching, they will obey yours also." As in v. 18, the word translated "if" (*ei*) indicates a condition of reality and could be translated "since" (because) in both places where it occurs here. Because Christ was persecuted, His disciple-servants can expect to be persecuted as well (cf. 1 Pet. 4:12-13). On the other hand, because some obeyed Christ's word (*ton logon*)—turning to Him for salvation (cf. John 3:36)—they would also obey the disciples. The disciples could expect to have fellowship with Christ in His sufferings and to share as well in His success.

15:21 The third reason given by Jesus for the world's hatred of believers is the world's ignorance of the Father. Jesus tells His disciples, "They will treat you this way because of my name, for they do not know the One who sent me." The inevitable hatred and persecution of Christ's followers by unbelievers is because unbelievers do not know God ("the One who sent me"). Rejection of the Son is the same as rejection of the Father (15:23), and it logically follows that those who reject both will reject Christ's disciples. For the significance of "my name," see comments on 14:13.

The Prediction of Hostility, 15:22-25

Jesus explains in vv. 22-25 that the world's hatred of Christ and His followers is inexcusable, yet inevitable, for it is in keeping with biblical prophecy.

15:22   Jesus appeals to His words (v. 22) and His works (v. 23) to demonstrate that the world has no excuse for rejecting Him. His appeal to His words is reflected in His statement "If I had not come and spoken to them, they would not be guilty of sin. Now, however, they have no excuse for their sin." Had Jesus not come and testified of His relationship with the Father, the Jewish people of the first century might be excused (i.e., "not guilty of sin") for rejecting Him. They would still be lost sinners in need of salvation, but they would not be guilty of the specific sin of rejecting Christ's words. However, because Jesus had come and spoken to the unbelieving world concerning His Person and work (5:18; 10:30), the people had no excuse for their sin (*hamartia*) of rejecting Him.

15:23   Jesus wants the disciples to understand clearly the gravity of rejecting His Person. "He who hates me hates my Father as well." By rejecting Jesus, they reject God the Father. And the opposite is also true (13:20). This suggests the closest possible relationship between the Father and Son. This is a clear statement about the pious and sincere worship of those who reject Jesus. To reject Jesus is to hate the true and living God.

15:24   Jesus' second point in demonstrating that the world has no excuse for rejecting Him is based on His works. He says, "If I had not done among them what no one else did, they would not be guilty of sin. But now they have seen these miracles, and yet they have hated both me and my Father." Had Jesus not performed His authenticating miracles or "works" (*ta erga*), those who rejected Him might have some excuse. But again, this was not the case. The miracles demonstrated again and again the truth of His Person (cf. 5:36; 10:37-38; 14:11; 20:30-31), but this testimony was consistently rejected. Sinning against the light of knowledge, those who rejected Him were left in sin and condemnation without excuse.

15:25   Verse 25 reveals that the world's hatred of Jesus was inevitable because it was prophesied in the Hebrew Scriptures. "But this is to fulfill what is written in their Law: 'They hated me without reason.'"

The words "those who hate me without reason" occur in Psalms 35:19 and 69:4. Both texts in the Septuagint read *oi misountes me dōrean*, "those hating me without a cause." Both passages speak of hatred and hostility that lack any reasonable basis. This is precisely the kind of hatred the unbelievers in the first century demonstrated toward Jesus, the divine Messiah. The term "Law" (*nomos*) is frequently used of the Pentateuch, but it refers more generally in this context to the Hebrew Scriptures.

THE RELATIONSHIP WITH THE HOLY SPIRIT, 15:26-27

Although the disciples had been called as witnesses to a hateful and hostile world (15:18-25), vv. 26-27 provide a word of encouragement. They did not face this task alone. The Holy Spirit would accompany them, bearing witness to the truth of Jesus.

15:26 Jesus reveals three things about the Holy Spirit: His titles, His origin, and His work. He is the Counselor (*ho paraklētos*), "one called alongside to help" (cf. 14:16). This title suggests He is one who will assist, empower, and encourage the believers. The designation "Spirit of truth" (cf. 14:17) indicates that He is characterized by and communicates truth. This aspect of His person is essential to His ministry of teaching the disciples (cf. 16:12-15).

Concerning the origin of the Holy Spirit, Jesus says He is one whom "I will send to you from the Father." Inasmuch as John 14:26 reveals that the Father will send the Spirit in Christ's name, it must be concluded that the Spirit is sent by both. The further statement that the Holy Spirit "goes out from the Father" was the basis for the decision of the Synod of Toledo (A.D. 589) to add the clause "and the Son" to the words of the Constantinople Creed (A.D. 381) regarding the "procession" of the Spirit.

The work of the Holy Spirit is revealed in the words "He will testify [*marturēsei*] about me." "He" (*ekeinos*) is in the emphatic position. In the face of hostility and unbelief, Jesus has a witness of the highest authority. The verb *martureō* simply means to testify or speak about someone or something. The witness of the Holy Spirit is elaborated by Jesus in 16:8-11.

15:27 The witness of the Holy Spirit would accompany the witness of the apostles. "And you also must testify, for you have been with me from the beginning." The form of the verb, *martureite*, may be taken as indicative ("you are bearing witness") or imperative ("you must bear witness"). Although the imperative seems to fit the general tenor of the passage (cf. 15:18, 20), Wescott's remarks reflect the difficulty of this translation problem.[19] The apostles would qualify as witnesses not only because of the indwelling Spirit (14:17) but also because of their personal knowledge of Christ. They had been with Him "from the beginning" of His ministry, the period commencing with His recognition and baptism by John (cf. 1:35ff.).

Verses 26-27 are foundational to the Christian's effective witness. First, believers must witness. Those who have been blessed with so much spiritually want to share the good news with others. Second, believers never witness alone. The Holy Spirit is always present, acting as a supportive partner, reinforcing the witness, and bringing about personal conviction.

HOMILETICAL SUGGESTIONS

John 15 provides an excellent text for an exposition of the believer's relationships—with Christ (15:1-11), with each other (15:12-17), with the unbelieving world (15:18-25), and with the Holy Spirit (15:26-27).

The believer's relationship with Christ (15:1-11) is depicted through the agricultural imagery of the vine and the branches. Because most people are not familiar with vineyards and grape growing, the cultural background should be fully developed in the exposition. The central truth here is that "fruit bearing results from abiding with Christ." Having established this basic premise, the sermon could focus on the kinds of fruit that should be seen in the Christian's life—answered prayer (v. 7), glorifying the Father (v. 8), a love relationship with God (v. 9), obedience to God's Word (v. 10), and full joy (v. 11).

The believer's relationship with other believers (15:12-17) develops the theme of *agapē* love, a concept that has been emphasized earlier (cf. 13:34-35). But within this section Jesus teaches on what it means to be His friend. Jesus mentions two conditions: complete obedience (v. 14) and personal knowledge. A friend of Jesus is one who knows Him intimately and obeys Him willingly.

The believer's relationship with the unbelieving world (15:18-25) is one of hatred and hostility. This is not a pleasant topic, but one we must face as Christians. There is an increasing lack of tolerance for Christian beliefs and perspectives in our society. Many have already

---

19. Westcott, *The Gospel According to St. John*, p. 225.

felt the sting of the world's hatred for Christ. This text provides consolation for a church facing increasing interference from government and society.

The believer's relationship with the Holy Spirit (15:26-27) is a tremendous encouragement in personal evangelism. The Holy Spirit is presented as a co-witness of the Person and work of Christ. This passage may be combined with others in a series on the ministries of the Holy Spirit.

JOHN
CHAPTER
SIXTEEN

WORK OF THE SPIRIT

Contextually, the first paragraph of chapter 16 continues the subject of the world's hostility, which was introduced in 15:18. Although a new chapter begins here, the United Bible Societies' Greek New Testament regards 16:1-4a as a continuation of 15:18-27.

THE MINISTRY OF THE HOLY SPIRIT, 16:1-15

Having promised the coming of the Holy Spirit as a co-witness (15:26-27), Jesus goes on in chapter 16 to provide further details concerning the ministry of the Spirit. He reveals that this work of witness will be done in the context of persecution (16:1-4).

THE PERSECUTION OF THE DISCIPLES, 16:1-4

Jesus returns to the idea of the world's hatred for His disciples (15:18) and reveals the intensity of that hostility.

16:1 Jesus has not been rambling in this great discourse. He has spoken with a definite purpose in mind. He has forewarned the disciples of coming persecution (15:18-25) in order that (*hina*) they "will not go astray." The expression "go astray" (aorist passive of *skandalizō*) is a metaphor that pictures one stumbling over an unexpected obstacle. Jesus was warning the disciples of the obstacles ahead so that they would not be taken by surprise and overcome by their trials. It is always easier to handle life's difficulties if they do not overtake us by complete surprise.

16:2   Jesus went on to reveal the extent of the trials the disciples could expect to face. To be "put out of the synagogue" was a form of excommunication. According to the Talmud, there were twenty-four offenses punishable by excommunication (*Berakot* 19a, Jerusalem Talmud *Mo'ed Katan* iii.1). For discussion on the three forms of excommunication described in the Talmud, see comments on 9:23. The most rigorous form of excommunication meant complete exclusion from the religious community and Jewish society.

Jesus added that a time will come when values will be so perverted that anyone who kills a follower of Christ "will think he is offering a service to God." The Greek word translated "service" (*latreia*) is used exclusively of "religious service" or "ritual" in the Septuagint (Ex. 12:25-26; 13:5; Josh. 22:27; see also Rom. 9:4; 12:1). This prediction was certainly realized in the life of Paul, who persecuted the early Christians out of a sincere zeal for serving God (cf. Acts 26:9-11; Phil. 3:6; 1 Tim. 1:13).

16:3   The persecution was certain, but the perversion of values was so extraordinary that an explanation was needed. Jesus explained "they will do such things because they have not known the Father or me." The word "because" (*hoti*) points to the reason for this hatred. The persecutors were ignorant of the Father and Son (cf. John 15:21). Although they may have known about God, their persecution of His followers indicated clearly that they had never really known (*ginōskō*) the Father as revealed by the Son.

16:4   Jesus gives His disciples the reason for His warning at this particular time. Until this point it had not been necessary to reveal such things. Jesus had been physically present with His disciples and had been available personally to guide and encourage those men. But with His departure imminent, it was necessary for the disciples to be forewarned so that they could cope with persecution when it came. The word "remember" (*mnēmoneuō*) means more than mere recall. It includes the idea of "keep in mind" or "think about."

The book of Acts indicates that Jesus' words served their purpose. When the apostles disobeyed the Sanhedrin's order to stop preaching about Him, they were flogged and commanded once again to speak no more in Jesus' name. Luke reports that they left the Council "rejoicing because they had been counted worthy of suffering disgrace for the Name. Day after day, in the Temple courts and from house to house, they never stopped teaching and proclaiming the good news that Jesus is the Christ" (Acts 5:41-42).

THE DEPARTURE OF JESUS, 16:5-7

Jesus had referred to His departure earlier in the discourse (13:33; 14:1-3). Now He returned to this subject and told the disciples why His departure was to their advantage.

16:5 Jesus here speaks of His departure as if it were already under way: "Now I am going [present tense] to him who sent me." The expression "him who sent me" (*ton pempsanta me*) is used repeatedly by Jesus to refer to the Father (cf. 5:24, 30, 36; also 14:12; 16:10, 17, 28).

Jesus' remark "Yet none of you asks me, 'Where are you going?'" is a bit troublesome because Peter asked this exact question in 13:36. This apparent contradiction has been used as an argument for re-arranging the discourse so that 15:1–16:33 precedes 13:31–14:31. But there are better alternatives. Perhaps Jesus' remark shows that the questioning was not persistent. Or perhaps the disciples' thoughts were on their own loss rather than on what the departure would mean to Him. As Morris suggests, perhaps Peter's question did not represent "a serious inquiry" as to Jesus' departure.[1] It is most natural, when trouble comes, to think of ourselves instead of others.

16:6 As with His earlier announcement (13:33), the words about Jesus' departure brought gloom to the disciples' faces and filled their hearts with sorrow (cf. 14:1). "Filled" (perfect active indicative of *pleroō*) indicates that there was room for nothing else. The word "sorrow" (*lupē*), used often in this chapter (16:20, 21, 22), occurs nowhere else in John. For the disciples, the departure of Jesus seemed like a terrible disaster, but in reality it would be to their benefit.

16:7 Jesus grabbed the disciples' attention with the emphatic words "But I tell you the truth" (cf. 1:51). Christ's departure was actually to their advantage, for without it there would be no coming of the Counselor (*ho paraklētos*), the Holy Spirit (cf. 14:16-17, 26; 15:26-27). Jesus uses a strong double negative (*ou me*) to emphasize that the Holy Spirit "will not come" apart from His departure.

Now, in what way is the indwelling presence of the Holy Spirit more advantageous than Christ's personal presence among His disciples? First, whereas Jesus could not always be with the disciples (cf.

---

1. Leon Morris, *The Gospel According to John*, NICNT (Grand Rapids: Eerdmans, 1971), p. 695.

John 6:17), the Holy Spirit is universally present in every believer (Rom. 8:9). Second, while Jesus was on earth, the disciples were sometimes fearful (cf. Mark 14:50; John 6:20). But after the coming of the Spirit they spoke for Christ with a new confidence and boldness (Acts 4:31). Third, whereas Jesus' stay on earth was temporary, the Holy Spirit would be with them "forever" (14:16). As Robertson points out, the Holy Spirit was already at work in the hearts of the disciples, but not in the full New Covenant sense (Jer. 31:31-34; Ezek. 36:25-28) that would take place after Christ's departure.[2] It is therefore quite a sobering thought to think that modern believers have a greater spiritual privilege than the apostles who lived and walked with Jesus.

THE WORK OF THE HOLY SPIRIT, 16:8-15

The death and departure of Jesus would prepare the way for an expanded ministry for the Holy Spirit in relationship to the world (16:8-11) and the believers (16:12-15).

16:8   In 16:8-11 Jesus expands the thought introduced in 15:26 regarding the Holy Spirit's witness to the unbelieving world. The Holy Spirit will bear witness to the Person and work of Christ by convicting the (unbelieving) world of guilt.

The word "convict" (*elegchō*) is an important word in this consideration. The word may be translated "convict," "reprove," or "rebuke." It implies a rebuke that brings conviction. In legal contexts the word means to cross-examine for the purpose of convincing or refuting an opponent. Here it is being used of awakening or proving guilt. More convincing than Perry Mason, the Holy Spirit will break down arguments, validate the evidence, elicit confession, and bring the unbeliever to conviction before Almighty God. The Holy Spirit will convict the world of guilt, convincing it of sin, righteousness, and judgment. It is important to recognize this as the Spirit's work, not man's. In our personal witness, it is often best simply to present the gospel and then wait while the Spirit begins to work. Just how the Holy Spirit brings conviction in relationship to these three issues is elaborated in vv. 9-11.

16:9   The "sin," "righteousness," and "judgment" mentioned in v. 8 are each introduced by the preposition *peri*, usually translated "because of," "with regard to," or "concerning" after verbs of judging or

2. A. T. Robertson, *Word Pictures in the New Testament* (Nashville: Broadman, 1932), 5:266.

censuring. The preposition *peri* is repeated in each verse (9-11) as the convicting work of the Spirit is further elaborated.

Jesus explains that the Holy Spirit will convict the world in regard to sin "because men do not believe in me." This can be taken to mean that their unbelief is an illustration of their sin. Morris remarks that the world's sin "received its classic expression when God sent His Son into the world and the world refused to believe in Him."[3] Plummer, on the other hand, regards the unbelief as the source of sin. "Sin is not limited to unbelief, but this is the beginning of it."[4] Robertson takes the text in the most straightforward manner, interpreting "sin" as the world's not believing in Jesus.[5] The Holy Spirit secures a verdict of guilty against the world because of the sin of unbelief. Certainly the greatest act of rebellion against God is the rejection of His beloved Son. It is the sin of unbelief that keeps so many from the joys of heaven.

16:10   The second ministry of the Holy Spirit in relationship to unbelievers is to convict them "in regard to righteousness." The word "righteousness" (*dikaiosunē*) occurs only here in John's gospel and refers to what is right in terms of God's will. Carson argues that the "righteousness" to which Jesus refers is that of the world that is "qualitatively inadequate and therefore must be repented of."[6] He suggests a parallel in Matthew 5:20, where Jesus tells the disciples that unless their righteousness surpasses that of the scribes and Pharisees, they will not enter the kingdom of heaven. This interpretation forges a convincing symmetry. The Paraclete convicts the world of its sin, of its righeousness, and of its judgment.

And yet it is significant that in Acts 3:14 Peter refers to Jesus as the "Holy and Righteous One." Jesus, the Righteous One, embodies the perfect standard of what is right as God has determined it. The explanation "because I am going to the Father, where you can see me no longer" clarifies this further. Christ's return to heaven, to be welcomed by the Father, is the ultimate proof that He is the perfect pattern of righteousness that God accepts. The Holy Spirit will convict unbelievers of their failure to accept the standard of righteousness

---

3. Morris, *The Gospel According to John*, p. 698.
4. A. Plummer, *The Gospel According to St. John* (Cambridge: At the University Press, 1899), p. 298.
5. Robertson, *Word Pictures in the New Testament*, 5:267.
6. D. A. Carson, "The Function of the Paraclete in John 16:7-11," *JBL* 98 (December 1979): 560.

that God approves—that righteousness exemplified in the Person of Christ, who remains the ultimate standard of righteousness for the world.

16:11   And finally, the Holy Spirit will convict the unbelieving world "in regard to judgment." This involves convincing the world of its liability for coming judgment. Jesus explains, "Because the prince of this world now stands condemned." The "prince of this world" (*ho archōn tou kosmou*) refers to Satan, who was judged at the cross (12:31). Now if Satan, a former angel and powerful spirit being, stands judged before God, what chance is there for man to escape judgment if God's grace is refused? There is absolutely no chance. Those who follow Satan will share his doom (cf. Matt. 25:41; Rev. 20:7-15). Few people cherish an intimate association with a loser. Satan is a loser, and those who unite themselves with Him through sin and unbelief will be lost as well.

There is a logical order presented here to the convicting ministry of the Holy Spirit in relationship to an unbeliever. First, the sinner needs to see his state of sin from God's perspective. Then, he needs to know that the righteousness Christ demonstrated provides the basis for salvation. Finally, the sinner must be reminded that if he refuses Christ's provision, he faces certain *judgment*. These verses could well provide a pattern for personal witness.

16:12   In John 14:26 Jesus tells the disciples that the Holy Spirit "will teach you all things." Now in vv. 12-15 Jesus elaborates on the teaching ministry of the Holy Spirit. He begins by informing the disciples, "I have much more to say to you, more than you can now bear." The word "bear" (*bastazō*) is used of Jesus carrying His cross (19:17) and is used figuratively of bearing anything burdensome (Acts 15:10). The word "now" (*arti*) is emphatic and contrasts the present case with future circumstances.

Why were the disciples unable to receive further teaching from Jesus at this time? Two suggestions are worthy of consideration. First, the disciples were limited in their ability to understand the truth because they had not yet received the illuminating ministry of the Holy Spirit. Second, apart from the indwelling ministry of the Spirit, they were not able to live out the implications of Jesus' teaching.

16:13   Anticipating the Spirit's work at Pentecost (Acts 2), Jesus announces that the "Spirit of truth" (cf. John 14:17) will "guide you into all truth." The word "guide" (*hodēgeō*) is actually made up of two words, "to lead" (*hēgeomai*) and "way" (*hodos*). The word indicates that the Holy Spirit, who is a source of truth, will lead the way into the truth as a guide. Note the words "all truth." There is no error, compromise, or variation in the truth He communicates. Such reliable teaching may be attributed to the fact that the Holy Spirit speaks "only what he hears" from Christ, and Christ speaks what He receives from the Father (7:16). Consequently, there is harmony and consistency in the revelation of the triune God. The Holy Spirit guided the apostles in what to write as divine revelation. By way of application, the Spirit continues to make clear (illuminate) the meaning of the inspired record (cf. 1 John 2:27).

A second ministry of the Spirit is mentioned in v. 13. Jesus informed the disciples that the Holy Spirit would also "tell you what is yet to come." The words "tell you" (*anagellō*) mean to "report" or "announce." The phrase "what is yet to come" refers to prophetic events. This promise was directed to apostles such as Peter and John to whom prophetic events would be revealed. For disciples today, the Holy Spirit gives them understanding of God's prophetic program as they study the apostolic writings.

16:14   A third ministry of the Holy Spirit is introduced in v. 14. Speaking of the Holy Spirit's ministry, Jesus says, "He will bring glory to me by taking from what is mine and making it known to you." The word "glorify" (*doxazō*) means to magnify or extol the reputation of another. The Holy Spirit will magnify Christ's reputation as He makes the truth of Christ's Person and work known. It is significant that the Holy Spirit works to glorify Christ rather than to draw attention to Himself. This truth may provide insight in determining what works are genuinely of the Holy Spirit.

16:15   Jesus explains how and why the Holy Spirit can reveal what the disciples need to know concerning Him. Jesus is in possession of "all [the truth] that belongs to the Father." For this reason, what the Spirit communicates may be fully relied upon. It is the truth of both the Father and the Son. Jesus assures the apostles that this truth will be communicated to them without deviation by the Holy Spirit. It is encouraging to know that we also have a teacher who is ever-present with us—the indwelling Spirit, whose "anointing teaches you about all things" (1 John 2:27).

SORROW TURNED TO JOY, 16:16-24

The disciples were about to experience the sorrow of seeing Jesus executed on a Roman cross. For them this would be a time of deep sadness. Jesus promised that although they would be sorrowful, their sorrow would be turned to joy on account of His resurrection.

16:16   Jesus announced to His disciples that, in a short time, "you will see me no more, and then after a little while you will see me." Was Jesus referring to His death followed by His postresurrection appearances or His ascension followed by His second coming? The announcement was not immediately clear to the disciples, nor has it been to the commentators. (For comments on the possible significance of the shift from *theōreite* to *opsesthe*, see v. 19.)

16:17   The disciples began questioning among themselves the meaning of Jesus' announcement. Obviously bewildered, they repeated the words of Jesus in v. 16 to themselves. The phrase "Because I am going to the Father" is drawn from 16:10. Wishing to prepare for v. 17 some copyists added the phrase in v. 16, where it is clearly not genuine. Coupling the phrase "Because I am going to the Father" with the words "after a little while" may indicate that the disciples saw a link between the two or were following through on a difficulty they felt earlier (16:10).[7] Jesus' departure was so imminent that John chose the present tense ("I am going").

16:18   The disciples' difficulty centered on the phrase "a little while" (*to mikron*). They continued asking (imperfect tense) one another the meaning of this key phrase. They had to confess their own lack of comprehension of Jesus' words. They simply had no idea what He was talking about. If the disciples had difficulty understanding the teaching of Jesus when they were in His presence, it is not surprising that we have difficulty with some of His teaching 2,000 years later.

16:19   Jesus recognized that the disciples were a bit perplexed and wanted to ask Him more. Before providing further insight (16:20), Jesus repeated His original statement (16:16). He made only a slight change in the negative particle from *ouketi* to *ou*.

Among the commentators there are three major views as to the meaning of Jesus' announcement in 16:16. Some have suggested that spiritual insight regarding the Person of Christ will follow His physical departure. Plummer writes, "When His bodily presence was with-

7. Morris, *The Gospel According to John*, p. 703.

drawn their view of Him was enlarged; no longer known after the flesh, He was seen and known by faith."[8] According to this view a distinction is made between the two verbs translated "see" in v. 16. The first "see" (*theōreō*) is interpreted to mean physical sight, and the second "see" (*oraō*) is taken to refer to spiritual sight or understanding. There is, however, no clear distinction between these two verbs in John's usage (cf. 1:39; 14:19; 20:18). They appear to be used as synonyms in vv. 16-17. Variation of vocabulary is a stylistic trait of John's writings.

A second interpretation takes Jesus' announcement to refer to His second coming, which will follow His ascension to heaven. But then the "little while" must be extended to nearly 2,000 years. It seems best to understand Jesus to be referring to the short time between His death and resurrection.[9] This view fits well with Jesus' similar remarks in 14:18-19. The point is, Christ's resurrection appearances would follow shortly after His death. Three days after His death, Jesus would appear to His disciples in His resurrection body.

16:20   Jesus provides further explanation of His announcement (16:16) in v. 20. The often repeated formula "I tell you the truth" (1:51) would cause the disciples to be alert for a key concept. Jesus explains, "You will weep and mourn while the world rejoices." The disciples would experience great sorrow at the crucifixion of Christ, whereas the unbelieving world would rejoice. But their grief would be short-lived. Jesus adds words of hope, "You will grieve, but your grief will turn to joy." The "but" (*alla*) reflects a strong contrast. The disciples' sorrow over the crucifixion would be surpassed by their rejoicing over the resurrection.

16:21   Jesus provides an illustration of the concept that sorrow precedes joy. Childbirth is first a cause of pain, but when the child is born, the pain and distress of labor is all but forgotten. The expression "she forgets the anguish" may be taken as hyperbole. Most mothers can remember the pain of labor. But such memories are far surpassed by the joy of bringing a healthy child into the world. The word "anguish" (*tēs thlipseōs*) is the basic word for tribulation or trouble (16:33) and is an apt term to describe the travail of labor.

8. Plummer, *The Gospel According to St. John*, p. 300.
9. Morris, *The Gospel According to John*, p. 702; F. F. Bruce, *The Gospel of John: Introduction, Exposition and Notes* (Grand Rapids: Eerdmans, 1983), p. 322; Merrill C. Tenney, "The Gospel of John," in *The Expositor's Bible Commentary*, ed. Frank Gaebelein (Grand Rapids: Zondervan, 1981), 9:159.

16:22   Jesus now applies the illustration to the experience of the disciples. "So, with you: Now is your time of grief, but I will see you again and you will rejoice and no one will take away your joy." The conjunction *oun* ("So, with you") links the illustration (v. 21) with the application (v. 22). The disciples would have sorrow over Christ's departure by death. But He would return to them in His resurrection body. The phrase "no one will take away your joy" contrasts their *temporary* sorrow over His death with their *permanent* joy over His resurrection. Their sorrow will depart, but their joy will remain.

This may be an appropriate place to distinguish between joy and happiness. Happiness is dependent on happenings, or favorable circumstances in our lives. Joy, on the other hand, is deeply rooted and grounded in a relationship with Jesus Christ. And this relationship never changes. Therefore, although believers may not always experience favorable circumstances, there is an ongoing basis for joy because of the presence of Christ in their lives.

16:23   Jesus instructs the disciples that in the day of His resurrection and thereafter ("In that day") they will have no need to question Him further about His teaching. There will be no need for questions such as, "Where are you going?" (13:36), "How can we know the way?" (14:5), or "What does he mean by 'a little while'?" (16:18). When the disciples receive the teaching ministry of the Holy Spirit (16:12-15), their questioning of Jesus will cease. Instead, they will bring their concerns directly to the Father. Prayer in Jesus' name (cf. 14:13-14; 15:16) is once again linked with effectual prayer.

Two different Greek words are translated "ask" in v. 23. The first word, *erōtaō*, is used here in the sense of asking a question. The second word is *aiteō*, used for making requests or asking favors. It is a word used of a subordinate person seeking something from a superior.

16:24   Jesus contrasts the disciples' experience with the new order about to be inaugurated by His return to the Father. In the past (before the Upper Room discourse) they had not prayed in Jesus' name. But from now on, things would be different. In view of His return to the Father, Jesus instructs the disciples, "Ask and you will receive, and your joy will be complete." The word "ask" (*aiteō*) is a present imperative suggesting that the request should be persistent and continual. For those who ask in Jesus' name—on the basis of His merits and influence as the Messiah and Son of God—there is promised answered prayer and full joy.

It is significant that the joy promised is linked with prayer. The last sentence in v. 24 could be translated, "Keep on asking, and you shall receive in order that [*hina*] your joy might be full." Believers are to pray in order that their joy may be complete. Perhaps when joy is lacking it is because believers have failed to pray. Just as earthly fathers desire the well-being and happiness of their children, so God, our heavenly Father, has these desires for us.

THE DISCOURSE SUMMARY AND CONCLUSION, 16:25-33

As Jesus approaches the end of the discourse He unites several themes to summarize and conclude His presentation. His final remarks were designed to encourage the disciples with the anticipation of sharing in Christ's victory (16:34).

THE DISCIPLES' FAITH, 16:25-30

In verses 25-30 Jesus encourages the faith of the perplexed and apprehensive disciples by promising to speak plainly about the Father after His resurrection.

16:25   Jesus contrasts His past speaking ministry with what the disciples could anticipate in the future. Up to this time in His ministry Jesus had been "speaking figuratively" to the disciples—through parables, allegories, and enigmatic sayings. The word translated "figuratively" is *paroimia*, meaning "proverb" or "dark saying," and is used especially of figures in which lofty ideas are concealed. The use of such enigmatic statements would soon cease. During his forty-day postresurrection ministry (Acts 1:3), Jesus would declare the truth of the Father to spiritually enlightened men. Instruction through parables and figures would then be unnecessary.

16:26   Jesus goes on in v. 26 to promise His disciples direct access to the Father. The words "In that day" (16:23) are usually taken to mean either after His resurrection or from Pentecost onward. Quite possibly Jesus is referring here to His resurrection and onward (cf. 16:25), when the disciples first received the Spirit's ministry (20:22). At that time it would no longer be necessary for Jesus to petition the Father in behalf of the disciples. In that day the disciples would appeal to the Father directly on the basis of Jesus' finished work.

16:27   Jesus explains that when the disciples request the Father's direction, God will respond because of their love for the Son and belief in His divine mission. The Greek word used for "love" here is *phileō* in contrast with *agapaō* in 14:21, 23. Although there is some difference in the root meaning of these words, John appears to use them synonymously. The Father's love for the disciples ("loves you") is in the present tense. It is persistent and continual. The words "you have loved" and "have believed" are in the perfect tense and indicate a settled conclusion and commitment.

16:28   Jesus declares His heavenly origin and heavenly destination. The verse contains a summary of the life of Christ—His mission ("I came from the Father"), His incarnation ("and entered the world"), His passion ("now I am leaving the world"), and His ascension ("and going back to the Father"). The word "entered" (*elēlutha*) is perfect tense, indicating the ongoing result of the incarnation. Christ will always be the God-man.

16:29   At this point in the discourse, the disciples begin to recognize that Jesus is speaking plainly. Perplexity over His previous teaching through "figures of speech" (*paroimia*, cf. 15:25) is now giving way to clearer understanding. "Now" (*nun*) is emphatic in the Greek sentence structure.

16:30   The disciples proceed to make a confident statement of their belief that Jesus is from God. "Now" is once again (cf. 16:29) in the place of emphasis in the Greek sentence structure. The disciples affirm Christ's omniscience: "Now we can see that you know all things." The words "you do not even need to have anyone ask you questions" refer to the fact that Jesus knew their very thoughts and was able to answer their questions even before they asked. Anticipating their questions, Jesus could answer them before they were spoken (16:19; cf. 2:24-25). Christ's full knowledge was convincing evidence of His divine origin. The disciples declare, "This makes us believe that you came from God."

THE COMING VICTORY, 16:31-33

The Upper Room discourse closes with the disciples' statement of faith and Christ's declaration of victory.

16:31   The words of Jesus "You believe at last!" can be understood grammatically as either a question ("Do you now believe?") or a statement of fact ("Now you believe"). The present tense indicative and imperative have the same verb form. The words "at last" (*arti*) may be translated "now" and contemplate the present situation in relation to the past or future. *Arti* could be translated "at this moment" or "at the present time." Jesus may be saying, "At this time you are trusting me." And by implication one might add, "But an hour of crisis is coming when that faith will be tested." Jesus was not questioning the reality of the disciples' faith. He was perhaps raising doubts as to its power and steadfastness.

16:32 Jesus goes on in v. 32 to speak of the disciples' future failure. He recognized that the long awaited "time" (2:4; 7:6, 30; 12:23; 13:1; 17:1) had virtually begun. The "time" (*hora*) refers to that hour when God would glorify the Son through His sacrificial death for sin (cf. 12:23-24; 17:1). For Jesus, it would be an hour of crisis. For the disciples, it would be a time of regrettable failure. Although they had professed faith in Christ and had committed themselves to Him (cf. Mark 14:31), they would all be scattered at His arrest. The word "scattered" (*skorpizō*) is used of sheep scampering (cf. 10:12). Although Zechariah 13:7 is not quoted here, there may be an implied allusion to it (cf. Mark 14:27). Abandoned by the disciples, Jesus would not be alone. The Father would be with him. And yet there was that moment on the cross when Jesus would cry out, "My God, my God, why have you forsaken me?" (Matt. 27:46). Becoming sin for the world, Jesus would be forsaken even by the Father, as God through Christ judged mankind's sin.

16:33 Jesus concludes His discourse by revealing the purpose of His instruction and the certainty of His victory. Jesus' purpose in telling the disciples "these things" (i.e., the entire discourse) is to provide them with "peace" (*eirēnē*; cf. 14:27). Verse 33 depicts the disciples as living within two spheres—"in me" and "in this world." The first is spiritual and eternal. The second is material and temporal. Temporal life in the world will be characterized by "trouble" (*thlipsis*) or "tribulation." The word is used in a general sense to speak of the "pressing affliction" that the disciples must endure as they identify with Christ in an unbelieving world (cf. 15:18-25). This is the pressure believers experience when they take a stand for Christ or speak out on a sensitive moral issue. Yet although believers face intense pressure from the world, they can enjoy internal peace in Christ.

Finally, in the face of the cross, Jesus claims victory over a troubled, unbelieving world. He announces triumphantly, "But take heart! I have overcome the world." Unbelievers view the crucifixion as symbolic of Christ's defeat. Jesus views it as the moment of victory. The pronoun "I" (*egō*) is emphatic. In the face of betrayal, disgrace, and death, Jesus claims the victory. And the victory Christ has accomplished at the cross is one in which believers share (1 Cor. 15:57; Col. 2:12; 1 John 5:4-5).

As long as they live on this earth believers will face pressure, hatred, and hostility. But Jesus' victory on the cross gives us confidence to keep the faith and press on with God's kingdom work. In the words of Paul, "We are more than conquerors through him who loved us" (Rom. 8:37).

HOMILETICAL SUGGESTIONS

The major contribution in the first half of John 16 is the work of the Holy Spirit in the world (16:8-11) and among believers (16:12-15). In relationship to the unbelieving world, the Spirit convicts. In relationship with the followers of Christ, the Spirit teaches. It is easy to overlook texts on the third Person of the Trinity. These passages provide opportunity to highlight His Person and work.

John 16:16-24 is an excellent text for helping people through hard times. There will be sadness in life this side of heaven. The disciples experienced it with the departure of Jesus. For Christians today it might be the loss of a loved one, the break up of a relationship, heartache over a rebellious child. There will be circumstances in life that are less than pleasant. The circumstances may not be "happy," but there can be deep and lasting joy for all those who know and love the Lord. The sadness fades and joy returns as believers focus on Him instead of their problems.

Verses 25-30 contain a statement of Christ's divine mission (v. 28) and the disciples' faith (v. 30). Taken together, these verses might provide a nice summary of the gospel and could be used in a brief homily or devotional.

JOHN
CHAPTER
SEVENTEEN

PRAYER WITH PURPOSE

OUR LORD'S PRAYER, CHAP. 17

Our Lord's prayer in John 17 is the crown and conclusion to the Upper Room discourse. It is commonly referred to as Jesus' "high priestly prayer," a designation it first received from the Lutheran theologian David Chytraeus (1530-1600).[1] The designation seems fitting, for in this prayer Jesus consecrates Himself for the work of the cross (17:19) and intercedes on behalf of those for whom the ultimate sacrifice is about to be offered (17:20).

This prayer is unique among the gospels. Other gospels mention Christ's praying, and some record His prayers. But John 17 contains the longest recorded prayer of Jesus. Spoken aloud (17:1) in the company of the disciples (18:1), this prayer provided consolation and instruction for those who heard. The place where it was spoken is not recorded. Jesus may have prayed this prayer in the upper room (but see comments on 14:31), on the way to Gethsemane, or possibly in the Temple courts as suggested by both Plummer and Westcott.[2] Josephus records that on the night of Passover the priests customarily opened the gates of the Temple beginning at midnight (*Antiquities*

---

1. F. F. Bruce, *The Gospel of John: Introduction, Exposition and Notes* (Grand Rapids: Eerdmans, 1983), p. 328.
2. A. Plummer, *The Gospel According to St. John* (Cambridge: At the University Press, 1899), p. 307; B. F. Westcott, *The Gospel According to St. John* (Grand Rapids: Eerdmans, 1973), p. 237.

18.29). Hence, a visit to the Temple by Jesus and the disciples, although not stated in the text, is certainly not improbable.

The prayer may be divided into three main sections. Jesus prays first for Himself (17:1-5), then for His disciples (17:6-19), and finally for future believers—all those who will believe on Him through the disciples' witness (17:20-26). This structure corresponds to Leviticus 16:17, where it is recorded that Aaron performed the day of atonement ritual for himself, his family, and for the whole community.[3]

JESUS' PRAYER FOR HIMSELF, 17:1-5

The theme of glory dominates the first section of the prayer. Jesus prays for Himself that He may be glorified that He in turn might bring glory to the Father (17:1, 5).

17:1   After He had finished His discourse, Jesus prayed. He did not close His eyes or bow His head. Instead, He "looked toward heaven," literally "lifted up His eyes." The word "eyes" (*ophthalmous*) is the word from which we derive the term *ophthalmologist*. His manner or "body language" reflected the position of petition. Jesus prayed, "Father, the time has come." Jesus had long anticipated this climactic moment (2:4; 7:6, 30; 12:23; 13:1). Now, with the cross before Him, Jesus recognized that the time had come for Him to complete the work for which He had been appointed.

His petition is reflected in the aorist imperative, "glorify your son." The word "glorify" (*doxazo*) is derived from *doxa* ("glory"), a word that refers to the estimation or opinion in which one is held. Here Jesus prays regarding His own reputation and attributes. His words "Glorify your son" petition the Father to bring into full display Jesus' divine character and attributes through His impending death and resurrection.

Note carefully that this request was not self-seeking. The purpose clause, introduced by *hina* ("that"), indicates that Jesus' request was motivated by a desire to glorify the Father. Christ's glorification would be but a means to enhancing the reputation of the Father. Paul may have the example of Jesus in view when he charged the Corinthians, "So whether you eat or drink or whatever you do, do it all for the glory of God" (1 Cor. 10:31).

3. Barclay M. Newman and Eugene A. Nida, *A Translator's Handbook on the Gospel of John* (London: United Bible Societies, 1980), p. 523.

17:2   Jesus uses a comparison to reveal the degree of glorification
He desires. The adverb *kathos* (translated "For" in the NIV) is most
frequently used to indicate comparison. It may be rendered "just as"
or "even as." Continuing the thought of His glory (17:1), Jesus requests that He be glorified to the same degree that He has been delegated authority over all mankind. He has been granted full authority
(5:19-29; 10:18) and requests full glory.

The purpose clause, introduced by "that" (*hina*), reveals the purpose for which Christ received His authority. The divine authority
possessed by Jesus was for the specific purpose of conferring "eternal
life" (3:15-16; 3:35-36; 5:24; 10:28). Yet this gift is not conferred indis-
criminately. It is granted only to the elect—those "given" to Christ by
the Father (cf. 6:37).

17:3   Verse 3 may seem like a nonessential footnote in Jesus' prayer,
yet it contains foundational truth concerning His Person and work. R.
E. Man has observed a chiastic structure in 17:1-5 that has its central
elements in the term "eternal life" (*aiōnios zōē*) and those who receive it (17:2-3).[4] The center point of the chiasm prepares for the focus on believers in the prayer as a whole (17:6-26).

It is clear that this prayer was designed for instruction as well as
petition. Here Jesus provides His definition of the eternal life He has
authority to confer. Here He equates eternal life with an intimate and
personal knowledge of God the Father and Christ His Son. The word
"know" (*ginōskō*) speaks of an intimate relationship, not just an
awareness of certain facts. The knowledge of God referred to here
comes through Jesus Christ (1:18). Because "know" is in the present
tense, Jesus must be referring to a growing and vital personal relationship with God.

It is noteworthy that the apostle Paul, first-century theologian
and veteran missionary, wanted to know Christ (Phil. 3:10). Moses had
a similar desire (Ex. 33:13). It seems clear that our knowledge of
Christ should not be static but growing. Many of us have known the
Lord for a long time. Is there that longing to know Him deeper and
more personally?

The expression "the only true God" (cf. 5:44; 1 John 5:20) reflects two fundamental tenets of monotheism. Jesus is the one and

---

4. Ronald E. Man, "The Value of Chiasm for New Testament Interpretation," *Bibliotheca Sacra*
   141 (April-June 1984): 150-51.

only God (Deut. 6:4), and among all the false gods of polytheism He is the true One (Ex. 20:3-6). The only other occurrence of the title "Jesus Christ" is in 1:17 (although see 20:31). The thought that God "sent" Jesus appears frequently in the fourth gospel and is prominent in chapter 17 (vv. 8, 18, 21, 23, 25).

17:4   Returning to the topic of His glorification, Jesus declares in v. 4 that the Father has been glorified as a result of His earthly ministry. The words "I have brought you glory" show that Jesus' life and ministry magnified the Father's reputation in the sight of others. It is significant that Jesus accomplished this "on earth," the very place where sin and rebellion have thrived.

Jesus explains further that the Father was glorified by His "completing the work" that God had appointed Him to accomplish. The word "completing," the aorist active participle of *teleioō*, "to finish," is based on the same Greek root as *teleō*, used in 19:30 where Jesus proclaims the completion of His redemptive work. At Jacob's well Jesus told His disciples, "My food is to do the will of him who sent me and to finish his work" (4:34). Now with the cross before Him, Jesus sensed the fulfillment of the task He had come to accomplish (19:30). There is a good principle here for believers: God is glorified through the accomplishments of His obedient servants. What work are we accomplishing today that will bring glory to our Father?

17:5   Jesus repeats and elaborates His original request. He prays, "And now, Father, glorify me in your presence with the glory I had with you before the world began." In His incarnation Jesus took on human flesh, and the divine glory He enjoyed as the second Person of the Trinity was veiled. At His transfiguration Jesus gave Peter, James, and John a revelation of the future glory He would enjoy in the kingdom (Matt. 17:1-2). Now, with His earthly ministry nearing completion, Jesus prays for a full restoration of His own preincarnate glory and the intimate fellowship He had enjoyed throughout eternity past.

The words translated "in your presence" (*para seautō*) speak of an experience beyond the present world and anticipate a return to the blessed fellowship the Father and Son shared before the incarnation (1:14). The words "which I had with you before the world began" affirm the preexistence and eternality of Jesus and are strong evidence for His deity as Son of God. As Jesus had glorified the Father on earth (17:4), now He sought to be glorified with the Father in heaven.

JESUS' PRAYER FOR THE DISCIPLES, 17:6-19

Having prayed for Himself, Jesus prays for His eleven faithful disciples. Here He focuses on the relationship of the disciples with the world and prays that the Father will keep them safe in view of Jesus' coming departure (17:11-12).

Their Progress in Faith, 17:6-8

As Jesus' thoughts turn to the disciples, He first describes their present status in relationship to the progress of belief.

17:6   Jesus prays, "I have revealed you to those whom you gave me out of the world." The word "reveal" (aorist tense of *phaneroō*) means "to make visible, clear, manifest or known." In the Greek text the object of the verb is "your name" (*sou to onoma*). The word "name" is used in the sense of "reputation" or "attributes." Jesus is here summarizing His life's work: the revelation of God's Person and character through His ministry. Although Jesus had a unique ability to reveal God to His followers, He does provide a good model for Christians at this point. It should be a goal of all Christians to reveal God through their words and actions.

The thought of the disciples being given to Jesus is prominent throughout this prayer (17:2, 9, 12, 24) and points to the sovereignty of God in both salvation and discipleship. Jesus acknowledges that those disciples whom God gave Him "have obeyed your [the Father's] word." The word "obeyed" (literally, "kept") is in the perfect tense, giving emphasis to the point of culmination and the existence of its finished results. The eleven disciples had responded by personal faith to the revelation God had given them in Christ.

17:7   The disciples recognized that "everything" (*panta*) given to Christ comes ultimately from the Father. The Father is the source of Christ's mission (12:44; 13:3), His authority (5:27), and His teaching (7:16; 8:28; 12:49).

17:8   Verse 8 provides the reason or logic behind the words of v. 7, as indicated by the Greek particle *hoti*, translated "For" in the NIV. The fact that the disciples received Christ's teaching ("the words") indicates their belief in His heavenly origin ("I came from you") and divine commission ("you sent me"). It has been suggested that the "words" (*rhēmata*) refer to "separate utterances" as distinct from *logos* (17:6), "the doctrine as a whole," but John, being prone to variation, may intend no significant difference in meaning between the two words.

Their Perils in this World, 17:9-16

In vv. 9-16 Jesus focuses on the relationship of the disciples and the world. Although they did not belong to the world, they had to remain in the world, and Jesus prays that the Father will protect them from the Evil One (v. 15).

17:9 Jesus prays (present tense, "I am praying"), making His request not for the unbelieving world (the *kosmos*) but for the little band of disciples the Father had given Him. His reason, or explanation, is revealed in the causal phrase "for they are yours." Although they had been entrusted to the Son (17:6), the disciples were God's own chosen ones.

Why would Jesus *not* pray for the *kosmos*? Certainly God loves the world and gave His son for it (3:16; 17:23). In His infinite wisdom and sovereignty God has chosen to bring the unbelieving world to faith through the disciples. Therefore, Jesus prays here for the disciples whose witness would bring salvation to the world.

17:10 Jesus recognizes that "all" that belongs to Him belongs to the Father, and all that belongs to the Father belongs to Him. The Father and Son are mutual sharers in everything, a concept that reflects Their perfect unity. The word "all" (*ta panta*) is neuter but refers here to persons and things, as indicated by the pronoun "them" at the end of the verse.

Jesus acknowledges that His "glory" (*doxazō*), the splendor of His character and reputation, has been revealed through the disciples. The perfect passive indicative of *doxazō* could be rendered "I stand glorified," emphasizing the ongoing impact of the disciples' personal faith and witness. They were successful in the work to which Paul calls believers (1 Cor. 10:31).

17:11 Verses 6-10 are introductory to Jesus' first request for the disciples, which appears here. Jesus is soon to depart for heaven, leaving the disciples on earth to face the hostility of those under Satan's sway. The words "and I am coming to you" must have delighted the heart of God as He anticipated receiving His Son in heaven with the Son's mission accomplished on earth.

The expression "Holy Father" (*pater hagie*) occurs nowhere else, although the concept of God as "the Holy One" is prominent in the Hebrew Scriptures. The concept of "separateness" lies at the root of the term "holy" (*hagios*). God is totally separate from all that is common or defiling.

Jesus' prayer for the disciples is a simple one: "Holy Father, protect them by the power of your name," or more literally rendered, "Holy Father, keep them in your name." The word "keep" (*tēreō*) is used elsewhere in the New Testament of keeping persons safe (Acts 16:23; 24:23; 25:4, 21). The preposition *en* ("in") may indicate location ("in," "within," "among") or agency ("by means of"). The "name" (*onoma*) of God in the Hebrew Scriptures may signify His character (as in 17:6) or His power (Ps. 20:1; 54:1; Prov. 18:10). The NIV has taken the second alternative in both cases, translating it "by the power of your name." If one takes the first alternative in both cases, Jesus prays that the disciples be kept in the knowledge of God's character as revealed in Christ.

The purpose of God's "keeping" the disciples is revealed in the last phrase, "that they may be one as we are one." Jesus desired that the disciples experience a unity among themselves that was patterned after the essential unity between the Father and Son (17:21, 23).

17:12 Jesus' concern for the disciples was motivated by His imminent departure. In v. 12 Jesus reflects on His past ministry among the disciples. "While I was with them, I protected them and kept them safe by that name you gave me." Because Jesus would no longer be personally present on earth to keep and guard the disciples, He committed the task to the Father.

Concerning the outcome of His work, Jesus remarks, "None has been lost except the one doomed to destruction so that Scripture would be fulfilled." His work with the eleven had been successful. He lost no one except Judas. And that "exception" was according to biblical prophecy (cf. Ps. 41:9). The expression "doomed to destruction" (*apōleia*) is the very antithesis of the concept of salvation and indicates that Judas was an unregenerate man (cf. John 3:15-16; 10:28; 2 Thess. 2:3; Rev. 17:8, 11).

It is hard to imagine that someone spent so much time with Jesus but did not personally believe and enter into saving faith. This reflects the depravity of the human heart and illustrates how it is easy to have a knowledge of God and His Word without knowing Him personally.

There was once a third-year student at Western Seminary in Portland, Oregon, where I teach, who realized that after all his Bible and theology courses he was personally unregenerate. By God's grace he did not graduate in that condition. He was led by one of his professors to *apply* the facts he knew so well and place his personal faith in Christ.

17:13   Here Jesus again reflects on His impending departure (cf. 17:11) and remarks on His reason for praying in the disciples' presence. Christ prayed aloud in the disciples' presence "so that they may have the full measure of my joy within them." The purpose clause is introduced by *hina* ("so that"). Jesus wanted the disciples to experience the full measure of His own joy. Jesus intended that they be comforted by the fact that He had committed them to the Father's safe keeping.

17:14   Verse 14 provides the grounds and motivation for the request of v. 15. As those who received God's revelation in Christ ("your word"), the disciples were hated by the unbelieving world (15:18-21). And like Jesus, they shared nothing in common with this unbelieving world system (*kosmos*). Christians today seem to fall short of this standard. Compromise with the world's ways and values often results in believers' being almost indistinct from unbelievers. Certainly this is reflected in the lack of Christian influence on our world.

17:15   In light of the world's hostility toward believers who are separated from the world and identified with Christ, Jesus petitions the Father, "My prayer is not that you take them out of the world but that you protect them from the evil one." Jesus did not pray that the disciples be removed from the world, for that is where they were needed. It is noteworthy that Moses, Elijah, and Jonah all prayed to be taken out of the world, but in no case was the request granted (Num. 11:15; 1 Kings 19:4; Jonah 4:3, 8).

Jesus did not pray that the disciples would be exempted from combat by being removed from the arena. He did pray that they be kept from the permanent and overriding influence of the enemy (*tou ponērou*). Some expositors believe that here Jesus is simply praying for the disciples to be kept from evil. But the definite article (*tou*) indicates that Jesus is referring to the evil one—Satan himself (Matt. 5:37; 1 John 5:19). Well aware of the activity of Satan and his dominion over the world, Jesus prays that His own disciples might be kept safe from Satan's power and influence as they carry out God's work in enemy territory.

Satan is alive and well on planet Earth. But believers have nothing to fear from the evil one. It is encouraging to know that God can and will protect them from Satan's evil designs (cf. 1 Pet. 5:8-9; 1 John 4:4).

17:16   Verse 16 repeats the thought of the last half of v. 14. The words "They are not of the world" served in v. 14 as the reason for the world's hatred. Here the same comment is used to introduce the next petition.

Their Sanctification in the Truth, 17:17-19

Verses 17-19 are concerned with the sanctification of Jesus and His disciples. Here Jesus offers His third request in behalf of the eleven.

17:17   Jesus prays, "Sanctify them by the truth; your word is truth." The word "sanctify" (*hagiazō*) literally means "to set apart." It can be used of persons or things. That which is set apart is withdrawn from ordinary use and is dedicated for a special purpose. Certain vessels from the potter's shop that were set aside for use by the priests officiating in the Temple became "holy vessels" (cf. Rom. 9:21). Sanctification has the idea of "dedication" or "consecration," and in a spiritual context implies separation from evil.

According to Scripture there are three aspects to a believer's sanctification—past, present, and future. Believers are *positionally* sanctified at the point of salvation (cf. 1 Cor. 1:2). They are *experientially* sanctified as they set themselves apart from the power and influence of sin (cf. 1 Thess. 4:3). And they will be *ultimately* sanctified when they see Christ in their glorified bodies (cf. 1 John 3:2). The only aspect of sanctification that believers can do anything about is the present aspect, and that is precisely what Jesus prays about in v. 17.

The disciples' sanctification is to be done "by the truth" (*en tē alētheia*). The preposition *en* can be interpreted in a locative ("in the sphere of") or instrumental ("by means of") sense. It is not necessary to choose between the grammatical options. Both may be in view. Perhaps Jesus was praying that the disciples be sanctified "in and through a knowledge of the truth." Believers will be sanctified in this life as they yield to God's will and obey His Word by the power of the Holy Spirit (Rom. 8:3-4).

The "truth" to which Jesus refers is "the word" (*ho logos*) or revelation that He received from the Father and made known to the disciples (17:8, 14). Although Jesus is not referring directly to the Hebrew Scriptures, His statement "Your word is truth" reflects His high view of the integrity of God's revelation and would certainly apply to sacred Scripture. The Word of God is the essence of truth (cf. 2 Tim. 3:15-16; 2 Pet. 1:20-21) and study of it is essential for those who would strive for personal holiness.

17:18   Verse 18 develops in a positive way the thought introduced in v. 15. The disciples were not going to be taken "out of the world" (17:15). Rather, Jesus was sending them "into the world." In keeping with the emphasis on the nations introduced in the Abrahamic Covenant (Gen. 12:3) and developed throughout Scripture (Isa. 41:1; 53:11-12; Amos 9:12), the disciples were commissioned as Christ's representatives to the world.

Note that Jesus' own mission forms a pattern for the apostles. As He was sent with a task to discharge, so the apostles were being sent into the world with a mission to accomplish. The comparative adverb "as" (*kathōs*) indicates that Christ was sending (*apostellō*) the disciples in the same way as the Father had sent the Son. Jesus may be referring here to His call and the appointment of His apostles as "fishers of men" (Matt. 4:19-20). It is also possible that these words anticipate the commissioning in 20:21 (where the present tense is used) as a certain fact.

17:19   Concluding His prayer for the disciples, Jesus declares in this verse, "For them I sanctify myself, that they too may be truly sanctified." Now in what way can the sinless Christ "sanctify" Himself? The answer lies in the meaning of the word *hagiazō*. If the word means "to be holy," there is an inherent problem. Jesus is sinless. He cannot be made more holy than He already is. But if the word means "to set apart," as was indicated in v. 17, then the meaning of v. 19 is clear. While living in this world Jesus "set himself apart" to the Father's will and purpose.

The last half of the verse indicates the intended purpose of Christ's sanctification. He set Himself apart to do God's will and to go to the cross to provide a basis for the disciples' own sanctification. Through His death the way was prepared for the disciples to be "set apart" to God, both in their salvation and service for their Lord.

THE PRAYER FOR FUTURE BELIEVERS, 17:20-24

Jesus concludes His prayer by praying for future disciples who will come to believe in Him through the ministry of the apostles. It is in this section that modern-day believers find the greatest personal application—here they find Christ's prayer for today's church.

For Unity, 17:20-23

17:20   Jesus prayed not only for His eleven faithful disciples but also for those who would come to believe in Him "through their message." In v. 20 Jesus speaks of those who come to trust Him through the message (*tou logou*) the apostles proclaim. He is speaking of the church—believers who through the ages have come to affirm the apostolic message that the resurrected Jesus is God's divine Son and Messiah. It is significant that Jesus anticipated that people would believe in Him (divine sovereignty and election) and that they would do so through the disciples' witness (personal evangelism). The sovereign and elective purposes of God, therefore, never make believers less responsible for personal outreach.

17:21 Jesus' prayer for future believers is that they might all be "one" (*hen*). Here He picks up and develops the thought introduced at the end of v. 11. The word "one" is in contrast to the parts of which the whole is made up and suggests the idea of oneness or unity (cf. Rom. 12:5; Gal. 3:28; Eph. 2:14). The words "just as" (*kathōs*) introduce the pattern for the unity. Jesus wants believers to experience a spiritual unity patterned after the unity shared by the Father and Son. In the Trinity there is a multiple of Persons—the Father, the Son, and the Holy Spirit—but one divine essence (Deut. 6:4; Matt. 28:19; John 10:30). So, too, in the Body of Christ there are many members, but they share in a unity of the Spirit (1 Cor. 12:13).

The purpose of the unity in the church—the Body of Christ—is at least twofold, as indicated by the two purpose clauses, both introduced by *hina* ("in order that"). The NIV obscures the first purpose clause by beginning a new sentence, "May they also be in us." The Greek text reads, "That all may be one, just as you, Father, are in me and I in you, that they also may be one in us, that the world might believe that you sent me." The first purpose of the unity is to promote the believers' fellowship with God ("that they also may be one in us"). The unity of believers allows them to share in a unity with the Father and Son. The second purpose for the believers' unity is evangelistic. Jesus prayed for the church to be united so that the world might believe (*pisteuō*) in His divine mission ("that you have sent me"). The present active subjunctive of *pisteuō* ("keep on believing") refers to a faith that is genuine and lasting.

Whereas the unity of believers has the potential to convince unbelievers of Christ's divine mission, it would seem clear from the text that disunity among believers would have the opposite effect. How often has the advance of the gospel been hindered by disunity and strife among believers? What a tragedy to have our witness to the world hindered by bitterness, internal strife, and an unwillingness to forgive. These attitudes are all too common in our churches today.

17:22   Verse 22 reveals the plan for achieving the unity for which Christ prayed. Jesus says, "I have given them the glory that you gave me, that they may be one as we are one." It is clear that the "glory" given to Jesus has been granted to believers. And this glory was given to the disciples for the purpose of creating unity ("that they may be one").

The major problem in this verse is what Jesus meant by "the glory." Kent suggests that Jesus is referring to the glory that believers share with Christ in heaven (Eph. 2:6).[5] Westcott interprets "glory" to refer to the full apprehension of God's purposes in Christ, which results in the believer's transformation and unity.[6] Plummer takes his cue from v. 24 and interprets this "glory" to refer to the glory of the ascended and glorified Christ.[7] Morris suggests that Jesus is referring to the glory of the path of humble service. He comments, "Just as His true glory was to follow the path of lowly service culminating in the cross, so for them the true glory lay in the path of lowly service wherever it might lead them."[8] Which of these options would result in unity among members of the Body of Christ? It seems that the view of Morris would best accomplish this objective. The view is consistent with the context of Jesus' life (Mark 10:45) and immediate teaching (cf. 13:1-17).

Serving one another certainly leads to expressions of appreciation and kindles a greater sense of unity. The path of greatness through humble service is the glory in which both Jesus and believers may share. Each believer must ask, "Are my attitudes and actions contributing to or hindering a sense of unity among believers?"

17:23   Verse 23 continues the thought of unity. The words "I in them and you in me" explain the meaning of "that they may be one as we are one" in v. 22. This is unity beyond human comprehension. God the Father is in Christ, and Christ indwells believers. In their unity as believers the disciples share in a unique and blessed fellowship with the Godhead.

5. Homer A. Kent, Jr., *Light in the Darkness* (Grand Rapids: Baker, 1974), p. 193.

6. Westcott, *The Gospel According to St. John*, pp. 146-247.

7. Plummer, *The Gospel According to St. John*, p. 314.

8. Leon Morris, *The Gospel According to John*, NICNT (Grand Rapids: Eerdmans, 1971), p. 734.

Continuing the thought of the unity of believers (17:22), Jesus reveals the ultimate objective of the unity for which He prayed. He desires that believers be "brought to complete unity." The periphrastic perfect of *teleioo* suggests a permanent state of unity. The purpose (*hina*), Jesus reveals, is "to let the world know [keep on knowing] that you sent me and have loved them even as you have loved me." Jesus intends the perfected state of unity among believers to impress the world in a significant and lasting way with Christ's divine mission ("you sent me") and God's supreme love ("have loved them").

In keeping with Jesus' prayer, the goal of the Body of Christ should be to grow into such a unity that the world will recognize believers as one. The display of such unity in our individualistic society will serve as a shining testimony to the world of the divine Person and work of Christ.

For Fellowship, 17:24

17:24   Jesus concludes His prayer for future believers by expressing His desire that they may be with Him in heaven to enjoy the splendor and majesty of His preincarnate glory. The expression "those you have given me" refers to believers (cf. 17:2) and reflects the sovereignty of God in appointing some to salvation. Jesus prays that those believers may be "with me," that is, in heaven (13:36; 14:3; Rom. 8:17; 2 Cor. 5:8; 1 Thess. 4:17). He also prays that they may "see my glory" (cf. 17:1, 5). Here Jesus is asking that those who know Him may "keep on beholding" (present tense of *theōreō*) His glorious reputation as demonstrated by His Person and work.

The "glory" (*doxa*) to which Christ refers is further defined in the last half of the sentence. The glory given Christ is the evidence of the Father's eternal love. The phrase "before the creation of the world" (Matt. 25:34; Luke 11:50) reflects the preexistence of Christ, who shared in a personal relationship with the Father from eternity past (cf. John 1:1). Bruce remarks, "The disciples had seen the divine glory in the incarnate Word on earth (John 1:14); they will see it more fully when they live in the presence of the glorified Lord—not, perhaps, because he will then be endowed with more of that glory but because they will be better able to behold it."[9]

9. Bruce, *The Gospel of John*, p. 336.

THE CONCLUDING BENEDICTION, 17:25-26

Jesus concludes His prayer by calling attention to the world's ignorance, His disciples' faith, and His own mission.

17:25   In v. 11 Jesus used the term "Holy Father," and here He addresses God as "Righteous Father" (*patēr dikaie*). God is righteous (Ps. 119:137; Jer. 12:1) because He does what is right and just. Jesus goes on to distinguish Himself and His disciples from the unbelieving world that "does not know" the Father. The word "know" (*ginōskō*) speaks of a personal, experiential knowledge, not just a knowledge of facts. The word appears five times in vv. 25-26. The world could not experience God because it had rejected the Father's revelation in the Son. Jesus made clear throughout His ministry that the only way to know the Father is through the Son (John 1:18; 14:6).

Jesus, in contrast to the world, knows the Father. And the disciples had fully and personally recognized the divine mission of Christ as sent from God.

17:26   Although the disciples had come to know God the Father through Christ, they had much more to learn. In v. 26 Jesus commits Himself to a perpetual mission of making the Father known. This work would be accomplished through the ministry of the Holy Spirit (cf. 16:12-15).

The twofold goal of Jesus' future revelation of the Father is disclosed in the purpose clause at the end of the verse, "in order that the love you have for me may be in them and that I myself may be in them." First, Jesus desired that the Father's love might indwell the disciples. The "love which you have for me" speaks of the quality of love that Jesus wants the disciples to experience. Jesus is praying that the quality and degree of love He has enjoyed in relationship with the Father might rule in the disciples' hearts, guiding them in their actions and relationships.

Second, Jesus desired that He "may be in them." Although He knew that He must go away (13:33; 14:2; 16:5), Jesus wanted to remain with the disciples. So He prayed that He might indwell them. Having known Christ in His physical body, they would now know Him according to His spiritual presence. As Jesus told His disciples before His ascension, "And surely I am with you always, to the very end of the age" (Matt. 28:20).

HOMILETICAL SUGGESTIONS

John 17, our Lord's high priestly prayer, divides nicely into three sections for preaching. Verses 1-5 record Christ's prayer for Himself and focus on His desire to glorify the Father. Christ's own desire in this regard provides an excellent pattern for believers (cf. 1 Cor. 10:31). Verse 3 provides a concise definition of eternal life and could serve as the key text for a message on this subject.

In vv. 6-9 Jesus prays for His disciples. This message could focus on His three requests: protect them by the power of Your name (v. 11); protect them from the evil one (v. 15); and sanctify them in the truth (v. 17). Although Jesus was praying for the eleven apostles, each one of these requests has practical implications for present-day believers. Verse 12 provides a sobering statement on the spiritual state of Judas and could be used to warn of the dangers of theological knowledge without personal faith.

The most exciting part of this chapter is the section where Jesus prays for future believers (vv. 20-24). Here Jesus prays for the church of today. His two requests, for unity (vv. 20-23) and for fellowship (v. 24), provide helpful insight in discerning the priorities of God for Christians. So often we focus on programs and activities while we neglect issues that must be resolved to build unity in the church and maintain fellowship with Christ. God is more concerned with the internal condition of the church than with its external structure or programs. If our unity is strong and fellowship is sweet, then God will be pleased and His church will grow.

JOHN
CHAPTER
EIGHTEEN

STEPS TO THE CROSS

THE CONSUMMATION OF UNBELIEF, CHAPS. 18-19

Chapters 18 and 19 record the arrest, trial, and crucifixion of Christ. In relationship to John's thematic development of belief and unbelief, this section illustrates the culmination of the unbelief (cf. 1:11; 6:64; 7:5; 12:37).

Yet even through these very difficult hours of His rejection Jesus is presented by John not as the victim but as the victor. He was in absolute control of the events that issued in His arrest, trial, and crucifixion. He delivered His own disciples from the arresting authorities (18:8-9). In the garden He could not be touched except by His permission (18:6). Even in death, His life was not taken from Him. John records that Jesus voluntarily yielded up His spirit (19:30). It was through these events that Jesus fulfilled His mission as the "lamb of God who takes away the sin of the world" (1:29).

In this section John turns again from discourse to narrative as he records that portion of his gospel that bears the closest resemblance to the synoptics.

THE ARREST IN THE GARDEN, 18:1-12

John has already introduced the reader to Judas the betrayer (6:70-71; 12:4; 13:2, 11, 21-27). Unlike the synoptic account, John does

315

not recount the arrangements made by Judas with the religious leaders to betray Jesus (Matt. 26:14-16; Mark 14:10-11; Luke 22:3-6).

18:1   When Jesus had finished His intercessory prayer (17:1-26), He departed with His disciples for the Garden of Gethsemane. Actually the word "garden" may be misleading. John's word *kēpos* (NIV "grove") may refer to a garden or orchard, not necessarily a place where flowers or vegetables are grown. The word used both in Matthew 26:36 and Mark 14:32 is *chōrion*, meaning "a piece of land" or "a place." The word "left" seems to indicate that Jesus remained in the upper room for the entirety of His discourse and prayer (see comments on 14:31). The Kidron[1] Valley (see 2 Sam. 15:23) lies east of Jerusalem and separates the city from the Mount of Olives. The valley has a small stream that flows during the winter, but the stream bed is dry most of the summer. The valley pursues a long, winding course through the wilderness to the Dead Sea.

Although John does not name the garden (for "Gethsemane," see Matt. 26:36; Mark 14:32), he records its location east of the Kidron and reports that there was an "olive grove" there. This detail coincides with the name "Gethsemane," which means "oil press." Because Luke records that the disciples went out "to the Mount of Olives" (Luke 22:39), it appears that the grove was located on the lower slopes of the Mount of Olives, across the Kidron from Jerusalem.

18:2   John remarks that Judas was familiar with Gethsemane because Jesus often met there with His disciples. It was a place of quiet retreat from the crowds who were continually following and questioning Him. The sanctity of this place was about to be violated by an infamous betrayal. Judas is literally described in the Greek text as "the one betraying" Him. The present tense of the participle *paradidōmi* ("to deliver over") suggests the vividness of an unfolding drama. The betrayal was actually in progress.

18:3   It was Judas who led the arresting officers to the olive grove where Jesus was with His disciples. The group that came to arrest Jesus included a detachment of Roman soldiers and some religious officials from the chief priests and Pharisees.

The word translated "detachment" is the Greek word *speira*, which is used to translate the Latin *cohors*, rendered in English "co-

---

1. A number of Greek manuscripts read *ton kedrōn*, "of the cedars," or *tou kedrou*, "of the cedar," but these readings are not widely accepted because the two variants have the appearance of corrections and there is no evidence that there were ever cedars in the valley.

hort." A cohort was a tenth of a Roman legion and normally was com-posed of six hundred men, although the number varied at different periods in Roman history. The Roman prefects of Judea had six co-horts at their command. Five were stationed in Caesarea and one in Jerusalem, probably at the fortress of Antonia. The Greek word *speira* does not require that the whole Roman cohort went to Gethsemane. Rather, a small detachment was sent with an officer in charge (see 18:12).

The "officials" (*huperetes*) or officers from the "chief priests" (see note on John 7:32) and "Pharisees" (see note on 1:24) were ap-parently members of the Temple guard (7:32). They were commis-sioned by the Sanhedrin, referred to here as "the chief priests and Pharisees" (cf. 11:57). The Temple guard, made up of Levites, guarded the entrances of the Temple and patrolled the Court of the Gentiles. They were at the disposal of the Sanhedrin, which met near the Tem-ple, and could be called upon to make arrests and execute punish-ments.[2]

The fact that members of the arresting party were armed with weapons suggests that they anticipated resistance and were prepared to thwart it.

18:4 Jesus was not taken by surprise at His arrest in the olive grove. John explains that Jesus knew precisely what was going to happen to Him (literally, "the things coming upon Him"). He knew what was ahead and carried out His actions accordingly. Instead of fleeing from the arresting officers, He went to them and asked, "Who is it you want?" Obviously, Jesus knew who the soldiers sought. But His question forced the authorities to state their business. John omits any reference to the kiss by Judas (Matt. 26:49; Mark 14:45; Luke 22:37). As Morris acknowl-edges, "He is not concerned to tell us everything that happened, but rather to show Jesus' complete control of the situation."[3]

18:5 The Temple guard answered Jesus' question (v. 4) with the words "Jesus of Nazareth." Although Jesus was born in Bethlehem (Mic. 5:2; Matt. 2:1), He grew up in the Galilean town of Nazareth (Matt. 2:23-24; John 1:45-46). Jesus' reply "I am he" (*egō eimi*) may be a simple self-identification, "I am Jesus," but His use of the expression in 8:58 suggests that much more is implied. Bruce suggests that the

---

2. Joachim Jeremias, *Jerusalem in the Time of Jesus* (Philadelphia: Fortress, 1969), pp. 209-10; M. *Middoth* 1.1.

3. Leon Morris, *The Gospel According to John*, NICNT (Grand Rapids: Eerdmans, 1971), p. 743.

phrase could have been understood on two levels.[4] On one level, it was a simple statement of identification. But the usage in John 8:58 (cf. also 6:20; 8:24) and the response of the arresting authorities here indicate that Jesus was identifying Himself with Israel's God, "I AM" (Ex. 3:14; cf. comments on John 8:58).

John notes that Judas the traitor was standing there "with them." He was not with the disciples. Although he had associated with Jesus, his true identity as a traitor and unbeliever was now quite apparent.

18:6   When Jesus identified Himself with the words "I am he" (*egō eimi*) the arresting officers immediately "drew back and fell to the ground." The precise implications of these words are not completely clear. It may be that the officers were simply overcome by the presence of Jesus, about whom they had heard so much. On the other hand, it is possible that Jesus exerted some miraculous manifestation of His power, which caused the guard's reaction. John seems to be linking the soldiers' response to Jesus' statement "I am he." The words *egō eimi* are seen elsewhere to refer to Christ's deity (cf. 6:20; 8:24, 28, 58), and this seems to be an implication here. Whatever the case, it is clear that Christ could not be touched by the Temple authorities except by His permission. He was in absolute control of the situation. He allowed the arrest even as He would permit the crucifixion.

18:7   John records that it was necessary for Jesus to speak a second time, "Who is it you want?" Once again they replied that they had been sent to arrest "Jesus of Nazareth."

18:8   After repeating His identification "I am he" (*egō eimi*), Jesus, the Good Shepherd, took steps to deliver His own. Apparently Jesus' followers had gathered around Him as He spoke with the arresting authorities. Perhaps gesturing toward His followers, He said, "If you are looking for me, then let these men go."

This verse contains John's third mention of "I am he" (*egō eimi*) in vv. 5-8. This is strong evidence that John is emphasizing Christ's deity (see also comments on 8:5 and 18:5).

18:9   Reflecting on Jesus' actions in behalf of His own, John recalls the words of His intercessory prayer. Comparing 17:12 (cf. also 6:39) with 18:9, one sees that the wording is not precisely the same. In keeping with his tendency toward variation, John changes "None have

4. F. F. Bruce, *The Gospel of John: Introduction, Exposition and Notes* (Grand Rapids: Eerdmans, 1983), p. 341.

been lost" (17:12) to "I have not lost one," emphasizing Christ's active part in protecting His own from danger. By delivering His own from arrest, the words expressed in His prayer were seen to be true ("fulfilled"). It is encouraging to know that Jesus has both the will and the power to protect His own through this life and into eternity (cf. 10:28-29).

18:10   Jesus' protection of His disciples from the Temple guards is remarkable in light of Peter's action in v. 10. Drawing a sword (*machaira*), Peter struck the right ear of Malchus, the high priest's servant.

Now what was Peter doing with a sword? Actually, the word "sword" (*machaira*) could be translated "a large knife," "short sword," or "dagger." The word is used in the Septuagint in Genesis 22:6 with reference to the sacrificial knife being used by Abraham. Peter did not have the large, broad *romphaia* that was carried by the Roman soldiers. Peter and John had been sent by Jesus to prepare the Passover (Luke 22:8), and it is likely that Peter still had the large, sacrificial knife that had been used for the sacrifice. This was probably one of the two "swords" produced by the disciples in Luke 22:36-38.

Earlier in the upper room Peter had expressed his willingness to "lay down" his life for Jesus (John 13:37). Impetuous Peter probably figured that there was no way he was going to get out of that olive grove alive and decided to take a few of Christ's enemies with him.

18:11   It must have been a tense moment when Malchus's ear dropped to the ground and Peter, the fisherman, stood facing the Temple guard with a bloody knife. But Jesus immediately intervened to protect Peter and the rest of the disciples. Luke, the physician, notes that Jesus said, "No more of this," and then touched Malchus's ear and healed him (Luke 22:51). It is amazing that Peter and the disciples got out of that garden alive.

John reports that Jesus instructed Peter to put away the sword and asked, "Shall I not drink the cup the Father has given me?" The synoptics record that Jesus prayed about "this cup" (Matt. 26:36-46; Mark 14:32-42; Luke 22:40-46) in the garden. Jesus apparently refers here to the same cup (*potērion*) and indicates that it is given to Him by "the Father." On the basis of Old Testament references (Ps. 75:8; Isa. 51:17; Jer. 25:15; Ezek. 23:31-33) that associate God's cup with sorrow and judgment, it has been suggested that the cup refers to Jesus' suffering and death. Perhaps the cup includes as well His bearing sin and separation from the Father (Matt. 27:46; 2 Cor. 5:21).

18:12   Although the disciples were not apprehended by either the Roman soldiers or the Jewish Temple guard ("officials"), Jesus was arrested and bound. The word "arrested" translates the Greek word *sullambanō*, "to grasp together" or "seize." Being arrested is not a pleasant experience, especially if you are innocent. Inasmuch as Jesus offered no resistance, it is not clear why they thought it necessary to bind Him. This may have been standard procedure. Perhaps they thought Jesus might use His miraculous powers and attempt an escape. All this could be construed as an example of the unnecessary use of force against an unarmed suspect. It could even serve as an admonition against the use of excessive force by Christian law officers.

THE RELIGIOUS TRIAL, 18:13-27

The trial of Jesus divides into two parts. Jesus first stood before the religious authorities, including Annas, Caiaphas, and the Sanhedrin. And because the Jews sought the death penalty for Jesus rather than some lesser punishment, the case was then submitted to the Roman civil authorities.

THE EXAMINATION BEFORE ANNAS, 18:13-23

According to the Mosaic law, the high priest was the most important member of the believing community because he was the only one authorized by God to offer sacrifices for the sins of the community on the Day of Atonement (Ex. 30:10; Lev. 16). This office was held by a descendant of Aaron and was passed on from father to son (cf. Ex. 28:1; Num. 18:1; 20:25-28). During King Herod's rule, however, the traditional pattern was often ignored as Herod arbitrarily dismissed and replaced the high priest (Josephus *Antiquities* 15.51). From then on, and continuing during Roman rule, the office ceased to be lifelong and hereditary. The office of high priest became wholly dependent on political authority.[5] But because the office of high priest was lifelong, the high priest retained a good measure of power and prestige among the Jewish population even after removal from office.

This provides some background for the situation reflected in John 18:13 where two men are regarded as having the authority of the high priest. Annas was appointed as high priest in A.D. 6 by Quirinius,

5. Jeremias, *Jerusalem in the Time of Jesus*, pp. 158-59.

governor of Syria, and was deposed nine years later by Valerius Gratus, prefect of Judea (Josephus *Antiquities* 18.26, 34, 95). Annas was succeeded by Ishmael ben Phiabia I (c. A.D. 15-16) and then by Annas's son Eleazar (c. A.D. 16-17). Following the term of Simon, son of Kamithos (A.D. 17-18), Joseph Caiaphas, who had married the daughter of Annas, was appointed to the office in A.D. 18 by Valerius Gratus. Caiaphas held the office until A.D. 36, when both Pilate and Caiaphas were removed from their respective offices by Lucius Vitellius, governor of Syria (Josephus *Antiquities* 18.89, 95).

Deliverance to Annas, 18:13-14

18:13   Because the office of high priest was held for life, it is not surprising that the matter of Jesus' arrest and trial was first brought before Annas, the father-in-law of Caiaphas, the high priest officially recognized by the Roman authorities. Annas, mentioned only here and in v. 24 in John's gospel, was a very powerful man. His influence was such that eventually five of his sons, as well as his son-in-law and grandson Matthias, became high priests. He was virtually regarded by the Jews as high priest, although Caiaphas held the title officially.[6] The words "That year" refer to that momentous year of Christ's crucifixion. According to the well-documented chronology of Harold Hoehner,[7] the year was A.D. 33.

18:14   John the apostle identifies Caiaphas as the one who unknowingly prophesied that "it would be good if one man died for the people" (cf. 11:49-50). The word "for" (*huper*) indicates substitution and strongly implies substitutionary atonement (cf. Mark 10:45; 2 Cor. 5:14). John's remark not only serves to identify Caiaphas but is also an indicator for the reader of what can be expected as the outcome of the trial. The outcome was certain. Events would lead rapidly to Jesus' death.

Denial by Peter, 18:15-18

18:15   Although all the disciples fled when Jesus was arrested (Matt. 26:56), Simon Peter and "another disciple" followed (the imperfect tense of the verb "following" [*akoloutheo*] provides a vivid picture of the action taking place) at a distance as Jesus was led to the house of

---

6. Luke regards both Annas and Caiaphas as holding the office of high priest (Luke 3:2).

7. Harold W. Hoehner, *Chronological Aspects of the Life of Christ* (Grand Rapids: Zondervan, 1970), pp. 95-114.

Annas, the high priest "emeritus." Several manuscripts read "the other disciple," but the evidence is in favor of "another" (*allos*). It is the almost universal opinion that the apostle John is referring to himself. This opinion is consistent with similar allusions to the gospel author in John 1:40; 13:23-25; 19:26; 20:2-8; 21:20-24 and the fact that John frequently accompanied Peter (Luke 22:8; Acts 3:1; 4:13; 8:14).

Because John was known to the high priest (*toi archierei*), he was able to gain access to the courtyard, or open space, in front of the house. Because his mother, Salome, may have been the sister of Mary (cf. Mark 15:24; John 19:25), and Mary was related to Elisabeth, a descendant of Aaron (Luke 1:5), it is possible that John was a member of a priestly family. This opinion is affirmed by Polycrates, bishop of Ephesus (A.D. 189-198), as recorded by Eusebius (*Historia Ecclesiastica* 3:31).

18:16   Although the nature and extent of John's acquaintance with the high priest is not explained by the author, the influence from this relationship was sufficient to secure Peter's entrance into the courtyard.

18:17   The servant girl on duty at the door of the courtyard may have known that John was a follower of Jesus and suspected that Peter was also. Perhaps it was Peter's hesitance that gave him away. The form of her question, "You are not one of his disciples, are you?" expects a negative answer and made it easy for Peter to say no. Perhaps Peter was nervous because of the unfamiliar surroundings and the presence of Temple guards and religious authorities. Fearful of the consequences of identifying himself as a disciple, Peter replied, "I am not." The negative particle *ouk* is in a place of emphasis. Peter was saying, "Not me!" It was the first of his three denials.

We tend to be hard on Peter for his denials, but who has not had a similar failing? Peter was facing a dangerous situation. He panicked and lied. Many of us have lied rather than be embarrassed or discovered. May God forgive us and help us to think before we speak. Lying dishonors God, is often discovered, and damages our witness. Tell the truth, tell it ever, cost you what it may.

18:18   Jerusalem is located in the Judean mountains about 2,500 feet above sea level, and spring nights—especially without cloud cover—can be quite cool. To take off the chill, a fire was burning in a brazier there in the courtyard. John's word "fire" (*anthrakian*), used only here and in John 21:9 in the New Testament, refers to "a heap of burning coals." Peter joined the "servants" of the high priest and other "officials" and warmed himself by the fire.

Questioning of Jesus, 18:19-23

18:19 The "high priest" may be assumed to refer to Annas (cf. 18:13, 24). He conducted a preliminary examination of Jesus before sending the case to Caiaphas. His questions focused on two primary issues: "his disciples (*tōn mathētōn*) and his teaching" (*tēs didachēs*). Annas wanted to know the extent of Jesus' following and about the doctrine He propagated. Jesus was suspected of involvement in some subversive movement, and Annas wanted to know the facts of the case.

18:20 Jesus explained quite simply to Annas that He had nothing to hide. His teaching had been presented publicly so that all could hear. The "world" (*kosmos*) refers here to everyone whom Jesus had come in contact with. The term calls attention to the universal application of Christ's message. Jesus had taught in the synagogues (Matt. 13:54; Mark 1:21; 6:2; Luke 6:6; John 6:59) and at the Temple (Matt. 21:23; Mark 11:27; 12:35; Luke 19:47; John 7:14; 8:20).

Jesus' statement "I said nothing in secret" should not be construed as a denial of private instruction (cf. 3:1-15; 4:7-26; 13:1–16:33). Rather, He was simply saying that He did not have two different messages—a public message concerning spiritual needs and a private message promoting political revolution.

18:21 Jesus seems to have challenged the legality of the proceedings. According to Mosaic law, a person was innocent until the evidence of witnesses confirmed his or her guilt (cf. Deut. 17:6; 19:15). The personal interrogation before Annas seems to have assumed Jesus' guilt. "Why question me?" He asked. "Ask those who heard me. Surely they know what I said." There were many in Jerusalem who were familiar with His doctrine and could answer the questions of the high priest. It was obvious that the officials were not seeking the truth but were merely looking for some incriminating charge to expedite their purposes (cf. 12:49-50).

18:22 When the questioning of Jesus did not achieve any results, one of the Jewish Temple guards (for "officials," see 18:3) standing nearby resorted to violence. Jesus was given a blow on the face. The word *rapisma* can refer to a blow with a rod or with the open hand. It is likely that Jesus was slapped by the official with the palm of the man's hand. This is the first of a series of abusive actions perpetrated against Jesus during His trial and crucifixion. The question, "Is this the way you answer the high priest?" constitutes a rebuke (cf. Ex. 22:28).

18:23   Jesus knew He had said nothing wrong (cf. Ex. 22:28) and challenged the high priest to prove the case against Him. His words "testify as to what is wrong" demand that Annas produce evidence of wrongdoing. But if no evidence against Him can be found, Jesus continued, "Why did you strike me?" (The word "strike" [*derō*] means "to flay the skin," "to beat," or "to thrash." It was clearly not a light tap.) Jesus did not ask this question of the official but rather of Annas, who was in charge of the proceedings and apparently viewed the action with approval.

EXAMINATION BEFORE CAIAPHAS, 18:24

The Sinaitic Syriac Version of the gospels has changed John's order of events to make it appear that Jesus went immediately from Annas to Caiaphas, and that what is recorded in John 18:15-27 all took place in the house of Caiaphas. This is accomplished by moving v. 24 to a position between vv. 13 and 14.[8] This reconstruction is an obvious attempt to harmonize John's gospel with the synoptic account. There is no Greek manuscript evidence for this shift. Although it seems unusual that John would not provide a more complete account of the examination before Caiaphas, it is best to avoid textual emendation.

18:24   Annas's attempt to find some incriminating evidence against Jesus was quite unsuccessful. So Annas sent Jesus, still bound (perfect passive participle of *deō*) with ropes, to be examined by Caiaphas, the official high priest and president of the Sanhedrin.

The synoptics record this second phase of Jesus' trial, which took place in the house of Caiaphas (Matt. 26:57-68; Mark 14:53-65; Luke 22:54). These secret and illegal proceedings resulted in a charge of blasphemy against Jesus (Matt. 26:65; Mark 14:64). The final stage of Jesus' religious trial took place in the early morning hours of April 3, A.D. 33, when the Sanhedrin, the Jewish supreme court, met to give its night verdict some semblance of officiality (cf. Matt. 27:1; Mark 15:1; Luke 22:66-71).

The biblical account of the religious trial of Jesus records a number of violations of Jewish law. First, the Sanhedrin convened in the house of Caiaphas (Matt. 26:57-59) rather than at its regular meeting

8. Bruce, *The Gospel of John*, p. 344.

place near the Temple (*Sanhedrin* 11*a*; *Middoth* 5.4). Second, the Sanhedrin met at night rather than the prescribed time during the day (Tosephta *Sanhedrin* 7.1). Third, contrary to official procedure, the Sanhedrin convened on the eve of a Sabbath and a festival (*Sanhedrin* 4.1; Josephus *Antiquities* 16.163). Fourth, special formalities required in cases involving a capital sentence (providing for the possibility of acquittal) were not followed (*Sanhedrin* 4.1). Fifth, the sentence of condemnation was pronounced on the same day as the morning trial. According to official policy, before pronouncing a verdict of guilty and imposing a sentence, the court was required to recess until the following day when it would reconvene to reexamine the evidence (*Sanhedrin* 4.1; 5.5).

Although the Sanhedrin seems to have violated its only laws in the trial of Jesus, Talmudic sources note that in exceptional cases the court was allowed to act in extralegal ways on a temporary basis when there was a compelling reason to do so.[9] Rabbi Eliezer tells of Shimon ben Shatach, head of the Sanhedrin, who executed eighty women for practicing witchcraft. By law the court was not permitted to perform more than one execution on a single day. Thus, Shimon ben Shatach's act was an exception. The compelling reason to set aside the law was concern that the relatives might attempt to free the women, and fear that they might use their witchcraft to escape.[10]

PETER'S SECOND AND THIRD DENIALS, 18:25-27

Each of the gospels records three denials of Jesus by Peter. There is little justification for the theory that Peter received two different warnings about denying Christ and in each warning was told that he would deny Christ three times, for a total of six denials.[11] Although there are minor differences in details, none of the accounts is contradictory, and the chronology of the three recorded denials is basically the same.

18:25 Verse 25 resumes the record of Peter's denials. If Annas and Caiaphas occupied separate wings of the same residence, the second and third denials probably took place in the same courtyard (cf. 18:15). John does not seem particularly interested in providing further

---

9. Artscroll Mishnah Series, *Sanhedrin* (Brooklyn, N.Y.: Mesorah Publications, 1987), p. 94.

10. Ibid., p. 100.

11. Johnson M. Cheney, *The Life of Christ in Stereo* (Portland, Oreg.: Western Baptist Seminary, 1969), pp. 218-19.

detail. Once again, someone (Matthew and Mark mention a "servant girl," Matt. 26:69; Mark 14:66) spoke to Peter: "You are not one of his disciples, are you?" Once again (cf. 18:17) a negative answer is expected, and Peter supplies it with the words *ouk eimi*, "Not me!"

18:26   Peter must have been sweating when one of the high priest's servants, a relative of the man whose ear Peter had cut off, approached him and said, "Didn't I see you with him in the olive grove?" This questioner is more assured, and the grammatical structure of his question indicates that an affirmative answer was anticipated.

18:27   For the third time Peter denied any association with Jesus. It was a response Peter would regret. At that moment a rooster "began to crow." The NIV is taking *phōneō* as an ingressive aorist, denoting the beginning of an action. This is a reasonable interpretation because roosters rarely crow just once. In fact, Mark records that the rooster crowed twice (Mark 14:72). The synoptics record that upon hearing the rooster crow, Peter remembered Jesus' announcement of His denial (Matt. 26:75; Mark 14:72; Luke 22:61). Luke provides an additional, significant detail. At the moment the rooster crowed, Jesus "turned and looked at Peter" (Luke 22:61). The eyes of Jesus must have penetrated his soul. Peter "went out and wept bitterly" (Luke 22:62).

Peter sinned a great sin, but he was not hardened by it. His heart was tender, and it grieved him that he had denied the Lord. Grief over sin, not just its consequences, reflects a heart that is near to God.

THE CIVIL TRIAL, 18:28–19:16

Had the Jewish leaders wanted only to give Jesus a beating or apply some punishment short of death, there would have been no necessity for a trial before the Roman authorities. But because they were intent upon applying the death penalty (Matt. 26:4; John 11:50-53), a trial by the Roman rulers of Judea was required (cf. 18:31).

The civil trial took place in the early morning hours of April 3, A.D. 33, and had three parts. Jesus stood before Pontius Pilate (18:28-38), before Herod Antipas (Luke 23:6-12), and again before Pilate (John 18:39–19:16).

BEFORE PILATE, 18:28-38

Following the expulsion of Herod's son Archelaus in A.D. 6, Judea became a Roman imperial province ruled by a prefect, or governor, appointed by the emperor. Pontius Pilate served as prefect from A.D. 6 to A.D. 36. He normally lived in Caesarea (Acts 23:25) but stayed in Jerusalem during the Jewish festivals to be available to handle a crisis and maintain order.

Pilate is described by his contemporary Philo (*Legatio ad Gaium* 301-2) and later by Josephus (*Antiquities* 18.55-59; *Jewish Wars* 2.169-77) as a greedy, inflexible, and cruel ruler. He created much antagonism between himself and the Jews on at least four occassions.[12] The first of these was shortly after his appointment when he and his soldiers brought standards into Jerusalem bearing the emperor's image (Josephus *Antiquities* 18.55-59). The second is recorded in Luke 13:1, which reports the killing of some Galileans while they were in Jerusalem offering sacrifices. The third was when Pilate used revenues from the Temple to construct an aqueduct to bring water to Jerusalem (Josephus *Antiquities* 18.60-62). The fourth occasion was when Pilate hung golden shields, apparently bearing the name of the emperor as a deity, in Herod's palace (Philo *Legatio ad Gaium* 299-305). The Jews objected so strongly that the emperor himself ordered them removed to the temple of Augustus at Caesarea.

18:28 After the trial before the Jewish authorities, Jesus was led from the presence of Caiaphas to the "palace of the Roman governor" (literally, "the Praetorium"). The Greek *praitōrion* is a Latin loanword that originally referred to the praetor's tent in camp and became a designation for the Roman governor's official residence. It is a matter of dispute whether John refers here to the palace of Herod in the western part of Jerusalem or to the Antonia fortress northwest of the Temple area.[13] The traditional view is that Jesus was tried before Pilate in the Antonia fortress.

It was "early" (*prōi*) in the morning when Jesus was brought before Pilate. It must have been quite early because Jesus' trial before Pilate was finished by 6:00 A.M. (cf. 19:14). John now relates a detail that has generated scholarly research and debate. He mentions that in order to avoid becoming ceremonially defiled by entering a Gentile dwelling, the Jews stayed out of the palace. According to the Mishnah,

---

12. R. Larry Overstreet, "Roman Law and the Trial of Christ," *Bibliotheca Sacra* 135 (October-December 1978): 324-25.

13. William F. Arndt and F. Wilbur Gingrich, *A Greek-English Lexicon of the New Testament*, 4th rev. ed. (Chicago: U. of Chicago, 1957), p. 704.

"The dwelling places of Gentiles are unclean" (*Oholoth* 18.7).[14] Such ceremonial uncleanness would prevent the Jews from eating the Passover.

Now the synoptic gospels indicate beyond reasonable doubt that Jesus ate the Passover (Matt. 26:17-20; Mark 14:16-17; Luke 22:13-14) with His disciples in the upper room Thursday evening, Nisan 14, and was crucified on the next day, Friday, Nisan 15. However, John 18:28 (also 19:14) indicates that on the day of Jesus' trial and crucifixion the Jews had not yet eaten the Passover. How could the Jews anticipate Passover on the evening of Jesus' death while Jesus and the disciples had already observed the feast? How do John's account and the synoptics fit together? For a lengthy discussion of the possibilities, see Morris's note, "Last Supper and Passover."[15]

Harold Hoehner's insightful study seems to offer the best theory for reconciling the data.[16] He suggests that two Passovers were observed by the Jews of Jesus' day on the basis of two different methods of reckoning a day. Earlier Israelites reckoned a day from sunrise to sunrise (cf. Gen. 19:34; Josephus *Antiquities* 3.248). Accordingly, the day begins in the morning after the preceding night. This method of reckoning was employed by Jesus and the synoptics and was perhaps the custom followed in Galilee.

In later Israelite reckoning it was the practice to count the day beginning with the evening at sunset (cf. Lev. 23:27; Deut. 16:4). This sunset to sunset reckoning appears to have been the official Jewish method of reckoning a day and was followed by the Judeans and used by John in his gospel.

According to this hypothesis, Jesus and His disciples observed Passover on Thursday, Nisan 14, with the Galileans. The Judeans sacrificed their Passover lambs Friday afternoon, Nisan 14 according to their reckoning, and observed the feast that evening. Other than the evidence for the two Jewish ways of reckoning, there is no explicit support for the theory in the New Testament or Mishnah, although it is interesting to note that the section of the Mishnah devoted to the Passover is entitled *Pesahim*, "Passovers." Numbers 9:1-14 does allow

---

14. The reason the houses of Gentiles are said to be unclean is that Gentiles were believed to "throw abortions down the drains" (Herbert Danby, *The Mishnah* [Oxford: Oxford U., 1933], p. 675, n. 10), hence the defilement would be the defilement of death, rendering the visitor unclean for seven days (Num. 19:11-14).

15. Morris, *The Gospel of John*, pp. 774-88.

16. Hoehner, *Chronological Aspects of the Life of Christ*, pp. 76-90.

THE TWO PASSOVERS
John 18:28

THURSDAY	Galilean Method Synoptic Reckoning Used by Jesus, His Disciples, and Pharisees	Judean Method John's Reckoning Used by Sadducees	Midnight
			Sunrise
	Nisan 14		
3-5 P.M. Passover Lamb Slain			Sunset
Last Supper		Nisan 14	
Jesus Arrested			Midnight
FRIDAY			
6 A.M. Jesus before Pilate	Nisan 15		Sunrise
9 A.M. Crucifixion			
12-3 P.M. Darkness			
3 P.M. Jesus Died		3-5 P.M. Passover Lamb Slain	
Jesus Buried			Sunset
		Nisan 15	
SATURDAY	▼	▼	Midnight

for a second Passover one month after Nisan 14 in the case of one who is unclean or on a distant journey. Perhaps this text served as the basis for what became a first-century tradition. Hoehner's hypothesis not only accounts for the data both in John 18:28 and the synoptics, but it also provides a precise fulfillment of Testament typology. According to this view, Jesus died on Friday afternoon at the time the Passover lambs of the Judeans were being sacrificed (19:36; cf. 1 Cor. 5:7).

18:29   Because the Jews would not enter the governor's residence (the Praetorium), Pilate went out to them and asked what formal charges (*katēgoria*) were being brought against Jesus. His question does not necessarily assume complete ignorance of the affairs of Jesus. Pilate was simply opening a proper legal inquiry.

18:30   The Jewish authorities were rather evasive in their reply. They apparently wanted Pilate to confirm their verdict without further examination. Certainly they would not trouble Pilate with this matter if Jesus "were not a criminal." The word translated "criminal" refers to one who is a persistent (present tense) evildoer (*kakon poiōn*).

18:31   Pilate had enough issues of state to attend to without involving himself in a petty Jewish controversy. Assuming that Jesus had violated some religious law or custom, he instructed the Jewish authorities to try Jesus by their "own law," an apparent reference to the regulations and procedures of the Sanhedrin.

Pilate's response demanded that the Jews clarify their request. Nothing less than the death penalty for Jesus would suffice. They wanted an execution, not a fair trial. Yet they had no authority to inflict the death penalty. When Judea became a Roman province in A.D. 6, the Jewish administration lost the authority to execute a capital sentence (Josephus *Jewish Wars* 2.117; cf. *Antiquities* 18.2; John 18:31). Sherwin-White notes, "The capital power was the most jealously guarded of all the attributes of government, not even entrusted to the principal assistants of the governors."[17] The one exception to this rule in Judea was in cases affecting the sanctity of the Temple (Josephus *Jewish Wars* 6.126; cf. Acts 6:23-24; 7:57-60). This may account for why the Sanhedrin sought to obtain false testimony against Jesus that He was plotting the destruction of the Jerusalem Temple (cf. Matt. 26:59-61).

---

17. A. N. Sherwin-White, *Roman Society and Roman Law in the New Testament* (Grand Rapids: Baker, 1978), p. 36.

18:32   John remarks in v. 32 that bringing the trial before the Roman authorities was significant in the fulfillment of Jesus' words concerning what kind of death (*thanatos*) He would die (cf. 3:14; 12:32-33). Had he been tried and executed by the Sanhedrin, He would have been stoned. But trial in Roman court meant death by crucifixion.

18:33   Having heard from the Jewish authorities, Pilate went back into the residence, or Praetorium (cf. v. 28), to question Jesus. He had undoubtedly heard of Jesus' claim to be Israel's Messiah. Although he was not interested in a religious dispute among the Jews, he was responsible to protect the interests of Rome. He had to find out if Jesus was a threat to Caesar.

Calling Jesus before his tribunal, Pilate asked, "Are you the king of the Jews?" In all four gospels these are the first words of Pilate to Jesus (cf. Matt. 27:11; Mark 15:2; Luke 23:3). In Pilate's question, the pronoun "you" is emphatic and may have been spoken with scorn, "*You* are the king of the Jews?"

18:34   Jesus answered Pilate's question with a question. "Is that your own idea," Jesus asked, "or did others talk to you about me?" Jesus was asking if Pilate was approaching the matter from a Roman ("your own idea") or a Jewish viewpoint ("did others talk to you?"). If Pilate was asking from a Roman viewpoint, his question might be phrased, "Are you, Jesus, a political king conspiring against Caesar?" In that case, the obvious answer was no. But perhaps Pilate had been prompted by the Jews and was asking if Jesus was the messianic king of Israel. In that case, the answer would be a resounding yes.

18:35   Pilate's retort, "Am I a Jew?" makes clear that he was asking his question from the Roman rather than Jewish point of view. Pilate was disclaiming any knowledge of Jesus except the information given him by the Jewish authorities who brought Jesus before Pilate's tribunal. His main concern was over what Jesus had done to warrant prosecution.

18:36   Jesus proceeds in v. 36 to answer Pilate's question (v. 33) from the Roman point of view. He admits that He has a "kingdom" (*basileia*), but not as the world commonly understands kingdoms. Jesus' kingdom is a different sort of kingdom than Pilate would be thinking of. The words "of this world" (*ek tou kosmou toutou*) mean that His kingdom does not take its origin or draw its power from the unbelieving world. Jesus goes on to explain that if His kingdom did draw its origin and power from this world, His servants would have used military means to prevent His arrest. They would be establishing Jesus' kingdom by warfare. But this was not the way of Christ's kingdom. Although Jesus' kingdom will eventually involve an earthly domain (cf. 2 Sam. 7:12-16; Rev. 20:4-6), it will not depend on men for its establishment and support.

18:37   Pilate was quick to realize that Jesus was indeed making a claim to kingship. "You are a king, then!" he exclaimed. Only a king would claim a kingdom. Ironically, Pilate recognized what the Jews refused to believe—that Jesus is Israel's king.

In His reply to Pilate, Jesus admitted, "You are right in saying I am a king." Then He proceeded to explain something of the nature of His divine mission and ministry. Jesus was born for kingship and came into the world to testify to the truth. The words "born" (*gennaō*) and "came" (*erchomai*) are in the perfect tense, expressing past events that continue in their effect. Jesus' ministry involved bearing witness to the truth—the truth of His own Person (cf. 1:14; 8:32; 14:6).

Concerning the citizens of His kingdom, Jesus added, "Everyone on the side of truth listens to me." Those who have their spiritual roots in the truth of Christ's Person draw from that rich reservoir for counsel and direction.

18:38   Pilate brushed aside the spiritually probing words of Jesus and closed this part of the examination with the words, "What is truth?" This is a question all must ask and few can answer. Note that Pilate did not ask what is *the* truth. He was not seriously interested in pursuing such a weighty question.

This was a significant moment of inquiry. It is sad that Pilate did not take a few minutes of his earthly life to get this issue resolved. Like Pilate, we are often so occupied with business and work that we neglect those issues that count for eternity. What is truth? Pilate entered eternity with the question unanswered.

Pilate had learned from Jesus what he really wanted to know. It was clear that Jesus was no political revolutionary and represented no danger to Rome. Once again he returned to the Jews who were waiting outside the Praetorium (cf. 18:28) and announced that he could find no legal basis for bringing an indictment against Jesus. The pronoun "I" is emphatic and sets Pilate in contrast with the Jewish audience.

BEFORE PILATE AGAIN, 18:39–19:16

Pilate probably learned at this point in the trial that Jesus was from Galilee, the region belonging to the jurisdiction of Herod Antipas, tetrarch of Galilee (B.C. 4–A.D. 39). Luke alone records that Pilate sent Jesus for a hearing before Antipas, who had longed to see Jesus and perhaps witness some miracle (Luke 23:8). This diplomatic courtesy did not advance the trial, but it did result in a reconciliation between Pilate and Antipas (Luke 23:12), whose relationship had been strained by the Galilean massacre (Luke 13:1).

The Attempt at Release, 18:39-40

18:39   Rather than releasing Jesus on the basis of His obvious innocence, Pilate suggested a course of action that was apparently designed to avoid insulting the Sanhedrin, which had already determined Jesus to be guilty (cf. John 18:30). Pilate appealed to the Jewish custom of releasing a prisoner at the time of Passover. Unfortunately, this custom is not mentioned outside the New Testament. The absence of secular evidence for the "custom" (*sunētheia*) of releasing a prisoner at Passover has led to the hypothesis that Jesus was brought before Pilate twice, first as Jesus Barabbas (i.e., Jesus, Son of the Father) and later as Jesus called Christos (i.e., the Anointed One, or Messiah).[18] According to this view, Jesus of Nazareth was known to His contemporaries as Jesus bar Abba(s), and there was not a separate person named Barabbas at the time of Jesus' trial.[19] Accordingly, the people were not granted a choice between two prisoners at all. Although this is an interesting hypothesis, it is quite speculative and does not do justice to the biblical text or the cultural background.

A possible allusion to the custom has been traced by some scholars to the Mishnah (*Pesahim* 8.6), where it is said that a Passover lamb may be sacrificed for "one whom they have promised to bring out of prison." But this passage might envisage the situation in which the prisoner was due for release shortly in the normal course of things.[20]

Presumably, the custom was one the Roman governors took over from their Herodian and Hasmonean predecessors. The release of a prisoner was apparently intended to commemorate the release of the

18. H. A. Rigg, Jr., "Barabbas," *JBL* 64 (1945): 428-32.
19. Stevan L. Davies, "Who Is Called Bar Abbas?" *New Testament Studies* 27 (1981): 260-62.
20. Bruce, *The Gospel of John*, p. 355.

Israelites from the Egyptian bondage at the first Passover. Plummer notes, "Prisoners were sometimes released at Rome at certain festivals, and it would be quite in harmony with the conciliatory policy of Rome to honour native festivals in this way in the case of subject nations."[21]

Pilate's chief concern at the early morning trial of Jesus was to minimize trouble rather than secure justice. If he pronounced Jesus innocent, he would no doubt offend the Jewish religious leaders. If he pronounced Jesus guilty, he would offend Jesus' supporters. But he could imply Jesus' guilt and then release Him on the basis of the Passover custom. It was a solution Pilate thought would satisfy everyone. The choice of the prisoner to be released was made by the people (Mark 15:6). And so he asked the question, "Do you want me to release 'the king of the Jews'?"

18:40   Things do not always turn out the way one expects them to. Although Pilate expected the people to cry out for Jesus to be released, they cried out (first aorist active of *kraugazō*, "to raise an outcry") instead, "Give us Barabbas!" Mark 15:11 notes that the chief priests stirred up the multitude to ask Pilate to release Barabbas instead of Jesus. No doubt the chief priests played on the people's sympathy with the cause for which Barabbas stood.

Barabbas, John informs the readers of his gospel, had been involved in an insurrection. The word he uses to describe Barabbas, *lēstēs*, speaks of one who is more dangerous to persons than to property. The word can be used of a "highwayman" or a "revolutionary." The term is used by Josephus to denote a Zealot insurgent (*Antiquities* 14.159f; 20.160-67). Mark 15:7 and Luke 23:19 mention that Barabbas had committed murder in connection with the insurrection. It is interesting to note that Barabbas had done what Jesus had refused to do— take the lead in an armed revolt against Rome.

HOMILETICAL SUGGESTIONS

John 18:13-27 records Jesus' trial before the religious authorities. The major message in this rather historical section concerns the denials of Peter (vv. 17, 25, 27). Peter experienced a major failure in his

---

21. A. Plummer, *The Gospel According to St. John* (Cambridge: At the University Press, 1899), p. 334.

loyalty and commitment to Christ. Many Christians can identify with Peter in this regard.

Peter did not stop living for Christ, however. He repented of his sin and was restored to fellowship with Jesus after the resurrection. Peter provides a good model for dealing with sin. We should not wallow in remorse but repent and get on with serving Christ and His kingdom.

Verses 28-38 record Jesus' trial before Pilate. This section is full of fascinating historical background and makes for interesting exposition. The primary message here concerns Pilate, who experiences a "close encounter" with the Son of God. It was a perfect opportunity for Pilate to learn more about Jesus and to place his faith in Him. But Pilate was interested in getting past this official business and back to his own affairs. Ironically and sadly, he was too busy with life to *live*. This passage could serve as an evangelistic text. There is also a helpful lesson about Christ's kingdom in v. 36. Although Christ's kingdom will have a physical culmination in the future, it is primarily a kingdom of spiritual rather than physical realities.

The last few verses of the chapter record Pilate's evaluation of Jesus (v. 38) and his offer of release (vv. 39-40). We find the world's approach to substitution. The guilty is released, and the innocent is condemned. God's redemptive program works differently. The guilty are forgiven and released while the innocent Lamb of God takes their place.

JOHN

CHAPTER NINETEEN

REDEMPTION ACCOMPLISHED!

BEFORE PILATE AGAIN (CONTINUED), 18:39–19:16

Chapter 19 continues John's account of the trial of Jesus before Pontius Pilate, prefect of Judea (A.D. 26-36). Although the Jewish leaders sought the death penalty for Jesus (18:31), Pilate recognized that Jesus had done nothing to warrant execution (19:38). Pilate would have liked to release Jesus, but he was concerned to avoid offending the Jewish leaders who had decisively concluded that Jesus must be put to death.

The Scourging of Jesus, 19:1-3

19:1 The trial of Jesus was rapidly reaching a crisis that Pilate wished to avoid. Apparently in an effort to satisfy the Jews, Pilate ordered that Jesus be "flogged" (*mastigoō*, from *mastix*, the Greek for "whip" or "scourge"). Scourging was a standard preliminary to a Roman execution. Only women, Roman senators, or soldiers (except in cases of execution) were exempt. The victim was stripped, bound to a post, and then beaten with a short whip, or flagellum, made of braided leather thongs to which were attached small iron balls and sharp pieces of bone.[1] Jewish law limited scourging to thirty-nine strokes

---

1. William D. Edwards, Wesley J. Gabel, and Floyd E. Hosmer, "On the Physical Death of Jesus," *The Journal of the American Medical Association* 255 (March 21, 1986): 1457.

(M. *Makkoth* 3.10). Because this was a preliminary to execution, care was taken not to kill the victim. Yet suffering under the scourge was intense. Josephus tells of a man whose bones were laid bare by scourging (*Jewish Wars* 6.303-4). Eusebius reports of how veins, arteries, entrails, and organs were exposed to sight by the scourge (*Historia Ecclesiastica* 4:15).

Pilate gave no explanation for the scourging of Jesus. Luke does report that Pilate said, "I will punish him and then release him" (Luke 23:16). Apparently he hoped the Jews would settle for this punishment and not press their demand for execution.

19:2 After the scourging of Jesus, the Roman soldiers decided to enjoy a few laughs at the expense of their victim. Because He claimed to be king of the Jews (cf. Luke 23:2-3; John 18:33-37), the soldiers decided to treat Him as royalty. To accomplish their purpose, they twisted some thorns into a makeshift crown (*stephanon*) and found a purple cloak, normally worn by military officers and men of high rank. Then they adorned Jesus with these "kingly" tokens to pay Him mock homage.

19:3 The soldiers mocked Jesus as they greeted Him with the words "Hail, king of the Jews!" The imperfect tense of the verbs "went up" (*erchomai*) and "saying" (*legō*) indicates that the mockery was continually repeated. Then the soldiers became physically abusive. They struck Jesus in the face. Matthew and Mark report that the soldiers knelt before Him and spat on Him (Matt. 27:30; Mark 15:19). To see His Son abused so must have brought deep sadness to the heart of God the Father. But what marvelous patience Jesus, the King of creation, demonstrated in the face of such physical abuse and humiliation. His example of patient endurance in the face of the world's hostility should serve as a motivation and encouragement to believers. Christ endured the greatest abuse and did not strike back in anger.

The Presentation of Jesus, 19:4-7

19:4 After the scourging of Jesus, Pilate once more came out of the Praetorium to speak to the Jews. He announced that he was presenting Jesus, beaten and mocked, "to let you know [purpose clause with *hina*] that I find no basis for a charge against him." Pilate was saying that Jesus was worthy of nothing more than ridicule. There was no criminal basis for further legal action.

19:5 When Jesus came out of the Praetorium wearing the crown of thorns and purple robe, Pilate introduced Him to the crowds, "Here is the man!" (*idou ho anthrōpos*). Pilate's words may have been spoken in a manner intended to elicit pity or to show contempt. He probably was attempting to demonstrate to the Jews the absurdity of executing such a weak and unintimidating man.

19:6   Although Pilate was hoping the spectacle would quench the crowd's thirst for blood, it seems only to have whetted the people's appetite. As soon as Jesus was presented to the crowd, the chief priests (cf. John 7:32) and religious officials shouted, "Crucify! Crucify!" The use of the aorist imperative of *stauroō*, "to crucify," communicated a sense of urgency.

Pilate was in no mood to placate the Jews further. His words "You take him and crucify him" reflect his impatience. Of course, the Jews had no authority to execute Jesus (cf. 18:31). Pilate was saying, "Tend to this yourselves—if you can." He then repeated his affirmation of Jesus' innocence (cf. 19:4). The pronoun "I" is in the emphatic position. Pilate contrasted his opinion with that of the Jews.

19:7   The Jews answered Pilate by pursuing another tactic. Although Pilate could see no violation of Roman law for which to execute Jesus, perhaps he could be persuaded to enforce Jewish law. So they appealed to the Mosaic law that calls for the death penalty for blasphemy (see Lev. 24:16). Because Jesus had "claimed to be the Son of God" (cf. John 5:18; 10:33) he had, in the opinion of the Jews, committed "blasphemy," a crime worthy of the capital sentence. Bruce explains that the imperial prefects not only had the responsibility to enforce Roman law, they were charged with respecting and (where necessary) enforcing Jewish religious law.[2] The Jews were seeking to persuade Pilate to enforce the Jewish law with Rome's authority.

Further Interrogation by Pilate, 19:8-11

19:8   Although Pilate was not a religious man, like most Romans he was certainly superstitious. When he realized that Jesus had made divine claims, "he was even more afraid." (The verb *phobeō*, "to be afraid," is the word from which the English *phobia* is derived.) Every Roman knew stories of gods or their offspring appearing in human form (cf. Acts 14:12). Pilate was already afraid that he was beginning to lose control of the situation. And now there was another reason to

---

2. F. F. Bruce, *The Gospel of John: Introduction, Exposition and Notes* (Grand Rapids: Eerdmans, 1983), p. 360.

fear. There was the distinct possibility that he was involved in judicial proceedings against a god.

19:9   Pilate entered the Praetorium again and further interrogated Jesus. "Where do you come from?" he asked. But Jesus was unwilling to answer. He had already alluded to His divine origin in 18:37, and unbelieving Pilate would not have understood even if Jesus had further explained. By His silence, Jesus was fulfilling Isaiah's prophecy "As a sheep before her shearers is silent, so he did not open his mouth" (Isa. 53:7).

19:10   Pilate did not appreciate being ignored. He was annoyed and somewhat surprised that Jesus refused to defend Himself. In order to force a response, Pilate reminded Jesus of his authority (*exousia*) "to free" or "to crucify" Him. It was a fundamental principle of Roman law that "no one who has power to condemn is without power to acquit" (Justinian *Digest* 50.17.37). Pilate had such authority and was willing to use it in this case. Any reasonable man would give such a judge his full cooperation.

19:11   Jesus responded to Pilate's boast by pointing out that the authority he possessed was not a sovereign right but had been "given to you from above." The words "from above" (*anōthen*) are used in John 3:3 to refer to a spiritual or heavenly birth. Here the reference is to God. Pilate was not an authority in and of himself. As in the case of all human rulers, Pilate's power was delegated by God (Dan. 4:17).

Although Pilate was guilty of sin, Jesus pointed out that the one who delivered Him over to Pilate was "guilty of greater sin." Jesus was not referring here to Judas, because he betrayed Jesus to the Jewish authorities. The reference was apparently to Caiaphas, the high priest, and head of the Jewish religious establishment. Jesus was probably basing His remark on the principle that greater privilege means greater accountability (cf. Matt. 11:20-24). Caiaphas was guilty of greater sin because he had the Hebrew Scriptures to point him to the truth of Jesus' messiahship.

There is a significant application of this verse for believers. There is greater accountability for those who know what is right and disobey than for those who disobey through ignorance. Christians who have been privileged to read and study God's Word will be judged in light of this opportunity. This constitutes a call and a challenge to Christian leaders to pursue personal holiness.

The Decision of Pilate, 19:12-16

19:12   It appears that the conversation with Jesus led Pilate to seek His acquittal. (The imperfect active indicative of *zēteō* suggests repeated efforts.) But he was stopped cold in that attempt when the Jews brought up an issue of Roman politics. "If you let this man go, you are no friend [*philos*] of Caesar. Anyone who claims to be a king opposes Caesar." The words "you are no friend of Caesar" must have stung Pilate's ears. The term "friend of Caesar" (Latin *Caesaris amicus*) was a notable term in the Roman politics.[3] It was used of those who were close associates of the emperor and could be sent to the provinces to conduct his affairs. But betrayal of the emperor meant the loss of this privileged relationship and ensured one's political doom.

Hoehner provides an excellent study of the significance of this term in Jesus' trial before Pilate.[4] It is probable that Pilate was appointed as prefect of Judea (A.D. 26) by Lucius Aelius Sejanus, the prefect of the Praetorian Guard. By A.D. 27 Tiberius had retired to the island of Capri, leaving Sejanus virtually in full control of the government. Philo reports that Sejanus was a dedicated anti-Semite who wanted to exterminate the Jewish race (*In Flaccum* 1; *Leg.* 159-61). Apparently Pilate implemented Sejanus's anti-Jewish policy in Judea (cf. Josephus *Antiquities* 18.55-59; *Jewish Wars* 2.169-77; Luke 13:1). Any complaints by the Jews to the emperor about Pilate's insulting abuses were merely intercepted by Sejanus.

This situation continued until the fall of A.D. 31, when Sejanus was about to usurp the throne and take over Roman rule. Eventually, Tiberius's suspicions were aroused. Sejanus was tricked into appearing before the Senate, where he was accused of treason and denounced. On that day, October 18, A.D. 31, Sejanus was executed.[5]

With the death of Sejanus, Pilate had an insecure political future. Having lost his friend and protector in Rome, he suddenly became very careful about giving his Jewish subjects grounds to make a complaint against him. That is why the words "you are no friend of Caesar" had such an impact on Pilate. He could not afford to jeopardize his political future for the sake of providing justice for a Galilean rabbi

---

3. A. N. Sherwin-White, *Roman Society and Roman Law in the New Testament* (Grand Rapids: Baker, 1978), p. 47.

4. Harold W. Hoehner, *Chronological Aspects of the Life of Christ* (Grand Rapids: Zondervan, 1970), pp. 105-11.

5. Ibid., pp. 108-9.

tangled in a controversy with the Jewish religious leaders. The people had spoken, and Pilate understood.

19:13   The possibility of losing his favored position in relationship to the Roman government was the key factor in convincing him to crucify Jesus. It was "when Pilate heard this" (ie., "you are no friend of Caesar," 19:12) that he brought Jesus out of the Praetorium to a place before the tribunal called "the Stone Pavement" (*lithostrōtos*). Pilate took his seat at a raised platform, known as the *bēma* ("judge's seat"), where a Roman magistrate or governor would sit in judgment. John notes parenthetically that the place was known in Aramaic (the commonly spoken language of Jews in the Second Temple period) as "Gabbatha," the meaning of which is still uncertain.[6] Wilkinson suggests that Gabbatha means "raised place," referring to a platform from which Pilate addressed the crowd (cf. Josephus *Jewish Wars* 2.175-76, 301, 308).[7] Whatever the meaning, it is clear that Gabbatha is not the Aramaic equivalent for the Greek *lithostrōtos*.

For many years the sisters of Our Lady of Zion have identified the Roman pavement beneath the Ecco Homo arch as the pavement where Jesus stood when Pilate said, "Here is the man!" (19:5). More recent archaeological study has confirmed that both the pavement and the arch date from the time of Hadrian's rebuilding of Jerusalem in A.D. 135 as Aelia Capitolina.

19:14   In the first section of v. 14 John provides details as to the day and hour of the proceedings against Jesus. In Jewish usage, the expression "day of Preparation" (*paraskeunē*) refers to Friday, the day to prepare for the Sabbath, when no work was permitted (Josephus *Antiquities* 16.163). Here the expression refers to the day of preparation for the Passover, which would be observed that evening by the Judeans (see comments on 18:28).

The time, namely the "sixth hour," is subject to considerable debate. The Romans, Greeks, and Jews customarily counted their hours from sunrise.[8] Accordingly, the "sixth hour" would be 12:00 noon. But for legal and contractual purposes the Romans reckoned their days from midnight to midnight. John, who is reporting on legal proceedings, may refer here to the "sixth hour" since midnight, or 6:00 A.M.

---

6. Suggested meanings include: "the hill of the House" (i.e., the mound on which the Temple was built), "the Ridge," or "platter."

7. John Wilkinson, *The Jerusalem Jesus Knew* (Nashville: Thomas Nelson, 1978), p. 141.

8. A. Plummer, *The Gospel According to St. John* (Cambridge: At the University Press), p. 341.

The difficulty with this approach is figuring how Jesus' civil trial could have taken place so early in the morning. In the early spring, the sun could be expected to rise in Palestine no earlier than about 5:30 A.M. It is unlikely that the Jews could have imposed on Pilate early enough to complete the trial by 6:00 A.M. The difficulty with identifying the "sixth hour" as "twelve noon" is Mark's note that Jesus was crucified at the "third hour" (Mark 15:25), apparently 9:00 A.M.

Miller seems to have resolved the difficulty of these time notations by interpreting them as approximations that can be reconciled in light of the author's usage and purpose.[9] He points out that John consistently numbers his hours from sunrise (cf. John 1:39; 4:6, 52). John's reference to "about" (*hōs*) the sixth hour refers to sometime before the middle of the day. Mark's "third hour" refers to that quarter of the day between 9:00 A.M. and noon. Mark sees the crucifixion of Jesus as a unit beginning with the scourging. John focuses on the decision of Pilate, which took place later in the proceedings. According to Miller's reasonable analysis, Jesus was crucified in the midmorning between nine and twelve o'clock. The time notices in both Mark and John are accurate, but they must not be pressed to a degree of precision beyond the intentions of the authors.

Before condemning Jesus to death, Pilate presented Him before His accusers. "Here is your king," Pilate announced to the Jews. The words were true. But for Pilate this was a less than subtle taunt against the religious authorities who had out-maneuvered him. It was as if Pilate were saying, "This beaten, bloody rabbi is all the 'king' you will see as long as I am prefect of Judah!"

19:15 Goaded by their hated Roman prefect, the Jews shouted, "Take him away! Take him away! Crucify him!" They would have nothing to do with King Jesus. Persisting in his taunt, Pilate asked, "Shall I crucify your king?" The depths of the spiritual degradation of the Jewish religious establishment is reflected in the response by the chief priests (cf. 7:32), "We have no king but Caesar." They embraced a pagan emperor rather than acknowledge Jesus—a descendant of David—as rightful king of Israel.

19:16 And so, at the insistence of the Jews, Pilate handed Jesus over "to be crucified" (purpose clause with *hina* and the aorist passive subjunctive of *stauroō*). Pilate placed Jesus in the custody of a small con-

9. Johnny V. Miller, "The Time of the Crucifixion," *JETS* 26 (June 1983): 157-66.

tingent of Roman soldiers who were charged with carrying out the execution.

THE CRUCIFIXION, 19:17-27

Crucifixion was not a Roman invention. The Assyrians, Phoenicians, and Persians all practiced crucifixion during the first millennium B.C.[10] And although the traditional method of execution among Jews was stoning (Deut. 21:21), the Hasmonean tyrant Alexander Jannaeus used this dreadful punishment on his own Jewish kinsmen (Josephus *Jewish Wars* 1.97). The Romans adopted crucifixion as the official punishment for non-Romans, particularly slaves. Crucifixion was later used by the Roman army to execute rebels. During the siege of Jerusalem in A.D. 70, Roman troops crucified as many as five hundred Jews a day for several months (Josephus *Jewish Wars* 5.449-52).

The person to be crucified was led to the execution site by a soldier who carried the *titulus*, an inscription written on wood (cf. John 19:20) bearing the victim's name and the crime for which he was being punished. The victim was then attached to the cross either by ropes or with nails. Without any body support, the victim would die from muscular spasms and asphyxiation in a period of several hours. In order to prolong the agony, the Romans devised a small seat and foot support.[11] By this means, the victims could be kept alive for several days. The cross itself could take various forms, including a single post or stake, the traditional cross, posts crossed to form an X, and a post with a crossbeam to form a T.

The discovery of the bones of a young Jew in an ossuary inscribed with the name "Yehohanan, the son of Hagakol" has significantly illuminated the matter of the position of the victim on the cross.[12] The heel bones were found pinned together by a seven-inch nail that was lodged in a knot and could not be pulled out after the young man died. The feet were amputated and buried with the knot into which the nail had been driven. Analysis of the skeletal remains indicates that Yehohanan's arms were nailed above the wrists to the

10. Vassilios Tzsaferis, "Crucifixion: The Archaeological Evidence," *Biblical Archaeology Review* (January-February 1985): 48.
11. Ibid, p. 49.
12. Joseph A. Fitzmyer, "Crucifixion in Ancient Palestine, Qumran Literature, and the New Testament," *Catholic Biblical Quarterly* 40 (1978): 493-513.

crossbeam. His legs were bent and twisted to one side, and a small *sedile*, or seat, supported only his left buttock.[13]

Death by crucifixion was in every sense *excruciating*, a term derived from the Latin *excruciatus*, meaning "from the cross." Although a crucified victim suffered terrible thirst and physical exhaustion, death usually came as a result of asphyxiation. Prolonged suspension from the cross caused fatigue and eventual paralysis of the diaphragm. The victim could linger on the cross several days using his legs as a point of leverage to thrust his body upwards and fill his lungs with air. In Palestine the executioner would often break the legs of the crucified person to hasten death and permit burial before nightfall (cf. Deut. 21:22-23; John 19:31-33). Breaking the legs would prevent upward thrusting and bring death by respiratory failure.

19:17   It was customary for condemned prisoners to bear the crossbeam to the crucifixion site. Carrying His own crosspiece, Jesus was led by the Roman soldiers to a place just outside the walled city of Jerusalem (cf. Heb. 13:12), known as "the place of the Skull." John also identifies the site by its Aramaic name, the language spoken by most first-century Jews. "Golgotha" is the Aramaic word for "skull." The familiar designation "Calvary" is derived from Latin *calvaria* ("skull") and found its way into the English language through the Latin Vulgate.[14]

The actual location of Golgotha is a matter of debate. When Hadrian reconstructed Jerusalem after the Second Revolt as Aelia Capitolina (A.D. 135), Christianity was considered a Jewish sect, and its holy sites were treated accordingly. Hadrian had a Roman temple built over the crucifixion site. This temple enabled Helena, Constantine's mother, to identify the place of the crucifixion and tomb of Jesus when she came to Jerusalem in A.D. 326. Hadrian's temple was removed and a magnificent basilica built in its place (A.D. 336). Although the Church of the Holy Sepulchre is inside the present walls of Jerusalem, excavations have revealed that the site was outside walled Jerusalem in the first century A.D.[15]

Charles Gordon, a British army officer, identified a rock formation north of the present city walls as the site of Golgotha, but his

---

13. For a different analysis, see J. Zias and E. Sekeles, "The Crucified Man from Giv'at ha-Mivtar: A Reappraisal," *Israel Exploration Journal* 35 (1985): 22-27.

14. Bruce, *The Gospel of John*, p. 367.

15. K. M. Kenyon, *Digging Up Jerusalem* (New York: Praeger, 1974), pp. 226-32, 261.

arguments are unconvincing, and the "Garden Tomb" lies in the middle of what was an extensive cemetery during the Iron Age. This tomb was originally constructed during the eighth or seventh century B.C. and reused for burial in the Byzantine period (fifth to seventh centuries A.D.).[16]

19:18   Although death by crucifixion was cruel and frightful, John does not emphasize that aspect. He simply records, "They crucified him." His readers were all too familiar with the horrors associated with this dreadful means of punishment. John does mention the two men who were crucified along with Jesus. Matthew and Mark call them "bandits" (*lēstai*), the same word John uses of Barabbas (John 18:40). John may include this comment as an illustration of how Jesus was "numbered with the transgressors" (Isa. 53:12).

19:19   It was customary for an inscription to be prepared that stated the condemned person's name and the crime for which he was being punished. In Latin this was known as the *titulus*, from which John's Greek word *titlos* ("notice") is borrowed.

The inscription is recorded in all four gospels, but with slight variation (Matt. 27:37; Mark 15:26; Luke 23:38). It seems as though each writer records only a portion of the inscription. The full statement may be reconstructed by combining the four accounts: "This is Jesus the Nazarene, the King of the Jews."[17]

19:20   The *titulus* was customarily attached to the cross so that those passing by could read the charges against the condemned man. John reports that many of the Jews read the sign, for the crucifixion site was in close proximity to the city of Jerusalem. The reading of the inscription was facilitated by its being written in three languages. Aramaic was the commonly spoken language of the first-century Jews. Latin was the official language of Rome. Greek was the spoken language of the Roman world, much as English is spoken throughout the world today.

19:21   The "chief priests" (cf. John 7:32) objected to the wording of the inscription and lodged a protest with Pilate. They had rejected Jesus as their king (cf. 18:39-40; 19:15) and did not want the *titulus* to proclaim Him "King of the Jews." They asked Pilate to write instead, "This man claimed to be king of the Jews." The difference may seem

---

16. Gabriel Barkay, "The Garden Tomb: Was Jesus Buried Here?" *Biblical Archaeology Review* (March-April 1986): 40-57.

17. Robert Thomas and Stanley N. Gundry, *A Harmony of the Gospels* (Chicago: Moody, 1978), p. 243.

slight to us but was significant to the Jews. They definitely did not want the *titulus* to proclaim the kingship of Jesus.

19:22   Pilate refused to alter the inscription. The official charge against Jesus would stand as written. Any official record would indicate that Jesus was crucified on charges of sedition.

In recording this incident John undoubtedly wants the readers to be aware that Jesus is King of the Jews, and that no objection, protest, or even crucifixion can deprive Him of His rightful position as sovereign. Even His crucifixion, by Roman decree, proclaims the kingship of Jesus. If the unbelieving Pontius Pilate could proclaim Jesus' kingship, why are Christians so often silent about this good news?

19:23   The clothes of the crucified victim were customarily appropriated by the soldiers in charge of the execution. Two main garments are mentioned. The "clothes," or cloak (*himation*), refers to the outer garment. The plural may have been used because the soldiers were able to divide the garment (probably at the seams) into four parts. The "undergarment" (*chitōn*) was a seamless tunic, or shirt, worn next to the skin. Josephus uses this word to describe the high priest's tunic that was woven in one piece (*Antiquities* 3.161).

19:24   Although Jesus' outer cloak was divided, the soldiers decided not to tear the seamless tunic. Instead they agreed to cast lots (*lachōmen*) to determine who among the four should take it. Lot casting was something like rolling dice and was a means of making decisions in ancient times (cf. Prov. 16:33; Acts 1:26).

John records that the action of the soldiers in dividing Jesus' clothes and casting lots for His inner tunic fulfilled messianic prophecy. He quotes Psalm 22:18 (LXX) as evidence for this most remarkable fulfillment. The fact that prophecy is being fulfilled during the crucifixion is evidence that Satan has not won a victory. God is still in control. He is using even the wicked actions of wicked people to accomplish His sovereign purposes (cf. Gen. 50:20).

19:25   John now draws the reader's attention to some special women standing near Jesus' cross. This simple reference brings a note of pathos to the scene. The tragedy of crucifixion is one thing. But here were friends and family members who shared in the grief as they watched the Lord suffering on the cross. As they had been with Him in the joys of life, they desired to be with Him in the pain of death. These loyal friends were there when Jesus needed them most. We all need —and need to be—friends like this.

There is a problem determining the number of women being mentioned. Jesus' mother, Mary, is mentioned first, though not by name. It is not clear whether "his mother's sister" is identical with or distinct from "Mary the wife of Clopas." It is probable they are distinct because it is unlikely any parents would name their two daughters by the same name. It is possible that "his mother's sister" is Salome (Mark 15:40), the mother of the sons of Zebedee (Matt. 27:56). Nothing is known of "Mary the wife of Clopas," although some have linked her with "Cleopas" of Luke 24:18.

Mary Magdalene would be the first to witness a resurrection appearance of Jesus (cf. John 20:10-18). The designation "Magdalene" indicates her place or origin of residence. Mary was from Magdala, identified with the present-day village of Migdal, about three miles north of Tiberias on the Sea of Galilee.

19:26 It is remarkable that in the midst of His own severe physical suffering Jesus had the grace to make some provision for His mother. Shortly before His death, He committed Mary to the care of John, "the disciple whom he loved" (see 13:23). Because Joseph is not mentioned, it is generally presumed that he has died. Jesus' half-brothers were still unbelievers and could not be counted on for spiritual support and encouragement. Jesus' words "Dear woman, here is your son" may be understood in the sense, "Consider him as your son."

19:27 Similarly, Jesus spoke to John, "Here is your mother." Jesus could be assured that His mother would be in good care with His beloved disciple. John records that "from that time on" he took Mary into his home, implying that he cared for her as his own mother.

Jesus honored His mother by making arrangements that she would be cared for in light of His own death. He was obedient to the fifth commandment, "Honor your father and your mother" (Ex. 20:12). Jesus' kindness and consideration toward His mother illustrates the concern believers should have toward the physical needs of family members. Paul declares in forceful words, "If anyone does not provide for his relatives, and especially for his immediate family, he has denied the faith and is worse than an unbeliever" (1 Tim. 5:8).

THE DEATH OF JESUS, 19:28-30

In this section John records the climax of redemptive history—the death of God's Lamb for the sins of the world. The biblical account of Christ's death provides the factual basis for the first key element of Paul's gospel, "that Christ died for our sins" (1 Cor. 15:3).

19:28   John affirms in v. 28 (as in 13:1) that Jesus was completely conscious of all that was taking place. He knew that "all" (*panta*) God had required of Him "was now completed" (perfect passive indicative of *teleō* (cf. 19:30). A similar thought is expressed in 17:4. The word "Later" (*meta touto*) indicates a short interval between what happened in vv. 25-27 and this next word from Jesus.

More than simply knowing what was taking place, Jesus was consciously in control of the circumstances. This is reflected in the words He spoke "so that the Scripture would be fulfilled." Intense thirst was one of the greatest agonies of crucifixion. It is not unusual that Jesus experienced thirst. But in speaking the words "I am thirsty" Jesus consciously intended to fulfill Scripture, specifically messianic prophecy. This is shown by the purpose clause with *hina* and the subjunctive of *teleioō*, "to finish" or "to accomplish." The Scripture to which John refers is most likely Psalm 69:21: "They . . . gave me vinegar for my thirst."

19:29   Earlier during the crucifixion Jesus had refused a drugged wine (Matt. 27:34), which, according to the Talmud, was customarily given by the women of Jerusalem to those being led to execution (*Sanhedrin* 43*a*). But now, in addition to fulfilling Scripture, He wished to speak a final word. A sip of wine would moisten His parched lips and throat and enable Him to be heard.

"Wine vinegar" (*oxos*) refers to a sour wine that served as the ordinary drink of common laborers and soldiers. It relieved thirst more effectively than water and was cheaper than regular wine. Giving Jesus sour wine should not be interpreted as a further act of cruelty. This was the customary drink of the soldiers and was readily available at the cross.

It was standard practice among Roman soldiers to carry a piece of sponge for use in lieu of a drinking cup. The sponge was soaked in the sour wine, pressed onto a stalk of "hyssop," and put to Jesus' lips. Hyssop, a small bush with blue flowers and highly aromatic leaves, was used in purification rituals (Ex. 12:22; Lev. 14:4; Num. 19:6, 18). Some have expressed concern that a stalk of hyssop (*hussōpō*) would not be long enough or strong enough to raise the wet sponge to Jesus' lips. An eleventh-century Greek manuscript substitutes a similar word "javelin" (*hussō*). But "hyssop" is no doubt the correct reading,[18] and a short stalk of the branch would have been sufficient for the task. It was only necessary for the feet of crucified victims to be clear of the ground. Contrary to popular paintings, they were not raised very high. There is no major difficulty with the reading "hyssop."

19:30   When Jesus had received the sour wine, He made one final declaration, *tetelestai*, "It is finished!" Matthew 27:50 mentions that Jesus cried out in "a loud voice" just before He died, an apparent reference to the final word recorded by John. *Telelestai* is the perfect passive indicative of *teleō*, which means "to bring to an end," "finish," or "complete" something. The word was used in ancient times in connection with the payment of rent or poll-tax. Receipts were often introduced by the Greek phrase *tetelestai*, indicating that the debt had been paid in full.[19]

With the use of *tetelestai* Jesus was declaring the completion of His life's work. The crucifixion did not thwart His mission. Rather, it accomplished it. Jesus did not hang His head in the agony of defeat. He was the victor, not the victim, on the cross. Jesus died in triumph, having accomplished in full the work the Father had sent Him to do. He had paid the final penalty for sin, securing redemption for lost men. What a glorious moment in salvation history.

Having completed His work, Jesus bowed His head and voluntarily yielded His spirit. No man took His life. The Greek word translated "gave up" (*paradidōmi*) expresses a voluntary act. Luke 23:46 records that Jesus' last words on the cross were a quotation from Psalm 31:5: "Father, into your hands I commit my spirit."

THE PIERCING OF JESUS, 19:31-37

This section records what took place at the crucifixion site after the death of Jesus. The account of the piercing of Jesus' side is unique to John's gospel.

19:31   John records that the day of Christ's crucifixion was "the day of Preparation" (*paraskeuē*), a familiar Jewish expression for Friday, the day when things had to be prepared for the Sabbath, when work was prohibited. The next day, beginning at sunset, was going to be a

18. Bruce M. Metzger, *A Textual Commentary on the New Testament* (London: United Bible Societies, 1971), p. 253.

19. J. H. Moulton and G. Milligan, *The Vocabulary of the Greek New Testament* (Grand Rapids: Eerdmans, 1930), p. 630.

"special Sabbath" (or "great Sabbath") because it would not only be the seventh day, but also the Passover of the Judeans (cf. comments on 18:28). It was in light of this approaching high holy day that the Jews wanted the bodies of the executed men removed from their crosses before sunset. This was in keeping with the Mosaic instruction that the corpse of a victim of execution should be buried on the day of death to avoid desecration of the land (Deut. 21:21).

Because the bodies needed to be removed before the Passover began, the Jews asked Pilate "to have the legs broken." The breaking of the legs, known in Latin by the technical term *crurifragium*, was not intended to intensify the agony of crucifixion but to hasten death. With the legs nailed to the cross the victim of crucifixion had a point of leverage to raise the body upward and fill the lungs with air. When the legs were broken, the point of leverage was removed, and the victim soon died of respiratory failure.[20] The leg bones of the crucified man found by archaeologists evidenced a fracture produced by a single, strong blow.

19:32   The men who were crucified with Jesus were still alive and could have lingered on their crosses for many hours or several days. According to Mark 15:44, Pilate was surprised that Jesus had died so quickly. In order to accelerate their deaths, John records that the soldiers broke the legs of the other two men.

19:33   The soldiers discovered that Jesus had already died (cf. 19:30), and so there was no need to break His legs. In view of this, some have argued that Jesus merely fainted and did not die. But these soldiers were accustomed to executions and were quite familiar with the signs of death. It was the professional opinion of seasoned executioners that Jesus was dead.

19:34   Instead of breaking His legs, one of the soldiers thrust his spear into the side of Jesus. This was not an act of brutality nor intended as a death blow. Rather, this post mortem piercing was intended to testify to the victim's death. Only after this testimonial was obtained was the body removed from the cross and handed over to the victim's relatives for burial.[21]

The significance of "the flow of blood and water" from Jesus' side is debated. One popular explanation is that the separation of blood and water (*aima kai hudōr*) indicates that Jesus died of car-

---

20. G. L. Borchert, "They Brake Not His Legs," *Christianity Today* (March 16, 1962), p. 12.
21. Tzaferis, "Crucifixion—the Archaeological Evidence," p. 53.

diac rupture. Others suggest that Jesus' death was multifactorial and related to shock, exhaustion asphyxia, and perhaps acute heart failure. The water probably represents serous pleural and pericardial fluid and would have been smaller in volume than the blood.[22] Some see theological significance in the water as representative of the cleansing from sin that resulted from Jesus' death. All unnecessary speculation aside, it is clear that John intends the readers to understand that there was a death in which blood was shed (cf. John 1:29).

19:35   The author of the fourth gospel provides a solemn testimony in v. 35 that he (John) is a reliable eyewitness of the matters about which he writes. The word "it" is not in the Greek text and should not be taken to refer only to the "flow of blood and water" (19:34). John is referring to all he has recorded regarding the crucifixion and death of Christ.

John never loses sight of the ultimate purpose in writing his gospel. In keeping with this purpose (cf. 20:30-31), he records this truthful testimony in order to (*hina*) elicit belief.

19:36   Once again (cf. 19:24), the apostle John sees God's purposes being accomplished even through the dreadful execution of Christ. The sovereignty of God is seen in that the circumstances of Jesus' death ("These things") took place in order to (purpose clause with *hina*) fulfill Scripture. As Paul states, Christ's death for sins was "according to the Scriptures" (1 Cor. 15:3).

The fact that Jesus' legs were not broken corresponds to the Passover lamb's being roasted and eaten without the breaking of bones (Ex. 12:46; Num. 9:12). The Scripture quotation "Not one of his bones will be broken" appears to be taken from the Septuagint translation of Psalm 34:20, where David describes how God watches over His own. It is probable that John intends the Passover allusion (cf. John 1:29; also 1 Cor. 5:7) but sees a direct fulfillment of Psalm 34:20.

19:37   The piercing of Jesus' side also brings another Scripture to John's mind: "They will look on the one they have pierced." The obvious Scripture reference is Zechariah 12:10, which describes prophetically the repentance of God's people Israel when they seek Jesus at His second coming and realize that He is the one they "pierced" (aorist active indicative of *ekkenteō*; cf. Rev. 1:7). John's quotation differs in every word from the Septuagint but agrees well with the Masoretic Hebrew text.

22. Edwards, Gabel, Hosmer, "On the Physical Death of Jesus Christ," p. 1463.

THE BURIAL OF JESUS, 19:38-42

The burial of Jesus is an important element of the gospel proclamation (cf. 1 Cor. 15:4). John's account of the burial serves to substantiate further the fact that Jesus actually died.

19:38   According to the synoptics, Jesus died around 3:00 P.M. (Matt. 27:46; Mark 15:34; Luke 23:44). Sometime later that afternoon, Joseph of Arimathea, a wealthy and prominent member of the Sanhedrin (Matt. 27:57; Mark 15:43), requested the body of Jesus and made arrangements for His burial. Arimathea was a Judean town (Luke 23:51), but its location is unknown. Luke reports that he was "a good and upright man" and had not consented to the Sanhedrin's action against Jesus (Luke 23:51).

John reports that Joseph was a disciple of Jesus but had not let this secret be known for fear of the Jewish leaders (cf. 12:43). From the viewpoint of Jewish culture, burial was quite important, and Joseph boldly (cf. Mark 15:43) stepped forward to tend to these arrangements. Although he was afraid of what others might think and do, he seems to have overcome his fear and publicly acted on his faith at this point. Many of us fear what the world will think or do if we act like Christians. Joseph's example is a good one for us to follow.

Ordinarily the body of an executed criminal was turned over to the family for burial, except in cases of rebellion against the state.[23] Jesus had been indicted for rebellion (cf. 18:37; 19:12, 21-22), and Joseph's prominence apparently enabled him to take custody of the body.

19:39   Joseph was accompanied by another prominent member of the Sanhedrin, Nicodemus (cf. 3:1). John reminds the readers of his gospel that this same man had first come to Jesus "at night" (3:2). Although John does not directly state the fact, Nicodemus was now making his association with Jesus public. It seems that he had come out of darkness into the light. Jesus' contact with this Jewish leader had not been unfruitful.

Nicodemus brought about seventy-five pounds of aromatic spices to the tomb in order to prepare Jesus' body for burial. It was the custom in ancient times to sprinkle powdered spices into the winding linen sheets that were used to wrap the body (Josephus *Antiquities* 17.199). Such spices would serve to cover the odor of the

---

23. Bruce, *The Gospel of John*, p. 378.

decaying body as arrangements were made for burial. Myrrh, a resinous gum from the bush *balsamodendron myrrha*, was prized for its aromatic qualities. Aloes, not mentioned elsewhere in the New Testament, is made from the fragrant leaves of the *Aloe succotrina* and was often used by the Egyptians for embalming.

19:40   John reports that Jesus' body was prepared for burial according to standard Jewish custom. The body of Jesus was wrapped "with the spices, in strips of linen." The description here seems to rule out the idea of a shroud, often associated with the burial of Jesus.

19:41   John alone mentions a garden in connection with the burial of Jesus. The words "at the place where Jesus was crucified" probably mean "in the immediate vicinity." It is unlikely that a crucifixion would take place in a garden. In the garden, possibly Joseph's, was a new tomb.

In Palestine, bodies were buried in natural caves or tombs that were carved out of the limestone. Niches or shelves were prepared where the bodies could be laid. The tomb was customarily sealed with a disc-shaped stone that could be rolled across the entrance. The tomb was usually a family tomb, and the niches would be reused as necessary. The bones of the previous occupant would simply be collected and placed in a bone-box, or "ossuary," that remained in the tomb.[24]

John stresses that the tomb in which Jesus was buried was one "in which no one had ever been laid." He uses a double negative (*oudepō oudeis*) to emphasize this fact. This tomb had not been defiled by the corruption associated with death (cf. Lev. 21:11; Num. 6:6; 19:11-13).

19:42   John's last comment concerning the burial of Jesus seems to indicate that it was something of a temporary measure. It was the "Jewish day of Preparation" (cf. John 19:31) for a Passover Sabbath, and sunset was fast approaching. Because the tomb was nearby, Jesus was laid there. Matthew records that this was Joseph's own tomb (Matt. 27:60). Although John does not mention it, the burial in Joseph's tomb fulfilled another prophecy. Instead of being buried in a common grave assigned to criminals, Jesus was "with the rich in his death" (Isa. 53:9).

---

24. For further study, see Ralph Gower, *The New Manners and Customs of Bible Times* (Chicago: Moody, 1987), pp. 72-74.

HOMILETICAL SUGGESTIONS

John 19 obviously commends itself to Easter season preaching. Verses 1-6 continue the record of Jesus' trial before Pilate. Here we see an example of an unjust trial. Jesus was repeatedly declared "innocent" (18:38; 19:4, 6). Yet Pilate sent Him to the cross instead of releasing Him. Much of life reflects this kind of injustice. Throughout the history of the church, believers have been subject to unjust treatment. But we are reminded by this text that (1) God is sovereign over such injustice; (2) God can use the injustices of mankind to accomplish His sovereign purposes; and (3) Jesus experienced injustice without grumbling or complaint.

The account of Christ's crucifixion (19:17-27) would of course provide an excellent text for a Good Friday service. Some details would provide good background on the nature of crucifixion, but preachers must be careful not to overdo and give too gruesome a description of Christ's death. He suffered greatly physically, but His greatest suffering was in the spiritual realm as He took our sin upon His holy Person.

The death of Jesus (19:28-30) marks the climax of redemptive history. This passage could either be a Good Friday message or the basis of a Lord's Supper meditation. The passage emphasizes the *voluntary* nature of Christ's death. The words "It is finished" are full of redemptive significance. Christ presented the once-for-all sacrifice (Heb. 9:26, 28; 10:4, 10, 12, 18) for sin.

Verses 38-39 mention Joseph of Arimathea and Nicodemus, who came forward to claim the body of Jesus and provide a proper burial. These texts provide material for biographical sermons. Both were hesitant and fearful at the beginnings of their association with Christ. But they overcame their fears and did a deed of kindness that reflects personal faith.

JOHN
CHAPTER
TWENTY

BELIEF IN THE LORD OF LIFE

THE CONFIRMATION OF BELIEF, 20:1-31

The resurrection of Jesus from the dead served to solidify and confirm the belief of the disciples (20:8, 27-28) and became the "good news" proclaimed by the apostles (1 Cor. 15:4). Apart from the physical resurrection of Jesus, there is no historical basis for Christianity. As the apostle Paul wrote, "if Christ has not been raised, your faith is futile; you are still in your sins" (1 Cor. 15:17).

Each gospel has its own unique resurrection narrative. Westcott does a good job in harmonizing the accounts.[1] The writers of the synoptic gospels focus their resurrection accounts on the witnesses of the empty tomb (Mark and Luke) or on the appearance of Jesus to His disciples (Matthew). John skillfully weaves these two aspects of the resurrection together, providing a nicely balanced account of the events.[2]

THE EMPTY TOMB, 20:1-10

It was in the early morning hours of Sunday, April 5, A.D. 33, that Jesus' disciples made the startling discovery that His tomb was empty.

---

1. B. F. Westcott, *The Gospel According to St. John* (Grand Rapids: Eerdmans, 1973), pp. 287-88.
2. Barclay M. Newman and Eugene A. Nida, *A Translator's Handbook on The Gospel of John* (London: United Bible Societies, 1980), pp. 601-2.

Had the tomb not been empty there would have been no factual basis for the proclamation of Christ's bodily resurrection.

20:1   Mary Magdalene and certain other women (note the plural "we" in v. 3, also Luke 24:1, 10) went to the tomb in the early hours of Sunday morning, "the first day of the week." They brought spices in order that they might anoint the body of Jesus (Mark 16:1). Perhaps they wanted to complete the job that was hastily done on the eve of Passover (cf. John 19:39-40). John points out that it was still dark when Mary Magdalene, who had apparently separated from the group, arrived and discovered that the tomb had been opened. The disc-shaped "stone" (*lithos*) that had sealed the tomb had been rolled from the entrance.

One wonders if the words "yet dark" (*skotias eti*) contain a subtle double reference to both the darkness of the morning and the spiritual darkness in the hearts of the disciples, which was about to be penetrated by the light of the resurrection (cf. 13:30).

For the Jews, Sunday (the day after the first Sabbath following Passover (cf. Lev. 23:11) would be the Feast of First Fruits. On this day the Jews would present the first sheaf of the barley harvest to the Lord in the Temple. This offering was both an expression of gratitude and an expression of faith that a full harvest was about to follow. It is significant that Jesus rose from the grave on the Feast of First Fruits. And so Paul presents Christ as the "first fruits" of the resurrection (1 Cor. 15:20-23).

20:2   Discovering that the tomb had been opened, Mary immediately ran to tell Simon Peter and the beloved disciple, John. She did not see the angel or hear the message he gave to the other women who arrived at the tomb after sunrise (Matt. 28:5-8; Mark 16:2-8; Luke 24:4-8).

Finding Peter and John, who were perhaps staying together, Mary reported that the tomb had been tampered with and the body of Jesus removed. The pronoun "they" is not defined. She was thinking generally of the enemies of Jesus, especially the religious leaders. Even though Jesus had predicted His resurrection (cf. Matt. 16:21; 17:23; 20:19; 26:32), it apparently did not occur to Mary that Jesus had been raised from the grave.

20:3   Although the hour was early, Peter and John ("the other disciple") wasted no time in heading out for the tomb. The imperfect tense of *erchomai* here indicates that they were "on the way" to the tomb.

20:4   Peter and John started off together, as indicated by the untranslated adverb *homou* ("together"), but John outran Peter and reached the tomb first (*prōtos*). For this reason it is often said that John was younger than Peter, but as Morris accurately points out, "speed and youth are not synonymous."[3] John may have been in better physical condition or knew of a shortcut.

20:5   John, who arrived first, bent down and looked (*blepō*) in through the low entrance, but he did not at first enter the tomb. (The apostle uses the present tense of *blepō* to record the action as presently and dramatically unfolding.) John does report that he saw the linen wrappings (*othonia*) that had been on the body of Jesus. One can well imagine what was going on in the mind of John. His brain was processing the data as quickly as possible. Why would the linen wrappings be here without the body? Any sign of forced entry? Any indication of foul play? Where is the body? What has happened here?

20:6   Peter arrived at the tomb shortly after John. There is no indication of a delay of more than a few seconds. Unlike John, Peter did not hesitate at the entrance of the sepulchre. He immediately pushed past John and entered the vault. He too observed the strips of linen lying where the body of Jesus had been placed. Robertson points out the distinction between the two words for "seeing" used by John in vv. 5-6.[4] In v. 5 John uses the word *blepō*, which denotes a mere glance. Here in v. 6 he uses the word *theōreō*, which seems to denote in this context a more careful observation.

20:7   In addition to the linen wrappings, Peter particularly noticed the burial cloth that had been on Jesus' head. Perhaps he even called this to John's attention. Lazarus had such a cloth wrapped around his head when he emerged from the tomb (11:44). Instead of being tossed aside, this item was "folded up by itself, separate from the linen." The word "folded" (*entulissō*) means "to wrap up" or "to coil about." It is unclear whether the linen headpiece was folded or simply left in the coiled state, as it would be on the head of a body.

On the basis of this comment some have suggested that Jesus rose up through the grave clothes without disturbing them.[5] It is suggested that the grave clothes observed by Peter and John retained the shape of a human form (though collapsed), and that the headpiece retained the circular shape of a head. This, then, is what caused John

3. Leon Morris, *The Gospel According to John*, NICNT (Grand Rapids: Eerdmans,1971), p. 832.

4. A. T. Robertson, *Word Pictures in the New Testament* (Nashville: Broadman, 1932), 5:309.

5. Homer A. Kent, Jr., *Light in the Darkness* (Grand Rapids: Baker, 1974), p. 217.

to believe. Although the language of the text does not demand this interpretation, it does allow for it.

One wonders, however, if John is not simply reporting that the grave clothes were not in disarray as one would expect if the body had been stolen. This interpretation may be the clearest and most straightforward approach. Whereas grave-robbers would have taken the body with the wrappings, or ripped and scattered them, John records Peter's observation that the burial cloth used on Jesus' head remained rolled or had been folded and set carefully aside.

20:8 John, the "other disciple," followed Peter into the tomb. The NIV's "Finally" seems to indicate some delay. The Greek *tote* is used to introduce that which follows next and simply means "then."

John records the climatic statement "He saw and believed" (*eiden kai episteusen*). The text does not specifically state *what* John saw and believed. Byrne argues that what John saw was the abandoned graveclothes and particularly the head cloth folded up by itself (cf. 20:7).[6] But was this the extent of what John "saw"? Seeing the empty grave must have had some impact upon his thinking. And what did John believe? Did he merely believe the words of Mary Magdalene, who had reported that the grave was empty? This would be anticlimatic and contrary to the thematic focus of this section—belief in the resurrection.

With a flash of insight John realized what must have happened. His growing faith came to culmination. Seeing the evidence before him, John believed that Jesus had risen from the dead and left the tomb. Comparing v. 8 with vv. 5-6, Robertson notes that Peter saw (*theoreo*) more after he entered the tomb than John did at first glance (*blepo*).[7] But v. 8 indicates that John saw into the meaning of it all better than Peter did. He was the first to believe that Jesus had risen from the tomb even before he saw Jesus. Byrne views John as a pattern for others who may come to faith in the resurrection of Jesus through the "signs," without seeing Jesus Himself.[8]

20:9 John explains parenthetically in v. 9 that the disciples ("they") did not yet understand the prophecies of Scripture that indicated Jesus would rise from the dead. Their understanding of the scriptural basis for the resurrection (cf. Ps. 2:7; 16:10; Isa. 52:10; 53:10-12) did

---

6. Brendan Byrne, "The Faith of the Beloved Disciple and the Community in John 20," *Journal for the Study of the New Testament* 23 (1985): 86-87.

7. Robertson, *Word Pictures in the New Testament*, 5:310.

8. Byrne, "Faith of the Beloved Disciple," pp. 90-91.

not come until later (cf. Luke 24:44-45; John 2:19-22; Ac

John is making a crucial point here. He is empha
disciples' belief in the resurrection preceded their und
the resurrection was foretold in Scripture. As Morris
first believers did not manufacture a resurrection story to agree with
their interpretation of messianic prophecy.[9] Rather, they were first
convinced that Christ had risen and *then* came to an understanding of
the scriptural teaching of this truth.

20:10   John concludes the testimony of his personal experience at
the tomb by reporting that the disciples went back to their homes.
John uses the term "disciples" (*mathētai*) to refer to himself and Peter. The words "to their homes" may suggest that they returned to
their homes in Galilee. The Greek reads "to themselves" (*pros au-
tous*). The emphasis is not on where they went but upon the fact that
they left the tomb. Peter and John probably returned to the place
where they were staying in Jerusalem.

We perhaps wonder how the disciples spent the rest of the day.
Later that morning they may have wondered if it had really happened
as they remembered. There may have been doubts. But there was
Mary's report (cf. v. 18). Should she be believed? There is often a "let
down" after a spiritual high point. Believers have all experienced this,
which was what the disciples were probably going through. At such
times it is important simply to keep living what we have come to believe and not allow our emotions to derail our faith.

THE APPEARANCE TO MARY MAGDALENE, 20:11-18

It is significant that the first resurrection appearance of Jesus was
to a woman. Judaism of the first century had a rather low view of
women's participation in religious matters. Although they might attend worship and individually pray, synagogue instruction was provided only for men. Indeed, Rabbi Eliezer said, "If a man gives his
daughter a knowledge of the Law it is as though he taught her le-
chery" (*Sota* 3.4). With Jesus, it was different. He had women friends
and disciples (Luke 8:2-3). And He showed His high regard for spiritually minded women by appearing first to Mary Magdalene. Although
Mark 16:9 records that this was the first resurrection appearance, John
alone reports the details.

9. Morris, *The Gospel According to John*, p. 835.

:11   Mary Magdalene returned to the tomb, apparently after the departure of Peter and John from the garden. Mary was weeping outside the entrance of the tomb, no doubt stricken with grief over the death of Jesus and confusion about the missing body. As she wept, she stooped to peer (*parakuptō*) into the tomb.

20:12   John reports that Mary beheld (*theōreō*) two angels, clothed in white and seated in the tomb. John uses the present tense "beholds" to describe vividly the action taking place. One angel was at the head and one at the foot of the ledge where the body of Jesus had been.

20:13   Unlike the "two men" of Luke 24:4-6, these angels do not announce the resurrection. Rather, they ask the question, "Woman, why are you crying?" Addressing Mary as "Woman" (*gunai*) was not harsh or disrespectful (see John 2:4; 20:15).

Mary responded by explaining her concern: "They have taken my Lord away, and I don't know where they have put him." This statement essentially repeats her words to Peter and John in 20:2. The encounter with the angels does not significantly advance the narrative, but their question gives Mary a chance to express her faith ("My Lord"). Her answer, however, also shows her ignorance of the resurrection.

20:14   At this point Mary turned around and saw (literally "beholds") Jesus standing before her. But like the disciples on the road to Emmaus (Luke 24:15-16), she did not realize it was Jesus. Although her vision may have been blurred by her tears, there seems to have been something different about Jesus after His resurrection (John 21:4, 12; cf. Matt. 28:17; Luke 24:36-39).

20:15   Then Jesus repeated the question the angels had asked, "Woman, why are you crying?" He added a question for which He knew the answer, "Who is it you are looking for?" It is significant that Jesus asked "who" (*tina*) rather than "what" (*ti*). As Morris remarks, "She was looking for a corpse whereas she should have been seeking a person."[10]

John reports that Mary mistook Jesus for a gardener (*ho kēpouros*). Because the tomb was located in a garden (John 19:41), Mary's assumption regarding this unidentified person is not surprising. She respectfully requested custody of the body of Jesus. Although

10. Ibid., p. 838.

not stated, it is implied that Mary was concerned to give the body a proper burial.

20:16 Mary finally recognized Jesus when He spoke her name, "Mary." Turning once again (cf. 20:14) toward the risen Lord she greeted Him in her native Aramaic tongue, "Rabboni." (For "Aramaic," see comment on 19:20). The term "Rabboni" was a respectful form of address more emphatic and perhaps more honorific than the simpler term "Rabbi,"[11] the traditional honorary title for recognized teachers of the law. The Aramaic *rab* means "great" or "great one." John renders the term loosely as "Teacher."

20:17 After greeting Jesus, Mary apparently embraced Him, perhaps taking hold of His feet, as did the disciples in Matthew 28:9. This was an expression of worship by one who loved the Lord. Mary's response makes me wonder how I will greet Jesus when I see Him in my resurrected body for the first time. Do I say "Hello"? Do I shake His hand? Do I give Him a hug? Do I bow at His feet? I do not know how I will respond. But I look forward to thanking Him who died for me.

Jesus then gave Mary two commands. He told her not to cling to Him and commanded her to deliver a message to the disciples. Tucked between these two commands is the problematic "For I have not yet returned to my Father."

Jesus first told Mary, "Do not hold on to me." The negative particle *mē* with the present imperative of *haptō* ("to cling" or "lay hold of") commands the cessation of an act in progress. The explanatory clause introduced by "for" (*gar*) follows. Complicated explanations have been offered as to why Mary could not touch Jesus before the ascension, especially because Thomas on the other hand was invited to touch Him (20:27). Perhaps Jesus knew Mary's thoughts and did not want her to conclude that He had returned to stay.

The best solution for the explanatory clause is offered by McGhee who suggests that the *gar* should be taken as the anticipatory conjunction "since" rather than the causal conjunction "for."[12] McGhee punctuates the text differently from traditional readings and renders v. 17 "Don't cling to me. Since I have not yet ascended to the Father, go to my brothers and tell them I am ascending to my Father and your Father and my God and your God." Accordingly, Jesus was simply stating

---

11. F. F. Bruce, *The Gospel of John: Introduction, Exposition and Notes* (Grand Rapids: Eerdmans, 1983), p. 389.

12. Michael McGhee, "A Less Theological Reading of John 20:17," *JBL* 105 (June 1986): 299-302.

a matter of fact (i.e., He had not yet ascended to the Father), not explaining why Mary should not cling to Him.

Jesus knew He was soon to be going to the Father, and He wanted Mary to deliver that news to the disciples. Mary was instructed to go and tell Jesus' "brothers," "I am returning to my Father and your Father, to my God and your God." It is obvious that Jesus' brothers refers here to the disciples (cf. Matt. 12:47-50) rather than the other sons of Mary, who were not yet believers (John 7:5). The present tense of the verb "am returning" (*anabainō*) indicates that Jesus was in the process of ascending. Jesus' return to the Father is a prominent theme in John's gospel (7:33; 14:12, 28; 16:5, 10, 28).

The words "my Father and your Father," "My God and your God" are taken by some to suggest a difference between Jesus' relationship with God and the disciples' relationship with God.[13] It is noted that Jesus says "my" and "your," not "our." Although there is certainly a uniqueness to Jesus' relationship with the Father, these phrases seem to emphasize commonality. The Father of Jesus was the heavenly Father of Mary. Jesus (as God's Son) and Mary (as a believer) shared in humanity and in a spiritual kinship with God the Father. In this sense Jesus is "one of us." At the same time we would be quick to emphasize that there is an important theological distinction between Jesus' relationship with God the Father and the relationship we enjoy as believers by adoption. As the divine Son of God and second Person of the Trinity, Jesus' relationship with the Father is absolutely unique. As God's Son He is in an eternal and coequal relationship with the Father. God is Mary's Father (and ours) through redemption and adoption.

20:18   Upon receiving Jesus' instructions, Mary went to the disciples and announced the good news of the resurrection. John uses the present active participle of *aggellō*, indicating continuous or repeated action ("announcing"). She declared, "I have seen the Lord," and faithfully reported the things Jesus had told her. The perfect tense of *horaō* ("seen") suggests that a lasting picture of the risen Lord had penetrated her mind's eye.

THE APPEARANCE TO THE TEN, 20:19-23

Later on resurrection Sunday Jesus appeared to other women (Matt. 28:9-10), to Simon Peter (Luke 24:33-35; 1 Cor. 15:5), and to the

13. Morris, *The Gospel According to John*, p. 842.

two disciples on the Emmaus road (Mark 16:12-13; Luke 24:13-32). It was late in the evening of that most memorable day when Jesus appeared to ten of His closest disciples.

20:19   The disciples gathered together in the evening, no doubt to discuss the wonderful events of the day. Peter had probably told the account of Jesus' appearance to him. There was excitement in the air, but also some fear. John reports that the "doors" (note the plural) of the house and the room in which they were gathered were locked "for fear of the Jews." And with good reason. A story was being circulated that the disciples had stolen the body of Jesus (Matt. 28:11-15). They could expect to be apprehended by the authorities. Indeed, Jesus had warned them of coming persecution (John 15:20; 16:1-2).

Suddenly Jesus appeared in the midst of the ten disciples and greeted them: "Peace be with you [*eirēnē humin*]!" It is fruitless to speculate whether Jesus' body just materialized in the midst of the disciples or whether He walked through the solid wall or opened the locked door. (The phrase *estē eis to meson* could be rendered "He stepped into the midst" [first aorist of *histēmi*].)

"Peace be with you" is a traditional Hebrew greeting (Judg. 6:23; 19:20; Dan. 10:19; Luke 10:5) that is still used in Israel today ("Shalom!"). For Jesus, this was more than a greeting. He was encouraging the disciples to appropriate the "peace" He had promised (John 14:27).

20:20   After greeting the disciples, He authenticated the genuineness of His resurrection body by displaying His wounds. He showed (first aorist of *deiknumi*, "to show" or "display") them His hands, which had been pierced by nails, and His side, which had been pierced by the lance (19:34). There was no mistaking Him. It was really Jesus. The disciples were overjoyed as the reality of His resurrection penetrated their minds. They had passed through a time of deep sorrow and were now experiencing the full joy Jesus had promised (cf. 16:20-22).

20:21   Jesus repeated His greeting, "Peace be with you!" He wanted the disciples to appropriate fully the deep and lasting peace that could be theirs. Then He commissioned the disciples for their future ministries. Jesus said, "As the Father has sent me, I am sending you." The Father's sending of Jesus the Son provided the pattern for the commissioning of the disciples. As God sent Jesus on a specific mission to speak as the Father's representative and with His authority, so the apostles were being sent by Jesus. More details regarding their specific responsibilities would be provided later (cf. Matt. 28:18-20).

20:22   John reports that Jesus, having commissioned the disciples, "breathed on them" (first aorist active indicative of *emphusaō*, "to breathe into" or "breathe upon") and said, "Receive the Holy Spirit." The text indicates that the Spirit was imparted by the breath of Jesus. The word *emphusaō* occurs only here in the New Testament, but it appears in the LXX translation of Genesis 2:7 where God "breathed" into Adam the breath of life. The breathing of Jesus upon the disciples was perhaps symbolic of His imparting to them something of His own life and Spirit. This was something of a "re-creation" event for the disciples. A new phase of their spiritual lives would begin with the New Covenant ministry of the Spirit (cf. Ezek. 36:27).

Following the lead of M. E. Isaacs,[14] Walt Russell suggests that the figure of Moses may lie behind John's description of Jesus' bequeathing the Holy Spirit to His disciples.[15] Numbers 11:24-25 records how God endowed the seventy elders with the same Spirit of prophecy that had been upon Moses. At various points in the gospel, John has demonstrated that Jesus is far greater than Moses (cf. 1:17-18; 6:32-35). Here in 20:22 this Mosaic imagery is brought to a climax as Jesus, the Greater Moses, bequeathed not just a temporary Spirit of prophecy but an abiding gift of the Holy Spirit.

This verse has presented some difficulty in regard to the giving of the Holy Spirit. It seems clear from Acts 2:1-17 that the Spirit came upon the disciples at Pentecost. Was there some bestowal of the Spirit at this time? Those who take John 20:22 as a promise of the Spirit's coming at Pentecost fail to appreciate the full significance of the symbolic gesture associated with Jesus' words. He breathed on them and said, "Receive the Holy Spirit." He did not say, "You will receive the Holy Spirit." As Plummer observes, the expression "plainly implies that some gift was offered and bestowed then and there."[16] It would seem likely that this bestowal of the gift of the Spirit was a preliminary provision for the disciples during the fifty days until Pentecost. Although not wanting to detract from the significance of Pentecost for the church, John apparently thought it was necessary to mention within his gospel the provision of the Holy Spirit that Jesus had promised

14. M. E. Isaacs, "The Prophetic Spirit in the Fourth Gospel," *Heythrop Journal* 24 (1983): 391-407.

15. Walt Russell, "The Holy Spirit's Ministry in the Fourth Gospel," *Grace Theological Journal* 8 (1987): 237-38.

16. A. Plummer, *The Gospel According to St. John* (Cambridge: At the University Press, 1899), p. 362.

His disciples (1:33; 7:37-39; 14:16-17, 26; 15:26-27; 16:13-15). The significance of this promise demanded an account of its fulfillment.

20:23   This verse has been used by the Roman Catholic church as the biblical basis for the priest's authority to forgive sins. It is quite clear from the Bible that God is the One who has the power and authority to forgive sins (Isa. 43:25). Jesus, of course, had this authority and demonstrated it during His ministry (Mark 2:5-10). Is Jesus now granting the disciples divine authority to forgive sins?

A proper interpretation of this verse can be determined only on the basis of a careful study of the Greek grammar. The verbs "are forgiven" (*aphieēmi*) and "are retained" (*krateō*; NIV "are not forgiven") are both in the perfect tense. The perfect tense portrays past action and affirms an existing result.[17] This means that God's action of forgiveness ("are forgiven") took place prior to the offering of forgiveness by Jesus' disciples. Mantey argues convincingly that both in Matthew 16:19 and John 20:23 the grammar used by Jesus did not provide the disciples with personal authority to forgive sin.[18] Robertson remarks, "What he commits to the disciples and to us is the power and privilege of giving assurance of the forgiveness of sins by God by correctly announcing the terms of forgiveness."[19] By proclaiming the gospel, a declaration of remission or retention of sins is made. Acceptance by faith brings God's forgiveness. Unbelief means that guilt remains. For Peter's understanding of 20:23, see Acts 2:38; 10:43.

God has blessed believers so that they might be a blessing to others. The greatest blessing anyone can experience is the joy of knowing that sins can be forgiven in Christ. By sharing this good news, Christians participate in the great promise of God to Abraham (Gen. 12:2-3) that through his descendants (spiritual and otherwise) the world will be blessed.

The Appearance to Thomas, 20:24-29

Five appearances of Jesus took place on resurrection day (to Mary Magdalene, to the women, to the disciples on the road to Emmaus, to Peter, and to the ten). The appearance of Jesus to Thomas marks

---

17. H. E. Dana and Julius R. Mantey, *A Manual Grammar of the Greek New Testament* (New York: Macmillan, 1927), pp. 200-201.

18. Julius R. Mantey, "Evidence That the Perfect Tense in John 20:23 and Matthew 16:19 Is Mistranslated," *JETS* 16 (1973): 129-38.

19. A. T. Robertson, *Word Pictures in the New Testament* (Nashville: Broadman, 1932), 5:315.

the first of five more specifically recorded resurrection appearances that took place before the ascension (cf. Matt. 28:16-20; John 21:1-25; Acts 1:3-12; 1 Cor. 15:7).

Far from seeking to invent a resurrection story, the example of Thomas illustrates that the disciples were somewhat reluctant to accept the fact of the resurrection. Only when confronted with the clear and irrefutable evidence did they come to faith.

20:24 This sixth resurrection appearance took place in the presence of the eleven apostles but was clearly for the benefit of Thomas, who had been absent when Christ appeared to the others on resurrection day. Thomas is referred to by his nickname, "Didymus," which is Greek for "twin" (cf. comments on 11:16; also 21:2). John does not report where Thomas was or why he missed the earlier appearance of Jesus. There is no indication of blame. The designation "one of the Twelve" continued in use even though Judas was dead (cf. Matt. 27:3-5).

20:25 The disciples who had witnessed Jesus' appearance on resurrection day reported to Thomas, "We have seen the Lord!" The word "told" (*legō*) is in the imperfect tense, which indicates repeated action—"They kept on telling."

Thomas was not going to be swayed by the rumors of excited disciples. He said, "Unless I see the nail marks in his hands and put my finger where the nails were, and put my hand into his side, I will not believe it." The expression "I will not believe it" contains a double negative (*ou mē*) for emphasis. Thomas was most certainly not going to believe apart from visual and physical evidence of the resurrection.

Thomas has often been criticized as a "doubter" and a "skeptic" for refusing to believe the bodily resurrection of Jesus without tangible proof. It should be remembered that none of the disciples had any concept of the resurrection prior to the event. Thomas was no exception. The reports were fantastic. But Thomas was a careful and calculating person. He had to be sure. He did not want to place his faith in a bogus resurrection.

20:26 One week later the disciples were gathered together again. The expression "one week later" is literally "eight days later," numbering according to the Jewish method of including both Sundays. The NIV renders the Greek *esō* ("inside") by the phrase "in the house." They were probably in a house, but the main point here is that Jesus' appearance took place behind locked doors (cf. John 20:19). Suddenly, Jesus came and stood in their midst and greeted them as before (cf. 20:19-21), "Peace be with you!" This must have been a thrilling moment for Thomas.

20:27   Knowing full well the struggles going on in Thomas's heart, Jesus invited him to explore with his hands ("Put your finger here") and his eyes ("see my hands") the reality of His resurrection body. Jesus then instructed Thomas, "Stop doubting and believe." The text reads literally, "Stop becoming unbelieving [*apistos*] but believing [*pistos*]."

20:28   Seeing the evidence of the resurrection there before him, Thomas renounced his doubt and confessed his faith in the risen Christ. His climatic words "My Lord and my God" reflect Thomas's newfound faith in Jesus as his personal Lord and God. Following the resurrection, when "Lord" (*kurios*) is ascribed to Jesus it serves as a designation of deity. There is no doubt here that Thomas was affirming both the lordship and deity of Christ. It can be noted that Jesus did not correct the apostle but accepted and approved his confession. John uses the words of Thomas to corroborate the prologue ("the Word was God") and further the purpose statement ("Jesus is the Christ, the Son of God").

20:29   The faith of Thomas was brought to culmination as a result of a personal appearance of the resurrected Jesus. The ascension of Jesus ten days before Pentecost would put an end to further such appearances. It is with a view to future believers who are not able to experience what Thomas beheld that Jesus pronounced the following blessing.

Jesus told Thomas, "Because you have seen me, you have believed." It was the sight, not the touch, that convinced him. The perfect tense of the verb "have believed" indicates a completed action with lasting results. Thomas was no different from the other disciples. He just "saw and believed" (20:8) a week after the others did. Both Thomas and the other ten had an encounter with the risen Lord. Now Jesus pronounced a special blessing upon those who come to faith apart from such an encounter.

Jesus said, "Blessed are those who have not seen and yet have believed." Jesus would not appear to all those who were following Him. Nor would He appear to future generations of disciples. Since the ascension of Christ, with the exception of the apostle Paul, all believers have come to faith in the risen Lord without seeing Him personally. Now it is through the Word of God and the proclamation of the gospel that people come to believe in Christ and appropriate His spiritual blessing. Those like Thomas who have come to faith through "seeing" are blessed. Those who have come to faith without "seeing" are blessed indeed.

THE PURPOSE OF THE GOSPEL, 20:30-31

Some New Testament scholars regard these verses as the original conclusion of John's gospel. Here John summarizes the purpose of his book. For a fresh study of the purpose of John's gospel, see Carson's insightful article.[20]

20:30 John reports that he was selective in recording the "miraculous signs" that appear in the gospel. Many other signs were performed by Jesus, which are not detailed here. Thirty-six miracles can be found recorded in the four gospels.[21] Of these, John records five that are unique to his gospel and two others that are recorded elsewhere (the feeding of the five thousand and walking on the sea, 6:1-14, 16-21).[22]

The term *sēmeion* is the term most used by John to refer to Jesus' miracles. The word indicates that the miracles are intended to signify something about Jesus.[23] Tenney points out that they were "revelatory in character," illustrating the Person and position of Christ as the incarnate Word.[24] They were not recorded as wonders to arouse curiosity but to point the reader to specific truths about Christ.

20:31 The clear purpose of John's written record of the miraculous signs of Jesus is to elicit belief in His Person. This is evident by the purpose clause indicated by *hina* and the present active subjunctive of *pisteuō*, "that you may believe." The term "believe" essentially means "to trust." The word never implies a mere intellectual knowledge or ascent to a proposition. Rather, *pisteuō* involves a personal response and faith commitment to Jesus as divine Savior/Lord.

Scholars have discussed whether John's purpose was to arouse faith for the first time or strengthen faith already present. This ques-

---

20. D. A. Carson, "The Purpose of the Fourth Gospel: John 20:31 Reconsidered," *Journal of Biblical Literature* 106(1987): 639-51.

21. For a list, see W. Graham Scroggie, *A Guide to the Gospels* (Old Tappan, N.J.: Revell, 1948), pp. 554-55.

22. The count of seven miracles does not include the resurrection of Jesus or the miraculous catch of fish recorded in the epilogue (21:4-11).

23. Merrill C. Tenney, "Topics from the Gospel of John: The Meaning of the Signs," *Bibliotheca Sacra* 132 (April 1975): 145-46.

24. Ibid., p. 158.

tion is complicated by the possibility of two different readings of *pisteuō*, the present subjunctive (*pisteuēte*) and the aorist subjunctive (*pisteusēte*). The aorist, strictly interpreted, suggests that the gospel was written so that unbelievers might come to faith. The present tense suggests that John's aim was to strengthen the faith of those who had already believed. Although the textual evidence is finely divided,[25] the majority of recent commentators prefer the present subjunctive. Carson, however, points to examples where the aorist subjunctive *pisteusēte* occurs with the sense of having faith corroborated (11:15), and where the present subjunctive *pisteuēte* refers to the entire process of coming to faith and continuing to believe (6:29).[26]

The two viewpoints (coming to faith and continuing to believe) are not mutually exclusive when one takes into consideration the progressive nature of faith (see Introduction, under Purpose) evidenced in John's gospel. For John, faith is something that begins, continues, grows, and matures. The fourth gospel would serve to elicit faith in some and strengthen faith in others. No doubt John had both in mind.

The substance of belief is presented in the words "that Jesus is the Christ, the Son of God." The term "Christ" (*Christos*), properly translated "Messiah" (anointed one), is actually a title, not a proper name. The miracles and other acts of Jesus show that He fulfills the expectations of the Messiah as anticipated by the prophecies of Hebrew Scripture. The miracles also authenticate that Jesus is the divine "Son of God" (cf. 5:36; 10:25, 38; 14:11).

The ultimate purpose of faith in Jesus is to possess life (*zōē*). This "life" is elsewhere defined as "eternal" (3:15, 36; 17:3). It is significant that John views life as the present possession of those who believe, not merely a reward to be received hereafter (cf. 5:24). Possession of life means abundant spiritual blessing for the present (cf. 10:10) and precludes perishing eternally (3:16). The words "in his name" mean that the blessing of "life" is available only on the basis of the reputation and work of Christ (cf. 14:13).

John wants his readers to learn that faith in Jesus, the divine Messiah, imparts "life." John has tasted of this "life" and has labored to share this grace-gift with others.

25. Bruce M. Metzger, *A Textual Commentary on the Greek New Testament* (London: United Bible Societies, 1971), p. 256.
26. Carson, "The Purpose of the Fourth Gospel," p. 640.

HOMILETICAL SUGGESTIONS

John 20 contains much material for Resurrection Day (Easter) messages. The highlight in the section on the empty tomb (20:1-10) is John's faith that was consummated when he understood the significance of the empty tomb (v. 8). A sermon on the subject could be called "The Discovery of an Empty Tomb." What if you were walking in a graveyard one day and you found an empty grave? What would you think? What would you think if you knew the former occupant? This is what happened to Mary, Peter, and John. This discovery led John to *believe* in the resurrected Christ.

John 20:11-18 records the first appearance of Jesus in His resurrection body. It is significant, I believe, that He appeared to a woman —and a woman of questionable background. This is "grace upon grace" (cf. 1:16). Even though the resurrection event is the most significant in this passage, Mary's response of worship may serve as the focus of an exposition on this text. We believe in the resurrection. But how do we respond to Jesus? Is the resurrected Jesus a mere doctrine to affirm or a Master to embrace? We see in this passage that belief in the resurrection leads to *adoration* of the Lord and *proclamation* of the good news.

The appearance to Thomas (20:24-29) illustrates how a skeptic came to place his faith in Christ. Jesus did not rebuke him for his lack of faith, but He encouraged him to take a step of faith. Thomas was convinced by what he saw, and he entered into personal faith. Verse 29 encourages others to follow the example of Thomas in placing faith in Jesus. And a blessing is promised to those who take this step of faith with less tangible evidence than presented to Thomas. It is not bad to be a "doubting Thomas" if, after examining the evidence, we too place our faith in Christ.

Verses 30-31 provide a statement of the purpose of the book and would serve well to introduce a series on the seven signs of the gospel. Borrowing the title of a popular apologetics book, the message could be entitled "Evidence That Demands a Verdict." This message could focus on the miraculous evidence presented by John and the purpose of his gospel—to elicit belief. This text would also serve well for an evangelistic message, presenting proofs for the Person of Jesus.

JOHN
CHAPTER
TWENTY ONE

BREAKFAST ON THE BEACH

THE RESPONSIBILITIES OF BELIEF, 21:1-25

It has been said that the apostle originally concluded his gospel with 20:31 but that chapter 21 was added later to report another miracle, give an account of Jesus' words concerning John, and clear up a misunderstanding (cf. 21:20-23).[1] Whether this is the case or not, there is no textual evidence that the gospel of John ever circulated independently of its final chapter.

Plummer points out that in terms of structure, chapter 21 serves as an epilogue, balancing the prologue (1:1-18) with the main body of the gospel lying between.[2] In addition to clearing up a misunderstanding concerning John, the epilogue is intended to show how the belief instilled in the disciples by the resurrection should be applied. Belief is to issue in service to others, motivated out of love for Christ.

THE APPEARANCE IN GALILEE, 21:1-14

The account opens with the disciples back in Galilee. They probably remained in Jerusalem for the Feast of Unleavened Bread (Lev.

---

1. See Barclay M. Newman and Eugene A. Nida, *A Translator's Handbook on the Gospel of John* (London: United Bible Societies, 1980), p. 623.
2. A. Plummer, *The Gospel According to St. John* (Cambridge: At the University Press, 1899), p. 367.

373

23:6-8) and then returned to Galilee. Jesus had commanded the disciples to leave for Galilee and promised that He would appear to them there (cf. Matt. 28:7, 10). According to Matthew, a particular mountain in Galilee had been designated as their place of rendezvous (Matt. 28:16).

THE RETURN TO FISHING, 21:1-3

The disciples proceeded to Galilee and decided to return to their previous employment while waiting for Jesus to come.

21:1   John reports that Jesus appeared again to His disciples. He uses the first aorist active indicative of *phaneroō*, "to manifest" or "to make visible," to describe this appearance. This is the third resurrection appearance in his gospel (cf. 20:11-18, 19-23, 24-29). This appearance took place near the Sea of Galilee, referred to by John as "the Sea of Tiberias" (cf. 6:1). The name "Tiberias" was associated with the lake because of the prominent city by that name on the southwestern shore.

21:2   John identifies five of the seven disciples who witnessed this resurrection appearance of Jesus. They include Simon Peter, Thomas (called Didymus, the "twin"), Nathanael, the two sons of Zebedee (James and John), and two unidentified disciples. Only here is it said that Nathanael was from the Galilean village of Cana where Jesus worked His first miracle (2:1). Cana is located about nine miles north of Nazareth, the childhood home of Jesus.

21:3   Perhaps Peter wearied of waiting for Jesus' arrival in Galilee. Perhaps the sight of fishing boats and the smell of wet nets drying in the sun reminded him of a way of life he had left to follow Jesus. Taking the lead, Peter announced to the others, "I am going out to fish."

Peter has been unduly criticized for returning to his former employment. Nothing in the account seems to suggest criticism by Jesus. Peter did not know what to do next. He knew that Jesus was coming, but he did not want to idle away time when it could be put to profitable use. He was not abandoning Jesus, just making good use of time. And the other disciples joined him for the outing.

As is still the custom on the Sea of Galilee, the disciples fished at night when the fish are actively feeding near the surface. And although the Sea of Galilee was noted for its fishing industry in the time of Jesus,[3] the disciples' night of labor was unrewarded. John records,

---

3. Michael Avi-Yonah, *The Holy Land* (Grand Rapids: Baker, 1966), pp. 205-6. Fish were salted at Taricheae or Migdal Nunaya ("Tower of the Fishers") for export.

probably with a bit of painful memory, that "they caught nothing" (*epiasan ouden*). Any fisherman can identify with the disappointment Peter and the other disciples must have experienced.

THE MIRACULOUS CATCH, 21:4-11

This miracle is reminiscent of the miraculous catch of fish that Peter, James, and John experienced just before they left their fishing business to follow Jesus (cf. Luke 5:1-11). Jesus concluded His earthly miracles with another great catch.

21:4   The dawn was breaking as Jesus appeared on the shore of the Sea of Galilee. The present participle of *ginomai* ("come to be," "happen") indicates that the dawn was in the process of breaking. Through the morning mist hanging over the water the disciples could see a figure standing near the still darkened shoreline (*aigialos*). John notes that, like Mary Magdalene (cf. 20:14), they did not realize at first that it was Jesus.

21:5   The second word of the Greek text of v. 5 is the inferential conjunction *oun*, "therefore." This indicates a logical link between vv. 4 and 5. Inasmuch as the disciples did not recognize him, Jesus called out a greeting. The greeting "children" (*paidia*, NIV "friends") seems a bit strange in speaking to adults. Although not a common form of address, the expression was used by those who felt a fatherly intimacy toward the ones being addressed (cf. 1 John 2:18; 3:7).

Jesus followed up the greeting with a question, "Haven't you any fish?" The word rendered "fish" is actually a more general word meaning "anything eaten with other food." Jesus was asking if they had caught anything to eat. It is obvious that fish was implied. The use of the negative particle *mē* with the present tense expects a negative answer. The unsuccessful fisherman never likes being asked about his fishing. The disciples answered Jesus' question with a simple no.

21:6   Jesus then gave the disciples a bit of advice. "Throw your net on the right side of the boat and you will find some." Now Peter and some of the other disciples were fisherman by profession. They were no doubt irritated at their lack of success during the night. And now a stranger on the shore was telling them how to do their job better. It takes a humble fisherman to accept advice from a nonfisherman. But Jesus, the Son of God and Creator, knew where the fish were. Perhaps the disciples thought the stranger on the shore could see a school of fish near the surface of the water. They put up no protest. One more cast after a long night of fishing would not do any harm.

Their obedience to the stranger's command was rewarded. The net was so full of fish that they could not haul it back into the boat. The imperfect tense of the verb *ischuō* ("to be able") pictures the disciples repeatedly tugging at the heavy net.

21:7   It was at this point that John, "the disciple whom Jesus loved" (cf. John 13:23; 19:26), realized there was something miraculous about what had happened and recognized the stranger as Jesus. He immediately told Peter, "It is the Lord."

Although John was the first to recognize Jesus, Peter was the first to act. He wrapped his outer garment around him and jumped into the water. The "outer garment" (*ependutēs*) occurs only here in the New Testament and refers to outer clothing without being more specific. The Greek text describes Peter as *gumnos*, a word that can mean "naked," "poorly dressed," or "without an outer garment." Peter had been stripped (probably to his loincloth) for work but wanted to be appropriately clad when he reached the shore to greet Jesus. Modesty had its place even in the life of a Galilean fisherman.

21:8   While Peter swam the hundred yards to shore, the rest of the disciples followed in the boat towing the net full of fish. The Greek word *ploiarion* is a diminutive form and means "little boat." A twenty-six-foot-long boat dated between the first century B.C. and the late first century A.D. has been excavated from the mud just off the northwest shore of the Sea of Galilee.[4] This discovery has provided greater understanding of Galilean boats and seafaring of nearly 2,000 years ago.

21:9   When the disciples arrived at the shore with the net full of fish, they saw a charcoal fire with fish and bread cooking over it. This must have smelled delicious to the tired and hungry fishermen. The text does not directly state that Jesus had started the fire and was preparing breakfast, but His instruction in v. 10 and invitation in v. 12 imply this. Whether this provision was made by miraculous or natural means is not indicated.

21:10   Jesus asked the disciples to bring some of the fish they had just caught. These would be roasted with the others (v. 9) to make a satisfying breakfast.

One wonders why Jesus asked them to bring some fish when He could have miraculously multiplied what was already cooking. Perhaps He wanted them to feel they had contributed in some way to the

---

4. Shelley Wachsmann, "The Galilee Boat," *Biblical Archaeology Review* (September/October 1988): 19-33.

meal. Most dinner guests like to contribute a dish to the meal, and Jesus may have simply been sensitive to this need.

21:11 Peter went to help the others with the fish. The text states that he "went up" (second aorist active indicative of *anabainō*, "to go up," "ascend"). Some commentators suggest Peter climbed aboard the boat to help pull the net in. Others suggest that he climbed up the steep bank. Because the net would be pulled behind the boat, Peter probably got into the boat and stood in the stern to retrieve the net. Then he apparently jumped into the water again to help drag the net to shore.

The net was full of large fish but was not torn. From Origen onward, the number 153 has been interpreted in symbolical and fanciful ways. The number has been used to teach about the Trinity, the perfection of the church, Christian conduct, and the church's missionary task.[5] Jerome cites the poet Oppian (c. A.D. 180) that there are 153 species of fish in the world and that the number means that every type of humanity is to come into the church. Unfortunately, Jerome was mistaken, for Oppian gives no such figure and the species he mentions do not add up to 153.[6] It is best to take the number literally without any symbolic meaning. It was a great catch and a memorable day. As fishermen are prone to talk about their best fishing outings, so John remembered as he wrote his gospel that this was the day they caught 153 fish.

An important lesson from this miracle should not go unnoticed. Only when the disciples obeyed Jesus were they successful in catching fish. So too, success in the Christian's ministry depends on obedience to Jesus. Consider what would have happened if the disciples had argued with the stranger on the shore. What if they had said, "We have been fishing all night and have already tried that!"? The miracle may not have been experienced if the disciples had not been quick to respond to the Lord's command.

THE BREAKFAST WITH JESUS, 21:12-14

There are special moments in life that are held forever in the memory. What a wonderful memory Jesus made for John and the other disciples as He invited them to breakfast on the beach.

---

5. J. M. Ross, "One Hundred and Fifty-Three Fishes," *The Expository Times* 100 (July 1989): 375.
6. Ibid.

21:12   The aroma of hot bread and sizzling fish must have stirred the appetites of the disciples. Jesus said to them, "Come and have breakfast" (*deute aristēsate*). Jews of the first century customarily ate two meals a day (cf. Luke 14:12), the breakfast and the main, or evening, meal.[7]

John notes that none of the disciples, knowing it was the risen Lord, ventured to ask Jesus, "Who are you?" There must have been something unusual about His appearance (cf. 20:15; 21:4) that made them wonder. They were undoubtedly experiencing a mixture of perplexity and awe. Plummer suggests, "They are convinced that He is the Lord, yet feel that He is changed, and reverence restrains them from curious questions."[8]

21:13   As is often the case with guests, the disciples may have appeared hesitant to begin serving themselves the meal. So Jesus went over, took the bread, and distributed it to the disciples. In the same manner, He served the roasted fish. He was acting as host at this recorded last meal with His disciples. The definite article used with "the bread" (*ton apton*) and "the fish" (*to opsarion*) indicates that Jesus served the bread and fish that were cooking on the coals when the disciples arrived on the shore (21:9). Their fish could be cooked later (cf. 21:10), but this was Jesus' provision. This early morning breakfast must have reminded the disciples of Jesus' miraculous provision for the five thousand when He multiplied the loaves and fish (cf. 6:1-14).

21:14   John concludes his account of this last recorded miracle of Jesus by noting that it was the third (*triton*) resurrection appearance of Jesus to His disciples (cf. 20:19-20, 24-29).

THE INSTRUCTION TO PETER, 21:15-19

This section is often entitled the restoration or reinstatement of Peter, alluding to Peter's denial of Christ during the trial. This would seem at first to make sense, the three questions "Do you love me?" answering to the three denials (cf. 18:17, 25, 26-27). However, Jesus had already met with Peter (Luke 24:34; 1 Cor. 15:5) and most likely had dealt with Peter's denial privately. Here Jesus deals with Peter's responsibility as a spiritual leader and instructs him concerning the motive for service and the ministry of a servant.

7. Ralph Gower, *The New Manners and Customs of Bible Times* (Chicago: Moody, 1987), p. 49.
8. A. Plummer, *The Gospel According to St. John* (Cambridge: At the University Press, 1899), p. 371.

21:15   When the disciples had finished eating breakfast, Jesus spoke to Peter. While He specifically addressed Peter, the conversation was public and undoubtedly for the benefit of the other disciples as well. Jesus asked, "Simon son of John" (1:42), "do you love me more than these?" What Jesus means by "these" (*toutōn*) was undoubtedly clear to Peter, but it is somewhat ambiguous in the text. Jesus could be referring to the boat, fishing net, and way of life represented by these things. But this implies that Peter's night of fishing constituted an abandonment of his commitment as a follower of Christ (cf. 21:3). Possibly Jesus was referring to Peter's earlier profession of devotion to Christ, "Even if all fall away on account of you, I never will" (Matt. 26:33; also Mark 14:29). But this view implies that Jesus is now bringing up the matter of Peter's disloyalty when it had probably been dealt with earlier (Luke 24:34; 1 Cor. 15:5). It is also possible that Jesus was referring to the love Peter had for his companions. In this case, Jesus would be asking Peter where his priorities lay—in earthly companionship or a heavenly relationship. Yet this seems to suggest that one cannot enjoy both. Regardless of which view is taken, the important thing to note is that Jesus was bringing to Peter's attention the priority of supreme love for Christ.

Peter responded to the question with an expression of his love, "Yes, Lord, you know that I love you." Peter's words "you know" (*su oidas*) imply, "Lord, you don't have to ask me this. You know my heart and the sincerity of my affection."

It is well known that Jesus and Peter use different words for love in vv. 15-17, and the significance of this is hotly debated among the commentators. In vv. 15 and 16 Jesus uses the word *agapaō*, whereas Peter responds in vv. 15-17 with the word *phileō*. Those who hold that a distinction is being made[9] point out that *agapaō* is a higher, volitional love that can be commanded. It seeks the good of its object even to the point of personal sacrifice, as in God's love for the world (John 3:16). This word refers not to a feeling but to a commitment. *Phileō*, on the other hand, is a warmer word and refers to a friendly or emotional love based on personal affection. Accordingly, Jesus questioned Peter about his commitment, and Peter repeatedly affirmed his affection.

---

9. William Hendriksen, *Exposition of the Gospel According to John* (Grand Rapids: Baker, 1953-54), 2:494-500; R. C. H. Lenski, *The Interpretation of St. John's Gospel* (Minneapolis: Augsburg, 1942), pp. 1418-20; Plummer, *The Gospel According to St. John*, p. 372; B. F. Westcott, *The Gospel According to St. John* (Grand Rapids: Eerdmans, 1973), p. 303.

Other commentators[10] argue that the change in words is stylistic and in keeping with John's pattern of slight variations without any actual difference in meaning.[11] According to this view, Jesus is asking the same question three times. In favor of the view it is noted that the verbs *agapaō* and *phileō* are used interchangeably in the Septuagint and that John himself uses the two verbs interchangeably elsewhere in his gospel (cf. 5:20). The fact that Jesus switches to Peter's word *phileō* in v. 17 may show that no distinction is intended.

It is difficult to be conclusive when reliable commentators take diametrically opposed viewpoints on an issue. However, McKay has made a good case for the view that the variation in words in John 21:15-17 is "not pointless" but constitutes "a contextual distinction which is not blatant, but gently significant."[12] McKay points out that even if the purpose of change is variation, it does not follow that there is no change of meaning. He argues that even if there is usually no difference in meaning between *agapaō* and *phileō*, one may not necessarily conclude that there is no difference in a particular context. Tenney concurs that in a particular context the difference between these words "is worth considering."[13] Even if the conversation took place in Aramaic (which would use different words) John has, by divine inspiration, accurately recorded the dialogue as he understood it.

When Jesus questioned Peter about his loving commitment (*agapaō*), Peter affirmed his loving friendship (*phileō*). Then Jesus commanded Peter, "Feed my lambs." Jesus appropriated pastoral imagery to instruct Peter concerning his responsibility as a follower and servant of Christ. This imagery was used by Jesus in John 10:1-18 and later by Peter in 1 Peter 5:2-4. The word "feed" (*boskō*) is used of herdsmen, who feed or tend their herds (Matt. 8:33; Luke 15:15). The verb means "to take care of" not merely "feed." The "lambs" (*arnion*) refer to Jesus' followers, particularly the young ones in the faith who are so prone to wander.

10. C. K. Barrett, *The Gospel According to St. John* (London: SPCK, 1962), p. 486; F. F. Bruce, *The Gospel of John: Introduction, Exposition and Notes* (Grand Rapids: Eerdmans, 1983), pp. 404-5; Leon Morris, *The Gospel According to John*, NICNT (Grand Rapids: Eerdmans, 1971), p. 873.

11. Leon Morris, *Studies in the Fourth Gospel* (Grand Rapids: Eerdmans, 1969), pp. 293-318.

12. K. L. McKay, "Style and Significance in the Language of John 21:15-17," *Novum Testamentum* 27 (1985): 319-33.

13. Merrill C. Tenney, "The Gospel of John," in *The Expositor's Bible Commentary*, ed. Frank Gaebelein (Grand Rapids: Zondervan, 1981), 9:202.

21:16   The fact that Jesus asked Peter the question a second time seems to suggest that he was not satisfied with the answer given. He dropped the words "more than these," perhaps to encourage a more positive response. Yet Peter answered exactly as in v. 15, "Yes, Lord, you know that I love [*phileō*] you." Then Jesus commanded Peter, "Take care of my sheep." This is quite similar to the command given by Jesus in v. 15, but different words are used. The word translated "take care of" (*poimainō*) means "to be a shepherd" or "tend" flocks. Both Paul and Peter use this word to speak of the spiritual duties of overseers (Acts 20:28; 1 Pet. 5:2).

The word "sheep" (*probation*) is a diminutive form of the more common word for sheep, *probaton*, and means "little sheep." Again, Jesus is referring to believers, perhaps those who are not yet fully mature in their faith.

21:17   When Jesus questioned Peter the third time, He used Peter's word *phileō*. The fact that John mentions that it was "the third time," may indicate that he did not intend any distinction between *agapaō* and *phileō*. On the other hand, the Greek text simply indicates that this is "the third time" Jesus spoke to Peter, not the third time He asked the question. Perhaps Jesus accommodated Himself to Peter's reserve in asking if his professed "loving friendship" was deep and genuine.

John notes that Peter "was hurt," or grieved (first aorist passive indicative of *lupeō*, "to cause pain or grief"), when Jesus used his own word to ask about his love. Certainly Jesus did not intend to cause Peter grief, but often growth and change takes place only as believers are confronted with the painful reality of their shortcomings. Believers should not be too timid to help in the growth or healing of another Christian, knowing that the process is sometimes painful.

When Peter had affirmed his love for Jesus, he was commanded "Feed my sheep." Here Jesus uses the word *boskō* ("feed") from v. 15 and the word *probation* ("little sheep") from v. 16. In view of John's affinity for variation, one should be careful not to make too much of the distinctions between these words. The present imperative of *boskō* indicates that the feeding process is to be repeated and regular. A meal or two now and then will not build strong sheep. Nor will a sermon now and then build strong Christians.

Verses 15-17 contain a significant message for Christians, particularly leaders. Jesus has outlined in no uncertain terms the ministry of

Peter and (by implication) all His disciples as well. Peter was to act as a shepherd in providing spiritual care for believers less mature in the faith. Peter later charged the elders of the church with the same responsibility (1 Pet. 5:2-4). And regardless of the debate over the words *agapaō* and *phileō*, it is clear that the motivation for such a ministry must be one's love for Christ. A sacrificial commitment to Christ is essential to being faithful to this challenging task.

21:18 Jesus here concludes His conversation with Peter by warning him what his service for Christ will cost. Jesus contrasts Peter's youthful freedom with the restrictions he will experience in old age. As a young man, Peter dressed himself and went wherever he wanted. But a day would come when he would no longer have control over his life and activities. He would "stretch out" (*ekteinō*, "to extend" or "stretch") his hands. This may refer to a gesture for "help." It has also been suggested that this refers to Peter's crucifixion. But the order of events would be odd unless "dress" (*zōnnumi*, "to gird") refers to the binding of Peter with ropes to the cross. To be led "where you do not want to go" is clearly a reference to death.

21:19 John explains parenthetically in v. 19 that Jesus' words in v. 18 indicated the "kind of death" Peter was to die. It is possible that Jesus intended His words to prophesy Peter's crucifixion, if this is the meaning of "stretch out your hands" in v. 18. On the other hand, Jesus could have simply been predicting that Peter would not die of old age. His commitment to Christ would ultimately mean martyrdom. Tertullian (c. A.D. 212) reports that Peter was crucified in Rome under Nero (*Scorpiace* 15) around A.D. 64. Eusebius cites Origen in saying that Peter was crucified with his head down (*Historia Ecclesiastica* 3:1).

Jesus refers to Peter's death as one that would "glorify God" (*doxasei ton theon*). Peter, who had struggled, would be so in tune with God's will and purposes that even in death he would magnify the character and reputation of God. What an example for believers.

It is encouraging to know that even a death can bring glory to God. A pastor friend of mine died of cancer this past year. I learned that his faith remained strong and that he testified of God's faithfulness to the end. There was no whining or complaining about a life and ministry that was about to end. This death glorified God.

Having spoken to Peter about his coming death, Jesus commanded him, "Follow me!" The present active imperative could be translated, "Keep on following me!"

THE CORRECTION CONCERNING JOHN, 21:20-23

Before concluding his gospel, John takes time to correct a misinterpretation of Jesus' words concerning him. Contextually, these verses continue the conversation between Peter and Jesus in the previous section (cf. 21:15-19).

21:20   It appears that Jesus and Peter were walking together away from the other disciples who had gathered for breakfast on the beach (21:12-14). Not wanting to miss any of the words or teachings of Jesus, John, "the disciple whom Jesus loved" (13:23), was following a short distance after them. John identifies himself further in terms of events that took place in the upper room the night before Christ's crucifixion. Reclining near Jesus' breast (13:23), John was the one who leaned back against Jesus and asked, "Lord, who is going to betray you?" The precise wording of John's question in 13:25 is "Lord, who is it?"

21:21   Looking back toward the disciples, Peter saw John following at a distance and asked, "Lord, what about him?" (literally, "Lord, but this one . . . what?"). Peter had just learned from Jesus that his ministry would cost him his life (cf. 21:18-19). Now he wondered what John could expect. What did the future hold for him?

21:22   Jesus' answer indicates that it was none of Peter's business what lay ahead for John. Peter was to focus his attention on his own responsibility—following Jesus. The rhetorical question, "If I want him to remain alive until I return, what is that to you?" reflects Jesus' anticipation of a second coming (cf. 14:3). The emphasis is more on the interval of waiting rather than on the coming of Christ. No matter how long John remained on earth—even until the second coming— that was none of Peter's concern. He had been given his duty, and Jesus repeated it, "You keep on following me" (present imperative of *akoutheō*). He added "you" for emphasis, in contrast with the earlier command (v. 19).

21:23   John now acknowledges a rumor that spread due to a simple misunderstanding of Jesus' words. It came to be believed among the Christians that the apostle John would not die (*apothnēskō*) but would live until Christ's second coming. Augustine refers with disapproval to some who asserted in his day "that the apostle John is still living, lying asleep rather than dead in his tomb at Ephesus" (*Homilies on the Gospel of John* 124). John points out the error, repeating verbatim the rhetorical question asked by Jesus in v. 22. Jesus had not said

John would live until the second coming. He had merely raised the possibility in the context of a hypothetical situation to emphasize that God's dealings with John were none of Peter's business.

THE AUTHENTICATION OF THE RECORD, 21:24-25

John concludes with a postscript that affirms the veracity of his gospel. Some would assert that these verses constitute an editorial appendix because of the plural "we know" (*oidamen*) in v. 24. This could have been a note added by the Ephesian elders before the publication of the gospel. But the use of the first person in v. 25 suggests that the author is John. Accordingly, he is simply referring in v. 24 to others who can vouch for his testimony. On the other hand, one could argue that the first person "I" in v. 25 refers to an anonymous editor. The external manuscript evidence indicates that these verses were included as part of John's original document. Plummer points out that no extant manuscript or version lacks v. 24, and all but Codex Sinaiticus include v. 25.[14] It is difficult to be certain on this final, technical detail. Johannine authorship will be assumed in these concluding comments.

21:24   Verse 24 reveals that the "disciple whom Jesus loved" (21:20) is none other than the author of the gospel. "These things" must refer not only to the narrative of chapter 21 but to the whole of the gospel. To suggest otherwise would leave v. 24 as a rather insignificant and anticlimatic footnote. In appropriating the first person plural ("we"), John joins hands with the other apostles, Ephesian elders, and witnesses to verify the truth of his record. What John wrote is true, and he is not alone in this affirmation.

21:25   John concludes his gospel with an acknowledgement of the vastness of the potential record of Jesus' life and ministry. As an author must be, John was selective. Jesus did many other things that have not fallen within the purpose of John's account (cf. 20:30-31). But if they were recorded, John suggests with grand hyperbole, "I suppose that even the whole world would not have room for the books that would be written." One is reminded of the lines from the hymn:

14. Plummer, *The Gospel According to St. John*, p. 377.

Could we with ink the ocean fill
   And were the skies of parchment made,
Were every blade of grass on earth a quill
   And every man a scribe by trade,
To write the love of God above
   Would drain the ocean dry,
Nor could the scroll contain the whole
   Though stretched from sky to sky.[15]

Although selective and limited, John's gospel has accomplished its purpose and will continue to do so as boys and girls, men and women, enter into life through personal faith in Jesus, our risen Redeemer and Lord.

HOMILETICAL SUGGESTIONS

Chapter 21 contains the epilogue and conclusion of the book and does provide good material for teaching and preaching. Jesus' appearance to His disciples in Galilee (21:1-14) seems to have been a more casual occasion than His appearances in Jerusalem. This gave more of an extended opportunity to renew their fellowship with the Lord after the separation that came from their fleeing at His arrest. Believers need times with Jesus and other Christians to have fellowship and to refresh their lives with a view to future ministry. Verses 1-14 provide a heart-warming example of such fellowship.

Jesus' instruction to Peter (21:15-19) provides an excellent text for a message on motivation for ministry. What motivates your ministry? Is it the promise of payment? Is it the thanks expressed by others? Is it the prestige of being in leadership? Here Jesus gets to the heart of the only proper motivation for ministry—a sacrificial and loving commitment for Christ. Three times Jesus asks Peter, "Do you love me?" Three times Jesus instructs Peter, "Care for my flock." It is quite clear that a love for Christ must be the motivation for ministry.

The correction concerning John (21:20-23) illustrates the danger of false rumors. Here John reports how a rumor got started. The rumor was that John would remain alive until the Lord's return. The passage serves to correct that rumor, and it more generally illustrates the danger of passing on misinformation.

15. "The Love of God" is a hymn attributed to F. M. Lehman, but the third stanza, quoted here, was written by an unknown writer.

SELECTED BIBLIOGRAPHY:
FOR FURTHER STUDY

Barrett, C. K. *Essays on John*. Philadelphia: Westminster, 1982.

_____. *The Gospel According to St. John*. London: SPCK, 1962. A scholarly commentary on the Greek text.

Bernard, J. H. *Gospel According to St. John*. International Critical Commentary. 2 vols. Edinburgh: T. & T. Clark, 1928. A critical and exegetical commentary on the Greek text.

Boice, James Montgomery. *The Gospel of John*. 5 vols. Grand Rapids: Zondervan, 1975-79. An insightful expositional commentary by an outstanding preacher.

Bowman, John. *The Fourth Gospel and the Jews*. Pittsburgh: Picwick, 1975.

Bowman, Robert M., Jr. *Jehovah's Witnesses, Jesus Christ, and the Gospel of John*. Grand Rapids: Baker, 1989.

Brown, Raymond E. *The Gospel According to John*. The Anchor Bible. 2 vols. Garden City, N.Y.: Doubleday, 1966, 1970. A cumbersome but exhaustive scholarly commentary. Brown interacts with virtually all previous critical scholarship and research.

Bruce, F. F. *The Gospel of John: Introduction, Exposition and Notes*. Grand Rapids: Eerdmans, 1983. Particularly helpful with historical and cultural background.

Carson, D. A. *The Farewell Discourse and Final Prayer of Jesus*. Grand Rapids: Baker, 1980.

_____. *The Gospel According to John.* Grand Rapids: Eerdmans, 1990.

Cook, W. Robert. *The Theology of John.* Chicago: Moody, 1979. A careful and detailed study of the theology of John's gospel, his three letters, and Revelation.

Culpepper, R. Alan. *Anatomy of the Fourth Gospel.* Philadelphia: Fortress, 1983.

Dodd, C. H. *The Interpretation of the Fourth Gospel.* Cambridge: At the University Press, 1953. A scholarly study of the background, leading themes, argument, and structure of John. He believes that John's gospel reflects Christianity at its earliest beginning.

Dods, Marcus. *The Gospel of St. John.* 3 vols. New York: A. C. Armstrong, 1902.

Duke, Paul D. *Irony in the Fourth Gospel.* Atlanta: John Knox, 1985.

Ellis, Peter F. *The Genius of John: A Composition-Critical Commentary.* Collegeville, Minn.: Liturgical, 1984.

Fortna, Robert T. *The Gospel of Signs: A Reconstruction of the Narrative Source Underlying the Fourth Gospel.* Cambridge: At the University Press, 1970.

Fredrikson, Roger L. *John.* The Communicator's Commentary. Waco, Tex.: Word, 1985.

Gruenler, Royce Gordon. *The Trinity in the Gospel of John: A Thematic Commentary on the Fourth Gospel.* Grand Rapids: Baker, 1986.

Haenchen, Ernst. *A Commentary on the Gospel of John.* Translated by Robert W. Funk. 3 vols. Philadelphia: Fortress, 1984.

Hendriksen, William. *An Exposition of the Gospel According to John.* 2 vols. Grand Rapids: Baker, 1954.

Hobbs, Herschel H. *An Exposition of the Gospel of John.* Grand Rapids: Baker, 1968.

Hoskyns, Edwyn Clement. *The Fourth Gospel.* 2d ed. London: Faber & Faber, 1947.

Käsemann, Ernst. *The Testament of Jesus According to John 17.* Translated by Gerhard Krodel. Philadelphia: Fortress, 1968.

Kent, Homer A., Jr. *Light in the Darkness: Studies in the Gospel of John.* Grand Rapids: Baker, 1974. A concise, conservative commentary.

Kysar, Robert. *John.* Augsburg Commentary on the New Testament. Minneapolis: Augsburg, 1986.

_____. *John: the Maverick Gospel.* Atlanta: John Knox, 1976.

Lee, Edwin Kenneth. *The Religious Thought of St. John.* London: SPCK, 1950. Essays on major thematic topics in John.

Lightfoot, R. H. *St. John's Gospel.* Oxford: At the Clarendon Press, 1983.

Lindars, Barnabas. *The Gospel of John.* New Century Bible. Greenwood, S. C.: Attic, 1972.

Lloyd-Jones, Martyn. *Saved in Eternity.* Westchester, Ill.: Crossway, 1988.

————. *Saved in the World.* Westchester, Ill.: Crossway, 1988.

————. *Sanctified Through the Truth.* Westchester, Ill.: Crossway, 1989.

Marsh, John. *Saint John.* Philadelphia: Westminster, 1968.

Martyn, J. Louis. *History and Theology in the Fourth Gospel.* Nashville: Abingdon, 1968.

Michaels, Ramsey J. *John: A Good News Commentary.* San Francisco: Harper & Row, 1984.

Morgan, G. Campbell. *The Gospel According to John.* Westwood, N. J.: Revell, n.d.

Morris, Leon. *The Gospel According to John.* NICNT. Grand Rapids: Eerdmans, 1971. The finest and most thorough evangelical commentary on John.

————. *Jesus Is the Christ: Studies in the Theology of John.* Grand Rapids: Eerdmans, 1989.

————. *Reflections on the Gospel of John.* 4 vols. Grand Rapids: Baker, 1986, 1987, 1988.

————. *Studies in the Fourth Gospel.* Grand Rapids: Eerdmans, 1969. An extensive treatment of authorship and other introductory issues.

Newbigin, Lesslie. *The Light Has Come: An Exposition of the Fourth Gospel.* Grand Rapids: Eerdmans, 1982.

Newman, Barclay M., and Eugene A. Nida. *A Translator's Handbook on the Gospel of John.* London: United Bible Societies, 1980. This volume is particularly helpful with translation and grammatical issues.

Nicol, W. *The SEMEIA in the Fourth Gospel.* Leiden: E. J. Brill, 1972.

O'Day, Gail R. *Revelaton in the Fourth Gospel.* Philadelphia: Fortress, 1986.

Painter, John. *Reading John's Gospel Today.* Atlanta: John Knox, 1975.

Plummer, A. *The Gospel According to St. John.* Cambridge: At the University Press, 1899. A brief but insightful exegetical commentary.

Robinson, John A. T. *The Priority of John.* London: SCM, 1985.

Rosscup, James E. *Abiding in Christ: Studies in John 15.* Grand Rapids: Zondervan, 1973.

Sanders, J. N. *The Gospel According to St. John.* Harper's New Testament Commentaries. New York: Harper & Row, 1968.

Schein, Bruce E. *Following the Way: The Setting of John's Gospel.* Minneapolis: Augsburg, 1980.

Sloyan, Gerard S. *John.* Atlanta: John Knox, 1988.

Smalley, Stephen S. *John: Evangelist and Interpreter.* Nashville: Thomas Nelson, 1978.

Tenney, Merrill C. "The Gospel of John." In *The Expositor's Bible Commentary*, edited by Frank Gaebelein. Vol. 9. Grand Rapids: Zondervan, 1981. An excellent resource by a lifelong student of the fourth gospel.

————. *John: The Gospel of Belief.* Grand Rapids: Eerdmans, 1948. Not a commentary but an analytical study of the text, giving special attention to the structure of the gospel.

Westcott, B. F. *The Gospel According to St. John.* Grand Rapids: Eerdmans, 1973. A classic exegetical commentary.

INDEX OF SUBJECTS

INDEX OF AUTHORS

INDEX OF SCRIPTURE AND ANCIENT WRITINGS